SANTA MONICA COLLEGE LIBRARY
3 5046 00165 2439

D0941542

ENCYCLOPEDIA *of* PANTOMIME

David Pickering, a graduate of St. Peter's College, Oxford in 1980, is a full-time writer and editor on the arts. He has collaborated on numerous dictionaries and encyclopedias and has also written several plays and novels as well as a pantomime version of *The Tinder Box*. Reference books he has edited include a *Dictionary of Theatre* (Sphere, 1988) and *Brewer's 20th Century Phrase and Fable* (Cassell, 1991).

David's love of the pantomime dates back to early visits to the theatres of Birmingham and Stratford-upon-Avon in the 1960s and he first became actively involved in their production as a follow-spot operator at the Palace Theatre, Redditch. Since then he has contributed as a writer, set designer, and actor to many amateur pantomime productions in Buckingham, where he lives with his wife Jan and two young sons. He is an enthusiastic member of the town's Old Gaolers amateur theatre company and has made over 120 stage appearances; his pantomime roles have included Buttons and the Squire. Current projects upon which he is working include an analytical and irreverent one-act play about the Ugly Sisters.

Of his many memories of the pantomime he particularly relishes the Demon King who boasted that he was responsible for the one dirty teaspoon always left in the washing-up bowl when it is emptied. As a set designer, he still wonders if anyone in the audience noticed the satellite dish he added to the rooftops of an 18th century village . . .

John Morley has often been described as the 'King of Pantomime' and has been acknowledged to be the foremost pantomime author of the postwar era. He wrote his first pantomime back in the 1940s as a morale-booster when on active service in Palestine with the Coldstream Guards and has never looked back since, with his many subsequent pantomimes being performed by countless professional and amateur companies throughout the world. His productions have entertained hundreds of thousands of children and adults over the years and have exerted a major influence upon the development of the genre, through (for instance) his expansion of the role of the pantomime villain.

John has written pantomimes for virtually all the leading panto performers of the last 50 years, many of whom have become close personal friends: they have ranged from Dame Anna Neagle and Arthur Askey to Terry Scott, Les Dawson, Danny La Rue, Roy Hudd, Frankie Howerd, Cilla Black, and Basil Brush. John admits he is unlikely to win an OBE for his efforts but is consoled by the inclusion of part of his script for *Dick Whittington* for study in the National Curriculum, alongside such luminaries as Shakespeare and Dickens.

In a long and successful career he has appeared many times as an actor in pantomime, as well as in fourteen West End musicals and plays by Noel Coward and many others. He has been quoted as saying pantomime is "all nonsense really" but his brand of "nonsense" packs houses every year from Brighton to Aberdeen (as well as in such outposts of the pantomime as Botswana, California, and Hong Kong). His *Aladdin*, seen at Nottingham's Theatre Royal between December 1980 and the end of April 1981, holds the record for the longest pantomime run of all time.

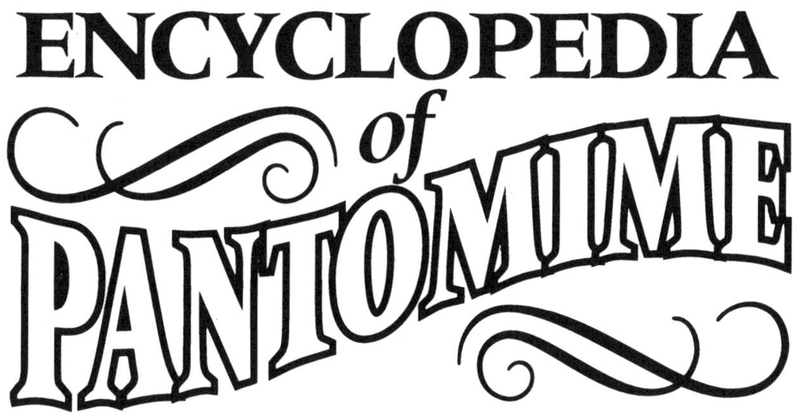

Editor
David Pickering

Adviser
John Morley

ISBN 1-873477-45-7

Published in the United Kingdom by Gale Research International Limited

A CIP catalogue record for this book is available from the British Library.

Typeset by Florencetype Ltd, Kewstoke, Avon

Printed in the United Kingdom by Unwin Brothers Ltd

Contents

Foreword

This encyclopedia represents the first attempt ever made to provide an accessible and comprehensive reference source for the pantomime and is intended for the use of students, enthusiasts, and general readers alike.

The book includes a detailed chronology following the curious development of the pantomime since its earliest roots in the *commedia dell'arte* and other ancient traditions, an essay on the state of the contemporary panto and a guide to writing pantomimes (both by the noted pantomime author John Morley), 'interviews' with the celebrated pantomime stars Roy Hudd and Jack Tripp, a selection of notable quotations about the pantomime, an A–Z section, an appendix covering related children's plays such as *Peter Pan* and *Treasure Island*, a bibliography, and a comprehensive index.

The A–Z section comprises some 600 entries covering not only the history of the pantomime, but also the plots and origins of famous panto stories, biographical entries, histories of famous pantomime venues, explanations of technical terms of particular relevance to the pantomime, and various miscellaneous articles on such topics as **amateur pantomime**, **awkward squads**, **entrances**, **jokes**, **music hall**, **songs**, **superstitions** and **topicality**.

It should be noted that in the case of plot summaries many variants are often used in the pantomime; in general the best known versions are given here (or the storyline of the original fairytale or other narrative on which pantomimes have been based).

Every attempt has been made to include extensive coverage of the contemporary pantomime in all its aspects, though apologies must go to any individuals or organizations not mentioned or only referred to in passing due to shortage of space.

In conclusion, my thanks go to John Morley, Roy Hudd, Jack Tripp, and to my many contacts in the theatre who have helped in this project; I would also like to express my gratitude to Lee Ripley Greenfield, Philippe Barbour, and Jenni Doig at Gale Research International for their able assistance.

David Pickering, 1993.

Picture Acknowledgements

The following illustrations and photographs are reproduced by courtesy of the Board of Trustees of the Victoria & Albert Museum: the cover illustration of the poster for *Cinderella*, Drury Lane, 1905, showing Cinderella with the Ugly Sisters; John Rich as Harlequin, 1753; Joe Grimaldi as Clown in *Mother Goose*, c. 1806; Grimaldi, as Clown, squaring up to a man made of vegetables in *Harlequin and Asmodeus*, 1810; Grimaldi as the Bold Dragoon in *Harlequin and the Red Dwarf; or, The Adamant Rock*, Covent Garden, 1812; Harlequinade from *The King of the Castle; or, Harlequin Prince Diamond and Princess Brighteyes*, Princess's Theatre, 1856; poster for *Bluebeard*, Covent Garden, 1860; George Conquest being shot from a Dragon's mouth and appearing as the Octopus in *Grim Goblin* at the Grecian Theatre, 1876; Charles Lauri as Puss, Drury Lane, 1887; Harry Payne as Clown in *The Double Harlequinade* at Drury Lane, 1890; the cast in *Queen of Hearts*, Drury Lane, 1892; Dan Leno as Idle Jack in *Dick Whittington*, Drury Lane, 1894; preparing for *The Forty Thieves*, Drury Lane, 1898; set for *The Sleeping Beauty*, Drury Lane, 1900; star trap; poster for *Cinderella*, Drury Lane, 1895; Vesta Tilley as Dick Whittington, Prince of Wales' Theatre, c. 1900; George Robey as pantomime dame; Arthur Askey as Widow Twankey in *Aladdin and the Wonderful Lamp*, London Palladium, 1964.

Photograph of Roy Hudd courtesy of the Evening Herald, Plymouth.

We would also like to thank the staff of The Theatre Museum for their kind assistance in the research for the illustrations and Roy Hudd, Jack Tripp and E&B Productions (Theatre) Ltd. for their help with photographs.

How to Write a Pantomime

by John Morley

There is a curious knack to writing pantomimes. It's not talent, it's not cleverness – but it does help to be a bit potty (which most theatre managers, for instance, are not – so they need a panto writer). British pantomime audiences are wonderfully eccentric and will accept even the most zany ideas, providing they are done in the traditional way, with all the corny jokes, over-the-top characters, and invitations for audience participation that they have enjoyed all their lives.

Posters advertising both amateur and professional pantomimes usually make a point of including the word 'traditional' and there are a number of long-established conventions that the pantomime writer must respect. There must be scope for attractive scenery, lavish costumes, singing and dancing, magic, exciting action, romance, and – most important of all – broad comedy of all kinds (both verbal and physical). The story must be plainly written and easy for all ages to follow, with as many spectacular touches as possible (from exploding cookers to bangs and flashes when the Demon King or other villain appears).

The comedy element is perhaps the most vital and must be carefully handled. The pantomimist seeks to please his audience, which must never be offended by controversial or 'unsuitable' material, especially when so many children make up the audience. Vulgar jokes are allowed, obscene ones aren't (there is a big difference between the two). If it is known in advance that 'blue' jokes will be included, ticket sales always suffer. At the same time the comedy must not swamp the telling of the central story, which must continue to progress with only the briefest of interruptions. Likewise dances and songs are best when they have some relevance to the plot in hand (for instance, the dancing of the guests at the ball in *Cinderella*). Audiences (especially the youngsters) will forgive many things, but not being bored, so songs must be contemporary and somehow or other the dialogue must lead into them. This can be tricky, as lyrics of pop songs aren't very subtle and on paper look banal; nevertheless, if Aladdin wants to sing a pop song (or his agent wants this) then the song in question must be fitted in so that it makes some kind of sense.

Audience participation is an essential feature of all good pantomimes. Scripts should provide at least one opportunity for each of the "It's behind you!" and "Oh yes it is – oh no it isn't!" exchanges and audiences – once they have got over their initial reserve – generally respond enthusiastically to join in in other ways (such as assisting with spells and warning the Goodies about impending danger). Failure to include these ritual routines all too often results in letters of complaint to local newspapers (which affects box office sales).

Despite the need to follow tradition in the above ways, there is still scope for much experimentation and scripts must be topical, with references to famous people and affairs of the day as well as to current fads and fashions in everything from clothes and music to the latest toys and television programmes.

There are a few basic differences between writing for an amateur and for a professional pantomime. Oddly enough, it is far more difficult to write a pantomime for a small-scale amateur production than it is for a professional theatre such as the London Palladium or for television. This is because with a smaller production you don't have the possibility of big dance routines or magnificent scenic displays to vary the action or to cover scene changes and the only option is often to write yet another comedy scene. There must also usually be fewer scenes in an amateur show, bearing in mind the restrictions on resources available in such venues as village halls and school assemblies.

Regardless of which plot is chosen the success of the piece will depend on the characters themselves. It's possible to identify a number of 'types' who feature in virtually every popular pantomime plot and who have been familiar figures on the panto stage for 200 years now. The most celebrated of them all is probably the Dame (Widow Twankey, Mrs Sinbad, Mother Goose, etc.), who is usually played by a man; she must have some good jokes, a comic song or two, and lots of chances to chat with the audience. Then there is the 'Simple Simon' part (Buttons, Idle Jack, Wishee-Washee, etc.), who again carries much of the comedy and must get the audience on his side, and the principal boy (Aladdin, Robinson Crusoe, Sinbad, etc.) who must be dashing, glamorous, and brave (and is usually played by a female). The principal girl is the heroine (Cinderella, the Sleeping Beauty, Maid Marian, etc.) who must be pretty and be given a chance to win the audience's sympathy. The magic of the pantomime is usually in the hands of the Fairy (the Fairy Godmother, the Fairy of the Bells, and sometimes even 'Fairy Nuff') and the chief villain (the Demon King, Abanazar, Wicked Wolf, etc.), whose henchmen may include a comedy double act (Broker's Men, bailiffs, robbers, etc.). Other characters include the father figure represented by Alderman Fitzwarren in *Dick Whittington and his Cat* or Baron Hardup in *Cinderella*. Most pantomime casts would not be complete without a 'skin part' – that is, an actor or actors playing an animal (such as a cat, cow, horse, or goose).

Having chosen a plot and assembled a cast, it's time to plan the pantomime itself. There is no single way of arranging the scenes of any pantomime and countless variations have been tried in the past. As long as events build to a thrilling climax, with lots of interest along the way, anything is possible. This is why people may see 10 versions of *Cinderella* and yet never see the story done the same way twice.

Traditionally pantomimes always started with a 'prologue' scene and this remains useful for stating what the moral of the story is going to be and for introducing the magical element that is going to play a major part in the plot later on. The 'Benevolent Agent' (perhaps the Fairy Godmother) enters – ideally in a pink spotlight – and pits her powers against the Demon King, Sheriff of Nottingham, King Rat, or equivalent 'baddie' – who appears in a green light – and the stage is now set for the unfolding of the central story.

To get things off to a bouncy start the Prologue should be followed by the opening chorus, a big song and dance number, which helps to break the ice and create something of a party atmosphere before the main comic characters are introduced. This is particularly useful to engage the interest of youngsters in the audience, who may have been expecting the stage to be no more than a giant television screen and are consequently rather overawed at the sight of live performers.

Immediately after this opening chorus, the plot should get under way as dramatically as possible. For instance, Cinderella discovers that her newly-arrived step-sisters are cruel and ugly; Alderman Fitzwarren finds that terrifying rats are running all over his shop; villagers in *Jack and the Beanstalk* discuss their terror of the giant Blunderbore who lives in a castle in the clouds; and Little Red Riding Hood discovers that the Wicked Wolf has tired of eating chickens and sheep and wants to include humans in his diet. These early scenes must be written in a hugely melodramatic style to appeal to youngsters in the audience, who need plots to be clearly and simply delivered, and to distract attention from what may be very spectacular larger-than-life scenery and costumes.

After all this drama the next scene needs to get the comedy of the evening (or afternoon) under way. Thus, Buttons, Idle Jack, Simple Simon, Wishee-Washee, and their equivalents make their first entrance and strike up an instant relationship with the audience. The most popular routines to accomplish this include those in which the audience is told to shout "Hello Buttons" (or Simon, etc.) whenever he enters. This is an open invitation for the children in the audience to get totally involved and by the time Buttons or his equivalent has had them practising the routine a few times (each time goading them to shout even louder) he will hopefully have won the audience over.

Now comes a quieter scene with the opening of the romantic subplot. This cannot afford to be more than a few lines long as youngsters in particular will quickly tire of such sentiment (especially if both heroine and principal boy are played by women). On no account must the two characters utter the dreaded words "I love you" as this will only provoke mirth among the younger sections of the audience and possibly embarrass the adults. It is best if the hero and heroine express their love for one another in song rather than in dialogue and thus after a few spoken lines they launch into a love duet – ideally, a song the audience knows and can perhaps sing along with. Thus, Maid Marian turns to Robin Hood not to tell him of her everlasting love but with such a plea as: "Robin, thank goodness you're here! My uncle the Sheriff has started to set fire to all the farms round Nottingham because the farmers can't pay the new taxes – what on earth are we going to do?" The music starts and Robin replies "Don't worry, Marian, I'll help them somehow" and they go into the song, by the end of which everyone in the audience will understand that the two are in love.

This romantic interlude is best followed by more comedy and it is at this point that the Dame, who everyone has been waiting to see, makes her entrance. Her deliberately outrageous, tasteless costume and comical manner should create an instant impression and good Dames can sometimes be left to establish their presence with lines and comic business of their own invention, though they will quickly return to the script to push the action forward. After introducing herself, the Dame will lament the misdeeds of her son Aladdin, Jack, Robinson Crusoe, Sinbad, etc. and dismiss him as a lazy good-for-nothing. She may then show off her dress to the audience, sometimes showing off her Victorian-style underwear as well, and perhaps find in a pocket some sweets to throw. This is where the under-tens shout and jump up and down and the pantomime becomes almost a party (which is what everyone wants). In *Cinderella*, of course, the comedy is provided by the Ugly Sisters (known in the trade as 'The Uglies'), who are typically featured in four scenes in each act as audiences always demand to see a lot of them; like the Dame, they also need breaks between their appearances to allow them time to change into increasingly outrageous costumes.

Up to this point all of the action – which may have taken as long as half an hour – has taken place in front of the same scenery and the scene needs to be wound up quickly, with a bit more plot. Thus, we learn that Dick Whittington and his cat have been taken on to work at Fitzwarren's stores; Sinbad has decided to set sail in pursuit of the sorcerer who has kidnapped the princess from Baghdad; Mother Goose is suddenly free from all her troubles because the magic goose has started to lay golden eggs; and Aladdin has been saved from the executioner's sword by Abanazar. With this news the stage is crowded with a throng of happy people who burst into a big song and dance number and exit, hopefully to enthusiastic applause.

At this point the first major scene change needs to take place, so – if the stage allows – a frontcloth is lowered and a 'carpenter's scene' takes place in the narrow area in front of it while the crew work hidden from view. These scenes usually carry the plot further on and typically involve a comedy duo such as the Broker's Men, who perform one of those comedy routines that often date back to the Victorian pantomime and beyond. Thus, one character convinces his dimwitted companion – against all logic – that the latter owes *him* money, rather than the other way round as the slower one thought, or the two characters sit beneath a 'Tree of Truth', which bombards them with acorns every time one of them tells a lie.

The whole stage is used for the third scene and the action returns to the main plot. Dick Whittington is accused of stealing money from the shop's safe and is thrown out of Fitzwarren's store; the Wicked Robbers try to kidnap the Babes; Mother Goose is seen in the trappings of her new wealth but reveals she is unhappy because she is not beautiful, so foolishly summons up the Demon King to improve her looks by magic; Aladdin is chased through his mother's laundrette by the Chinese Policemen; and Cinderella's Ugly Sisters get ready for the ball (a famous example of the 'slosh scene' in which the action depends upon the hurling of flour, buckets of water, paint, and other messy objects – though not too messy, or the dancers will slip over during the next scene).

The fourth scene is played in front of a frontcloth and can vary in form. It can equally successfully be another dialogue scene continuing the story, a musical interlude in which some pop song or other number is performed, or perhaps a comedy routine involving the Dame and Simple Simon or his equivalent.

Act One closes with the climactic fifth scene, which leads on to the interval. This must be both exciting and visually thrilling, recalling the fabulous 'transformation scenes' of Victorian pantomime. In *Cinderella* this is the scene where the Fairy Godmother steps in and transforms a pumpkin into a coach (preferably with real ponies) while the humble kitchen magically changes into Fairyland. In *Sinbad the Sailor* this is where Sinbad arrives in the

Valley of Diamonds, while in *Aladdin* the hero finds the magic lamp (with the aid of the audience) and conjures up the Genie, who turns the sinister cave into the dazzling "alcove of a thousand dreams" resplendent with jewels and treasure. In *Dick Whittington*, the hero has his dream as he sleeps on Highgate Hill and is transported to the Hall of Chivalry where he enters in magnificent clothes as the Lord Mayor of London.

Perhaps the most famous (and the most difficult to present) of all these transformation scenes in the modern pantomime is that in *Jack and the Beanstalk*, for it is at this point that the beanstalk must be seen to sprout out of the ground and shoot up towards the roof of the theatre (sturdily enough for Jack to begin to climb it as the lights fade). In all cases, the scene ends with the stage filling with dancers and singers in magnificent costumes, who perform a rousing number and group themselves into a 'tableau' as the hero waves to the audience and the curtain descends.

The first act should have lasted no longer than one hour, which is as long as most audiences (familiar with the hour-long entertainments seen on television) can concentrate. If the final scene of the act has been successful, the audience will be alive with a hubbub of excited conversation and business at the ice cream kiosks will be brisk (to the satisfaction of the theatre management): the better the pantomime, the noisier the interval.

The first half of the second act (which should also not exceed an hour in length) is often where writers have their greatest problems, for the audience's attention must be re-engaged at a point where the plot has just reached a climax and another one does not immediately present itself. Usually it is best to press on rapidly with the plot. Following the pattern set in the first act, the opening scene takes place on the full stage. *Cinderella* offers one of the best openings to a second act, with the spectacular ball scene, which combines spectacle with the comedy potential of the Ugly Sisters (who may even perform an impromptu cabaret act to impress the prince) and the romantic subplot concerning Cinderella herself and Prince Charming. In *Jack and the Beanstalk* the action continues with Jack arriving at the giant's castle, while in *Dick Whittington and his Cat* Dick arrives in Morocco where he has to grapple with a plague of rats.

This scene is followed by one in which a frontcloth is used and can be a song or a comedy interlude. Some of the comic interludes used today date back to Joey Grimaldi's time, when the great Clown regularly brought the house down with his comedy brass bands, drill routines, and other set pieces still performed.

The full stage area is used in the next scene, with the plot moving ahead at a fast pace to keep audiences interested and prevent the youngsters from getting restless. Yet again a Joey Grimaldi scene may be used with, for instance, the Ugly Sisters coming face to face with a ghost in their bedroom (in fact, this style of scene is still called a 'Joey-Joey' in memory of Grimaldi and earlier this century it had a profound influence upon the silent film comedy routines of the 'Keystone Cops').

At this point it is time to let the audience get in on the action and a few of the principals gather before a frontcloth to lead a 'singalong' in which the two halves of the audience are encouraged to outsing each other. Another popular ploy is the inviting of various younger members of the audience (perhaps those with birthdays) to come up on stage to meet the Dame or other characters. Handled by an expert, this exchange produces some of the funniest moments of the show.

Following the singalong the action moves swiftly on to the final scene, in which the forces of good finally confront those of evil (in the person of giants, witches, wicked fairies, and demon kings). The Baddies are defeated after a great struggle (Jack disposes of his giant, Dick and his cat overcome King Rat, the Prince identifies Cinders as his unknown lover, etc.) and the Goodies are all reunited. Defeated Baddies are humiliated, exiled, or agree to change their ways and assorted pairs of lovers declare their feelings for one another. Endings, of course, must always be happy ones (even the Baddies usually get off pretty lightly and vow to be back again next year).

The music then swells and the cast launch into the Grand Finale, which though short (just two minutes from start to end) is by tradition the most spectacular in the show. Entering in groups or pairs, the entire cast re-appear on stage dressed in the most extravagant costumes yet seen and take their bows as the audience applaud. According to tradition, the last two characters to enter in this 'walkdown' are the Principal Boy and the Principal Girl. As the applause dies down the Principal Boy delivers the last couplet of the pantomime (which is never spoken in rehearsal as it brings terrible bad luck if it is). As often as not, this runs "Did you enjoy the pantomime?", to which the audience hopefully replies "Yes!", and then the very last line, which ends with the rhyme "God Bless!". The audience applauds again and demands that the curtain be raised several times so that they may have one last glimpse of the performers. Even the most modest little provincial pantomime will be honoured in this way, with wild cheering and applause as though it was the close of a glamorous first night in London's West End. You see, even though no other nation can make head nor tail of it, to the British there's nothing like a pantomime . . .

Pantomime Today

by John Morley

At the close of World War II, the professional pantomime was still much as it had been back in 1900: a large-scale enterprise characterised by lavish scenery and costumes, big orchestras, and casts of over a hundred. Popular comedians of the calibre of Arthur Askey had inherited the roles once graced by Dan Leno and other contemporaries and large sums of money still seemed to be available for the construction of spectacular sets that harked back to the great days of the Victorian and Edwardian pantomime at Drury Lane.

The greatest changes in the pantomime since 1950 have been the result of ever-increasing financial pressure and the modern pantomime, though stronger in many aspects, is a different affair from its predecessor of 50 years ago.

In terms of spectacle the pantomime of the immediate post-war era was a breathtaking event. Typical of many shows seen around the country at that time was a version of *The Sleeping Beauty*, which was staged in Birmingham starring Evelyn Laye. This epic production culminated in a Grand Finale that opened with Harlequin (already an exile from most pantomimes) tapping a vast hanging tapestry with his 'slapstick' and thus transforming it into a staircase down which came a magnificently-costumed cast of a hundred, to rapturous applause.

Such scenes caused a sensation, but have long since been consigned to history due to changed financial circumstances. The cost of the timber from which such a staircase would be made for a pantomime today alone precludes its use (modern scenery is made of canvas, with little timber). Even the staircase upon which Cinderella loses her slipper is a fairly modest structure nowadays. The fact that the tapestry staircase of *The Sleeping Beauty* needed a dozen or so stage hands to work it is another reason why such scenes have been dropped in recent decades.

Also lost to the modern pantomime is the old tradition that depended upon the spectacular use of traps (a central feature of the Victorian pantomime). Birmingham's *The Sleeping Beauty*, for instance, was memorable for an entrance by the Wicked Witch, who burst up through a golden throne. Her entrance was achieved by means of a star trap, which was operated by six stage hands who dropped heavy weights thus propelling the Witch upwards on a small platform and six feet into the air above the stage.

Such traps carried their own dangers: performers standing in the wrong place on the platform risked serious injury as they were shot upwards. Equity, the actors' union, prohibited the use of such traps many years ago after an accident to Arthur Askey. Arthur (for whom I wrote many pantomimes) once told me how he had been walking across the stage at the London Palladium after a rehearsal and fallen through a 'grave trap', which someone had forgotten to bolt. The result of his fall onto the concrete floor below was eight weeks in intensive care at St. George's Hospital, in great agony, and the closing of the trapdoors for ever.

Equity's decision was sad but inevitable. Even if the employment of such traps had not been ended in the interests of safety, they would have fallen into disuse anyway because – as mentioned before – of the large numbers of stage crew required to operate them (suffice it to say that a stage hand at the London Coliseum Opera House now earns as much as some of the principal singers). In the same way the flying ballet of former years was now only permitted if very high insurance was taken out on the performers involved. Casts of a hundred or more are also a thing of the past in the professional theatre at least, again because of the cost involved, and the large orchestras once commonplace have been replaced by much smaller ensembles (or even by a single player operating a synthesiser).

Because pantomime remains so expensive to present, managements frequently choose to play safe by staging a guaranteed popular story. The top six pantomimes today are *Cinderella* and *Aladdin*, then *Dick Whittington*, *Jack and the Beanstalk*, *Babes in the Wood*, and *Mother Goose*. Also popular, though less safe at the box office, are such titles as *Robinson Crusoe*, *Snow White*, *Goldilocks*, *Humpty-Dumpty*, *Sinbad the Sailor*, *Little Red Riding Hood*, and *Puss in Boots*.

Fifty years ago managements were more adventurous, staging such rival productions as *Old King Cole*, *Jack and Jill*, *Ali Baba*, and so forth, but market research has since revealed that ticket-buyers (it's always Mother who buys the panto tickets) tend to select stories that they already know something about. Around 20 years ago, for instance, I wrote *Goody Two-Shoes* for Les Dawson at the Grand Theatre, Leeds. Les was even then a top comedian (from the Leeds area himself) but no one knew the story because there is no well-established adaptation of it and, despite good press notices, tickets did not sell.

Jack and Jill was a popular story as a three-hour pantomime back in 1945, but what would happen to it now? First, no one knows the story (the original nursery rhyme being short on plot) and second, no modern audience would put up with a production lasting more than two hours (excluding the long interval).

The decreasing length of the modern pantomime probably reflects the influence of the television drama, which is commonly an hour in length. Television viewers have grown accustomed to having a break after an hour's viewing and expect the pantomime to conform to the same pattern, with two one-hour sections broken by an interval at the halfway point. More television is watched in the UK than in virtually any other nation (perhaps due to our weather!) and viewing habits undoubtedly show themselves in the theatre when after an hour fathers need a drink, mothers an ice-cream, and children the loo.

The most publicised development of recent years is the 'invasion' of celebrities as compared to pantomime artistes. The need for managements to be certain of good takings even before the first night has prompted the importation of stars from all walks of life. These have ranged from such sportsmen as Ian Botham and Frank Bruno to Australian soap opera actors, who have been recruited regardless of whether they can 'play panto' or not (unfortunately some of them can't). It's a big jump to go from an underplayed 'natural' television performance to the broad pantomime style and it does not help that the expense of hiring such stars requires managements to save money elsewhere – often by reducing rehearsal time (all artistes are paid a rehearsal salary). Many provincial pantos receive only two weeks preparation (whereas in 1950 casts would rehearse for a panto at the Palladium for over a month). If the cast is the same as last year's then rehearsals may be all over in just eight days (even though a pantomime is in effect a full-scale musical).

Thus far, the development of the pantomime since the war would appear to have been all down hill, with less lavish scenery, smaller casts, a narrower range of plots, the outlawing of traps, greater restrictions upon length, the use of inexperienced actors and reduced rehearsals. However, there is a distinct silver lining to the clouds thrown up by financial constraint in recent decades, and that is the 'baddie'.

One of the strengths of the contemporary pantomime is the quality of the modern 'Baddie', whose improvement as a role in the past 50 or so years was a side-product of a dangerous development that threatened one of the most cherished of all pantomime traditions – that of the principal boy (the hero) being played by a female. In the 1950s and 1960s this 200-year-old convention (derived originally from the bacchanalia of ancient Rome) that dictated that the hero was played by a pretty girl was temporarily overturned when numerous pop singers and other male stars were cast in the part (among them Englebert Humperdinck as Robinson Crusoe and Frankie Vaughan as the hero of *Puss in Boots*, both at the Palladium). These interlopers were often the first to admit that they could not act but nonetheless the female principal boy soon became a threatened species and for a while the tradition seemed doomed.

It was soon realised that it was unwise to trust these new stars with much dialogue and somebody else had to be found to deliver the plot. The natural choice was the villain (who in the 1950s had little to do of any interest). So I started to expand the role in my own pantomimes and audiences responded with enthusiasm to revitalised baddies who quickly emerged as one of the main attractions.

The change had another benefit as well, for theatrical agents saw that here was a part that would appeal to their 'straight' (in other words, non-singing and non-dancing) performers. Thus, the pantomime was suddenly enriched by such unlikely stars as the dignified and elegant Dame Anna Neagle, who made a delightful Fairy Godmother (speaking the mock-Victorian lines I wrote for her with great gusto), and even Sir John Gielgud. Gielgud agreed to play the King of Gooseland in a charity panto I had written for Drury Lane, explaining to the flabbergasted media "It's high time I was part of our ancient tradition called Pantomime" and adding that he wanted lots of photographs of himself in the "unusual though flattering" costume he had to wear.

Other notable recruits included Peter Gilmore, then playing the lead in television's sailing-ship saga *The Onedin Line*, who told me he'd like to play Blackbeard the Pirate in *Robinson Crusoe*. He did, splendidly decked out with black eyepatch and smiling a hideous leer. Keith Baron played the Sheriff of Nottingham, while Nicholas Parsons had such fun as the villain that he moved on to play the Dame in *Jack and the Beanstalk*. Andrew Sachs, of television's *Fawlty Towers*, played King Rat, and Honor Blackman, of James Bond and *The Avengers* fame, played Queen Rat a year later. Other baddies have included Gareth Hunt and John Nettles (of the Royal Shakespeare Company).

The presence of such stars in the part of baddie upgraded the formerly fairly modest part to star status, an ironic consequence of casting male pop stars who couldn't act as principal boy (a fashion that largely faded after a few years anyway). From my own point of view, the development of the villain was a great help as it provided somebody to carry the plot. Comics understandably dislike doing this, as Ken Dodd – I think it was Ken Dodd – once told me during rehearsals of *Dick Whittington* at Birmingham's Alexandra Theatre: "Why waste the time that could be spent telling a good joke with something as boring as a plot line of dialogue?" Frankie Howerd, appearing in *Robinson Crusoe* at the same theatre, once said the same thing. (Frankie, incidentally, always wanted a comedy scene with an animal, following the great success he had talking to Daisy the Cow – complete with ridiculous wooden udder – in *Jack and the Beanstalk*; in various pantomimes we provided him with opportunities to chat with camels, bears, and even gorillas.)

Other more heartening aspects of the contemporary pantomime include the continued emergence of fine individual performers in such roles as the panto Dame and the unfailing enthusiasm with which present-day audiences (in contrast to the quieter ones of the 1940s) take up the invitation to join in. The awareness of a reduced concentration span among modern audiences might also have contributed to punchier faster-moving plots and pacier direction as directors seek to meet the expectations of audiences used to the breathless style of much television and cinema.

In fact, despite the high costs, the pantomime remains one of the most reliable money-earners for the modern theatre, compensating for the losses too often made on productions of Ibsen, Chekhov, and even Shakespeare. Critics over the years have damned the panto for its vulgarity and low-brow content, but at this fundamental level it is clearly the serious drama's most valuable friend, keeping theatres open and actors in work.

The amateur pantomime has mirrored many of the above developments, with higher and higher standards of production being achieved in imitation of the standards of television's light entertainment. No one knows how many amateur productions are staged each year, but the territory covered by the amateur theatre is vast, with almost every local community putting together a show.

I've 200 amateur pantomimes performed each year, many of them outside the UK. Wherever English is spoken, it seems, so is the pantomime performed; bemused local populations are invited to the British pantomime in places as far apart as California, Hong Kong, and Spain. Heaven knows what they make of the verbal crossfire and the sight of wildly applauding Brits during the Grand Finale, except to conclude perhaps that the British are, quite definitely, no question about it, mad. But then pantomime *is* mad. That is its charm and why it remains so popular with a nation that produced both the seaside postcard and Frankenstein's monster!

Pantomime will never die, for three reasons. One is that it appeals especially to the young. The child aged anywhere from two to twelve who enjoys the pantomime now will be back in the audience in another 20 years or so with his own children, lured by his nostalgia for his own youth and by his certainty that his own offspring will enjoy it as he did (even though he probably went off it when he became a teenager). Another reason is the health of the amateur pantomime, which is shielded from the financial strictures threatening professional companies and is largely impervious to the distortions of fads and fashions that sometimes affect the professional form. Thirdly, and most important of all, is the fact that the modern pantomime is part of the national psyche: without it we just wouldn't be British...

When I was in the Coldstream Guards in 1950 and morale among British forces in Israel/Palestine was low, the Commanding Officer said the Guardsmen needed a morale booster, something to cheer everyone up. So we evolved a panto called *Dick Whittington and his Kit*. No one in a battalion of over a thousand men seemed to think the idea the least bit odd.

My own career in the pantomime had begun.

The Pantomime Performer

with Roy Hudd and Jack Tripp

Roy Hudd is one of the most popular of performers in the contemporary pantomime and has a wide experience of the genre, working in the capacity of actor, writer, and director. Audiences never fail to warm to his lively stage persona and he remains one of the most effective 'box-office draws' available to theatre managements. He is well-respected both inside and outside the profession for his knowledge of the history of the pantomime and the music hall and is also familiar to millions for his many television appearances, which have ranged from children's programmes to Dennis Potter's *Lipstick on your Collar* (1993). (For fuller details of Roy Hudd's pantomime career consult A–Z section.)

How did you first become involved in pantomime?
As a member of a boys' club amateur concert party in Croydon. It was run by an ex-pro Tommy Dennis and the standard was high. My first appearance was as the Dame's sidekick and I've never played in drag since!

Has the pantomime changed since your first appearance in it?
No – the ingredients are just the same.

How does acting in pantomime differ from acting in other forms of theatre and what is the secret of a good pantomime performance?
It has to be broader and simpler of course. The audience tells you if you've given a good pantomime performance – your rapport with them is the ultimate litmus paper.

Which are your favourite pantomimes and which roles do you most like to play?
I think everyone's is 'Cinderella' – and certainly every comic's favourite part is Buttons – the combination of laughs and pathos – though Billy Dainty said it was his favourite part because he only had to wear one costume!

Who do you consider to be the finest panto performers of the modern era?
Certainly Jack Tripp – the most complete Dame. Funny, a wonderful dancer, loved by the kids and grown-ups because he's a totally believable Mum – not a trace of the drag act.

There must have been many memorable moments during your career in pantomime. Which do you most cherish?
I think a sweet little six-year-old shouting out as I was being rejected by Cinderella 'Go on, Cinders – give him one!'

As a writer, director, and performer of pantomime, how healthy is the contemporary panto and how do you see it developing in the future?
The future looks good for panto – really because it is such a rag bag of an entertainment that anything can be fitted into it, including popular stars and contemporary special effects. The story must always be predominant though – it *mustn't* be sent up. The children *want* to be able to follow a plot.

* * *

Jack Tripp must be numbered among the greatest of all Pantomime Dames and is perhaps the most notable living heir of Dan Leno and his contemporaries. He learnt his craft as Dame from such accomplished actors as Douglas Byng in the 1940s and has since developed his performance around his skills as a comedian and dancer without stepping over the line into pastiche by over-exaggerating the character. He is a stalwart defender of the 'traditional' pantomime and year after year proves that a Pantomime Dame can still be a subtly played, richly believable character who appeals to adults and children alike. (For fuller details of Jack Tripp's pantomime career see A–Z section).

How did you first become involved in pantomime?
Pantomime has played a big part in my theatrical career. I had a wonderful introduction to panto when I was offered the part of Billy – the Dame's son – in *Goody Two-Shoes* at the King's Theatre, Edinburgh. My 'Mother' was none other than the famous Douglas Byng, one of the great Pantomime Dames – a marvellous introduction to panto. After playing four consecutive years in the same production, I had learnt a great deal about pantomime and was later offered the Dame part in a new production of *Goody Two-Shoes*, playing Glasgow and Edinburgh – again for the famous Howard and Wyndham pantomime circuit. After this I was booked by one of the best pantomime producers, Derek Salberg. This led to 12 consecutive years playing various subjects. I was always cast as Dame, with some of the big names in the business – I was 'Mother' to Beryl Reid, Leslie Crowther, Roy Castle, Ted Rogers, Les Dawson, Barbara Windsor, Anita Harris, The Batchelors, and many more top names. That all led to working for the past seven years with, I consider, one of the finest pantomime artistes of them all – Roy Hudd.

Has the pantomime changed since your first appearance in it?
Good pantomime productions have not changed a great deal over the past few decades – with the exception of a few pop stars playing the leading roles and now famous boxers and cricketers (yes, even a politician) playing parts. I have to say, I do disagree with this. Also, there are not so many speciality acts included in the productions – but overall they are just as good, providing the pantomimes are put on by managements who care about the book (script) and select the right artistes (such as those of Duncan Weldon and, today, Paul Elliott).

How does acting in pantomime differ from acting in other forms of theatre and what is the secret of a good pantomime performance?
Acting in pantomime is very hard work – one of the hardest jobs being playing to masses of children 'flat out' twice daily. Probably the most difficult thing is adjusting the performance to the audience. For instance, a Saturday morning

matinee audience is mainly children and the visual comedy works best (the gorilla, the ghost, the chase, the "behind you's"), whereas a Saturday night audience is mainly adult and the reverse has to happen, with the visuals cut to a minimum and the verbal gags coming into their own. The secret of a good pantomime performance is some of each or a little bit of everything to try to please everybody from three to ninety-three – not easy.

Which are your favourite pantomimes and which roles do you most like to play?
My favourite pantomime is *Mother Goose* – in which Derek Salberg gave me the opportunity to play the wonderful Dame character, which calls for acting as well as comedy and has great pathos (lovely for children). The character's glamorous transformation and then her change back again to being poor and ugly, but happy – and the scenes with the Goose – are all great stuff. Unfortunately managements will not give me the opportunity to play that subject today because they feel that the part must be played by the top billing star of the show – which I am not. I also love my current subject – *Babes in the Wood*, written by Roy Hudd. *Aladdin* is great and *Jack and the Beanstalk* – properly approached, they are all good, providing the storyline is brought out in the script, as one of the best pantomime writers, John Morley, knows so well (he's written many for me). *Cinderella* is probably the most popular, but as there is no Dame part I don't know much about that production. I tried Ugly Sister once, but I would not play it again – the Dame has much more warmth.

How do you approach the role of Pantomime Dame?
My approach to the role of Dame is really summed up in a very kind notice by Eric Shorter, the critic for *The Daily Telegraph*, who came to Plymouth to see *Aladdin* at the Theatre Royal: "Dames in pantomime ought to be demure. They need finesse on all occasions. No clowning and above all no attempt at female impersonations. To see Jack Tripp is to learn something of the nature of the endangered species for Mr Tripp's redhead is as resolutely masculine as (say) Arthur Askey in his heyday. He is both dignified and dainty in Roger Redfarn's spectacular and shapely idea of *Aladdin*." This pleased me so much because it is exactly what I aim to achieve – to be clean and crisp in both gags and costume and to be sincere with the plot, for the children's sake.

There must have been many memorable moments during your career in pantomime. Which do you most cherish?
I remember playing Wolverhampton in about my third pantomime season, as Dame, and an incident when the publicity photographs were being put up Front of House. Two women were looking at the photographs. One said "Oh, look – Jack Tripp". The other said "Jack Tripp? Who's that?" Her friend replied "You know, we've seen him before – she's good." Praise indeed. Recently, very recently in fact, we had the first morning call at the theatre to meet the press and were hoping that we would get good notices after our opening night. A very young lad, on what must have been his first reporting job, came up to me and, I swear, said "Mr Tripp, what pleasure do you get out of wearing women's clothes?" I replied "None whatsoever" and finished the interview. Later I thought – and we are at the mercy of someone like this to give his criticism in the local press!

As one of the most successful pantomime performers of the modern era, how healthy is the contemporary panto and how do you see it developing in the future?

Very healthy. Pantomime will always be a great British institution: it is the one period during the year when the provincial theatres play to packed houses. Up and coming young talent will always replace the oldies – I was up and coming when I worked with Douglas Byng. Whilst we have pantomime artistes like Roy Hudd, producers like Paul Elliott, writers like John Morley, and directors like Roger Redfarn, panto will survive. And for anybody wanting to play Dame – don't overdo the make-up, don't wear enormous boobs, wear outrageous but not ridiculous clothes, and wait until you are middle-aged. A very young performer can look too pretty as Dame, but a middle-aged performer looks more amusing and just like a man dressed up as a woman should look. Long live panto!

Quotations about the Pantomime

"A new Italian mimic scene between a Scaramouch and a Harlequin, a country farmer, his wife and others."

John Weaver, introducing the first of his 'pantomimes' (1717).

"A most exquisite entertainment."

Henry Fielding, of pantomime in the early 18th century.

"The worst and dullest company into which an audience has ever been introduced."

Samuel Richardson, on the 'Immortals' in the pantomime (*c.* 1740).

"The sneering Knave usurps Apollo's Crown . . . Pull, pull the parti-coloured tyrant down!"

Anonymous critic of Harlequin, *British Frenzy; or, the Mock-Apollo.*

"But if an empty house, the actor's curse,
Shews us our Lears and Hamlets lose their force,
Unwilling we must change the nobler scene,
And, in our turn, present you Harlequin . . .
If want comes on, importance must retreat;
Our first great ruling passion – is to eat."

David Garrick, apologising for the introduction of pantomime at Drury Lane (1750).

"Heart of oak are our ships,
Heart of oak are our men,
We always are ready,
Steady, boys, steady!
We'll fight and we'll conquer again and again!"

'Heart of Oak', from *Harlequin's Invasion; or, A Christmas Gambol* (1759).

"But why a speaking Harlequin? –
'Tis wrong, The wits will say, to give the fool a tongue . . .
But now the motley coat, and sword of wood,
Require a tongue to make them understood."

David Garrick, introducing a talking Harlequin (1759).

"How unlike the pantomimes of Rich, which were full of wit, and coherent, and carried on a story! . . . I see I understand nothing from astronomy to a harlequin-farce!"

Horace Walpole, on Sheridan's *Robinson Crusoe* (1781).

"Here we are again!"

Joseph Grimaldi, making his entrance as Clown (*c.* 1800).

"I am Grim all day, but I make you laugh at night."

Joseph Grimaldi.

"It's all in my way, you know, I play the fool to shew others the absurdity of it."

Joseph Grimaldi, in *Fashion's Fools* (1809).

"Shall sapient managers new scenes produce
From Cherry, Skeffington, and Mother Goose?
While Shakespeare, Otway, Massinger, forgot,
On stalls must moulder, or in closets rot?"

George Gordon, Lord Byron, *English Bards and Scotch Reviewers* (1809).

I'm not in mood for crying,
Care's a silly calf,
If to get fat you're trying,
The only way's to laugh."

Joseph Grimaldi, 'Tippity Witchet' (1810).

"I'll make one that's far more real."

Drury Lane carpenter, on seeing a live elephant in a rival production at Covent Garden (1811).

"A little old woman her living she got
By selling hot codlins hot, hot, hot:
And this little old woman who codlins sold,
Though her codlins were hot she felt herself cold,
So to keep herself warm she thought it no sin
To fetch for herself a quatern of – GIN!"

Joseph Grimaldi, 'Hot Codlins' (1819).

"Amusing . . . whether he have to rob a pieman or open an oyster, imitate a chimney-sweep or a dandy, grasp a red-hot poker or devour a pudding, take snuff, sneeze, make love, mimic a tragedian, cheat his master, pick a pocket, beat a watchman, or nurse a child."

Horatio Smith, of Joseph Grimaldi, *Drama* (1822).

"Everybody 'pooh-poohs' the pantomime, but everybody goes to see it. It is voted 'sad nonsense' and played every night for two months."

The Times (1823).

"Like vaulting ambition, I have overleaped myself and pay the penalty in advanced old age. It is four years since I jumped my last jump, filched my last sausage and set in for retirement . . . "

Joseph Grimaldi, farewell speech (1828).

"I never saw anyone to equal him. There was so much *mind* in everything he did. It was said of Garrick that, when he played a drunken man, he was 'all over drunk', Grimaldi was 'all over Clown'".

Charles Dibdin, of Joseph Grimaldi (*c.* 1828).

"Thou didst not preach to make us wise –
Thou hadst no finger in our schooling –
Thou didst not 'lure us to the skies' –
Thy simple, simple trade was – Fooling!"

Thomas Hood, of Joseph Grimaldi (*c.* 1830).

"Handsome just above the knee,
The legs of Madame Vestris."

Chorus of popular song (*c*. 1830).

"It is agreed on all hands that Pantomimes are not what they were . . . the Clown retains some of his character still, but the rest has become a mere mass of gratuitous absurdity without object."

Leigh Hunt, in the *Tatler* (1831).

"He that says he does not like a Pantomime either says what he does not think or is not so wise as he fancies himself . . . Not to like pantomime is not to like love, not to take a holiday, not to remember we have been children ourselves."

Leigh Hunt (*c*. 1831).

"Old friends, I've the old prayer to make, before it is too late,
With your old kindness please to view this change in our old state,
Our old mythology, we thought, was getting out of date,
And so we've left Olympus old, and all its gods so great,
For a fine old English fairy tale, all of the olden time!"

J. R. Planché, *Riquet with the Tuft* (1836).

"We believe in Garrick, whom we never saw, and those to come may believe in Grimaldi; for, though in a low department of art, he was the most wonderful creature of his day, and far more unapproachable in his excellence than Kean and Kemble in theirs."

H. D. Miles (1838).

"Let us at once confess to a fondness for pantomimes . . . we revel in pantomimes."

Charles Dickens.

"The delights – the ten thousand million delights of a pantomime."

Charles Dickens, *Memoirs of Joseph Grimaldi*, introduction (1838).

"A pantomime is to us, a mirror of life."

Charles Dickens.

"Pantomimes are a farrago of nonsense suited only to the vulgar and illiterate."

Theatrical Inquisitor (1841).

"Pantomimes are grave matters nowadays. Very little roaring, or giggling, or grinning, or any frivolity of that sort, is to be got out of a modern harlequinade."

The Times (1842).

"Pantomime is no longer what it used to be."

The Times (1846).

"Poor Arlecchino took a prance
To merry England, via France;
Came just in Christmas-pudding time,
And welcomed was by Pantomime.
But Pantomime's best days are fled:
Grimaldi, Barnes, Bologna – dead!"

J. R. Planché, *The New Planet* (1847).

"An entirely new Allegorical, Beautiful, Comical, Diverting, Educational, Fanciful, Gorgeous, Hyperbolical, Intellectual, Jovial, Keen, Laughable, Merry, Novel, Original, Peculiar, Quizzical, Romantic, Splendid, Transcendent, Unobjectionable, Volatile, Waggish, X-travagant, Youthful, and Zig-Zaggy Grand Comic Christmas Pantomime."

E. L. Blanchard, his billing for *Little Jack Horner; or, Harlequin A. B. C.* (1857).

"Society goes to them on the sly and it is the general subject of conversation for a month at least. A good Pantomime epitomises the events and ideas of the moment. It must be up to date, scourge the people's bugbear and flatter its idol. It has full licence to be coarse and would be disappointing if it were not."

Francis Wey, *Diary* (1858).

"The lower orders rush there in mobs, and in shirtsleeves applaud frantically, drink ginger beer, munch apples, crack nuts, call actors by their Christian names and throw orange peel and apples by way of bouquets."

Charles Mathews, of the audience at the Royal Victoria Theatre (later the Old Vic) (*c.* 1860).

"Wise men of all ages have affirmed that laughter is a good thing. It clears the lungs, shakes up the diaphragm and loosens the fetters of the brain. How then shall we get a good hearty laugh? If we want a good roar, if we want to make our lungs crow like chanticleer, we must go and see a Christmas pantomime. There is no fun like it after all."

Andrew Halliday, *Comical Fellows or the History and the Mystery of the Pantomime* (1863).

"All the stockings gone in ladders – then the sausages and bladders,
And the chromes, and greens, and madders, that I've seen five thousand times;
And the glitter, gauze, and spangle, and the Clown turned in the mangle,
And the everlasting jingle of the mutilated rhymes."

W. S. Gilbert, 'Bab Ballads' (1865).

"In West London, Harlequin is an ornament of the season like a glittering hoar-frost; in East London he is the ideal. Pass on to the suburbs and provinces, onwards to any extremity of the island in which a theatre is to be found and there a Christmas Pantomime, well got up according to local resources, is to be found in its proper season . . . this particular species of entertainment, although Italian in origin, has become as natural to the unsophisticated as the Oriental turkey is to every Briton who tastes a Christmas dinner."

The Times (1867).

"Good little man, you'll make headway."

Charles Dickens, to Dan Leno (1869).

"What a strange, admirable, absurd, inscrutable thing is our English Pantomime. What an intensely national thing it has grown up to be. How we have loved it in our day and cherish it still for the sake of the mirth and delight it imparts to our little ones and the soothing sadness with which it inspires us as it calls up our days of innocent revel!"

George Augustus Sala (*c.* 1870).

"Year after year Mr. Beverley's powers were tasked to outdo his former outdoings. The *last* scene became the first in the estimation of the management. The most complicated machinery, the most costly materials, were annually put into requisition, until their bacon was so buttered that it was impossible to save it. As to me, I was positively painted out."

J. R. Planché, *Recollections and Reflections* (1872).

"Pantomime is dying on account of the marvellous complexity of mechanism, painting, limelight, coloured fire and ballet girls which we now call a Transformation Scene . . . Pantomime, as our fathers and grandfathers knew it, is a thing of the past."

The Graphic (1877).

"Though pantomime seems at present to hold its own, I do not see how it can continue to do so."

The Theatre (1882).

"To Drury Lane to see *Sinbad* . . . hardly anything done as I had intended, or spoken as I had written: the music-hall element crushing out the rest, and the good old fairy tales never to be again illustrated as they should be."

E. L. Blanchard, quoted in *Life and Reminiscences* (1891).

"I sympathise with the small boy who refused to go to Drury Lane Pantomime because he knew that Augustus Harris was only going to surpass himself."

H. G. Hibbert, *A Playgoer's Memories*, of Drury Lane pantomime in the 1890s.

"If we didn't laugh at him, we'd cry our eyes out."

Marie Lloyd, of Dan Leno (*c.* 1891).

"He said he was the son of a Scottish marquis and his mother had been a housemaid . . . he told me that the greatest ambition of his life was to play Shakespeare – he wanted me to make a contract with him to play in Shakespeare for five years. His body was trembling and his hands were icy cold and I realised as he spoke, that something strange had happened to him."

Constance Collier, of Dan Leno shortly before his breakdown (1902).

"Pantomime will never again be what it was."

Sir Max Beerbohm (1903).

"And we hope to appear
For many a year,
In the panto of old Drury Lane."

Dan Leno and Herbert Campbell in *Humpty-Dumpty*,
shortly before they both died (1904).

"To find anything like a close parallel to his style we should probably have to go back to the Italian *commedia dell'arte*."

The Times, obituary for Dan Leno (1904).

"Oh, for an hour of Herod."

Anthony Hope, during the first performance of *Peter Pan* (1904).

"A child who has never seen a pantomime, or an adult who has never seen a play, is a public danger."

George Bernard Shaw, letter (1905).

"No, no, not to be replaced by a *pantomime*!"

Ivor Novello, on learning that his enormously successful musical *Glamorous Night* was to be taken off to make way for a Drury Lane panto (1934).

"The one art-form that has been invented in England."

Sir Max Beerbohm, of the pantomime.

"If we rang down the curtain without giving the kiddies their ten minutes of red-hot poker, sausages and the rest of it there would be a riot."

Frederick Melville (*c*. 1930).

"My detestation of pantomime at Christmas has grown steadily from December to December."

George Bernard Shaw.

"I admit that a pantomime once kept me shrieking with laughter for half an hour and in thorough good humour for the rest of the evening. Its subject was Sinbad the Sailor and what made me laugh so shamelessly was an outrageously vulgar exploitation of the humours of sea-sickness."

George Bernard Shaw.

"I deplore the habit of Christmas playgoers flocking to the pantomime."

J. B. Priestley.

"I don't like playing in pantomime. All I have to say, in every scene, is 'Hullo mother' to a man."

Pat Kirkwood.

"The secret to playing a pantomime principal boy is complete sincerity."

Evelyn Laye.

"When a Principal Boy swings one shapely leg forward and thumps a well-kept fist into the opposite palm, she is imitating some lost vision of man . . . she is not trying to create an illusion of manhood."

Dorothy Ward (*c*. 1950).

"It is a miracle that in these days of cynicism and sophistication something so essentially simple in character not only thrives but flourishes more strongly than ever."

Tom Arnold, pantomime impresario (*c*. 1950).

"I just put on my wig like a hat and go on stage."

Arthur Askey, on the subtleties of playing a pantomime dame.

"I quite wanted to play the principal boy once, although I don't imagine that will happen now."

Glenda Jackson (1991).

"Like all theatre, if you play it for what it's worth, it's terrific. I can't think of anything that has more elements in it – melodrama and singing and comedy."

Ray Cooney (1991).

"I suppose in a way they're a bit like folk songs, the Lord's Prayer, or whatever. They're handed down from one generation to the next. You talk to anybody in the business, and usually it was the panto that inspired them in the first place. It looked like so much fun, and it still is."

Roy Hudd (1991).

Chronology

1st century BC–5th century AD The term 'pantomime' (from the Greek, meaning 'We can act everything') is first used in reference to the performers who presented popular and often bawdy solo comic entertainments throughout the Roman Empire (otherwise unconnected to the English pantomime tradition). Cross-dressing becomes a feature of the Bacchanalia, with slaves dressing in the clothes of their masters and mistresses.

14th–16th centuries The study of Roman and Greek theatre is nurtured during the Renaissance and promotes the convention of cross-dressing in the English theatre, in which all female roles are taken by boys and men. The *commedia dell'arte* tradition combining dance, dialogue, and knockabout comedy develops in Italy.

1602 An Italian *commedia dell'arte* company performs at the court of Elizabeth I. Meanwhile Italian companies settle permanently in Paris, where the tradition continues to develop.

1660 English theatre revives following the Restoration of Charles II.

1673 Tiberio Fiorillo's *commedia dell'arte* company, one of several to come from France to post-Restoration England, creates a sensation in London.

1685 Characters from the *commedia dell'arte* make their first significant appearance in a play by an indigenous English playwright (William Mountford's *Doctor Faustus*). Subsequently *commedia dell'arte* characters also figure in plays by such writers as Aphra Behn and Edward Ravenscroft.

1688 Christopher Rich acquires a share in the management of Drury Lane, subsequently moving to the Lincoln's Inn Fields Theatre.

1700 Christopher Rich invites French troupes to perform Italian Night Scenes at Drury Lane and establishes a new theatrical fashion.

1702 (or later) John Weaver stages *The Cheats; or, The Tavern Bilkers*, in which he exploits the conventions of Italian Night Scenes and attempts to revive the *pantomimus* tradition of ancient Rome.

1714 John Rich, who is to dominate the early history of the pantomime, inherits the run-down Lincoln's Inn Fields Theatre on his father's death.

1717 John Weaver stages his ballet-pantomime *The Loves of Mars and Venus* (the first production actually billed as a 'pantomime') and joins John Rich at Lincoln's Inn. Rich stages *Harlequin Sorcerer*, the first of a series of innovative pantomimes combining scenes based on Classical mythology or folklore with silent scenes (interspersed with songs and dances) depicting the comic adventures of the lovers Harlequin and Columbine as they are pursued by other characters derived from the *commedia dell'arte* – the first 'harlequinades'. His productions are staged as afterpieces and form the final part of a long evening during which farces, tragedies, and a variety of other entertainments may be presented.

1723 John Rich's *Necromancer; or, Harlequin and Doctor Faustus* enjoys enormous success and establishes Lincoln's Inn as the leading venue in London.

1732 John Rich opens the Theatre Royal, Covent Garden, where he remains the leading pantomime producer and Harlequin for another 30 years.

1737 The Licensing Act confirms the sole right of the two Patent Theatres (Covent Garden and Drury Lane) to present spoken drama.

1750 David Garrick stages his first pantomime, *Queen Mab*, at Drury Lane, in response to the rival success of Covent Garden. Subsequent Drury Lane pantomimes are distinguished by scenery painted by the great scene designer De Loutherbourg and by a controversial attempt (1759) to introduce a speaking Harlequin (Henry Woodward).

1773 First performance of *Jack the Giant Killer* (as a Christmas play at Drury Lane).

1779 Spoken lines play a more prominent role in *The Touchstone; or, Harlequin Traveller* at Covent Garden (where such dialogue is permitted).

1780 George Colman's *The Genius of Nonsense* promotes the use of fairy-tales as source material and subsequently plots are drawn from all manner of folk traditions and from popular literature. Meanwhile the comic emphasis of the harlequinade gradually shifts from Harlequin to Pierrot (notably through the performances of Carlo Delpini).

1781 First performance of *Robinson Crusoe* (in a version by R. B. Sheridan at Drury Lane), in which scenes from the harlequinade are no longer interwoven with the 'mythological' narrative but are given separately after the 'Opening'. The two parts of the entertainment are linked by a 'transformation scene' (in which the characters of the Opening are now revealed in the form of Harlequin and his fellows). The infant Joseph Grimaldi makes his stage debut.

1786 *Robinson Crusoe* and *Harlequin's Invasion* become the first pantomimes to be staged in the USA (at the John Street Theatre, New York).

1788 First pantomime production of *Aladdin and his Wonderful Lamp* (at Covent Garden). Outside the two Patent Theatres other venues get round the Licensing Act by presenting 'burlettas' (which include many 'straight' dramas disguised as burlettas by the inclusion of musical interludes); increasingly pantomimes incorporate spoken passages.

1791 First performance of *Bluebeard* (at Covent Garden).

1793 First performance (as an opera) of *The Babes in the Wood* (at the Haymarket).

1800 Joseph Grimaldi makes his first appearance as Clown – a restyled Pierrot – at Sadler's Wells and James Byrne adopts a distinctive diamond-patched coat to play Harlequin (the colour of each patch representing a particular emotion). The harlequinade approaches its peak and the pantomime, presented chiefly at Christmas and Easter, becomes the major item of the evening's entertainment. Pantomime dames played by men become an increasingly common sight.

1803 First performance of *Little Red Riding Hood* (at Sadler's Wells).

1804 First performance of *Cinderella* (at Drury Lane).

1806 Grimaldi is acclaimed as Clown in *Mother Goose* and in his hands the harlequinade enters its golden era, with Clown as its most popular character. Such writers as Charles Farley and the Dibdins sharpen the satirical content of the pantomime in collaboration with Grimaldi. First performance of *The Sleeping Beauty* (at Drury Lane).

1814 First performances of *Dick Whittington and his Cat* (at Covent Garden) and *Sinbad the Sailor* (at Drury Lane).

1815 The part of principal boy in a pantomime is played by a woman for the first time (in Charles Farley's *Harlequin and Fortunio* at Covent Garden).

1818 First performance of *Puss in Boots* (at Covent Garden).

1819 Eliza Povey, the first female principal boy known by name, takes the role of Idle Jack in the first performance of *Jack and the Beanstalk* (at Drury Lane). Still a very young girl, she and her successor Elizabeth Poole play juvenile heroes (unlike the principal boys of later times).

1823 Grimaldi retires through ill-health (making his last regular appearance on tour in Birmingham). Clarkson Stanfield is engaged as a scene painter at Drury Lane and subsequently becomes famous for his dioramas.

1827 Pantomimes staged at Covent Garden and Drury Lane cost up to £1000 apiece.

1828 Grimaldi makes two celebrated farewell appearances.

1830 Madame Vestris takes over the Olympic Theatre (becoming the first woman to manage a London theatre) and enjoys immediate success in *Olympic Revels*, the first of an acclaimed series of burlesque extravaganzas by J. R. Planché. The genre subsequently has a profound influence upon the pantomime proper and hastens the adoption of spoken dialogue, the use of more lavish scenery, and the decline of the harlequinade. The popularity of Vestris in male roles promotes the concept of the thigh-slapping female principal boy.

1831 A production of *Mother Goose* is toured to New York; the audience, however, fails to understand the play and it is not a success.

1836 Planché presents his first extravaganza based on a fairytale, *Riquet with the Tuft*.

1837 Grimaldi dies. With managements having proved unable to find anyone capable of matching him as Clown the emphasis switches from comedy to spectacle; speciality acts are seen with increasing frequency and the harlequinade continues to contract as the restyled opening expands.

1843 The Theatre Regulation Act allows all theatres to present a range of theatrical entertainments, subject only to approval by the Lord Chamberlain, thus ending the Patent Theatres' monopoly of spoken drama.

1844 First performance of a pantomime by E. L. Blanchard, later known as the 'Prince of Openings', whose charming and elegantly written works raise the Victorian pantomime to new heights.

1846 First pantomime performance of *Ali Baba and the Forty Thieves* (at Astley's Amphitheatre).

1849 William Beverley designs the first of many dazzling transformation scenes, for Planché's *The Island of Jewels*.

1850s Virtually all pantomimes – now uniquely associated with the Christmas season – incorporate dialogue, putting further pressure on the harlequinade. As venues stage shorter and shorter harlequinades, performers in them are paid less than actors in the opening. The first mature female principal boys appear in the pantomime (the honour of the very first possibly going to a 'Miss Saunders' in 1847 or a 'Miss Ellington' in 1852).

1861 First performance of H. J. Byron's classic burlesque *Aladdin*, which introduces the character Widow Twankey. The production's success confirms the popularity of the female principal boy and promotes the casting of men in the role of dame on a regular basis.

1868 George L. Fox's production of *Humpty-Dumpty* runs for over 1,200 performances at the Olympic Theatre, New York, making it the most successful pantomime in US history.

1869 The Vokes family begin a 10-year domination of the pantomimes at Drury Lane.

1870s Performances of pantomime, which is at a height of popularity and prestige, can last up to three hours or more. Pantomimists increasingly aim to please juvenile audiences, though striving at the same time to offer something for all ages. Besides the Patent Theatres, other leading homes of the pantomime include the Britannia, Grecian, and Surrey Theatres. Pantomime runs regularly last for many weeks at venues throughout the UK.

1879 Augustus Harris becomes manager of Drury Lane and goes on to stage a series of the most sumptuous pantomimes yet seen, complete with speciality acts, flying ballets, spectacular scenery, celebrated principal boys, and casts of several hundred. He also makes the pantomime the sole item of the evening's entertainments and strengthens it by recruiting leading music hall performers, leading to complaints that the pantomime is being vulgarised.

1883 The ever-shrinking harlequinade is finally dropped from the Drury Lane pantomime for the first time despite attempts by Blanchard and others to keep it alive by doubling and tripling the characters involved.

1886 Dan Leno appears in pantomime for the first time, playing the Dame in *Jack and the Beanstalk* at the Surrey Theatre.

1887 The last of Covent Garden's regular annual pantomimes is staged (the tradition was subsequently revived on two occasions).

1888 E. L. Blanchard dies. Dan Leno wins acclaim in the first of the 16 consecutive annual pantomimes at Drury Lane in which he starred. Other stars of this golden age of Drury Lane pantomime include Marie Lloyd, Little Tich, and Herbert Campbell.

1896 Augustus Harris, considered the father of the modern pantomime, dies, but the tradition of spectacular Drury Lane productions continues under Arthur Collins.

1900 Collins presents *The Sleeping Beauty and the Beast*, the first of J. Hickory Wood's celebrated pantomimes, which effectively set the pattern for pantomime scripts for future years.

1904 Both Dan Leno (creator of the modern pantomime dame) and fellow-comedian Herbert Campbell die. Under Collins a new generation of comedians, including Harry Randall, Wilkie Bard, and George Graves enjoy enormous success at Drury Lane. First performance of J. M. Barrie's *Peter Pan*.

1909 The Melville brothers become managers of the Lyceum Theatre and begin an almost unbroken run of highly successful old-fashioned pantomimes that does not finally come to an end until 1939. They are the last

London management to stage brief harlequinades as an integral part of their pantomimes.

1912–15 Collins casts male performers in the role of principal boy in four successive pantomimes at Drury Lane, but the experiment does not catch on.

1920 In the face of competition from the musical comedy, Drury Lane does not stage its annual pantomime for the first time in nearly 70 years and subsequently only revives the tradition on an occasional basis (in 1929 and 1934).

1930s Through the work of such producers as Julian Wylie a new balance is struck between the comedy element in the pantomime and the fairytale narrative, which is given greater emphasis.

1939 The surviving Melville brother, Frederick, dies and the Lyceum's long pantomime tradition ends.

1948 The London Palladium starts to emerge as the most prestigious home of the pantomime in the capital.

1950s Norman Wisdom and other male stars are cast in the role of principal boy, threatening the tradition of the female principal boy. The use of traps and flying ballets virtually ends due to safety considerations.

1960s The cost of staging a major West End pantomime rises to anything up to £100,000; subsequently fewer and fewer West End venues are used. Stars from television and the world of pop music are increasingly presented in leading roles (with mixed results); as a side-effect of this the part of the villain is expanded to accomodate accomplished panto performers. Notable dames include Danny La Rue, who breaks the tradition of the unsophisticated comical dame by playing the role as a drag queen with great success.

1971 Cilla Black's success as principal boy signals a return to the female principal boy at most venues.

1970s The increasing use of 'blue' material by pantomime comedians threatens the future of the pantomime as a family entertainment, but the trend is eventually reversed and the panto quickly recovers its reputation and enters a boom period.

1980–81 John Morley's *Aladdin*, staged at the Theatre Royal, Nottingham, sets a new record for a pantomime run.

1983 The National Theatre adds pantomime to its programme with *Cinderella*, but the production is not a success.

1984 Rising costs mean just one professional pantomime is staged in London's West End, but another 30 are seen in the environs, with 70 in the provinces and another 22 in Scotland, Wales, and Northern Ireland (together with numerous amateur shows). Casts everywhere grow smaller to save money and the element of spectacle likewise declines.

1992 John Morley's *Dick Whittington* is chosen for study as part of the National Curriculum.

1992–93 There is no West End pantomime for the first time in living memory due to high costs, but productions elsewhere in the country continue to prosper and include celebrity guests ranging from sportsmen to stars of Australian soap operas. The most frequently seen pantomimes presented in some 200 professional productions are: *Cinderella* (30 productions), *Aladdin* (30), *Jack and the Beanstalk* (20), *Dick Whittington* (20), *Snow White* (12), and *Babes in the Wood* (11). Amateur companies continue to present countless pantomimes, often to a high standard, throughout the world.

A

Abanazar In *Aladdin and his Wonderful Lamp*, the wicked sorcerer who tries to steal the magic lamp from Aladdin. In early versions of the tale he was described simply as the 'African Magician' until in 1813, in a production presented at Covent Garden, he was finally identified as Abanazar. In some versions he was aided in his evil schemes by a dumb slave called **Kasrac**. Popular performers of the part have ranged from Fred Vokes in 1874 and George Graves in 1909 to John Nettles in 1984 and Gareth Hunt in 1992. Like other villainous roles Abanazar was played relatively straight in the Victorian pantomime but is now presented as a more appealing character who gets enormous enjoyment out of the power he has. Abanazars in the contemporary pantomime make quite sure of getting a lively response from their audiences by explaining that they hate all children and threatening to poison their ice cream in the interval.

abandoned children The theme of abandoned children is central to the pantomimes *Babes in the Wood*, *Hansel and Gretel*, and *Hop o' My Thumb* as well as being a familiar feature of folk traditions worldwide. Usually such stories concern children abandoned (usually in deep woods) for reasons of poverty, jealousy, or fear of prophecies concerning their future. In most tales the children survive with the help of various sympathetic animals and return to reveal the guilt of their relatives. It has been argued that the motif of abandoned children in fairytales represents the lesson that the time comes in every child's life when he or she must rely upon their own wits to make their way in the world.

abracadabra The magic word that is traditionally spoken by sorcerers, fairy godmothers, witches, and conjurors at the climactic moment of a spell or stage illusion. The word has a surprisingly long history, with the earliest mention of it being made in the 2nd century BC in the writings of the Gnostic physician Severus Sammonicus. Thought to be of Cabbalistic origin, the word was believed to provide protection against fevers and other medical ailments, as well as generally to guard against ill luck. Patients wore an amulet or inscribed parchment bearing the word repeated several times, each time with the last letter removed until the last line read simply 'A'. The theory behind the charm was that as the word decreased in length, so the evil influence operating on the patient was reduced.

It has been suggested that the word itself may have been formed from the initials of the Hebrew words Ab (Father), Ben (Son), and Ruach A Cadsch (Holy Ghost). Alternatively the word may once have been the name of a feared demon, now long-forgotten. In the modern pantomime 'abracadabra' is more often replaced by some more comical phrase (such as "Izzy-wizzy, let's get busy") but retains its magical significance.

acrobatics The pantomime has always incorporated acrobatics as a feature of the knockabout comedy that has distinguished its history since the earliest days. As HARLEQUIN, JOHN RICH set a high standard with his energetic and highly inventive clowning and it became the convention for performers of the role of Harlequin and later of Clown and Pantaloon to execute numerous death-defying leaps and tumbles. Many performers, including the great JOSEPH GRIMALDI, suffered frequent injuries in the course of these acrobatics, but they remained the essence of the comedy of the harlequinade to the very end.

Grimaldi was not, in fact, the most acrobatic of Clowns and relied upon a more subtle humour on the whole. Some of his contemporaries, however, made acrobatic feats the chief attraction of their performance – ROBERT BRADBURY, for instance, executed some almost incredible stunts, which included spectacular leaps from the FLIES down to the stage below (he protected himself from injury by wearing a number of pads to cushion his falls). Notable acrobats of other eras included the clown GEORGE WIELAND, the various members of the VOKES FAMILY, and FRED CONQUEST, who was famous for his popular but perilous prowl round the balcony of the dress circle in the role of CAT.

All Harlequins in the late 19th century were expected to be adept at leaping through concealed TRAPS and their most spectacular efforts were advertised in advance to attract larger audiences. It has always been common practice to add to the spectacle of the pantomime by inviting SPECIALITY ACTS of various kinds to participate and over the years these have included acrobats of every description, from high-wire walkers to trick cyclists. Such acts still appear in the pantomime today, though with less frequency and often to the exasperation of audiences who resent the interruption to the plot that their acts cause.

act One of the parts into which the pantomime (and other forms of drama) are usually divided. The earliest pantomimes (lasting anything from one to two hours and comprising only a part of the evening's entertainment, which might last five hours) were delivered as one act, which was generally split into 18 SCENES. In the modern pantomime, however, a show has two acts, allowing opportunities for major set changes to be made and for refreshments to be purchased (most theatre managements insist upon taking a percentage of the considerable profits made from the selling of ice creams in the interval).

Adelphi Theatre A theatre in the Strand, London, which was once famous for its spectacular pantomimes. The theatre began life as the **Sans Pareil Theatre** in 1806, being renamed the Adelphi in 1819, the **Theatre Royal New Adelphi** in 1829, the **Royal Adelphi Theatre** in 1867, the **Century Theatre** in 1901, the Royal Adelphi Theatre in 1902, and simply the Adelphi in 1940.

The theatre was particularly well known for its pantomimes in the Victorian era; famous productions included *Mother Shipton* (1855), starring MADAME CÉLESTE as COLUMBINE, and *The Children of the Wood* (1874), in which the comedian JAMES FAWN first sang 'Tommy Make Room for your Uncle'. Among other stars to appear at the theatre in the 19th century were NELSON LEE, who played HARLEQUIN in one of his own pantomimes in the 1830s, and the Clowns RICHARD FLEXMORE and Watty Hildyard. Somewhat against his image as a musician of great intellectual seriousness, the composer Richard Wagner greatly enjoyed a visit to the pantomime here in 1855.

Ultimately the Adelphi, which is usually remembered for the 'Adelphi dramas' of J. B. BUCKSTONE, switched to musical comedy and revue and the theatre's long tradition of pantomime came to an end.

ad lib To deliver lines of one's own invention on the spur of the moment. This basic acting skill is particularly relevant to the pantomime where the physical nature of the action can easily lead to unpredictable events and mishaps, which must be 'covered' by the performers on stage.

The early pantomime was largely silent, but as DIALOGUE came to be adopted more widely in the late 18th century so skill at ad libbing gradually acquired new importance. There was relatively little opportunity for it in the later 19th century when scripts were written in elaborate rhymed verse, but the introduction from the 1860s onwards of MUSIC HALL artists, who were skilled in such extemporising, restored the importance of spontaneous wit.

Contemporary pantomimes are performed to relatively complete scripts but actors are allowed considerable licence to add their own humorous observations, which might simply be responses to taunts or queries from the audience or jokes at the expense of the government or personalities currently in the news (*see* TOPICALITY).

The best performers have a fund of instant responses for use in times of emergency and the most memorable moments in 20th-century pantomime history include numerous instances of able performers turning potential disaster into hilarity through an inspired ad lib. Typical of such instances was a production of *SINBAD THE SAILOR*, which featured Johnny Beattie as dame – on the first night none of the four comedians in the show could climb up the side of the Terrible Whale as intended, as the creature had been covered with slippery black plastic: the comedians were rendered helpless with laughter (as was the audience) and it was left to Beattie to save the day by coming downstage and delivering a sequence of topical gags until order was restored. *See also* CATCHPHRASES.

advertising The naming of particular commercial products or shops and the like in exchange for payment or some other benefit. Advertising has been an important factor in theatre finance for at least 300 years and is of particular relevance to the pantomime, one of the costliest but most financially rewarding forms of British drama.

When the pantomime first began to attract large audiences drawn from all sectors of socicty in the early 18th century owners of various businesses quickly realised the potential the pantomime offered for building up commercial reputations. Subsequently all manner of brand names were trotted out, sometimes purely for comic effect but more often because an advertiser had paid for his product, hotel, or other business to be favourably mentioned.

The names of these commercial enterprises frequently adorned the shop windows and doorways that were essential features of the knockabout comedy of the HARLEQUINADE and it was not unheard of for characters to interrupt the action to deliver impromptu elegies in praise of certain commodities or services offered by local tradesmen. Well-known examples of the practice in the past have included references to the various companies that ran street gaslights in the early 19th century and CHARLES DIBDIN's *Thirty Thousand; or, Harlequin's Lottery* (1810), which incorporated plentiful references to the newly-launched National Lottery (the plot revolved around the winner of £30,000 on the lottery).

Insurance companies often sponsored pantomimes in the early 19th century. This was to the advantage of the pantomimists, who made the most of the comic possibilities arising from the fact that the insurance companies then ran the country's fire-fighting forces. JOSEPH GRIMALDI, for instance, was famous for his stirring song 'Hope' – though the last line made it clear he was in fact singing about the Hope Life Insurance Company.

Later in the Victorian era performers playing Clown stepped out of character to do some SWEET-THROWING, announcing the names of the sponsors who had provided the sweets as they tossed bags of nuts and candies into the audience. Many deals were struck between commercial concerns and individual performers, scene-painters, and writers (rather than the theatre managements themselves) through which a certain amount of the product being advertised would be given in payment for such mentions on the stage. It was quite common for actors to exchange such deals among themselves according to which commodity each preferred.

Such links with trade continued into the 20th century: a production of *SLEEPING BEAUTY* in 1929 featured a set based on the children's Meccano construction toy, while another pantomime of the same decade, *BABES IN THE WOOD*, had the two babes dressed as the 'Bisto Kids' associated with Bisto gravy. More recent pantomimes have featured such characters as Fairy Liquid (and have gleaned another soap-inspired witticism through the line "Can I kiss your palm, Olive?").

Advertising in the contemporary pantomime is generally more discreet than hitherto and confined to sponsorship of the theatres or productions themselves or to programme credits (often in return for goods or services provided to the theatre). Brand names are, however, still often quoted in jokes without anyone objecting, though modern managements, mindful of possible legal problems, sometimes insist upon such trade names being given in a garbled form.

aerial diorama *See* DIORAMA.

afterpiece A short theatrical entertainment that was formerly presented at the close of an evening's programme. Such pieces were usually light comedies or dance shows designed as light relief after a full-blown tragedy or other serious production. It was as afterpieces that the ITALIAN NIGHT SCENES and early HARLEQUINADES were seen in the first half of the 18th century, although as time passed the popularity of the harlequinade made the afterpiece the central event of the evening and noisy audiences would often make no secret of their impatience for the preceding entertainments to end. The management at DRURY LANE finally acknowledged reality in 1879 when AUGUSTUS HARRIS made his pantomimes the sole item of an evening's programme. *See also* FOREPIECE.

Aladdin The PRINCIPAL BOY in *ALADDIN AND HIS WONDERFUL LAMP*. Aladdin is the feckless son of a lowly laundrywoman (*see* WIDOW TWANKEY) but goes on to win wealth and the hand of the Sultan's daughter through the aid of a magic LAMP and the help of two GENIES. Notable early performers of the part included Mrs. Charles Kemble and MARIE WILTON; subsequently HETTY KING and more recently such performers as CILLA BLACK, Isla St. Clair, and Lorraine Chase have proved popular in the role. Males have appeared as Aladdin with increasing frequency in recent years, including among their ranks NORMAN WISDOM and Cliff Richard.

Aladdin and his Wonderful Lamp One of the most enduring of all pantomimes, second only to *CINDERELLA* in popularity. Associated with the *ARABIAN NIGHTS ENTERTAINMENTS*, though only included in the original manuscripts as a supplementary tale, the story was first performed as a pantomime in a version by John O'Keeffe at COVENT GARDEN on Boxing Day 1788, at a time when the public was obsessed with a taste for all things oriental.

The action in O'Keeffe's version revolved around CARLO DELPINI as PIERROT; the music was composed by the Theatre Royal's resident composer William Shield. The costumes used in the production were a startling combination of Chinese, Japanese, and Persian styles and similarly colourful (though historically fairly inaccurate) costumes have been used in performances of the story ever since.

The tale soon became a favourite in the repertory of many theatres, the Theatre Royal itself returning to it in a further non-pantomime production directed by CHARLES FARLEY in 1813, this time with Mrs. Charles Kemble playing ALADDIN and JOSEPH GRIMALDI as Kasrac.

Aladdin as modern audiences recognise it, however, is descended from H. J. BYRON's classic EXTRAVAGANZA *Aladdin or the Wonderful Scamp*, which was first seen at the Strand Theatre in 1861. Celebrated productions since then have included the 1874 version seen at DRURY LANE, in which all the main roles were played by members of the famous VOKES FAMILY. The 1956–57 production seen at the LONDON PALLADIUM was significant in that it starred the comedian NORMAN WISDOM as PRINCIPAL BOY, establishing a trend for male principal boys that was to dominate the pantomime through the late 1950s and 1960s. Like most pantomimes still performed, *Aladdin* exists in many different variants. Virtually all the most popular pantomime writers in the postwar period have included a version of the tale in their repertoire (a script by JOHN MORLEY was even performed with a Chinese cast in Hong Kong).

As well as the exotic location, the most successful common elements of the plot include the clowning of WIDOW TWANKEY, thc LAUNDRY SCENE in which Aladdin is pursued by two CHINESE POLICEMEN through various concealed TRAPS, and the magical appearances of the two GENIES. Film versions of the story include the somewhat lacklustre movie *The Wonders of Aladdin* (1961), starring Donald O'Connor and Vittorio De Sica, and a spectacular full-length Disney cartoon (1992). *See also* RUN.

Story Aladdin is the penniless son of Widow Twankey, who manages the local laundry in Peking. He is constantly in trouble for his unruly ways and a great trial to his long-suffering mother (as is the dim-witted WISHEE-WASHEE). Aladdin's adventures begin when ABANAZAR, a sorcerer from Egypt or Morocco, pretends to be his long-lost uncle and saves Aladdin from the executioner's sword. It is then easy for him to persuade Aladdin to go down into a cave to fetch a magic LAMP that has been left there. The sorcerer hands him a signet ring with the promise that it will preserve him from harm.

Once in the cave, Aladdin quickly finds the lamp; when he refuses, however, to hand up the lamp until he is safely above ground, the evil Abanazar flies into a rage and seals the entrance to the cave. Now trapped underground, Aladdin rubs the signet ring and thereby conjures up the Genie of the Ring, who grants his wish to be released from the cave. When Aladdin (or his mother) subsequently rubs the magic lamp in an attempt to clean it, he calls up a second, even more powerful genie, who grants him any wish he desires. At Aladdin's request for great wealth the Genie magically transforms the cave into an "Alcove of a thousand jewels" (at which point the first act usually ends).

Aladdin and his mother are now able to live in luxury, with Widow Twankey indulging her taste for lavish costumes and jewellery, while Aladdin entertains hopes of marrying the Emperor of China's daughter, Lady BADROUBALDOUR. The Emperor is shocked at Aladdin's presumption and makes impossible demands of him, saying that he must build overnight a marvellous palace for his daughter if he is to win her hand (plots vary greatly at this point). If he fails he will be executed. The Genie of the Lamp carries out the task and Aladdin is betrothed to the Emperor's daughter. (In the original tale, it is stipulated that the palace must have 24 windows studded with precious jewels; the 24th window is deliberately left bare by the Genie for the Emperor to decorate in a similar manner, but his resources prove inadequate for the task).

Abanazar, meanwhile, schemes to retrieve the lamp in the disguise of a travelling merchant and tours the streets of Peking with the cry "New lamps for old!" The Emperor's daughter, unaware of the now-neglected lamp's magical properties, exchanges it with the sorcerer, who orders the Genie to transport Aladdin and his family to the deserts of Africa (often Egypt, where the inevitable Mummy and Camel provide further comic relief). Aladdin uses the sorcerer's ring to summon up the Genie of the Ring, who returns them to Peking (sometimes via magic carpet). Aladdin succeeds in unmasking the sorcerer (in the original version he is poisoned, but in the pantomime he is more usually put to work in Widow Twankey's laundry or otherwise humiliated). All live happily ever after, with several pairs of characters becoming betrothed, sometimes including Widow Twankey to the Emperor himself.

Origins Several elements of the story are common to other pantomime plots (notably *The Tinder Box*) and are derived from ancient folkloric sources. The lamp appears in both Asiatic and European tales, while the cave with its various treasures and the magical transportation of the hero and his bride on their wedding night belong to Arabic tradition. In an Indian version the hero receives and recovers the lamp by different means – often through the intervention of some sympathetic animal for whom he has previously performed some favour. In a version from Bohemia he is aided by a dog, cat, and snake, whose lives he has saved. The hero is then given a magic watch (in an Albanian version it is a wishing stone), which provides him with a palace and the hand of the king's daughter. When the princess subsequently uses the watch to create a palace for herself out at sea, the animals attempt to retrieve it but drop it in the water, from which it is nonetheless recovered by a fish.

Ali Baba The central character in *ALI BABA AND THE FORTY THIEVES*, who learns the magic formula to open the robbers' cave and is then protected from their revenge by the slave girl Morgiana. A poor wood-gatherer who happens upon the robbers' secret hoard of gold by accident, Ali Baba has to contend with the greed of his brother Kasim and a plot to secure his own murder before he is able to relax and enjoy his new-found wealth. *See also* OPEN SESAME.

Ali Baba and the Forty Thieves A traditional pantomime in which the poor ALI BABA steals a robber band's store of gold and subsequently escapes retribution with the help of the servant girl Morgiana. The story was first seen on English stages as a melodrama based on one of the supplementary tales associated with the *ARABIAN NIGHTS ENTERTAINMENTS*. The earliest versions of it included a BURLESQUE seen at the LYCEUM THEATRE in 1844 as *Open Sesame; or, A Night with the Forty Thieves*.

As a pantomime proper its history dates back to 1846, when a version of the tale was presented at ASTLEY'S AMPHITHEATRE as *The Forty Thieves; or, Harlequin Ali Baba and the Robbers' Cave*, an EQUESTRIAN DRAMA by NELSON LEE, in which most of the characters, including the thieves, entered on horseback. The story subsequently became a great favourite and productions of *Ali Baba and the Forty Thieves* were among the most lavish presented on the Victorian stage, with vast bejewelled caves, oriental dancing, and even, in a version at the Lyceum Theatre, Edinburgh in 1885, a troupe of trick cyclists. Equally spectacular was the version staged at DRURY LANE in 1898 as *The Forty Thieves*, which featured classic comic performances by DAN LENO and HERBERT CAMPBELL.

Successful productions in the first half of the 20th century included two further versions presented at the Lyceum (1924–25 and 1935–36). In more recent times the pantomime has been seen less frequently on the professional stage, largely because of the expense involved in hiring a full cast of robbers – although many modern productions have attempted to find some way round this (the simplest solution being to avoid having all the robbers on the stage at the same time). Another feature that militates against frequent revivals is the superstition of obscure origin that the play brings bad luck to those involved in it.

Film versions of the story date back to 1902 and include *Ali Baba Goes To Town* (1937), starring Eddie Cantor, *Ali Baba and the Forty Thieves* (1944), starring Jon Hall, *Son of Ali Baba* (1952), starring Tony Curtis, *The Adventures of Hajji Baba* (1956), starring John Derek, and *Sword of Ali Baba* (1964), starring Peter Mann.

Story Ali Baba, a penniless woodcutter, is out gathering firewood one day when he comes across a robber band hiding away a hoard of stolen gold. At the command OPEN SESAME a large rock moves aside, revealing the entrance to a cave in which the thieves conceal their booty. Having sealed the cave with the command "shut sesame", the robbers ride off and Ali Baba decides to try his luck, repeating the magic formula. The rock moves aside and inside he finds a fabulous store of gold, silks, carpets, and other treasures. Quickly, Ali Baba loads his asses with riches and makes good his escape.

Once home, Ali Baba keeps news of his wealth to himself but arouses the suspicions of his brother Kasim and his wife. When Ali Baba returns some scales he has borrowed from Kasim's wife to weigh his money he fails to notice that a gold piece has stuck to some wax she has hidden in the bowl and his secret is out. Kasim forces Ali Baba to tell how he got his riches and immediately sets out with ten mules. He finds the cave and gains entrance using the magic formula but then forgets the words required to open the door again and is still in the cave when the robbers return. Kasim is killed by the thieves – in modern pantomime versions he is more often taken prisoner or else magically restored to life – and his body is quartered and hung on the inside of the cave door, where Ali Baba later finds it. When Kasim's body disappears, the thieves realise that someone else knows their secret and they soon arrive at Ali Baba's house.

The leader of the robbers disguises himself as an oil merchant (or sometimes as an old woman) and his men hide themselves in oil jars with orders to remain there until the signal is given for them to come out and kill Ali Baba; one oil jar is filled with oil to complete the deception. The merchant then arranges for Ali Baba to store the oil jars in his house. As the robbers lie in wait for their signal, Ali Baba's servant girl Morgiana approaches one of the jars in order to refill a lamp with oil (in many pantomimes Morgiana is made a FAIRY GODMOTHER character and the DAME plays the servant girl). The robber inside assumes it must be his leader and asks if it is time to come out. Morgiana replies "Not yet" and quickly boils up a cauldron of oil taken from the one filled jar. She then pours the boiling oil into each of the other jars, scalding the robbers to death (in the pantomime, they are generally excused such a grisly death and overpowered by itching powder or otherwise humiliated by more humane – and comic – means).

Ali Baba is duly grateful to Morgiana for saving his life and promises her his son in marriage (in some pantomime versions, he marries her himself). The role of Ali Baba's son is often treated as a part for a PRINCIPAL BOY, while Ali Baba and his brother are generally played by men.

Origins Like many other pantomimes, the story of Ali Baba often has elements taken from other pantomimes grafted onto it, but the central story comes straight from the *ARABIAN NIGHTS ENTERTAINMENTS*, which itself has links with much earlier myths common to Indian, Arabian, African, Estonian, and Finnish legend. A similar ruse to that adopted by the robbers in hiding themselves in the oil jars is employed by the warriors in the Welsh epic called the *Mabinogion*, who hide themselves in leather sacks in order to ambush Bran when he visits Ireland to rescue Branwen; Cypriot folklore also boasts a story in which an ogre conceals his men in bales. Other features of the story that are common to a wide range of myths from various countries include the magic formula, the underground treasure chamber, and the borrowed scales.

amateur pantomime The presentation of annual pantomimes remains one of the staple activities of numerous amateur theatre groups throughout the UK (and in other parts of the world where the influence of the pantomime has been extended). Mirroring the experience of the professional theatre, performances of pantomime are considered important in the programmes of all kinds of amateur companies as they provide funding for productions of other kinds throughout the rest of the year.

There is a long and glorious tradition of amateur pantomime, with such distinguished exponents as CHARLES DICKENS among those to present such productions on a regular basis back in the 19th century, although many shows were the subject of derision from critics who found them lacking in virtually all departments. In the modern age, when pantomime has struggled to retain its traditional hold on the West End (there was not a single professional production in the West End in the 1992–93 season), the amateur theatre – through such leading companies as the Questors of Ealing – has continued to maintain the pantomime tradition, often at a standard comparing very well with that of professional companies.

Improvements in standards have been particularly noticeable since World War II, arguably a side-effect of the influence of high-quality television light entertainment. Though lacking the resources of professional companies, amateur pantomimes are sheltered from the often debilitating necessity to tailor scripts for CELEBRITY STARS and often have a sense of frivolity and liveliness that can be lacking on the professional stage. Amateur directors also have a very clear idea of what their audience wants and despite financial restrictions can draw on much larger casts than could possibly be afforded in the professional theatre (one of the best examples of this being the ballroom scene in *Cinderella* in which the amateur director can crowd the stage with members of the chorus, whereas the professional director is lucky if he can finance even half-a-dozen guests). In recent years increasing pressure has been put on the acting unions to allow amateur performers to play in such scenes in professional productions in order to solve this problem, without much success to date.

Scripts in the amateur pantomime are often very good, being either self-written or by the same authors who write for the professional theatre (many professional pantomime writers deliberately design their scripts so that they are equally suited to performance in a major theatre complete with all technical resources and in a local village hall with virtually no resources whatsoever).

One indication of the current strength of the amateur pantomime is the fact that it continues to prosper even when in competition with a professional show nearby, luring healthy audiences through its local reputation for relatively low ticket prices, high standards of production, and choice of strong scripts (personal contacts are also helpful). Spoof pantomimes (rarely seen on the professional stage) are an eccentricity that also flourishes on the amateur stage, with many 'alternative' shows being presented by student drama groups, rugby clubs, etc. (*see* PARODIES).

Andersen, Hans Christian (1805–75) Danish author, whose fairytales have on many occasions been used as the basis for successful pantomimes and children's plays. The son of a shoemaker, Andersen trained as an actor in Copenhagen and then (1828) attended the university there before travelling throughout Europe and taking up a career as a writer of novels, plays, and travel books.

The 138 fairytales that he wrote between 1835 and 1872 are notable for their often tragic tone and moralising interpretations of ancient folk myths and were intended to be read by adults and children alike. They included such celebrated stories as *The Snow Queen*, *The Little Mermaid*, *The Tinder Box*, and *The Ugly Duckling*.

The publication of the stories in England did much to revive public interest in the fairytale and they were eagerly latched onto by pantomimists. Several pantomimes and children's plays in the past have been constructed by combining a number of Andersen's tales with a link provided by a narrator (a device also adopted in the hit film *Hans Christian Andersen* (1952), which starred Danny Kaye).

As a teller of fairytales Andersen ranks alongside the GRIMM BROTHERS as the best regarded writer in modern literature. His death was hastened by injuries he received after falling out of bed in 1872.

Andreini, Francesco (1548–1624) Italian actor-manager and playwright, who was the senior member of a celebrated family of *COMMEDIA DELL'ARTE* players. As head of the Gelosi acting company, he was much acclaimed in the role of young lover and later in his career as Il Capitano, which role he created. He appeared both in Italy and several times in France in the late 16th century. He retired from the stage on the early death of his wife **Isabella Andreini** (Isabella Canali; 1562–1604), who was also admired as an actress with the company.

Their son, **Giovann Battista Andreini** (*c*. 1579–1654) was a noted actor and playwright. Popularly known as Lelio, the role he continued to play until the age of 73, he is thought to have been a cofounder of the Fedeli company, which played to acclaim in both Italy and France.

animals *See* DOG DRAMA; EQUESTRIAN DRAMA; SKIN PARTS.

apple A poisoned apple plays a major role in the plot of *SNOW WHITE AND THE SEVEN DWARFS*, in which Snow White is tricked by the disguised queen into taking a bite out of the poisoned red half of an apple and is thus sent into a deep drugged sleep, from which she is finally woken by a KISS. The apple has considerable folkloric significance; in various traditions it has been regarded as a symbol of immortality, chastity, magic, sexual awakening, temptation, fertility, and knowledge. It has also been used as a love charm and as protection against illness.

aquatic drama A theatrical genre of the early 19th century, in which large amounts of real water played a major role in the action of various entertainments, including pantomimes. Such productions were first staged in the circuses of Paris but subsequently they became a regular feature of the playbills of London's SADLER'S WELLS, where the stage area could be flooded with water from the New River nearby. The alterations necessary for such novel entertainments were made at the Wells in 1804 and over the years that followed many successful productions were presented as aquatic dramas. These included a number of highly acclaimed pantomimes by CHARLES DIBDIN, who deliberately adapted his plots to make full use of the possibilities offered by a flooded stage.

Besides Dibdin's pantomimes *Harlequin and the Water Kelpe* (1806), *Fashion's Fools; or, Aquatic Harlequin* (1809), and *The Mermaid; or, Harlequin Pearl-Diver* (1815), notable productions included *London; or, Harlequin and Time* (1813), which lured capacity audiences with a combination of waterborne marvels and the comic skills of the great JOSEPH GRIMALDI. Although the water was not deep, entire galleons could be launched and floated across the stage, while further spectacles included submarine grottoes and Neptune's palace as well as real waterfalls and ornamental fountains, which were often used to great effect in the climactic TRANSFORMATION SCENE.

The success of the aquatic drama at Sadler's Wells prompted many other leading venues – including COVENT GARDEN – to instal water tanks of varying dimensions so that they too could present waterborne spectacles. Covent Garden's production of *Jack in the Box* (1829) featured a real waterfall using 39 tuns of water. Specialist firms hire out equipment for fountains and waterfalls for use in the contemporary pantomime, allowing managements to thrill audiences with spectacular water effects in the first act and perhaps a comedy bathroom in which the plumbing goes disastrously wrong in the second. *See also* NAUTICAL DRAMA.

Arabian Nights Entertainments A collection of folk stories from Arabia, from which were taken the plots of several classic pantomimes. Alternatively titled the *Thousand and One Nights* (although the original Arabic title suggests an infinite number of tales rather than 1001), the collection was based on an Egyptian text written around the 15th century and is thought to have descended ultimately from Persian legend, although the tales themselves may have been derived from a wide range of cultures, including those of the Egyptians, the Indians, the Jews, and the Arabians themselves (being first put together as far back as the 8th century AD).

According to the myths surrounding the tales, they were first told by Scheherazade, bride of Sultan Schahriah, to delay her execution. The Sultan had vowed to take a new wife each night and have her strangled in the morning in revenge for his first wife's infidelity. Scheherazade volunteered to become his next wife and each night told the Sultan one of the tales, each tale leading on to the next one, until finally the delighted Sultan changed his mind about executing her.

The stories were first introduced to Europe through a French translation from a Syrian text by Antoine Galland, who compiled a 12-volume set between 1704 and 1717. English translations of separate tales followed almost immediately, with *SINBAD THE SAILOR* making its appearance in 1712 and *ALADDIN AND HIS WONDERFUL LAMP* and *ALI BABA AND THE FORTY THIEVES* in 1721–22.

The first full English translations were made by R. Heron (1792) and W. Beloe (1795); later versions based on a 17th-century Egyptian text included those of Henry Torrens (1838), E. W. Lane (1839–41), John Payne (1882–84), and Sir Richard Burton's complete edition of 1885–88. The success of the tales contributed much to the English passion for all things Oriental at the start of the 19th century (inspiring the construction of the Royal Pavilion at Brighton and the Pagoda in Kew Gardens among other extraordinary buildings) and had a profound influence upon the development of the pantomime.

Arlecchino One of the stock characters of the Italian *COMMEDIA DELL'ARTE* tradition, from whom the English HARLEQUIN ultimately developed. Together with BRIGHELLA, Arlecchino was one of the principal *ZANNI* characters responsible for the knockabout comedy on which the *commedia dell'arte* largely depended.

He was originally played as a blundering idiot from the region of Bergamo in northern Italy, which was renowned for its rustic fools, and his traits included cowardice, lust, and gluttony (it is thought possible that his name was originally *al lecchino* – the glutton).

Arlecchino was always played in a costume consisting of a belted and much-patched white rag coat with a small black mask and he also carried a wooden sword (descended from the comic phallus of ancient Roman comedy). Performers of the role had to be talented dancers and acrobats (as indicated by the hare's foot worn in his cap). The most celebrated included Tristano Martinelli and Giuseppe Biancolelli, who played the part in Paris, adding an element of pathos to the character and combining the traits of Arlecchino and Brighella to create the more sophisticated **Arlequin** – cunning, impudent, elegant, worldly-wise, and talking with a distinctive croaking voice. *See also* COMÉDIE-ITALIENNE.

Arlequin *See* ARLECCHINO.

arranger *See* DIRECTOR.

Askey, Arthur (Arthur Bowden; 1900–82) British comedian, born in Liverpool, who enjoyed a long career as one of the most popular pantomime stars of the 20th century. Nicknamed 'Big-hearted Arthur' (or 'Big-hearted Martha' when appearing as a DAME), Askey made his debut in a touring concert party in 1924 and established himself as a household name through the radio comedy show *Bandwagon*, which was first broadcast in 1938. He made regular appearances in pantomime, usually in the role of dame (notably as WIDOW TWANKEY), although he also played many other comedy roles, including BUTTONS, to great effect. Among the most successful pantomimes in which he starred was *ALADDIN AND HIS WONDERFUL LAMP* (1964) and many spectacular productions at the LONDON PALLADIUM. His irrepressible good humour and easy relationship with his audience made the diminutive Askey one of the biggest box office draws of his time, even when he was well into his seventies.

Astley's Amphitheatre A former theatre in the Westminster Bridge Road, London, where pantomimes were presented regularly as EQUESTRIAN DRAMA. Astley's Amphitheatre was as much a circus as it was a theatre and began life (in 1769) as a venue for acrobatic displays as well as equestrian entertainments. Its founder, Philip Astley (1742–1814), was a retired cavalry officer who was himself noted for his skilled riding.

The original building was destroyed by fire on several occasions but continued to prosper (from 1804 as the **Royal Amphitheatre of Arts**) under the management of ANDREW DUCROW. Ducrow combined equestrian entertainments with melodramas, among which were several plays that were subsequently to become famous as pantomimes (including *ALI BABA AND THE FORTY THIEVES*). Stars who appeared there in conventional pantomime included JOSEPH GRIMALDI and JACK BOLOGNA. Burnt down again in 1841, the theatre was renamed **Batty's Amphitheatre**, the **Theatre Royal, Westminster**, and

Sanger's Grand National Amphitheatre and remained a popular home of pantomime until demolition in 1895.

atellana A form of early Roman drama (or *fabula*) that is thought to have contributed remotely to the development of the *COMMEDIA DELL'ARTE* during the Renaissance. The *atellana* revolved around the comic antics of stock clown characters (notably MACCUS) and, in common with the *commedia dell'arte*, was distinguished by its rustic setting, bawdy humour, and use of masks and disguises; like its Renaissance counterpart it is thought to have depended heavily upon IMPROVISATION.

auction scene *See MOTHER GOOSE.*

audience The pantomime audience has changed considerably over its 300-year history. For at least the first hundred years audiences comprised mainly adults, drawn from all classes (from the very poor right up to the royal family), who flocked to marvel at the spectacles on offer and to delight in the comic antics of the harlequinade. Among the monarchs to be bewitched by the pantomime have been George III, who was a great admirer of Grimaldi, and Edward VII, who summoned Leno to give a private performance at Sandringham; the young Princesses Elizabeth and Margaret were also enthusiastic visitors to the pantomime (and even performed in one at Windsor Castle).

The contemporary pantomime audience is usually cheerful but restrained and well-behaved. It was not always thus, however, and audiences of the 18th and 19th centuries were noted for their wild spirit. The evening's entertainment was often uproarious, with fights, slanging matches, and other forms of cheerful mayhem breaking out on a regular basis at even the most prestigious venues (there were often injuries and even the occasional death as eager theatre-goers battled their way to the best seats in crowded auditoria).

One of the reasons for the often wild behaviour of audiences back in the 18th and 19th centuries was boredom and impatience generated by the fact that they were frequently obliged to sit through lengthy 'improving' FOREPIECES, of which little sense could be made in view of the faulty acoustics of most theatres of the age. They were usually much more attentive once the slapstick comedy of the pantomime began.

Audiences of around 3000 were commonplace at both COVENT GARDEN and DRURY LANE, where during a successful pantomime the theatres would be full to capacity every night for as many as 35 nights in a row. Entertainments that failed to please were rewarded with catcalls, a barrage of orange peel and nuts, and demands to bring the curtain down forthwith. In more successful shows fights would break out frequently as people jostled for a better view and the expectation of seeing a hearty brawl was part of the attraction for many who attended the pantomime in the 18th and 19th centuries. The heat in crowded auditoria was intense and tempers quickly frayed. Objects were frequently hurled from one part of the auditorium to another, though usually without causing injury, and there were even instances of a rope of neckties being made to raise dropped items from the pit to the galleries above.

The unruliest part of the house was generally the gods, and the verdict of this section of the audience on an opening night (usually Boxing Night) could spell success or disaster to a production. Most daunting of all were the occupants of the gods at the OLD VIC (then the Royal Victoria

Theatre) where audiences were drawn chiefly from the 'lower orders' and behaved even less decorously than those in other London theatres; they showered the stage with apples and orange peel and were in the habit of noisily addressing the actors by their Christian names.

Behaviour improved somewhat in the later Victorian era and by the 1880s critics were complaining that audiences were showing reluctance to comply with invitations to sing along, but the arrival of the music hall artists helped to restore something of the old vitality. The 20th-century pantomime audience has a very high proportion of children, although care is usually taken to ensure that there is enough to keep accompanying adults interested and entertained.

audience participation The involvement of the AUDIENCE in the action presented on stage, a crucial element in the success of any pantomime. Strangers to the pantomime tradition are always startled by the degree to which British audiences are accustomed to shouting out stock responses to questions and taunts from members of the cast in a manner that would be unthinkable in virtually any other form of theatre. Pantomime villains regularly invite audiences to take part in a shouting match, the two sides exchanging shouts of "Oh no, it isn't!" and "Oh yes, it is!" and the like. Other standard responses include the shouts of "Behind you!" with which the audience attempt to warn a befuddled dame of some approaching danger and catchphrases yelled out on the entrance of BUTTONS or other leading characters. Among other essential features are the full-scale singing contests in which the two halves of the audience are encouraged to outsing the other, with the assistance of selected members of the cast (*see* SINGALONG).

Such lively traditions were promoted by the influence of the riotous world of the music hall in the late 19th century although audiences in the Grimaldi era were equally willing to join in with the songs they knew and the tradition of noisy participation of all kinds harks back to conventions of medieval theatre both in England and abroad. Heated opinions have been exchanged over how far such participation should be taken: prolonged shouting matches and invitations for children celebrating a birthday to come on stage, for instance, can bring the plot to a complete standstill and reduce less enthusiastic members of the audience to a state of frustrated embarrassment.

In some pantomimes the audience's role in the action can be very direct, assisting in finding Aladdin's LAMP, for instance, guarding the Golden Goose, keeping an eye on Buttons' boots, or foiling the plans of the villains by, for example, dazzling them by holding up specially-provided slips of silver paper to reflect the stage lights into their eyes. Villains are jeered and hissed at their every entrance and impromptu threats delivered by irate toddlers are part and parcel of the humour of every good production. Even normally reserved adults can be beguiled into joining in. Such good-humoured impromptu exchanges hark back to the pre-Victorian theatre, when audiences (particularly on Boxing Day) were often noisy and even violent. *See also* CATCHPHRASES.

audition A test at which actors and actresses are asked to show their suitability for a particular role. Performers – who may have been personally invited to the audition or may have responded to advertisements in various trade publications – are asked to demonstrate before the director (or casting director) their skills as singers and dancers as well as actors. Subsequent auditions may also be held before a final choice of performers (and possibly understudies) is announced. Casting for professional pantomimes may take place many months before a production actually goes into rehearsal (sometimes more than a year in advance of the first night).

auditorium The main body of a theatre, in which the AUDIENCE sits. Formerly also called the **auditory** or **spectatory** in the 19th century, the auditorium has changed in shape over the years. In the classical theatre it was an open horseshoe or semicircular area surrounding the stage and was often cut into a hillside, which provided convenient tiered seating and also good acoustic properties. The Elizabethan theatre generally had a circular auditorium, but by the time of the development of the pantomime audiences were generally accommodated in a deep rectangle in front of a PROSCENIUM ARCH, which separated the stage from the auditorium itself. An earlier convention that allowed distinguished patrons of a theatre to sit on benches situated at the sides of the stage itself had already fallen more or less into disuse and was finally outlawed by DAVID GARRICK. Wealthier members of the audience could pay extra to sit in a BOX rather than in the PIT or GALLERY where the cheaper seats were. *See also* BALCONY; CIRCLE; STALLS.

Augustus Druriolanus *See* HARRIS, SIR AUGUSTUS HENRY GLOSSOP.

Aulnoy, Marie-Cathérine Le Jumel de Barneville de la Motte, Comtesse d' (*c*. 1650–1705) French author, who wrote a number of fairytales that were later turned into popular pantomimes. Madame d'Aulnoy was married into a respected Norman family at a young age but many years later retired to a convent (or possibly to Spain) after apparently plotting the execution of her husband for high treason. She published a romantic novel based on a folktale in 1690 and went on to produce in all 25 fairytales, among other writings. She was in much demand in fashionable circles for her recitations of well-known fairytales, which she may have reworked by adding details from the mythology of Normandy and other native French sources. Many of her stories were gathered together as the tales of **Mother Bunch**, an equivalent of the MOTHER GOOSE figure associated with the tales of CHARLES PERRAULT.

Successful pantomimes based on her fairytales included *Mother Bunch and the Yellow Dwarf*, which was staged in London in 1807 and EXTRAVAGANZAS written by J. R. PLANCHÉ in the 1840s and 1850s; in an attempt to restore Madame d'Aulnoy's versions in their original condition Planché compiled a translation of them in 1855. As well as *THE YELLOW DWARF*, her best-known tales on the pantomime stage included *THE WHITE CAT*.

awkward squad A stock comedy scene of the contemporary pantomime, that dates back nearly 200 years. Typically the scene revolves around the hilarious attempts of the DAME to marshal a body of volunteers or incompetent troops into an efficient fighting force with which to march against the villains of the story. Such scenes are standard in *MOTHER GOOSE* and other pantomimes and are sometimes further embellished with the addition of guest 'soldiers' from the audience.

The first such awkward squads were seen in the pantomime in the early 1800s, when the British Army was faring relatively badly against Napoleonic France. The Army's failures were particularly embarrassing when seen in the context of the victories achieved by Nelson's Navy and by the time the Army had finally improved its record with glory at Waterloo and elsewhere the pantomime had already made Britain's land forces a favourite target for good-natured satire. JOSEPH GRIMALDI in particular convulsed audiences with his chaotic attempts as Clown to drill his men, who were as unlikely a body of heroes as was imaginable. Representatives from the Horse Guards who witnessed the scene sent angry letters to the theatre where Grimaldi was appearing, but the popularity of the scene ensured its survival, and he revived it again and again in successive productions (in *Harlequin and the Swans* (1813) he even went to the extent of replacing his living recruits with animated barrels).

B

Babes in the Wood, The One of the most popular traditional pantomimes, which relates the story of two children who are abandoned in a deep forest by order of their Wicked Uncle. Based on an old English ballad registered in 1595 (and now preserved in the British Museum), the story was first presented on the stage in 1793, when *The Children in the Wood*, an opera, was performed at the Haymarket.

In this early version the two babes survived their ordeal and were restored to their parents but other early pantomime versions often stuck to the more gloomy conclusion of the original ballad. The babes both succumbed to the elements in *Harlequin and Cock Robin; or, the Babes in the Wood*, a spectacular production culminating in a stunning performance by a team of tightrope walkers that was presented at DRURY LANE in 1827, and in a further version seen at the Haymarket in 1856.

COVENT GARDEN'S 1874 pantomime *The Babes in the Wood and the Big Bed of Ware* also retained the unhappy ending and had the wicked uncle responsible for the deaths of the two babes meeting his own end while sleeping in the famous Bed of Ware. Other Victorian versions had the babes being rescued from their fate by ROBIN HOOD (who first appeared in the story in a production of 1867 and is sometimes played by a man) and in modern interpretations of the tale the children invariably survive to unmask their evil uncle.

The parts of the two children have been interpreted by a wide variety of actors, from small children to comedians; one of the most memorable productions featured the classic comic partnership of DAN LENO and HERBERT CAMPBELL, who appeared as the babes in a DRURY LANE version of 1897.

The story has maintained its popularity over the years: a version staged at the Stoll Theatre in London in 1941–42 attracted 2,500 people twice daily. Recent reworkings of the tale include pantomimes by such noted writers as Paul Reakes, Alan Brown, Verne Morgan, JOHN MORLEY, and DAVID WOOD.

Story When their father dies, two young children (whose names vary from one version to another) are entrusted to the care of their uncle (often identified in the pantomime as a wicked baron). The uncle, however, is eager to acquire the fortune left to the children and knows that it will pass to him if the children should die. Accordingly, he persuades two cronies to take the children deep into the woods and to murder them there. One of the would-be murderers relents, however, at the last moment and instead kills his companion and leaves the unharmed children to their fate (alternatively the lives of the babes are protected by a guardian fairy). The children find blackberries to eat and when they sleep the birds cover them with leaves to keep them warm (the original ballad ends at this point with their deaths).

In most modern versions of the tale, they are then discovered by Robin Hood and Maid Marian, who may also, somewhat conveniently, be the children's nurse. The evil deeds of the children's uncle are subsequently unmasked and he is obliged to repent of his wickedness as all are happily reunited. In many modern versions the Sheriff of Nottingham is also implicated in the affair and plays the role of chief villain (sometimes he is identified as the wicked uncle to whose keeping the babes are entrusted).

Origins The central theme of abandoned children belongs to the mythology of many folk cultures (as does the magical aid offered by the sympathetic birds) although the immediate source for the plot of the well-known pantomime is a celebrated English ballad, which claimed to be based on real events.

According to the ballad, first recorded by the Stationers' Hall in 1595 as *The Children in the Wood; or, the Norfolk Gentleman's Last Will and Testament*, a wealthy widower from Watton in Norfolk left his two children to the care of his brother, who subsequently plotted their deaths. On his orders two "ruffians strong" took the children into the depths of nearby Wayland Wood, where one of them took pity on the babes and instead murdered his companion before making off, on the pretence that he was going in search of food. The children survived for a time by eating blackberries but eventually died and a robin redbreast covered their bodies with leaves (a reference to the ancient superstition that robins never suffer a dead body to remain unburied). Ill luck then dogged the children's uncle with the deaths of his own sons, the loss of his farm and animals, and finally his own demise in gaol, while the remaining murderer was condemned to death after his arrest for highway robbery and confession to his part in the children's deaths.

The fact that some pantomimes of the past gave the children Italianate names suggests that there may have been a play of Italian origin upon which the ballad itself was based. The story may alternatively have had its roots in anti-Catholic propaganda (the Wicked Uncle being made out to be a Catholic). Ancient stone carvings telling the story are kept in a library close to the ruined Griston Hall, where the Wicked Uncle of history actually lived.

bacchanalia The ritualistic celebrations in honour of Bacchus, the Roman god of nature and wine, that played an important role in the development of comic drama and established certain conventions that are still observed today in the pantomime. The bawdy humour of the simple dramatic entertainments presented in the course of these celebrations, the practice of cross-dressing (slaves were allowed to wear the clothes of their masters and mistresses), and the depiction of satyrs as half-men half-animals were among the features of these early spectacles that came eventually to be revived in the Italian COMMEDIA DELL'ARTE during the Renaissance and were thus transmitted to the English pantomime (which has ironically acquired its own ritual significance through its association with CHRISTMAS). *See also* PLAUTUS, TITUS MACCIUS.

Badroubaldour, Lady The Emperor of China's daughter in *ALADDIN AND HIS WONDERFUL LAMP*, with whom ALADDIN falls in love. In the modern pantomime the role is invariably played by a female, although this was not the case in some of the earliest productions when the part was occasionally portrayed by male performers and once, in a version at the Royal Princess's Theatre in 1856, by a man on stilts.

bailiffs *See* BROKER'S MEN.

balcony The upper level of seating in the auditorium, often where the best seats in the house are. *See also* GALLERY.

ball *See CINDERELLA*.

ballad A folk song of the type familiar to the cultures of most European nations. English folk ballads in particular furnished the pantomime with a number of plots, some of which were also shared by the ballad traditions of Scandinavia and other countries. Many ballads told the story of the adventures of ROBIN HOOD, while others related the events that were to form the basis of the pantomime *THE BABES IN THE WOOD*. One of the most popular ballads to be parodied was the melodramatic tale of *Black Ey'd Susan*, which reached the pantomime after being successfully adapted as a play by Douglas Jerrold. Such ballads were available in printed form from the 16th century onwards and varied widely from the tragic to the whimsical and downright bawdy.

ballet-pantomime *See* ITALIAN NIGHT SCENES.

Bard, Wilkie (William Augustus Smith; 1870–1944) English comedian and singer, born in Manchester, who became one of the most popular of all pantomime DAMES. Bard began his career as an amateur after working as a clerk in a textile firm, subsequently appearing in Manchester's free-and-easies under the name 'Will Gibbard' and then arriving in London, where he adopted a distinctive bald wig and spotted eyebrows. He made his pantomime debut at Manchester's Gaiety Theatre in 1906, in the role of WIDOW TWANKEY, and won immediate acclaim. His many subsequent pantomime triumphs included two appearances at DRURY LANE, in 1908 as IDLE JACK and in 1909 as Widow Twankey (opposite GEORGE GRAVES as ABANAZAR).

Famous for such songs as 'I Want to Sing in Opera' and 'Popping In and Out', he became the first PIERROT to earn £100 a week. It was through his success with such songs as 'She Sells Sea Shells, on the Sea Shore' and 'The Leith Police Dismisseth Us' that the vogue for tongue-twisting songs in the pantomime took root. He continued to delight pantomime audiences with his timing and his rich, inimitable voice until he retired shortly before his death.

Barnes, James (1788–1838) English actor, who was much admired in the role of PANTALOON. Barnes made his debut with the DRURY LANE company while they were in temporary residence at the LYCEUM THEATRE in 1809 and subsequently made the role his own, appearing alongside the great JOSEPH GRIMALDI both at COVENT GARDEN and SADLER'S WELLS. He was unrivalled in his depiction of Pantaloon as a feeble-minded old man and numbered among his many admirers such notable figures as Leigh Hunt and J. R. PLANCHÉ. The exertions of his role, which like Grimaldi he often performed at two theatres nightly, contributed to his early death at the age of 50.

Baroness The second wife of BARON HARDUP and WICKED STEPMOTHER to Cinders in *CINDERELLA*. This was once one of the great comic roles of the pantomime, being played by such prominent performers as JOSEPH GRIMALDI prior to his transformation into CLOWN. Although subsequent stars such as DAN LENO also appeared in the role years later, the part gradually lost ground as the UGLY SISTERS became the comic focus of the story; in many modern versions of the tale the Baroness is omitted altogether.

Baron Hardup CINDERELLA's father, who is completely dominated by his second wife (*see* BARONESS) and by his two step-daughters (*see* UGLY SISTERS). In most modern productions of the story he feels keenly for Cinderella's distress but is too feeble (or drunk) to do anything about it. His domestic problems are compounded by the fact that he is virtually penniless, hence his name, which has also been given in various versions of the story as Baron Balderdash (as in H. J. BYRON's pantomime of 1860), Baron Stoneybroke, and Baron Pas de Largent. In the days of the HARLEQUINADE the actor playing the Baron was usually transformed into CLOWN. Popular Barons over the years have included the comedian GEORGE JACKLEY. Equivalents of the Baron in other pantomime stories include Alderman Fitzwarren in *DICK WHITTINGTON AND HIS CAT*.

Bathing the Baby Traditional knockabout routine that was one of the most celebrated of JOSEPH GRIMALDI's comedy acts, in the role of CLOWN. The routine, which long survived Grimaldi himself, comprised a series of gags during the course of which Clown cheerfully maltreated an infant in a hilarious parody of the usual feeding and cleaning routines. 'Babies' were tossed, cleaned with mops, squeezed through mangles, fed with giant ladles, washed with boiling water, and otherwise misused to the glee of audiences in countless pantomimes. Public taste eventually protested against the routine in the late Victorian era, although distant echoes of it are preserved in the contemporary pantomime in the comical attempts of an incompetent dame (in the role of NURSE) to care for the infant royal princess in *SLEEPING BEAUTY*. JOHN MORLEY recently also revived the scene in his version of *JACK AND THE BEANSTALK*.

beans The magic beans that IDLE JACK acquires in exchange for his mother's cow and which subsequently sprout into the BEANSTALK by means of which he climbs up to the GIANT's castle above the clouds. Beans have long had significance in the folklore of many cultures. The Romans are known to have offered beans to the dead on what was called the Bean Calends, while the Greeks had a taboo against eating them. Beans also have ritual significance in Japanese tradition and among various Indian and African peoples. In several stories from around the world beans grow into ladders to the sky as in the pantomime. In an updated reworking of the story by DAVID WOOD (as *Jack and the Giant*) Jack meets some spacemen and exchanges the cow for some tins of baked beans (which he thinks are rocket boosters) and a baked bean tin tree appears.

beanstalk The beanstalk that Jack climbs in *JACK AND THE BEANSTALK* has an ancient lineage in folklore worldwide. Beanstalks that grow overnight are found in folk tales from British, Tuscan, Breton, Flemish, Slavonic, Jamaican, Philippine, and Fijian cultures and there are obvious links with the biblical story of Jacob's ladder as well as with the world-tree of Norse myth. In various different stories, the hero concerned ascends the beanstalk (or other ladder) to the sky to retrieve a friend or lover, obtain riches as Jack does, to catch the sun, or simply to see what lies at the end of it. Sometimes the means of ascent is a rope; in other myths it is a giant cabbage, a road, a tower, or a ladder of sunbeams. In an early version of the pantomime tale the beanstalk is so huge that there are entire towns built on its leaves and Jack pauses in his climb to refresh himself at an inn.

Beauty and the Beast Enduringly popular pantomime concerning the story of a girl whose selfless love for a hideous monster transforms him into a handsome lover. The story is based on an ancient legend common to several cultural traditions and was first presented on the English stage in something approaching its modern form by J. R. PLANCHÉ at COVENT GARDEN in 1841, although it had previously been seen in a variety of adaptations in earlier decades (in 1821, for instance, at the ADELPHI as *Beauty and the Beast; or, Harlequin and the Magic Rose*).

Celebrated productions over the years have included the 1900 DRURY LANE pantomime *The Sleeping Beauty and the Beast* starring DAN LENO and HERBERT CAMPBELL and two versions presented at the LYCEUM THEATRE by the MELVILLE BROTHERS (1928–29 and 1937–38). More recent versions include one by David Cregan and a children's play based on the plot by Nicholas Stuart Gray – although the story is performed less now because of the similarity it bears to *CINDERELLA* (with its feeble father and two sisters etc.). The story was filmed with great success by Jean Cocteau in 1946 and has also been rendered as a full-length cartoon by the Disney studios.

Story A penniless merchant sets out to regain his lost fortune and asks his three daughters what they would like him to bring home for them. The two eldest (rather unpleasant) daughters ask for expensive presents, but the youngest – called Beauty – asks for just a rose. The merchant has no success in regaining his wealth and on the way home passes a mysterious castle, where he is entertained by an unseen host. In the garden he spies a beautiful rose; remembering his daughter's request, he picks it and is at once threatened by the owner of the castle – a hideous monster – who demands one of his daughters in punishment for the theft.

The merchant sorrowfully tells his daughters of his experience and Beauty offers to go to the Beast. The Beast is touched by Beauty's selflessness and treats her with kindness, till eventually she falls in love with him, despite his ugliness. The Beast allows Beauty to go home to visit her sick father but warns her not to stay too long, for he will die of grief. She lingers, however, and when she finally returns to the castle, Beauty finds that the Beast is dying.

Her grief breaks the spell that binds the Beast and he is restored to the handsome young prince he really is (in the days of the harlequinade he would be transformed into Harlequin). The tale conventionally ends with the marriage of the two lovers, the restoration of the father's fortune, and the punishment of the two greedy sisters (in the original fairytale they are turned into statues). Several pantomime versions add a comic housekeeper in the service of Beauty's father, thus providing a part for a DAME.

Origins Before the evolution of the pantomime the story existed in the form of fairytales by such authors as

Madame Marie Leprince de Beaumont (1711–80), whose version was translated into English in 1757, and CHARLES PERRAULT. These were in turn derived from a long-established cycle of beast-marriage stories shared by the mythology of the Basques, the Swiss, the Germans, the English, the Italians, the Portuguese, the Lithuanian, the Magyar, the Indian, and the Kaffir peoples. Variants on the theme include the Basque version in which the Beast is a huge snake, the Lithuanian story in which he is a white wolf, and the Magyar tale in which he is a pig. The story of *THE FROG PRINCE* by the GRIMM BROTHERS is also thought to have been derived from these sources.

behind you! *See* AUDIENCE PARTICIPATION.

Behn, Aphra (1640–89) English playwright and novelist, whose play *The Emperor of the Moon* influenced the early development of the pantomime in England. Mrs. Behn, an adventuress whose other works included the comedy *The Rover* (1678), based her play on a French original derived in turn from a scenario of the Italian *COMMEDIA DELL'ARTE*, the conventions of which had only recently been imported from France for the first time. Prominent among the characters in the piece were SCARAMOUCHE, HARLEQUIN, and Mopsophil (essentially the COLUMBINE role). The play incorporated several comic routines borrowed directly from the *commedia dell'arte*, some of which depended upon TRICKWORK involving special stage props. With the growing popularity of Harlequin the play was revived on the London stage several times over the next 20 years and promoted the familiarity of English audiences with the genre.

Benevolent Agent The FAIRY GODMOTHER or other supernatural character who oversees the magic of the pantomime. The Benevolent Agent once played a crucial part in every pantomime, halting the action in order to signal the TRANSFORMATION SCENE that bridged the OPENING and the HARLEQUINADE. At the touch of her magic wand the often breathtaking business of transforming both characters and scenery would begin and, at the end of the harlequinade, it was usually the Benevolent Agent once again who magically restored the fortunes of the beleagured lovers and transported all the characters to the Bower of Bliss or other paradise in the concluding scene.

The Benevolent Agent was usually female, although the part might also be played by a man (anticipating the development towards the end of the 19th century of the modern DAME). In the famous 1806 production of *MOTHER GOOSE* at COVENT GARDEN, for instance, the role was fulfilled by Mother Goose herself (played by Samuel Simmons). In many pantomimes the Benevolent Agent appeared in great splendour in a magnificent chariot drawn by mythical creatures; occasionally he or she would actually be identified as a character from legend, such as Neptune or Orpheus. With the disappearance of the harlequinade in the 20th century the Benevolent Agent (now often played by actresses of mature years) declined in importance and she is frequently treated as a comic figure who is too incompetent to make her spells work without the assistance of the hero, heroine, and members of the audience.

Bessy A character from the ancient Fool Plough ceremonies of northern England, who was arguably one of the antecedents of the modern DAME. A comic old woman, she was invariably played by a ludicrously attired male performer. She also appeared in mummers' parades and in sword dances and was variously called Bess or Besom-Bet.

Beverley, William Roxby (*c.* 1811–89) English scene painter, who was highly regarded for his settings for both pantomimes and EXTRAVAGANZAS, which were to have a fundamental effect upon the whole history of the genre. Having gained early experience as an actor and scene painter under his father (who was manager of the Theatre Royal, Manchester) and as a pupil of the great scene painter and nautical artist CLARKSON STANFIELD, Beverley worked on scenery for the LYCEUM THEATRE before being appointed (1853) scene painter at COVENT GARDEN. The following year he moved to DRURY LANE, where he assumed responsibility for the theatre's sets for the next 30 years.

It was largely through the spectacular effect of his scenery for such entertainments as J. R. PLANCHÉ's *The Island of Jewels* (1849), in which the falling leaves of a palm tree revealed a group of fairies supporting a coronet of jewels, and for every one of the pantomimes of E. L. BLANCHARD between 1853 and 1883 that the TRANSFORMATION SCENE became such an important feature of the Victorian pantomime tradition. This in turn helped to shift the focus of the pantomime from comedy to spectacle (putting another nail in the coffin of the harlequinade).

Beverley's imaginative brushwork became the toast of critics and audiences alike and he was especially praised for his frequent incorporation of living figures in stunning tableaux, as seen in such productions as *Peter Wilkins; or, Harlequin and the Flying Women of Loadstone Lake* (1859). The Drury Lane management allowed Beverley full scope to indulge his talents and many writers, including Planché himself, complained that their own contribution was being all but ignored. Beverley also won acclaim for his scenic designs for the Shakespearean productions of Charles Kean.

Big Crash *See* SOUND EFFECTS.

Big Heads The huge masks that were formerly worn by members of the cast as a disguise throughout the entire OPENING prior to the TRANSFORMATION SCENE.

Such masks accentuated character and were extremely useful in effecting a rapid transformation into the characters of the HARLEQUINADE. Such Big Heads were commonly seen in pantomimes of the early 19th century when they were an important weapon in the continual battle between the theatres to claim the most spectacular production; only the actress who was to be revealed as Columbine did not wear one.

Often grotesque in appearance, the masks themselves were generally made of papier-maché and were highly detailed, the work of skilled artists backstage. The main drawback lay in the fact that the voices of the performers wearing the masks were so muffled that little sense could be made of their words and the audience had to rely upon understanding their gestures to follow their meaning. They also made the performers playing them anonymous, which was no advantage when players of the calibre of JOSEPH GRIMALDI were on stage. With the exception of the occasional giant or nursery rhyme character, their use gradually petered out towards the end of the 19th century, by which time the transformation scene was itself also passing into history.

Black, Cilla (Priscilla Maria Veronica White; 1943–) English singer and television personality, born in Liverpool, who became one of the pantomime's most popular PRINCIPAL BOYS of recent years. Having established herself as a pop singer in the 1960s, she embarked upon a highly successful career as a television presenter and appeared regularly in pantomime in such roles as IDLE JACK and ALADDIN. Her natural good humour proved her greatest asset, although her real significance to the development of the pantomime lies in the fact that her success helped to restore the part of the principal boy to female performers after a period of ten years or more in which – in London at least – it had been interpreted mainly by male performers.

Blanchard, Edward Leman (1820–89) English author, whose pantomimes dominated the Victorian theatre for nearly 40 years. The son of a comedian attached to the company at COVENT GARDEN, Blanchard began writing for the stage at the age of 16 and by the time he was 20 had penned around 30 plays, burlesques, and pantomimes (some under the pseudonym Francesco Frost). He was one of the first writers to specialise in pantomimes and was in time recognised as one of the finest, being nicknamed 'The Prince of Openings', the 'King of the Pantomime Writers', and the 'Hero of a Hundred Pantomimes'. Ironically Blanchard himself disliked the description 'pantomime' and called his works 'annuals'.

Written in rhyming couplets, his scripts were used in many of the most spectacular London productions, notably those presented at DRURY LANE, where pantomimes by his hand were given annually every year for 37 years (beginning in 1852 with *Harlequin Hudibras; or, Old Dame Durden and the Droll Days of the Merry Monarch* and ending in 1888 with *BABES IN THE WOOD*, in which DAN LENO made his Drury Lane debut).

Blanchard's first pantomime reached the stage in 1844 and by the time of his death he had collaborated on over 100 productions, with at least two of his pantomimes being seen in London every year between 1850 and 1880 (in 1874 no less than four of his pantomimes were being presented simultaneously in London theatres). His pantomimes for Drury Lane were doubly notable, winning praise not only for the quality of the scripts, but also for the spectacular scenery that WILLIAM BEVERLEY contributed (every one of Blanchard's productions there between 1852 and 1883 was staged with designs by Beverley).

One of his regular collaborators was T. L. GREENWOOD, who like Blanchard was descended from a noted theatrical family and had penned many pantomimes on his own account; they wrote together under the pseudonym the **Brothers Grinn**. Typically, Blanchard's scripts were inventive, literary, elegantly written, and enriched with witty puns, with the plot itself – usually based upon a famous fairytale – being given full emphasis. Blanchard was particularly admired for the elevated tone of his imaginative opening scenes, which could vary in setting from a 'curiosity shop' to 'The Atmosphere, 45 miles above the Earth's Surface', and for his ability to dovetail one fairytale with another. Many of his stories were clearly allegorical and, in keeping with the popular Victorian image, put forward strong moral lessons to be learnt.

Although his pantomimes represented a watershed between the productions of the pre-Victorian theatre and the modern entertainment, Blanchard was something of a traditionalist and regretted many of the changes he found himself being a party to. His pantomimes, which included all the best known plots from *Cinderella, or Harlequin and the Fairy Slipper* to *SINBAD*, generally included a traditional HARLEQUINADE and Blanchard did all he could to keep it alive, to the extent of doubling – and even tripling – the number of performers in it in the hope that sheer spectacle would ensure its survival (*see* DOUBLE HARLEQUINADE). It was all to no avail, however, and Blanchard's *Cinderella* in 1883 was the first Drury Lane pantomime to be staged without a harlequinade.

The author also opposed the recruitment of stars from the MUSIC HALL to bolster the pantomime's popular appeal, arguing that the licence such performers took with his scripts and their frequent 'gagging' had a vulgarising effect and pushed the fairytale element too far into the background. In this too his voice went unheard and the Lane's new manager, AUGUSTUS HARRIS, pressed ahead with such reforms, referring to his reluctant author somewhat begrudgingly as 'The Old Man of the Sea'. Blanchard himself was required to adapt several pantomimes to accomodate certain stars, his *ALADDIN* of 1874, for instance, providing members of the VOKES FAMILY with opportunities to demonstrate their skills as eccentric dancers.

The invasion by music hall artists spelt the end of the poetic, morally elevating pantomime of which Blanchard was king and towards the end of his life the author grew increasingly bitter at the way in which his carefully wrought works were rewritten by theatre managements to cater for changing tastes, regarding any payment he received as compensation for the damage done to his literary reputation.

As well as being a prolific writer of pantomimes (and of the bills and programmes associated with them), Blanchard also wrote much theatre criticism and was for 14 years drama critic for *The Daily Telegraph*; his other writing included advertisements, sermons, riddles, guide books, and all manner of other commissions (though he never made much money from his unceasing labour). His diary provides a fascinating insight into the way in which he produced pantomimes with such rapidity and into his reaction to the development of the genre in the Victorian era.

Blanche, Ada (1862–1953) English actress who became a popular star of the MUSIC HALL before being invited by AUGUSTUS HARRIS to appear in pantomime at DRURY LANE. Petite and energetic, she was particularly admired in the role of PRINCIPAL BOY, appearing in the role of Little Boy Blue in *Little Bo-Peep, Little Red Riding-Hood and Hop o' My Thumb* in 1892 and subsequently playing similar parts in the annual pantomime there every year until 1897. Her success in such roles as Aladdin led critics to acclaim her the finest principal boy of her day. Her niece, Marie Blanche, was the last actress to play principal boy under the management of ARTHUR COLLINS.

Bluebeard The villainous central character in the popular 19th century pantomime *BLUEBEARD*. Tradition links the fictional Bluebeard with the real Gilles de Rais (1404–40), a French nobleman who was accused of the murder of a large number of children. He fought beside Joan of Arc but subsequently became interested in alchemy and in the pursuit of his studies of witchcraft caused the deaths of as many as 200 women and children. He admitted his guilt under torture and was hanged. Others link the fictional character with Henry VIII, who was equally ruthless when his wives failed to please him. Other possible models include Comorre the Cursed, a 6th-century Breton chieftain who was in the habit of murdering his wives when he discovered they were expecting a child.

Bluebeard Pantomime story, about a mythical wife-murderer, that was frequently seen on the 19th century stage. The tale was presented on the English stage as a MELODRAMA at COVENT GARDEN in 1791 but was subsequently turned into a pantomime by CHARLES DIBDIN the younger under the title *Harlequin and Bluebeard*, at SADLER'S WELLS.

Later versions included an EXTRAVAGANZA by J. R. PLANCHÉ, an adaptation by H. J. BYRON, and one of the 'annuals' of E. L. BLANCHARD (1871), in which G. H. MACDERMOTT enjoyed considerable success. In 1879 the story was chosen by AUGUSTUS HARRIS as his first pantomime at Drury Lane. DAN LENO subsequently enjoyed great acclaim playing Sister Anne in the tale at the Lane in 1902.

Once a standard of the Victorian pantomime canon, the tale has only rarely been revived since (possibly due at least in part to its reputation as an 'unlucky' pantomime). It has also inspired operas by the composers André Grétry (1789), Jacques Offenbach (1866), Paul Dukas (1907), and Béla Bartók (1918).

Story Bluebeard, who is variously depicted as a king, rich merchant, or sorcerer, of French, English, or even Turkish nationality, has a blue beard that makes him hideous to women. He is, however, capable of charming them into agreeing to marry him and he takes three (sometimes seven) sisters as his wife in turn. When he decides to go on a lengthy journey he hands his latest wife the keys to his castle with the instructions that she may open any door she likes but one.

Inevitably, his wife is overcome with curiosity and unlocks the door to the forbidden chamber. Inside she discovers the bodies of Bluebeard's previous wives, who have been foully murdered. The key with which she opened the door has become indelibly stained with blood and when Bluebeard returns he realises from this that his new wife has disobeyed his orders. He vows to kill her and is about to do so when his wife's two brothers – warned to hasten to the castle by her sister Anne – burst in and kill him.

Alternatively, the earlier wives are found not to be dead, but have been imprisoned in the castle dungeon (where they have been fed on human flesh), from which their young sister rescues them. She conceals the two sisters in a sack, which she tells Bluebeard contains gold, and persuades him to take it to her father. She herself dons a suit of feathers and flies to her father to forewarn her brothers of the truth.

Origins Planché based his version of the story of Bluebeard upon the fairytale related by CHARLES PERRAULT in his *Contes du Temps* (1697), which was itself derived from ancient folkloric origins and was first translated into English in 1729. Details of the plot vary widely from one source to another. In Norse tradition Bluebeard is a troll, while in the Italian version he is the Devil himself; in the Greek variant he is a personification of Death who murders those who do not share his taste for human flesh.

Other writers who made their own versions of the story included the GRIMM BROTHERS. Such details as the locked door that must not be opened are shared by a number of folktales of ancient origins and are interpreted by psychologists as having special relevance in what may have been intended as a parable about sexual infidelity and forgiveness.

Blunderbore (1) One of the GIANTS confronted by Jack in *JACK THE GIANT-KILLER*. (2) The giant in *JACK AND THE BEANSTALK*. In an acclaimed production at DRURY LANE in 1899, starring DAN LENO, he was renamed Blunderboer, in reference to the Boer War then being waged in South Africa. In response to Paul Kruger's boast that he could put the whole British Army in his pocket, an army of khaki-clad British soldiers (played by children) marched triumphantly out of the dead giant's pocket, to universal applause. He is sometimes so big that he is in fact part of the scenery, with a huge hand that can be lowered to scoop up the terrified princess.

Boleno, Harry (Harry Mason; d. 1875) English comedian, who won acclaim in the role of CLOWN in the 19th century. Defying his parents, he began his career in the theatre while still a boy and played his first small role during JOSEPH GRIMALDI's second benefit. Subsequently he graduated to the part of Clown in 1840, in which role he appeared in Bath, Dublin, and Liverpool before playing it at DRURY LANE, where he starred in no less than 14 pantomimes. He was particularly admired for his skill as a comic dancer. He retired in 1873 after a last appearance at the SURREY THEATRE.

Bologna, Jack (John Peter Bologna; 1781–1846) English actor, of Italian extraction, who excelled in the role of HARLEQUIN. Born into a family of professional dancers who emigrated to England in 1786, he was highly acclaimed in the part in pantomime at SADLER'S WELLS and COVENT GARDEN, appearing alongside such noted contemporaries as JOSEPH GRIMALDI (his close friend and relation by marriage) and James Barnes. Considered the finest Harlequin of his day, he was one of the cast in the immensely successful and influential 1806 Covent Garden production of *MOTHER GOOSE*. He was eventually succeeded in the part by THOMAS ELLAR in 1816 (one of Bologna's sons inherited the role in the 1850s). Towards the end of his career, Bologna also worked as a conjuror and dancing teacher, making return visits to Sadler's Wells as late as 1838.

booth A small temporary theatre at a fair or other public event that was used by travelling performers in the early history of European drama. A common sight at fairs in England and France and elsewhere until the 19th century, such booths staged a wide range of entertainment, from clowning to Punch and Judy shows.

In relation to the development of the pantomime, such booths at the Parisian fairs of Saint-Germain and Saint-Laurent were important in that they witnessed the emergence of a French version of the Italian *COMMEDIA DELL'ARTE*, which was ultimately to be transmitted to England through the ITALIAN NIGHT SCENES of JOHN WEAVER. The popularity of the French booth theatres prompted the Comédie-Française to seek (and get) an official order forbidding players at the booths to speak dialogue, hence the tradition of mute HARLEQUINS that subsequently took root in the booths of English fairgrounds and ultimately at LINCOLN'S INN and elsewhere in the pantomime itself.

Among the well-known travelling booth theatres of the early 19th century was that run by John Richardson (1760–1836), which presented pantomimes and other entertainments up to 20 times a day and was witnessed by the young CHARLES DICKENS. *See* COMÉDIE-ITALIENNE.

boots *See HOP O' MY THUMB*; *PUSS IN BOOTS*.

Bo-Peep *See LITTLE BO-PEEP*.

Bowery Theatre A former theatre in New York, where many pantomimes were staged during the 19th century. Opened in 1826, the theatre played host in 1831 to the classic *MOTHER GOOSE* production in which JOSEPH GRIMALDI had won great acclaim as CLOWN back in 1806. The company from London included E. J. Parsloe as Clown and the father of E. L. BLANCHARD among other noted performers, but the visit was not a success and the production met with incomprehension (and ended with Parsloe's death).

Nonetheless the Bowery Theatre went on to become the most important home of pantomime in the USA with such productions being staged as part of a mixed programme of spectacles, melodramas, and similar entertainments. Most notable of all were the pantomimes of the theatre's manager GEORGE L. FOX, whose pantomimes staged at the venue between 1850 and 1867 (with himself as Clown and his brother Charles Kemble Fox as Pantaloon) represented the high point of pantomime in the USA.

The venue burned down in 1828, 1836, 1838, and 1845 and in 1858 was renamed the Old Bowery Theatre. It closed in 1878 and reopened as the Thalia Theatre, finally closing permanently in 1929 after two more fires.

box An enclosed area of seating, where the most expensively priced seats are to be found. Such boxes, usually housing half a dozen seats or less, became a feature of English theatres in the 17th century, ranged down both sides and sometimes across the back of the auditorium. In the days when the auditorium remained lit throughout a performance, a box provided an excellent place for fops and society ladies to show off their charms and were accordingly much sought-after. Ironically, though a seat in a box is traditionally considered more desirable than a seat elsewhere, boxes frequently offer a less than ideal view of the stage.

box office The area in a theatre where tickets can be purchased for a pantomime or other production. It is also possible at most theatres to buy tickets by telephone.

Bradbury, Robert (1777–1831) English actor, who won acclaim in the role of CLOWN in the pantomime in the early 19th century. One of the more successful of JOSEPH GRIMALDI's contemporaries, Bradbury was renowned for his acrobatic performances, in which he appeared to risk serious injury (in fact, he wore nine resilient pads on his body to cushion the effect of his collisions with scenery etc.). He began his career in the theatre as a stage carpenter in Manchester but later sought fame as a performer, appearing initially in the parts of PIERROT and PANTALOON before establishing himself in the part of Clown at both SADLER'S WELLS and at other leading houses.

He developed a unique style as Clown, which relied far more on physical feats than did the humour of Grimaldi (who never wore pads). Critics generally considered Grimaldi's mastery of the role unchallenged and Bradbury came off a poor second when the two actors shared the role of Clown in an extraordinary production around 1810. Bradbury was praised nonetheless for his daring leaps and death-defying tumbling and continued in demand at leading venues. He was also noted for his TRICKS OF CONSTRUCTION, the most celebrated of which included his conversion of two giant gingerbread men into dandies, which then came to life (he was himself popularly known as the 'Brummell of Clowns' because of his weakness for extravagant dress and jewellery).

He courted controversy throughout his life and had something of a reputation as an eccentric and a bully. The most notorious incident in his career took place in 1818 when, during a performance of *Harlequin and the Dandy Club* at DRURY LANE, he allowed himself to be goaded into public retaliation by interruptions from an army major in the audience who had taken offence at allusions to a recent kidnapping; as a result he was not hired again by the two major theatres, although he continued to appear at lesser venues and in the provinces.

breeches parts *See* PRINCIPAL BOY.

Brighella One of the *ZANNI* characters of the Italian *COMMEDIA DELL'ARTE* tradition, who formerly comprised the other half of a comic partnership with ARLECCHINO. Like Arlecchino, Brighella had his roots in the old Italian joke that anyone from the region of Bergamo in northern Italy, where the two hail from, is a congenital idiot. Brighella was depicted as a servant with rather more brains than the dim-witted Arlecchino and completely unprincipled in the cause of making easy money, usually by robbery, deception, or lies. He was easily identified through his costume, which was decorated with green and white stripes; he also carried a dagger and often played a guitar.

Leading performers of the role, who always wore a mask, were invariably accomplished acrobats and dancers. As time went on Brighella's role gradually diminished as his character became increasingly sentimental. Although Brighella had little direct impact upon the English HARLEQUINADE, his presence exerted itself through the survival of comic routines previously perfected between him and the longer-lived Arlecchino, who by then had become an amalgam of both characters as Arlequin.

bristle trap One of the many varieties of TRAPS used in pantomime. The entrance to a bristle trap is concealed by overlapping bristles or foliage through which a performer may make an unexpected exit or entrance.

Britannia Theatre A former theatre in Hoxton, London, which was once second only to DRURY LANE and COVENT GARDEN for its pantomimes. Opened in 1841 as the **Britannia Saloon**, it graduated from being one of London's song-and-supper rooms into a music hall and in 1843 became a theatre. It was rebuilt and reopened in 1856 and became one of the most prosperous London venues on the strength of the many successful plays and pantomimes that were presented under the management of SAM LANE and after his death under that of his widow Sara Lane (who starred as PRINCIPAL BOY there into her old age). Other stars included five generations of the remarkable LUPINO family (two of whom married into the Lane clan), MARIE LLOYD, and G. H. MACDERMOTT.

Nicknamed the 'Old Brit', the theatre was particularly renowned for staging relatively small-scale pantomimes outside the conventional canon of well-known works; popular successes there included such entertainments as *Queen Dodo*, *The Magic Dragon*, and *King Klondyke*, which starred the 12-year-old Lily Elsie (later to win fame as The Merry Widow) and ran for a record-breaking three months.

The harlequinade was a feature of all the Britannia pantomimes and Clowns seen at the theatre were among the best survivors of the tradition. Regular visitors to the theatre in its younger days included CHARLES DICKENS. The Britannia eventually reverted to a music hall in the early 20th century and was then used as a cinema before being destroyed by bombs in World War II.

Broker's Men The two comic bailiffs of *CINDERELLA*, who threaten to remove the Baron's furniture and other belongings but are usually foiled by the ingenuity of BUTTONS and his various confederates. First introduced as a 'Chorus of Broker's Men' in a version staged in Sunderland in 1880, the roles provided slapstick comedians from the music hall with an ideal opportunity for knockabout comedy and eccentric characterisation. They appeared on the London stage at Sanger's Amphitheatre in 1883 and in 1895 were interpreted by the Griffiths Brothers at DRURY LANE; they have since become established characters in a number of other pantomimes, notably *MOTHER GOOSE*, and are often played by well-known comedy duos.

Brothers Grimm *See* GRIMM BROTHERS.

Brothers Grinn *See* BLANCHARD, E. L.; GREENWOOD, T. L.

Buckstone, John Baldwin (1802–79) English pantomime writer, actor, and manager, who was the author of many highly successful pantomimes seen on the Victorian stage. He began as an actor in comedy at the SURREY THEATRE and received encouragement from the great tragedian Edmund Kean, winning particular acclaim for his creation of the role of Gnatbrain in Douglas Jerrold's celebrated nautical drama *Black Ey'd Susan* (1829). Subsequently he consolidated his reputation as one of the leading comic actors of his day and became one of the pillars of the company led by MADAME VESTRIS and CHARLES MATHEWS.

As a writer of pantomimes he had works performed as early as 1830, when his *Grimalkin the Great* was staged at the ADELPHI THEATRE. As manager of the HAYMARKET from 1853 until his death, he presented many more notable pantomimes. He was also the author of around 160 farces, operettas, burlettas, and other works, the most successful of which included *Luke the Labourer* (1826), which promoted the popularity of the melodrama. His ghost is said to haunt the Haymarket to this day.

burla A stock comic interlude that was a characteristic of performances of the *COMMEDIA DELL'ARTE*. Such impromptu comic exchanges (which represented a more sophisticated form of the *LAZZI*) gave the performers, especially the *ZANNI*, an opportunity to indulge in a little slapstick humour (usually in the form of a practical joke played on one of the other characters) without having to worry about the constraints of plot. The word *burla* itself was subsequently transmuted into the terms 'burletta' and 'burlesque'.

burlesque A form of light-hearted satirical comedy that developed in the English theatre (and elsewhere) in the late 17th century and which influenced the pantomime tradition in the 19th century through the plays of H. J. BYRON, SIR FRANCIS BURNAND, and others. The essence of burlesque was the comic lampooning of some dramatic style, social class, or theatrical genre.

Early targets included heroic drama, in the Duke of Buckingham's *The Rehearsal* (1671), opera, in John Gay's *The Beggar's Opera* (1728), and sentimental theatre, in Sheridan's *The Critic* (1779). The satirical element became somewhat less biting in the 19th century but found a rich new vein of source material in the MELODRAMA, which inspired countless writers to new heights of parody. The nautical dramas of such authors as Douglas Jerrold – notably *Black Ey'd Susan* in the 1820s – and popular operas, such as von Weber's *Der Freischütz*, were favourite targets of burlesque writers, while others included Mozart's *Don Giovanni*, Jonathan Swift's *GULLIVER'S TRAVELS*, and the tragedies of William Shakespeare.

Ultimately the burlesque was translated into the EXTRAVAGANZAS of J. R. PLANCHÉ and rendered as never before in the spectacular productions of MADAME VESTRIS. The success of these entertainments impressed the pantomimists and the burlesque in all its various forms eventually came to replace the conventional OPENING of the pantomime, which consequently took on a new life of its own.

Among the earliest attempts to merge the burlesque with the pantomime was Mark Lemon's highly popular *JACK AND THE BEANSTALK; OR, HARLEQUIN AND MOTHER GOOSE AT HOME AGAIN*, which was staged at the ADELPHI THEATRE in 1855; characters of the piece included a personification of Burlesque itself, who promised to help entertain the audience. Among Lemon's most notable successors was Alfred Hollingshead (1827–1904), whose many burlesques included a version of *ALADDIN*. The operettas of Offenbach and Gilbert and Sullivan were directly influenced by burlesque and eventually contributed to the development of musical comedy.

Burlesque has an equally long history in the USA, where its popularity was confirmed during a sensational tour by an English troupe led by LYDIA THOMPSON in 1868 (their repertoire including a lively burlesque of the story of *ALI BABA*). Over the years, however, the US version of burlesque diverged somewhat from the English original and became a form of variety show which depended largely upon the appearance of glamorous scantily-clad females. *See also* BURLETTA; CRITICS; PARODIES; SATIRE.

burletta A broad category of drama encompassing rhymed satirical comedy, musical farce, and BURLESQUE that was one of the most popular forms of entertainment on the early Victorian stage. The LICENSING ACT of 1737 dictated that only the Theatres Royal at DRURY LANE and COVENT GARDEN (and the HAYMARKET in the summer only) had the right to stage spoken drama, thus restricting several lesser theatres to performances of burlettas, which legally had to contain at least five musical items in each act. Ironically the immediate effect of the ruling was to encourage the opening of many new venues for the performance of such entertainments, which offered an opportunity to get round the exclusive right of the Patent Theatres to present spoken dialogue. Many otherwise 'straight' dramas were thus embellished with musical interludes and enacted at theatres licensed only to present burlettas.

The success of J. R. PLANCHÉ's *Olympic Revels*, billed as a 'burlesque burletta', at the OLYMPIC THEATRE in 1830 opened a new era in London theatrical history and paved the way for the gradual absorption of the burletta with its witty lyrics and fantastical plots (many based on tales from English folklore) into the pantomime proper. Many pieces billed as burlettas prior to the change in the licensing laws in 1843 were in fact EXTRAVAGANZAS, including most of Planché's celebrated entertainments.

Burnand, Sir Francis Cowley (1836–1917) British playwright and editor of *Punch*, who was the author of numerous BURLESQUES, pantomimes, and adaptations of French plays. Educated at Eton, where he made the first steps in his career as a writer for the stage, he enjoyed his greatest success in 1866 with a burlesque of the nautical melodrama *Black-Ey'd Susan*. The production ran for over a year with Burnand himself winning acclaim as one of the actors. His other productions included such pantomimes as *Valentine and Orson; or, Harlequin and the Magic Shield*, which was seen at COVENT GARDEN in 1880 with the VOKES FAMILY leading the cast, and his 1905 version of *CINDERELLA* at DRURY LANE. He was also the founder of the Amateur Dramatic Club at Cambridge.

Butcher A minor character of the HARLEQUINADE, from whose shop CLOWN customarily stole various pies and haunches of meat. The Butcher was just one of Clown's traditional victims and was invariably easily outwitted in his attempts to prevent Clown helping himself to strings of sausages etc.

Buttons The page-boy in *CINDERELLA*, who proves to be the heroine's one faithful friend in her darkest hour before her FAIRY GODMOTHER steps in to help. Buttons was a creation of the pantomime writer H. J. BYRON, who introduced him in his classic 1860 version *Cinderella; or, The Lover, the Lackey, and the Little Glass Slipper* as 'Buttoni'. At other times he has answered to such names as Alfonso, Billy, Chips, Hobbedehoy, Jack Pickles, Pedro (in which identity JOSEPH GRIMALDI appeared back in 1820), Peter, Pimples, Podgio, Puffpaste, Tickleum, and Twiddles. Writers reverted to Buttons (the universal nickname of page-boys after the row of buttons fastening their jackets) after he was seen under that name in three highly successful versions staged at the LYCEUM THEATRE in 1915, 1918, and 1921, when the part was played in turn by Harry Weldon, George Bass, and Johnny Danvers. Many other pantomime stars have subsequently excelled in the role, the most notable among them including ARTHUR ASKEY, whose mischievous good humour and small stature were ideally suited to the part, and TOMMY STEELE. Others in recent years have ranged from Ronnie Corbett and ROY HUDD to Des O'Connor and Rolf Harris.

Byng, Douglas (1893–1987) English comedian and singer, born in Nottingham, who became a major star of revue and cabaret and one of the most popular of all pantomime DAMES. Byng began his theatrical career as a costume designer but made his professional debut as a performer in 1914, as a member of a concert party. He gradually established himself as a comedian and singer of outrageously camp comic songs, which he wrote himself.

He made his first appearance in pantomime in 1921, when he starred in *ALADDIN* at the LONDON PALLADIUM and soon won recognition as one of the most accomplished dames of his era. This was in spite of a curious nervous ailment that caused his right arm to fly suddenly upwards and his head to flick to one side; the condition proved incurable but Byng successfully incorporated it into his act. His most successful dame roles included Eliza the Cook in *Dick Whittington*, which he played at the New Oxford Theatre in 1924, forming a memorable partnership with Wilkie Bard – his song 'Oriental Emma of the 'Arem' (the first comic song he had ever written) was the hit of the show.

Despite the fact that some critics thought Byng's humour too sophisticated for young audiences (he was banned several times by the BBC) he remained hugely popular and was the star of no less than 27 Christmas pantomimes. He was particularly noted for his comic costumes, which included a 'fur' cape made entirely from bathroom loofahs. As a cabaret star he topped the bill of the famous Cochran revues between 1925 and 1931; his first solo variety appearance was in a one-man burlesque entitled *Cinders, or Hop o' My Thumb*. During World War II he toured widely as a member of ENSA.

Byrne, James (1756–1845) English actor and dancer, who was one of the most celebrated performers ever to take the role of Harlequin. Born into a family of professional dancers, he was hailed for his grace and acrobatic prowess in the part and was described as the finest Harlequin since John Rich himself. Byrne received early training as a dancer and performed at Drury Lane while still a boy; later he also appeared at Covent Garden and in the provinces as well as visiting the USA before settling at Drury Lane as ballet-master in the 1800–01 season.

It was Byrne who for a performance of *Harlequin Amulet; or, the Magic of Mona* in 1800 created the character's distinctive close-fitting patched one-piece costume with black eye mask. The costume, which was decorated with a profusion of shiny metal spangles, created a sensation and became the standard outfit for all subsequent Harlequins (it failed, however, to wrest the focus of the harlequinade away from the usurper Clown, who was currently being transformed by Joseph Grimaldi).

Other innovations introduced by Byrne during the same production included his largely dispensing with the conventional 'attitudes' (poses in which a finger pointed to a particular coloured spangle indicated a certain emotion) to which Harlequin had been confined in recent decades.

Byron, H(enry) J(ames) (1834–84) British playwright, theatre manager, and actor, who was a prolific writer of extravaganzas, pantomime openings, melodramas, and burlesques. Born in Manchester, the son of the British consul to Haiti, Byron gave up studies in medicine and law for the theatre and was best known for his highly successful comedies, which included the long-running farce *Our Boys* (1875). As a writer for the pantomime he was highly influential, perfecting the burlesque style that was first attempted in the pantomime in the 1840s.

Among his most significant burlesques – many of which were written for the Strand Theatre and starred Marie Wilton – were *Aladdin and His Wonderful Lamp; or, the Genie of the Ring* (1856), which saw the first appearance of Widow Twankey under that name, and *Cinderella; or, The Lover, the Lackey, and the Little Glass Slipper* (1860), in which he not only introduced Buttons but also developed the characters of the Ugly Sisters.

All his pantomimes were notable for their awful but also highly inventive puns, of which Byron was considered a master. As a theatre manager, he took over three venues in Liverpool but was declared bankrupt in 1868.

C

Camel One of the most popular of the SKIN PARTS. The camel has long had supernatural significance in folklore, being considered sacred by Arab peoples, where 'camel' is a word of endearment, and also in India. The pantomime tradition, however, generally capitalises upon the common view of the creature as wilful, stupid, greedy, disdainful, and bad-tempered. He features in the desert scenes of *ALADDIN AND HIS WONDERFUL LAMP.*

Campbell, Herbert (1846–1904) English comedian, who became a popular star of pantomime after establishing his reputation as one of the great performers in the MUSIC HALL (he also appeared in minstrel shows and even in straight theatre). An enormous man who weighed 19 stone and was over six feet tall, he made his first appearance in pantomime in 1871, at the Theatre Royal, Liverpool, and was subsequently much acclaimed for the topical duets he sang with HARRY NICHOLLS at the GRECIAN THEATRE and, from 1883, at DRURY LANE.

It was at the latter theatre that Campbell, with his proven comic skills and imposing frame, found his ideal partner in the diminutive DAN LENO, with whom he went on to enjoy enormous success in a celebrated series of 14 consecutive pantomimes in the 1890s and 1900s. Where Leno was small and wistful Campbell was huge and booming, making him the perfect comic foil to Leno's bright wit. Highlights of their classic partnership included the topical duets lampooning political figures and other well-known public personalities that they sang in every pantomime.

Campbell's many roles at Drury Lane ranged from one of the babes in *BABES IN THE WOOD* and King Screwdolph in *THE SLEEPING BEAUTY AND THE BEAST* to Will Atkins in *ROBINSON CRUSOE*, the BARON in *CINDERELLA*, and Goody Thumb, wife to Leno's Daddy Thumb in *Little Bo-Peep, Little Red Riding-Hood and Hop o' My Thumb*.

The pair's final appearance was in early 1904 in *HUMPTY-DUMPTY*; within months both were dead – Leno dying insane from the pressures of his career and Campbell as the result of an accident – and a golden period in the history of the pantomime was over.

Capitano, Il *See COMMEDIA DELL' ARTE.*

carpenter's scene A sparsely set scene that takes place in front of a frontcloth, thus allowing the stage crew an opportunity to change the scenery for the next scene without the need for a break in the action. Such carpenter's scenes are characteristic of the modern pantomime, during the course of which there may be as many as half a dozen or more such interludes.

Some carpenter's scenes are more relevant to the main plot than others; back in 1904, when it was realised at a late stage that an extra carpenter's scene was required in the first production of the children's play *Peter Pan*, the actor playing Captain Hook appeared before the closed curtain and proceeded to present a series of hilarious parodies of leading performers of the day.

Frequently the scene is given over to a song or to a comedy double-act, who might perform one of the traditional routines that date back many decades (including those in which logic is turned upside down so that one character 'proves' the other is not present or otherwise that rather than owing five pounds to the other character, he is actually *owed* five pounds).

catchphrases The pantomime has produced a lengthy list of popular catchphrases over the years. Some of these spring from the scripts themselves (no performance of *Ali Baba and the Forty Thieves* would be complete without a cry of "Open Sesame!" and every Abanazar offers "New lamps for old") while others are of ancient lineage. Joseph Grimaldi's greeting "Here we are again!" when entering as Clown belongs to pantomime history now that the harlequinade has disappeared, but for nearly 200 years it heralded the arrival of the clowns.

Many other now-forgotten catchphrases were once familiar to pantomime audiences everywhere. A great number of these were, to the modern eye at least, totally nonsensical: in the early years of the 20th century, for instance, popular catchphrases that were yelled out on entrances or when the comedy was perceived to be flagging included "Get your hair cut!", "Ain't he like our Fred?", and "Go and cut yourself a piece of cake".

Among the best known catchphrases of the contemporary pantomime are certain well-established exchanges between members of the cast and the audience (*see* audience participation). Most pantomimes allow audiences at least one opportunity to indulge in a ritual "Oh, yes it is! – Oh, no it isn't!" shouting match and shortsighted dames are well versed in failing to spot characters standing in their shadow despite enthusiastic shouts of "Behind you!" from all parts of an auditorium. Other catchphrases are introduced in the course of single pantomimes and may vary from parodies of famous slogans to comical greetings that are shouted out each time certain characters appear.

Still more catchphrases have been imported with particular performers, examples varying from Sandy Powell's "Can you hear me, mother?" and Arthur Askey's cheerful "Hello playmates!" to Danny La Rue's "Wotcher!" and John Inman's "I'm free!", with which he first became famous as a television star.

cats The most well-known pantomime cats are the eponymous hero of *Puss in Boots* and the hero's companion in *Dick Whittington*. There has been much debate over the origins of Dick Whittington's cat (usually called Tommy in the pantomime), of which the earliest records date back to two plays of 1605. According to one theory, the coal-carrying barges upon which the real Dick Whittington built his fortune were informally known as 'cats' and that the animal of the pantomime arose through some confusion resulting from this. Others prefer the explanation that the animal came into being as a result of a mistranslation of the French term *achat*, meaning 'bargain'. It is also possible that the cat arrived simply through confusion with the cat-hero in *Puss in Boots* or was borrowed from a Portuguese folktale about a young hero who with his cat rids the palace of an Indian prince of rats.

Whatever the case, Dick Whittington's cat was an essential detail of the stories surrounding his name by the early 17th century. In the pantomime, Dick Whittington's Cat often enjoys greater success with the audience than his master and many experienced performers have learnt to fight shy of the role of Dick for fear of having all their scenes 'stolen' by this feline companion.

Elsewhere cats generally appear as witches' familiars, as in *Mother Shipton*, and are celebrated for their supernatural powers (in British folklore, a black cat signifies great good fortune, although conversely seeing a black cat promises ill luck in the folk traditions of both Russia and the USA). Among those to take the part was the young JOSEPH GRIMALDI, who at the age of five appeared in the role in *Hurly Burly* at DRURY LANE; his costume was so unwieldy that he was unable to see where he was going and he fell through a trapdoor, breaking his collarbone and being forced to rest from the pantomime for several weeks.

The popularity of such feline characters was never more clearly defined than in CHARLES LAURI's appearances as a cat in *CINDERELLA* at the LYCEUM THEATRE in the 1893-94 season, when the cat ousted the role of BUTTONS as Cinders' closest ally.

Catskin A storytelling tradition of ancient European and Asiatic folkloric origins from which the familiar story of *CINDERELLA* developed. The Catskin cycle of stories generally concerned a young girl who flees incestuous marriage with her father, wearing a cloak made from the skin of a cat or other animal, and who then seeks to evade identification by working in a lowly capacity in the royal household. In all the various stories linked to the tradition she is eventually unmasked by a prince after attending a splendid ball, sometimes when he recognises a ring or other present he gave her. The two are happily married and the girl's father is punished.

cauldron trap One of the many stage TRAPS formerly used in the pantomime. The cauldron trap is sited upstage and gets its name from its use for the three witches in Shakespeare's *Macbeth*.

cave *See ALADDIN AND HIS WONDERFUL LAMP*; *ALI BABA AND THE FORTY THIEVES*.

celebrity stars The use of celebrities from the worlds of the serious theatre, sports, politics, pop music, etc. to add appeal to the advertised cast of a pantomime goes back a long way. Such ploys date back at least to the 1830s, when the failure of London managements to find anyone to inherit the mantle of the great JOSEPH GRIMALDI prompted them to attempt to lure audiences with new attractions. Thus it was that (to the dismay of many critics) familiar plots would be interrupted so that all manner of acclaimed 'variety artists' could be presented (often on the thinnest of pretexts). Pantomimes of the 1830s and 1840s, when the element of spectacle became paramount, were suddenly awash with singers, child dancers, tightrope-walkers, and fireworks technicians (*see* SPECIALITY ACTS).

Subsequently the pantomime was once again enriched, or polluted according to the conflicting responses of members of contemporary audiences, when AUGUSTUS HARRIS and other managers enticed major stars of the MUSIC HALL into the pantomime towards the end of the century. Such imports as MARIE LLOYD and DAN LENO brought obvious skills with them, as did guests from the 'straight' theatre – one of the most distinguished of whom was the great Shakespearean actress FAY COMPTON – and from the world of dance (examples having included Dame Alicia Markova, Sir Anton Dolin, and more recently Wayne Sleep).

The phenomenon of the celebrity star has gathered pace since World War II, with many major professional productions relying upon nationally-known figures from TELEVISION or other spheres to bolster box-office receipts. Against expectations, the results have sometimes been fruitful, as in the case of the fashion model Twiggy, who played a distinctive cockney CINDERELLA, and the singer TOMMY STEELE.

More often, however, celebrities drawn from outside the theatre have been found to be badly wanting in the necessary skills required. Guests from the world of pop music in particular proved to be strong box office attractions in the 1950s and 1960s but all too often turned out to lack the acting ability to communicate well on stage and many critics saw their importation as setting a dangerous precedent (especially as it displaced the female PRINCIPAL BOY, the part most youthful celebrity stars were invited to take). The fad went largely out of fashion within a few years and since then guest stars, unless they have some demonstrable talent as actors, are generally cast in such supporting roles as kings and genies, where they can do the least damage.

Some performers have become almost as well known for their appearances in pantomime as they previously were in other fields. In recent years further stars have been recruited particularly from the world of sport, among whom the cricketer Ian Botham (who once turned down an important overseas tour to appear in pantomime as King Satupon) and the boxer Frank Bruno attracted the most attention. Television actors remain the most common imports, though, with pantomimes of the 1980s and 1990s being dominated by waves of celebrity guests from detective series, comedy shows, and both English and Australian soap operas.

Céleste, Céline (1814–82) French actress, who was highly acclaimed for her many performances in pantomime in London and is believed by some to have been the first of the modern PRINCIPAL BOYS. Celebrated in France and the USA as a dancer and straight actress, she shared in the management of the ADELPHI THEATRE for some years, appearing there with great success in such pantomimes as *JACK AND THE BEANSTALK; OR, HARLEQUIN AND MOTHER GOOSE AT HOME AGAIN* (1855), in which she played Jack. It seems, in fact, that at least two other mature actresses played principal boy before her and that numerous others had played similar breeches roles in related forms of theatre for decades previously; her success in the role did, however, help to consolidate the concept of females as male heroes in the pantomime. She was also manager of the LYCEUM THEATRE from 1859 to 1861.

Champion Clog Dancer of the World *See* LENO, DAN.

chapbook A small booklet, containing popular folktales and other stories (as well as political and religious comment), of the type once sold throughout England for just a few pennies. Chapbooks could be purchased from travelling sellers from the 16th to the 19th centuries and contained well-known ballads, fairytales, and romances. The plots of these stories were frequently adapted for use in the pantomime, thus hastening the replacement of Classical mythology by folktales in typical OPENINGS. Many translations of European fairytales were first communicated to a mass English readership through the chapbooks, among them the tales of MOTHER BUNCH and those associated with MOTHER GOOSE.

The most popular texts covered by the chapbooks included the stories of *DICK WHITTINGTON*, *THE BABES IN THE WOOD*, and *BLUEBEARD*. Few early chapbooks were written specifically for children but many telling favourite nursery rhymes such as *OLD MOTHER HUBBARD*, *JACK THE GIANT KILLER*, and *COCK ROBIN* were aimed at younger readers after 1800.

Among other stories were abridged versions of popular classics, including *ROBINSON CRUSOE*. The quality of the chapbooks varied greatly but they served to promote folk stories among the poorer classes and proved a ready source of material for many pantomimists. The last chapbooks were published in the mid-19th century, when their place was largely assumed by the penny dreadful.

chase scene Traditional SLAPSTICK scene of the pantomime, in which the cast engage in a riotous pursuit of the DAME, or some other character. Such scenes date back to very beginnings of the pantomime and earlier to the *COMMEDIA DELL'ARTE*. In the 18th and 19th centuries (when they were referred to as **spill and pelt** scenes) they were a central feature of the HARLEQUINADE – itself a protracted chase sequence – and were often choreographed to the last detail so that the stage swarmed with figures colliding, falling over each other, and otherwise coming to grief as a result of the machinations of HARLEQUIN and CLOWN.

Some of the most spectacular chase scenes ever staged were those that were characteristic of the pantomimes at the GRECIAN THEATRE under the management of GEORGE CONQUEST towards the end of the 19th century; in these the DEMON KING was pursued through an impressive array of traps and other devices that required displays of great acrobatic skill from the performers.

Modern pantomimes generally attempt fairly modest chase scenes in which a long chain of characters rush headlong in and out of wings (and sometimes into the auditorium) to traditional 'chase music' in the manner of the silent movies of the early 20th century (which had been influenced themselves by the pantomime experience of such leading performers as Stan Laurel).

children Child performers have been associated with the pantomime since the beginning. Ever since the early 18th century children have played the parts of fairies, animals, sprites, and other generally non-talking roles and there are even records of companies that were composed entirely of such young performers. In the Victorian era children were central to some of the most famous spectacles seen in the pantomime on the London stage, among them being the celebrated climactic scene of *JACK AND THE BEANSTALK* seen at DRURY LANE in 1899, which had an army of children dressed in the uniform of Britain's soldiers then fighting in south Africa emerging from the dead giant's pockets.

Child performers frequently appear in contemporary professional productions, though rarely in any great numbers; amateur pantomimes, on the other hand, frequently provide opportunities for anything up to 30 or 40 children to make brief appearances. Children also make up a much higher proportion of the audience in the contemporary pantomime than they did in past centuries, when adults and youngsters alike clamoured to see JOSEPH GRIMALDI and other leading performers. As a result, to appease the sensibilities of the young, pantomime stories are often less violent than in their original form and happy endings are now obligatory (though somewhat perversely children have always preferred thoroughly evil baddies and realistic monsters and giants to the 'nicer' scenes).

It was in the last century that such writers as E. L. BLANCHARD addressed themselves specifically to the children in their audiences and adapted their tales so that they conveyed a distinct moral lesson for the young (though still striving to maintain the pantomime's appeal to adults). The incorporation of MUSIC HALL stars (who were not known for their restraint when it came to more risqué material) did threaten the status of the pantomime as a family entertainment towards the end of the century, but managements reacted to this and ever since then (with something of a hiccup in the 1970s, when stand-up comedians once more began to experiment with 'blue' material) the pantomime has remained the one form of live theatre guaranteed to be suitable for all ages. The matinée was also a Victorian innovation designed to cater for the needs of the younger audience, who could not be expected to concentrate on a full evening's performance which might last up to five hours.

Chinese Policemen The comedy double-act that became a familiar component of *ALADDIN AND HIS WONDERFUL LAMP* towards the end of the 19th century. The Chinese Policemen, usually two in number, became popular as the hero's bungling pursuers and rejoiced in such names as Bobbee and Coppee (they have since been rechristened many times, as Ping and Pong and Bamboo and Typhoo among other variations). Celebrated performers in the roles, who are generally skilled in the arts of SLAPSTICK comedy and TRICKWORK, have included such teams as the popular GRIFFITHS BROTHERS in the late 19th century and, in more recent times, Hope and Keane and Mike and Bernie Winters.

The Chinese Policemen remain survivors of a long tradition in the pantomime of making fun of all representatives of authority. As long ago as the late 18th century pantomimists were making jokes at the expense of magistrates and watchmen and when the first official police force was formed in 1829 it too became the subject of much scurrilous attention. Even earlier a similar flouting of the authorities was a characteristic element of the humour of the *COMMEDIA DELL'ARTE*. Then, as now, the forces of law and order in the pantomime have rarely succeeded in laying hands on the miscreants.

chorus The body of performers who play minor roles supporting the principal actors and actresses. The earliest choruses were an important element in Classical Greek drama although subsequently they played a smaller role (usually as a commentator on the main action) in Renaissance theatre. In the pantomime the chorus features primarily in crowd scenes and song-and-dance routines, rarely having more than a few lines of dialogue between them.

The heyday of the pantomime chorus was in the late 19th century when such major theatres as DRURY LANE often employed choruses totalling several hundred, all dressed in extravagant (and expensive) costumes. Considerations of cost have prevented the use of large choruses in recent years and professional productions have often been criticised for presenting 'crowd' scenes with a chorus of just three or four (or even less). 'Equity-waiving', a special arrangement with the actors' trade union to allow non-professionals to appear alongside professional players, is seen as a way round this in the future. The situation is somewhat different in the case of the amateur pantomime, in which the chorus is generally much larger (which also boosts the numbers of tickets sold to relatives and friends).

Christmas The festive period that marks the start of the traditional pantomime season. Many of the earliest pantomimes were presented around Christmas but this was by no means a universal custom, with pantomimes being equally often produced at other times of the year. Back in the early 19th century the beginning of the pantomime season dated from 9 November (the Lord Mayor's Day in London), with a new pantomime starting on Boxing Day; further pantomimes were then staged around Easter and again in July. The Lord Mayor's Day pantomime was dropped from the programme in the 1830s, but it was not until the repeal of the Licensing Act in 1843 that Christmas became the accepted time for such entertainment.

The rival EXTRAVAGANZAS of MADAME VESTRIS and J. R. PLANCHÉ were also staged at Christmas at the OLYMPIC THEATRE, but were moved to Easter when they became part of the bill at COVENT GARDEN, where a proper HARLEQUINADE (which the extravaganza did not boast) was considered an essential feature of a Christmas entertainment. A trip to the pantomime became a ritual part of the Victorian Christmas and devotees would often go to several different shows before the season was over (CHARLES DICKENS regularly took in a dozen pantomimes each year).

Only rarely are pantomimes now presented at any time other than Christmas, usually heavily disguised as 'plays for children'. This association with Christmas inevitably entailed the incorporation of various Christmas traditions: children invited on stage may well be asked what they had for Christmas and Father Christmas himself is a common visitor, although long runs can mean that he is dropped once the Yuletide festivities are over.

Chu-Chin-Chow Musical comedy, which was based on the pantomime *ALI BABA AND THE FORTY THIEVES*. This adaptation of the popular pantomime story proved to be one of the great successes of early 20th-century English theatre, enjoying a record-breaking run at His Majesty's Theatre from 1916. The script was written by Oscar Ashe, who also played the robber-chief, with music composed by Frederic Norton.

Cibber, Colley (1671–1757) English actor-manager and playwright, who as one of the managers of DRURY LANE permitted the first pantomimes to be performed there in the 1750s. Cibber, one of the most influential theatrical figures of his time and the author of such plays as *Love's Last Shift* (1696) and *The Careless Husband* (1702), was one of the famous triumvirate of managers who took over the theatre in 1711 and did much to promote the venue as the most important theatre in the country. He was made poet laureate in 1730 and was subsequently obliged to agree – very much against his wishes – that the theatre should present its first pantomime in 1750, in response to the success such entertainments were enjoying at the LINCOLN'S INN FIELDS THEATRE. Garrick's *Queen Mab* was well received, but Cibber felt constrained to issue a public apology for presenting such 'lowly' fare at the most prestigious theatre of them all, explaining that it was either that or starvation for the entire company.

Cinderella The heroine, called 'Cinders' by her friends, in *CINDERELLA*, the most popular of all pantomime stories. She is known by several other names in different versions of the story around the world. As the Ash Girl, she is called Aschenputtel in Germany, Cendrillon in France, and Cenerentola in Italy. Her name reflects her unhappy condition, cruelly overworked and left to sit among the ashes while her stepsisters indulge in every luxury (the link between unhappiness and ashes dates back to Classical times).

In the early history of the pantomime, she was variously called Angelina (as in Rossini's comic opera) and Finetta (as in the original tale by MADAME D'AULNOY). In some variants of the familiar story she is a GOOSE GIRL and receives supernatural aid from her dead mother. In the days of the HARLEQUINADE the actress playing Cinderella was usually transformed into COLUMBINE.

Perhaps the most admired of all actresses to take the role was ELLALINE TERRISS, who starred as Cinders in what was called at the time a 'perfect' production staged at the LYCEUM THEATRE during the 1893–94 season. She has had countless successors of varying abilities, the most recent of which have included Dana, Bonnie Langford and Annabel Croft.

Cinderella The most famous of all pantomime stories and indeed one of the most widely-known folktales in the world. As a pantomime, the story was first seen in England at DRURY LANE in 1804 – billed as a 'New Grand Allegorical Pantomime Spectacle' – and again at the LYCEUM THEATRE in 1809, although it was not until 1820, in a production given at COVENT GARDEN, that the plot and cast list began to resemble that of the familiar pantomime of today.

Entitled *Harlequin and Cinderella; or, The Little Glass Slipper*, this version owed much to Rossini's opera *La Cenerentola*, which had been presented in London earlier that year complete with an incompetent BARON (to which rank Rossini was the first to raise Cinderella's father), stepsisters, prince, and valet DANDINI. The pantomime of 1820 was significant in that it added a BARONESS (played by JOSEPH GRIMALDI) and a FAIRY.

H. J. BYRON's 'fairy burlesque extravaganza' *Cinderella; or, The Lover, the Lackey, and the Little Glass Slipper* was staged at the Royal Strand Theatre in 1860 and not only introduced BUTTONS but also developed the characters of the UGLY SISTERS. Later additions included the BROKER'S MEN. Particularly successful versions that followed included the 1893–94 production at the Lyceum, which was subsequently toured to New York and even eclipsed a rival version of the same story at Drury Lane, despite the fact that the latter starred the immortal partnership of HERBERT CAMPBELL and DAN LENO.

Over 90 productions of the tale were staged in the 19th century and it has long been recognised that *Cinderella* will attract larger audiences than any other pantomime. Modern productions have included the spectacular 1958 musical staged at the London COLISEUM and written by Rodgers and Hammerstein as well as reworkings by such leading contemporary writers as DAVID WOOD, JOHN MORLEY, Alan Brown (1986), and David Cregan (1989). A production staged at the National Theatre in 1983 was a rare failure and had to be withdrawn.

Film versions include a classic full-length Disney cartoon (1950) and *The Slipper and the Rose* (1976), a somewhat leaden but lavish musical starring Richard Chamberlain, Gemma Craven, and Annette Crosbie. The story has also inspired music by Prokofiev and several ballets, including one choreographed by Sir Frederick Ashton.

Story Cinderella is the daughter of the hapless BARON HARDUP who is completely dominated by his wife, Cinderella's WICKED STEPMOTHER, and her two stepsisters (*see* UGLY SISTERS). Her role in the household is that of a miserable drudge, forced to perform menial tasks while her stepsisters preen themselves and squabble over their imagined beauty. When an invitation to a royal ball arrives Cinderella is excluded and she is obliged to help deck her stepsisters out for the big event.

After the rest of the family have set out, Cinderella weeps in despair until comforted by her FAIRY GODMOTHER, who promises that she shall go to the ball after all. She uses her magic to provide a pumpkin-coach, complete with attendants and horses, and for Cinderella herself a beautiful dress with two tiny glass slippers. Thus attired, Cinderella immediately catches the eye of the prince – usually called PRINCE CHARMING – and they dance together. The Fairy Godmother has warned Cinderella, however, to leave the ball by midnight, for then all will be as it was before. The clock strikes twelve and Cinderella flees – losing one of her glass slippers.

The kingdom is scoured for the girl whose foot will fit the glass slipper but to no avail until finally the shoe is brought to Baron Hardup's house. The two stepsisters eagerly try the slipper on, but it is far too small (one of the most frequently tried ruses has one of the sisters producting a false leg as her own and for a delightful, horrifying moment the shoe fits). Cinderella then tries the slipper and it fits perfectly. The two sisters are left to regret their earlier unkindnesses while Cinderella marries the prince. Cinderella's stepmother is either humiliated or otherwise forced to leave the baron's house for ever.

Origins The story of Cinderella is found in the folklore of all the world's major cultures; 500 versions of the tale have been identified in Europe alone. It is likely that the story was first told in the Orient and the earliest known version is Chinese, thought to date to the 9th century AD. In this, the tale of *Yu Yang Ts Tsu*, the heroine is mistreated by her stepmother until a mysterious man provides her with fine clothes and golden shoes and she becomes the king's wife. The story also bears some similarity to the ancient Greek legend of Rhodope, who loses one of her slippers to an eagle, who takes it to the King of Memphis; he is so touched by the slipper's delicate beauty that he falls in love with the unseen wearer.

Details of the plot vary widely: in a Turkish variant Cinderella cooks an omelette that is magically transformed into a magic carpet, on which she then travels to the ball. In Hindu folklore the story is interpreted as an allegory for the mysterious workings of nature, with Cinderella representing the dawn, her wicked relatives clouds, and the Prince the reviving sun. European versions also differ in a number of ways: in Romanian legend, for instance, Cinderella is the daughter of an emperor but is forced to live in a pigsty, while in the Swedish version she is offered supernatural aid not by a fairy godmother, but by an ox. A Scottish version, entitled *Rashin Coatie*, has Cinders meeting her prince at a church at Christmas.

The story's circulation was promoted by a GRIMM BROTHERS version, entitled *Aschenputtel* and was told by CHARLES PERRAULT in his *TALES OF MOTHER GOOSE*, although the story had previously been published in England in 1721 in a collection of tales compiled by MADAME D'AULNOY, under the title 'The Story of Finetta the Cinder-Girl'. The tale was the subject of the very first serious study ever made of such oral traditions, being discussed by Marian Roalfe Cox in 1893, and since then it has been dissected by numerous folklorists and examined for its social and sexual content. *See also* GLASS SLIPPER.

Cinquevalli, Paul (Paul Kestner; 1859–1918) English juggler, born in Poland, who became one of the most popular SPECIALITY ACTS of the late Victorian pantomime. Cinquevalli took up juggling after an accident prevented him from developing his career as a trapeze artist and in time he became the most skilled juggler ever seen.

Having established himself as a popular star of the MUSIC HALL, he was invited to appear in a number of pantomimes at DRURY LANE and elsewhere. In one of his most admired routines he demonstrated sleights of hand with a saveloy sausage to an astounded WIDOW TWANKEY (played by DAN LENO). He was also famed for his skill as a contortionist, and it was claimed that he could play billiards perfectly, using his own back as a table.

circle The upper tier of seating in an auditorium. If there are two such tiers, then they are usually called the dress circle and the upper circle. *See also* BALCONY; GALLERY.

circus A form of touring theatrical entertainment in which a series of acts, including performances by clowns, animals, and trapeze artists, is presented in a huge tent (the 'big top'). The history of the circus is closely linked to that of the pantomime, with many circus performers – among them tightrope walkers, stage magicians, and trick cyclists – being presented in the pantomime as SPECIALITY ACTS (often to the detriment of the plot). Circus performers also made appearances in BURLESQUE, DOG DRAMA, EQUESTRIAN DRAMA, MUSIC HALL, and even in MELODRAMA in the 19th century, though the 20th century has seen a decline in the use of such acts in the pantomime itself (partly due to growing public resistance to any kind of animal act that might be suspected of involving some degree of cruelty).

The common heritage of the two genres is nowhere more clearly seen than in the circus clown, where the memory of JOSEPH GRIMALDI is preserved (albeit in a highly diluted form) long after the Clown character he made famous disappeared from the pantomime.

cloak The red riding cloak of the heroine in *LITTLE RED RIDING HOOD* is an integral feature of the story and no version of the tale would be complete without it. In the very earliest versions of the fairytale upon which the pantomime was based Red Riding Hood is described as wearing a red cap, which suits her colouring perfectly; psychologists have conjectured that the fact that the cap is red (indicative of passion) hints at the hidden sexual relevance of the story and the underlying message that the young should not be exposed to certain strong emotions until they are of an age to cope with them. Some pantomime writers have given the cloak magical powers (as in the version by David Cregan, in which it is hoped the cloak will work a transformation on the character of a singularly wayward Little Red Riding Hood).

Clown A character of the HARLEQUINADE, the irreverent servant and comic sidekick of PANTALOON, who in time replaced PIERROT and took over from HARLEQUIN himself as the most important figure in the pantomime. He began life as one or more of the *ZANNI* characters of the *COMMEDIA DELL'ARTE* – in which he was known by such names as Gingurto and Coviello – and subsequently accompanied his fellows into the French and English traditions, though still remaining a relatively minor comic part. His incorporation into the English harlequinade did, however, echo earlier clownish characters of native English theatre who had masqueraded under various disguises in mystery plays, miracle plays, and even in the comedies of William Shakespeare (in which pieces such clowns as Richard Tarleton and Will Kempe were popular).

Redefined by the *commedia dell'arte* tradition, Clown made his earliest appearances on the English stage in JOHN WEAVER's *Perseus and Andromeda* (1725). Jemmy Spiller, a friend of Hogarth, won acclaim in the role in the pantomimes of JOHN RICH and CARLO DELPINI made the part more central to the action when he played it towards the end of the 18th century. It was, however, left to one of their successors in the role to make it the most prominent in the whole of the harlequinade.

JOSEPH GRIMALDI (capitalising upon his father's development of the role) effected this transformation in the early 19th century, experimenting with the now-traditional white make-up used by clowns in the circus and elsewhere and bringing to the role – previously that of a clumsy rural oaf – a new sublety and wit. Unlike earlier performers in the role he dropped some of the more elementary tumbling required of the part and devised for the character a body of original comic routines that captivated audiences everywhere with their ingenuity and humour.

In his hands the Clown became the archetypal rebel who undermines the subterfuges of his master and devotes himself to the satisfaction of his own gluttony, lust, and (often criminal) appetite for mischief. Enlisted to accompany Pantaloon and the Dandy Lover in their pursuit of Harlequin and Columbine, Grimaldi's Clown was easily distracted by the sight of food, drink, women, and any opportunity to create comic mayhem, though becoming himself the hapless victim of the magic wielded by Harlequin's slapstick.

Prior to the TRANSFORMATION SCENE the actor who played Clown was usually cast in the role of the hero's rival suitor, who might be a servant in the father's household or a minor court official (Grimaldi appeared in such roles as the SQUIRE and Queen). Tools of the specialist performer of the part included a red-hot poker, a string of (stolen) sausages, and some butter, which was used to prepare butter-slide grease traps for victims; performers of the role of Clown were also generally personally responsible for devising the slapstick business of the harlequinade.

Competent Clowns had more opportunity to stamp their own personality on the part than had other actors in the harlequinade, but the standard set by 'Joey' was high. After Grimaldi many performers attempted and failed to emulate his unique mastery of the part; among the more successful were his pupil TOM MATTHEWS, PAUL HERRING, PAULO REDIGÉ, ROBERT BRADBURY, HARRY BOLENO, JEFFERINI, 'NIMBLE' GEORGE WIELAND, James Huline, RICHARD FLEXMORE, HARRY PAYNE, 'WHIMSICAL' WALKER, and members of the CONQUEST, LUPINO, and LAURI families. There was even a female Clown, a Miss Cuthbert, who enjoyed some popularity in the 1850s. The first to play Clown in the USA was E. J. Parsloe, who took the role in the 1831 tour of Grimaldi's old hit, *Mother Goose*, to New York; the visit was not a success and Parsloe himself died after the third night.

Styles varied considerably: some Clowns talked, others executed death-defying acrobatics, and others still modelled their acts closely upon that of the matchless Grimaldi. Clowns were often expected to utilise real animals in their acts and appeared with troupes of trained dogs and monkeys (Grimaldi himself was admired for his skill and inventiveness in such scenes). Such songs as TIPPITY WITCHET and HOT CODLINS, which Grimaldi made famous, were uniquely associated with the part and were delivered on innumerable occasions long after Grimaldi's death.

Ironically, Grimaldi's success in the role may well have contributed to the decline of the harlequinade as a whole, for upon his retirement no one could be found to equal him and consequently the emphasis switched from the comedy of the harlequinade to the spectacle of the expanded OPENING. The cruel treatment meted out by the greedy practical joker Clown to babies and policemen alike may also have contributed to a decline in the popularity of his adventures with respectable Victorian audiences who were increasingly inclined to express outrage at such behaviour.

Popular comedians of the stature of DAN LENO eventually usurped Clown's role and he was reduced to a grotesque figure who made a brief appearance to throw sweets to children in the audience. With the disappearance of the harlequinade in the 1930s, Clown – once the embodiment of the chaotic saturnalia that was the early pantomime – was exiled to the circus, where many of the routines developed by Grimaldi and his successors are preserved (though only as the very palest shadow of what they once were). Other relics of Clown's long reign over the English pantomime include the fictional Wilkins Micawber in CHARLES DICKENS's novel *David Copperfield*, who was, according to some critics, drawn from the character of the early Victorian Clown. *See also* JOEY.

coach *See* PUMPKIN.

Cock Robin English nursery rhyme that was sometimes used as the basis for popular pantomimes in the 19th century. One of the most provocative productions of the story was that presented as *Harlequin Cock-Robin and Jenny Wren* (by W. S. GILBERT) at the LYCEUM THEATRE in 1867, in which the role of PRINCIPAL BOY was played by Mabel Gray, a well-known London prostitute.

Story All pantomime versions of the brief rhyme about the death of Cock Robin at the hands of Jenny Wren combined a number of similar nursery rhymes and other subplots. Gilbert's version was typical, introducing various supernatural evil characters as enemies of Cock Robin and architects of his downfall (his characters included Fresh Air, the Demon Miasma, and various birds, bears, and fairies).

Origins The original nursery rhyme upon which the pantomime was based first appeared in print around 1744 and was popularly supposed to refer to the fall of the government of Robert Walpole two years earlier. It is thought, though, that the rhyme may be much older and may even be descended from ancient Norse myth as a song about the death of the Norse god Balder.

Colin The traditional name of the PRINCIPAL BOY in *MOTHER GOOSE*. Colin has been treated by most arrangers as a role for a female principal boy since 1870 and is conventionally the rustic hero-son of the DAME or else a suitor for the hand of her daughter (as in the classic 1902 version by J. HICKORY WOOD). The name Colin has long had associations with rural England and in medieval times was a name particularly favoured by the peasant classes; the poet Edmund Spenser, for instance, used the name for the shepherd boy in *The Shepherd's Calender* back in 1579 and again in the pastoral epic entitled *Colin Clout's Come Home Again* in 1595.

Coliseum Theatre A theatre in St. Martin's Lane, London, where a series of highly successful pantomimes was presented in the middle years of the 20th century. Opened in 1904 as a music hall, the theatre did not flourish at first and closed for a time in 1906 before building a reputation as a venue for high class drama featuring such great stars as Sarah Bernhardt and Ellen Terry. Diaghilev's Ballets Russes occupied the theatre for three years in the 1920s, after which it presented (from 1932) a mixed programme of musical comedies and pantomimes, which were the most spectacular in London, making full use of the theatre's revolving stage (the first in the capital) and huge auditorium.

The Coliseum pantomimes maintained their reputation for lavish spectacle even during the years of World War II (when it was occupied by EMILE LITTLER): a production of *CINDERELLA* in 1941 boasted a chorus of 60 and a glittering exhibition of 560 costumes. A production of *HUMPTY-DUMPTY* starring PAT KIRKWOOD a year later was equally sumptuous. The theatre was converted for use as a cinema in 1961 and eventually became the home of the Sadler's Wells Opera Company (now the English National Opera).

Collins, Arthur (1863–1932) English theatre manager, who succeeded SIR AUGUSTUS HARRIS as manager of DRURY LANE after Harris's death in 1896. Collins began his theatrical career as a scene-painter at the Lane but later rose to become Harris's assistant. As manager, Collins determined to maintain the theatre's great reputation as a pantomime venue and successfully presented a long series of spectacular productions featuring major stars of the MUSIC HALL.

In particular, he won acclaim for his work with the great DAN LENO, who produced his best performances under Collins. Unlike Harris, who had been content to allow Leno a free hand, Collins worked closely with the great star and provided him with material ideally suited to his comic persona, the scripts themselves being written by Collins's collaborator J. HICKORY WOOD. His most successful productions included the sensational 1899 version of *JACK AND THE BEANSTALK*, which culminated in an army of children dressed as British soldiers emerging from one of the dead giant's pockets – one of the most memorable scenic coups ever seen on the pantomime stage.

The Leno era ended with his death in 1904 but Collins continued to uphold the Drury Lane pantomime tradition (after initial disappointment with his 1904 production of *The White Cat*, his only failure) and ushered in a new style of production in which stars of musical comedy and operetta appeared in many leading roles, with the result that the musical content of the pantomime was lifted to sublime new heights. For a time he also reversed the convention of females always appearing as PRINCIPAL BOY when, in 1912, he invited the baritone Wilfred Douthitt to play Prince Auriol in *THE SLEEPING BEAUTY*. He invited Douthitt back in 1913 and subsequently cast the operetta star Bertram Wallis and the balladeer Eric Marshall as principal boy – though female principal boys reclaimed their ascendancy soon after. Collins continued to oversee the annual Drury Lane pantomime until the last regular production in 1919, finally retiring in 1924.

Collins, Lottie (1866–1910) English singer, who became one of the leading PRINCIPAL GIRLS of the late Victorian pantomime. Having begun her career as a skipping-rope dancer, she became a solo performer in the MUSIC HALL in 1881 and rocketed to fame in 1891 with the song TA-RA-RA-BOOM-DE-AY, which she first sang in *DICK WHITTINGTON* at the Grand Theatre, Islington. The song remained the centrepiece of her performances for the rest of her pantomime career and confirmed her status as one of the most admired pantomime stars of the 1890s.

Colman, George (1732–94) English playwright and theatre manager, called the Elder to avoid confusion with his son (also a playwright), who influenced the early development of the pantomime while manager (1767–74) of COVENT GARDEN. It was Colman who first suggested, in 1754, that NURSERY RHYMES and similar native folktales – specifically *BABES IN THE WOOD* – might furnish pantomime writers with suitable plots, though it was only towards the end of the century that his idea was taken up with any seriousness.

His own *Genius of Nonsense* (1780) was one of the first pantomimes to offer an OPENING based on a fairytale rather than upon Classical mythology. At other times he criticised the pantomimes of his day, especially objecting to the introduction of DIALOGUE. After leaving Covent Garden Colman (who had previously been one of the managers at DRURY LANE) took over the HAYMARKET, but he is usually remembered today for his collaboration with DAVID GARRICK on *The Clandestine Marriage* and for his 30 or so other plays and adaptations.

Columbine The pretty sweetheart of HARLEQUIN in the English HARLEQUINADE. She began as Columbina, a servant girl who was one of the stock characters in the *COMMEDIA DELL'ARTE*, in which her turbulent romance with ARLECCHINO provided a lively comic subplot. Originally she often appeared under a number of different names, including Carmosina, Diamantina, Nespolia, and Rosetta before being identified universally as Columbina. When the *commedia dell'arte* was reinterpreted by performers in France, Columbine was elevated to the role of romantic heroine, even acquiring her own maid.

In the pantomime, the actress playing one of the lovers in the OPENING would be 'revealed' as Columbine in the TRANSFORMATION SCENE. With Harlequin, she would then be pursued through a lengthy series of scenes by the other leading characters of the harlequinade before the final reconciliation brought the lovers together. Flirty and capricious, Columbine is the daughter of PANTALOON, who strongly disapproves of her alliance with Harlequin, by whom he is invariably outsmarted.

Performers of the role of Columbine were not required to be great acrobats and never spoke (they were occasionally allowed a song) but did have to be pretty, graceful, and accomplished dancers. In the early history of the pantomime performers of the role wore contemporary dress, but from the middle of the 19th century they were usually costumed in the short skirts popularised in the ballet by the Italian dancer Marie Taglioni. Famous actresses who appeared in the role in the 19th century included MADAME VESTRIS, MADAME CÉLESTE, and Rose Leclerq. The herb columbine, incidentally, is an emblem of folly and the abandoned lover.

Comédie-Italienne French theatrical company, whose development of the French version of the Italian *COMMEDIA DELL'ARTE* was to have a profound influence upon the growth of the HARLEQUINADE in England. The company began life as the celebrated troupe led by Tiberio Fiorilli at the Petit Bourbon theatre close to the Louvre, one of several Italian companies that enjoyed significant success in Paris in the late 17th century. In response to the enormous popularity of Fiorilli's company, Louis XIV granted it royal protection and in 1680 the renamed Comédie-Italienne settled at the Hôtel de Bourgogne, which had been newly vacated by the rival Comédie-Française.

Led by such acclaimed performers as Domenico Biancolelli (*c*. 1637–88) and Angelo Costantini (*c*. 1655–1729), the company attracted huge audiences and embarked on a gradual transformation of the conventional *commedia*, relying increasingly upon scripts written by French playwrights rather than upon improvisation. Performances at the theatre were halted abruptly in 1697 when members of the company were expelled from France for allegedly offending Madame de Maintenon, but the troupe was re-formed in 1716 and subsequently continued to develop its own style of playing independent of its Italian origins.

The company turned eventually to sentimental comedy, drawing on written scripts provided for them by such writers as Pierre Carlet de Chamblain de Marivaux (1688–1763), author of such pieces as *Arlequin Poli par l'Amour* (1720). As well as adopting a more sentimental tone than their Italian models, the players with the Comédie-Italienne also reduced the number of principal characters and subtly altered the balance between them as well as giving them new names – ARLECCHINO, Scaramuccia, Pantalone, and Columbina becoming Arlequin, SCARAMOUCHE, PANTALOON, and COLUMBINE respectively. Most significantly of all, Pedrolino was redefined in the form of the melancholy PIERROT. The use of masks was also restricted and, after dialogue was banned by Royal Patent (at the request of the Comédie-Française) greater emphasis was placed upon dumb-play (although the players attempted to get round the regulations by the use of placards etc.).

The company was granted a royal pension in 1723, after which it moved further still from its origins in the *commedia dell'arte*, ultimately merging in 1762 with the Opéra-Comique to present comic opera and vaudeville.

commedia dell'arte Italian theatrical tradition from which the HARLEQUINADE ultimately developed. The *commedia dell'arte*, which evolved in the middle of the 16th century in the BOOTH theatres of Italy, may or may not have been descended from the BACCHANALIA of the Romans but certainly it shared the robust humour and use of stock characters that characterised the plays of Plautus and his contemporaries. Other influences included the *commedia erudita* of Renaissance Italy, the clowning of court jesters, and the performances of travelling minstrels and actors back in medieval times.

The action of the *commedia dell'arte* was based on brief skeleton plots (scenarios) and performers had to be expert in the techniques of improvisation. Typically the plots themselves revolved around the romantic intrigues of various pairs of lovers, the outwitting of gullible masters by their servants, and the lustful aspirations of old men towards various pretty young women, the whole being enriched by mistaken identities, comic deceptions, and disguises.

Among the leading characters were **Pantalone** (*see* PANTALOON), **Il Capitano** (a swaggering but cowardly soldier), **Il Dottore** (a pedantic physician or lawyer often called Gratiano), and the *ZANNI* (a pair or more of wily servants from whose ranks came such figures as ARLECCHINO, BRIGHELLA, and PULCINELLA). The *zanni* provided most of the comedy while romantic interest was provided by a young hero (known by such names as Flavio or Oratio) and the heroine, who was usually identified as the daughter or ward of Pantalone or Gratiano and was called Isabella or Silvia among other names. Other characters closely involved in the central romantic intrigue included the heroine's maid Columbina (*see* COLUMBINE). Most of the parts were played with a distinctive MASK (covering the upper half of the face) and costume, which meant that the character concerned was instantly recognised by the audience and further detailed characterisation was unnecessary.

Although the Italian *commedia* was not originally silent (a change that was forced upon it in its French reincarnation) the emphasis was nonetheless firmly on comic physical action rather than dialogue. Every production provided ample opportunities for acrobatics, stock comic interruptions (*see LAZZI*), and broad-humoured practical jokes (*see BURLA*). Performers were also skilled mimics, singers, and dancers. Many celebrated companies sprung up in Italy to present such entertainments; the most famous included the Accesi of Mantua, the Confidenti, who toured Europe with their shows, the Desiosi, the Fedeli, who were rapturously received in Paris in 1613 and 1614, the Gelosi, and the Uniti.

Actors with such companies frequently inherited their roles from their parents and many performers were related. Among the greatest of them were Francesco Gabrielli (1588–*c*. 1636), Tristano Martinelli (*c*. 1557–1630), and Flamineo Scala (fl. 1600–21). Drusiano Martinelli (d. *c*. 1607) brought a *commedia dell'arte* company to London in 1577, while records exist of another troupe performing before Elizabeth I herself in 1602. It was, however, in France that the genre really took root (productions in England being hampered by, among other things, the prohibition against female performers). It was through this French tradition (*see* COMÉDIE-ITALIENNE) that the *commedia dell'arte* was communicated to the English stage, albeit in a somewhat altered form.

By the end of the 17th century several French troupes had taken their art to England, appearing at fairs and booth theatres to rapturous applause (to the irritation of many English playwrights who bemoaned what they saw as a vulgarisation of their art). Soon such performances were being seen in some of London's leading venues under the title ITALIAN NIGHT SCENES and characters from the *commedia dell'arte* were finding their way into dramas written by indigenous English playwrights. The first English writer to incorporate characters from the *commedia* in his plays was probably WILLIAM MOUNTFORD, who introduced several of them in his version of *Doctor Faustus* in 1685.

As well as having a profound influence upon the pantomime, the *commedia dell'arte* also had a pronounced effect upon the 'legitimate' theatre in England, influencing the drama of Ben Jonson and William Shakespeare among others. The origins of the Punch and Judy show are also to be found in *commedia dell'arte* characters. The genre itself had fallen from fashion in Italy by the end of the 18th century, but through the harlequinade many of the characters and techniques upon which the *commedia dell'arte* depended survived into the 20th century.

Compton, Fay (Virginia Lillian Emmeline Compton; 1894–1978) English actress, who excelled in straight drama and comedy but was also popular for her performances in pantomime. A member of a distinguished theatrical family, she was acclaimed in both Shakespearean and light comedy roles and was lured to the pantomime by the producer Julian Wylie. Her subsequent triumph as PRINCIPAL BOY (in the role of PRINCE CHARMING) in 1942 confirmed her abilities as an actress in a wide range of theatre and endeared her to London audiences, as well as making it more acceptable for 'serious' actors to venture into pantomime. Her other pantomime roles included that of ROBIN HOOD.

Conquest family English theatrical family that began a long association with the pantomime early in the 19th century. **Benjamin Conquest** (Benjamin Oliver; 1812–72) was a star of the SADLER'S WELLS THEATRE in the 1830s and also managed the GRECIAN THEATRE, which he opened in 1851, in collaboration with his son, **George Augustus Oliver Conquest** (1837–1901).

George Conquest was the most notable member of the family, being a theatre manager, noted translator and adaptor of French plays, and also the author of several melodramas, but being best known for his many pantomimes, in which he appeared himself to great acclaim. He was particularly admired in SKIN PARTS, of which he was regarded a master. His most brilliant impersonations of the animal kingdom (in preparation for which he spent many hours at the Zoological Gardens in London) included appearances in the role of a monkey, in the pantomime *Grim Goblin* (1876), as well as interpetations of giants, dwarfs, and even an octopus and a porcupine, among other extraordinary roles.

Conquest's great talent as an acrobat was of immense value and he made the costumes he wore himself with equal skill (he claimed that the remarkable disguise he wore as a spider crab took him nearly a year to construct). Audiences flocked to marvel at his inventive creations and to gasp at his daring leaps and tumbles (it was said that he had broken every bone in his body during the course of his career). The Grecian Theatre prospered under his control from 1872 until he sold it in 1879 and two years later he took over the Surrey Theatre in Blackfriars, which in turn became one of the most popular pantomime venues in the city.

It was George Conquest who first recognised the talent of DAN LENO and engaged him to appear in pantomime at the Surrey in 1886; other discoveries included HERBERT CAMPBELL and G. H. MACDERMOTT among other comedians. Pantomimes presented by George Conquest and other members of the family were notable for their originality and for the prominence given to the HARLEQUINADE.

George's three sons followed him into the pantomime: George Benjamin Conquest (1858–1926) was popular as DAME while Fred Conquest (1871–1941) and Arthur Conquest (1875–1945) won acclaim in skin parts. Fred was especially acclaimed in the role of GOOSE, with which part his name became uniquely identified, while Arthur's finest roles included Daphne the Chimpanzee. Fred and Arthur took over the Surrey Theatre when their father died and eventually passed it on to their brother George (who subsequently became manager of the BRITANNIA THEATRE in 1910).

Cook The DAME in *DICK WHITTINGTON*. Warmhearted, cantankerous, and a great favourite with audiences over many years, she played no role in the original legend and was an invention of the pantomime writers, who had her mistreating the unfortunate Dick prior to him gaining his fortune. She has masqueraded under a great many different names, among them Dame Dorothy Drippington, in T. L. GREENWOOD's *Whittington and His Cat; or, Old Dame Fortune, and Harlequin Lord Mayor* (1852), and Sarah the Cook or Sarah Suet in a great many modern adaptations. Records exist of a man playing the part as far back as 1731, when the story was staged at Southwark Fair. Most of the great dames have included the role of Cook in their repertoire; others to have undertaken the role are reputed to have included – somewhat surprisingly – the great tragedian SIR HENRY IRVING and in more recent times JACK TRIPP.

Cormoran One of the GIANTS that Jack faces in *JACK THE GIANT-KILLER*. According to Cornish legend, Jack received an ornate belt from King Arthur after he killed the giant by luring him into a concealed pit.

corner trap A variety of TRAP positioned downstage on either side of the acting area through which stationary standing figures could be raised. They were particularly useful in the pantomime for appearances by fairies and other supernatural characters.

Corsican trap *See* GHOST GLIDE.

cosmorama *See* DIORAMA.

costume Pantomime costumes include some of the most bizarre and magnificent outfits ever seen upon the stage, with endless opportunities being offered by mixed casts of supernatural beings, outrageous DAMES and UGLY SISTERS, processions of historical figures, and all manner of giants, ogres, dwarfs, and demons.

Back in the 17th century actors upon the English stage generally appeared in contemporary dress, but this convention was gradually dropped during the course of the 18th century. Costumes for characters in the HARLEQUINADE were dictated by conventions inherited from the *COMMEDIA DELL'ARTE*, but there was still room for development even under these restrictions, with, for instance, the creation of Harlequin's distinctive diamond-patched coat (first worn by James Byrne in 1800) and variations in the exotic costumes adopted by Clown over the years.

Costumes in the 18th- and early 19th-century pantomime reflected fashions in society as a whole and in the 1790s, for instance, many performers were appearing in fanciful versions of Eastern dress (including turbans, veils, and turned-up slippers) in response to the contemporary taste for things Oriental (the amalgam of Chinese, Japanese, and Persian costume then arrived at remains virtually unchanged to the present day in the traditional costumes of *ALADDIN*). Other styles of costume loosely drawn from life included the elaborate outfits donned by the DANDY LOVER in the 1820s and 1830s; these were even more eccentric than those worn by the fops of the day and anticipated the development of the costume as a tool in the armoury of the modern pantomime humorist. JOSEPH GRIMALDI, always with an eye for a bit of satirical fun, scored an immense hit lampooning the outfits donned by the fashionable hunting fraternity, riding a mock horse and wearing a ludicrous riding cap with an enormous peak (which kept falling off).

J. R. PLANCHÉ was the first arranger to insist upon some degree of historical authenticity in the costumes provided for his extravaganzas in the 1830s – an innovation that was to have far-reaching consequences throughout the theatre. Costumes have never been more extravagant and elaborate than they were in the pantomimes of AUGUSTUS HARRIS at DRURY LANE in the closing years of the 19th century. Harris spared no expense on clothing every member of his cast from principals to chorus in the most fabulous outfits; he was also insistent that all costumes were historically accurate, setting a high standard for subsequent producers. Examples of the scale and care involved in his productions include the costumes required for *SINBAD THE SAILOR* (1882), among which were scores of miniature military uniforms, correct to the last detail, to be worn by an army of children impersonating the British Army's triumphant return from a campaign in Egypt that year. Other characters in the pantomime requiring the most lavish costumes included a procession of every British monarch since William I.

Financial considerations have largely precluded costumes of the same brilliance being seen *en masse* with any regularity in the 20th-century pantomime, though designers of great reputation have, on occasion, contributed ideas (among them the royal wedding dress designers, the Emmanuels). The MELVILLE BROTHERS signalled a sea change in the pantomime when they opted to rent costumes for their pantomimes, rather than having them specially made, preferring to reserve their money for spectacular scenery and the hire of leading performers. Modern pantomime costumes can cost anything up to £1000 each and are consequently intended (with careful cleaning) to last anything up to ten years (*see also* SKIN PARTS).

GEORGE LACY and DOUGLAS BYNG were largely responsible for establishing the tradition that the dame should wear a series of increasingly flamboyant and outrageous costumes, which now provides one of the characteristic running gags of the contemporary pantomime (modern dames may wear as many as a dozen different outfits ranging from mock girl guide uniforms to Superwoman catsuits in the course of a single performance). The costumes of PRINCIPAL BOYS are similarly dictated by convention though according to tradition they are expected to provide their own tights (a not inconsiderable expense in past years). The most magnificent costumes are still by tradition kept for the Grand Finale in which they may only appear for two or three minutes while the cast take their bow and wish the audience good night.

Coveney, Harriet (1827–92) English singer and actress, who was among the very first MUSIC HALL artistes to win acclaim in the Victorian pantomime, notably as PRINCIPAL BOY. The daughter of stage performers at the HAYMARKET, she made her stage debut as a child and at the age of 14 appeared in E. L. BLANCHARD'S *Arcadia* (1841). Subsequently she established herself as a popular principal boy at DRURY LANE, acting alongside the VOKES FAMILY in such pantomimes as *ALADDIN AND HIS WONDERFUL LAMP* (1874), in which she played WIDOW TWANKEY. In a career that lasted over 50 years she played a total of 1800 parts.

Covent Garden The London theatre, now formally called the Royal Opera House, which began its life as the home of the enormously popular and influential pantomimes of JOHN RICH and remained one of the leading pantomime venues in the city for the next 150 years. Rich opened the first Covent Garden theatre in 1732, as the Theatre Royal, Covent Garden, in order to stage even more spectacular pantomime entertainments then he had at the LINCOLN'S INN FIELDS THEATRE. For the next 50 years the theatre – jealously protecting its right as a Royal Patent holder to stage spoken drama – remained London's most prestigious pantomime venue, despite competition from DRURY LANE.

Milestones in the Covent Garden pantomime included the first pantomime version of *ALADDIN* in 1788 (with further productions of the story in 1813 and 1826). The oldest surviving pantomime staged at the theatre is *Harlequin's Magnet*, an AQUATIC DRAMA staged in 1805 after the stage had been fitted with water tanks in response to the success of such waterborne pantomimes at SADLER'S WELLS.

In the early 19th century the pantomimes of THOMAS DIBDIN (staged by CHARLES FARLEY) were highly successful, but never more so than when they featured performances by the supreme Clown of them all, JOSEPH GRIMALDI. Grimaldi was lured to the theatre in 1806 after a disagreement with the Drury Lane management where he had previously appeared and made his Covent Garden debut in *Valentine and Orson*, after which he enjoyed unparalleled success as Clown in Dibdin's *Harlequin and Mother Goose; or, the Golden Egg*; it was staged once more at the theatre in 1807 and, after Covent Garden was destroyed by fire, at the HAYMARKET in 1808.

Significant pantomimes starring Grimaldi at the rebuilt Covent Garden in following years included *Harlequin Asmodeus; or, Cupid on*

Crutches (1810), *Harlequin and the Red Dwarf* (1812), Farley's *Harlequin and the Swans; or, The Bath of Beauty* (1813), with Grimaldi as the hilarious Doctor Tumble Tuzzy, and *Harlequin and Fortunio* (1815), in which Grimaldi sang 'An Oyster Crossed in Love' and a female performer first appeared in the role of PRINCIPAL BOY. With Grimaldi as Clown, Covent Garden set a new standard for the pantomime and the style of the Garden's pantomimes, in which the elements of spectacle, satire, and slapstick were finely balanced, influencing productions seen at numerous other theatres.

Other landmark productions of the period included *Harlequin Whittington; or, The Lord Mayor of London* (1814), which was the first pantomime production of the tale, *Harlequin and Cinderella*, which was seen at Easter in 1820 and introduced the characters of the BARONESS and the FAIRY GODMOTHER, and the introduction of the very first DIORAMA in *Harlequin and Friar Bacon* (also 1820).

There were occasional failures, inevitably, and the 1817 production of *The Marquis de Carabas; or, Puss in Boots*, had to be taken off after audiences rioted and demanded that the run be ended. Also significant, although unsuccessful at the time, was the 1830 production of *Harlequin Pat and Harlequin Bat; or, The Giant's Causeway*, in which the OPENING was written entirely in prose for the first time.

The tradition continued through the management in the 1830s of the tragedian William Charles Macready, who was among those who realised that a successful pantomime brought in more money than 'straight' drama ever could. In 1839 the theatre witnessed the next great development in the pantomime tradition when the partnership of MADAME VESTRIS and J. R. PLANCHÉ arrived to continue the highly popular series of EXTRAVAGANZAS that they had previously inaugurated at the rival OLYMPIC THEATRE. Their spectacular productions became a regular attraction at Easter and exerted a major influence upon the changing shape of the pantomime itself, recreating the OPENING and putting new pressure upon the HARLEQUINADE.

Subsequently major pantomime attractions at the theatre included the celebrated VOKES FAMILY, who starred at Covent Garden in 1880 at the end of their joint careers. The following seven years witnessed some of the most extravagant pantomimes ever staged, with stunning scenery, huge casts, and elaborate ballet sequences in answer to the prevailing Victorian taste for spectacle. Nonetheless, a change in policy in 1887 brought it all to an end and since then only two pantomimes have been staged at Covent Garden, which is now devoted to productions of opera and ballet. In 1920 the theatre staged the previous year's DRURY LANE production when the latter theatre replaced its annual pantomime with a spectacular drama and in 1938 Francis Laidler's production of *Red Riding Hood* was seen there.

Cow The cow exchanged by Jack for a handful of BEANS in the pantomime *JACK AND THE BEANSTALK*. Variously identified as Daisy, Gertie, or by a host of other names, the Cow is the best loved of all the SKIN PARTS. The Cow, who must be sold at the market to relieve the sorry financial plight of Jack and his mother, provides one of the highlights of the early scenes of the story and is unfailingly popular with younger members of the audience. Usually played by two actors, the Cow is often played for sympathy and frequently 'steals' the scenes in which she appears (often with a comic tap dance). Notable performers of the role over the years have included ARTHUR CONQUEST and the GRIFFITHS BROTHERS. The scene in which Jack sells Daisy has never been more touchingly interpreted than it was in performances featuring DOROTHY WARD, whose moving farewell regularly moved children and adults alike to tears (the scene was so celebrated that it was even performed in a Royal Variety Show). FRANKIE HOWERD also excelled in the scene.

critic A writer who contributes reviews and other articles upon the theatre to a newspaper or other publication, radio or television programme. Opinions about the pantomime have been divided ever since the earliest days of the genre, with distinguished critics siding with both camps for and against. The dominance of the innovative pantomimes of JOHN RICH in the early 18th century was particularly resented by many critics, who feared that 'serious' drama would lose audiences as a result.

Among those to attack Rich's productions was Alexander Pope, who 'honoured' Rich by listing him as one of the Dunces of *The Dunciad*. COLLEY CIBBER called the pantomimes of the 1720s "monstrous medlies", but was obliged out of necessity to join the ranks of those presenting them. Similarly, DAVID GARRICK protested against the public's enthusiasm for the genre and called such shows "mummery and toys" but oversaw the first DRURY LANE pantomime himself in 1750. Subsequently the novelist Samuel Richardson called the 'immortals' (the divinities who played such an important part in the early pantomime) "the worst and dullest company into which an audience has ever been introduced" while Henry Fielding wrote a hostile BURLESQUE based on Rich's pantomimes and elaborated on his theme in the novel *Tom Jones* (1749), declaring that pantomime was in every way dull entertainment.

When dialogue was first introduced in 1779 the playwright George Colman could say nothing better about it than it was "dullness and dialogue come together" and there has been no shortage of critics ever since (usually to the effect that the contemporary pantomime is in every way inferior to the pantomime of yesteryear and surely on its last legs). One of the most vociferous critics in the early 19th century was Lord Byron, who attacked the popularity of the pantomime (and especially THOMAS DIBDIN's *MOTHER GOOSE*) in his 'English Bards and Scotch Reviewers'; he was not, however, above visiting the pantomime himself on a fairly regular basis and numbered several pantomime stars – including Grimaldi (to whose benefits he readily contributed) – among his acquaintances.

The criticisms of such notable figures have never had much effect upon the readiness of the public to flock to the pantomime, as the *Times* observed in 1823 when it dryly remarked on the fact that "Every body 'pooh-poohs' the pantomime, but every body goes to see it." Sometimes the critics have genuinely reflected public reaction to the pantomime. In the Victorian era, for example, the press spoke for many when it suggested on many occasions that the HARLEQUINADE should now be dropped altogether – although it lingered on regardless at certain theatres until the 1930s.

In contrast, the pantomime can claim an impressive array of equally impassioned supporters. The great essayist Leigh Hunt was enthusiastic in his support for the genre, proclaiming that those who professed to dislike it were either liars or fools. Other keen supporters have included such prestigious writers as William Hazlitt, William Thackeray and CHARLES DICKENS, who may have used characters from the pantomime as models for his own fictional creations. *See also* AUDIENCE; BURLESQUE; PARODIES.

cross-dressing *See* DAME; PRINCIPAL BOY.

Crusoe, Mrs. The DAME in *ROBINSON CRUSOE*. The character is, of course, an invention of the pantomime and over the years she has arrived at Crusoe's desert island under a variety of pretexts, often as the ship's cook. Celebrated interpreters of the role have included the Scottish actor Ramsey Danvers.

cue A sentence or other signal (perhaps a special effect or lighting change) upon which a performer makes his entrance or delivers one of his own lines or performs some other action. The ability to pick up cues rapidly is one of the skills required of all performers and successful technical effects often also depend upon the stage crew knowing their cues well. *See also* SLAPSTICK.

curtain The heavy cloth that conceals the stage from the view of the audience before and after a performance and during the interval. The lowering of a frontcloth during the course of the action allows stage crew to change the set unobserved (*see* CARPENTER'S SCENE). A safety curtain of special fireproof material must be lowered between acts as it will prevent any backstage fire spreading into the auditorium (formerly an advertisement curtain was also sometimes lowered).

curtain music The music that is played as an overture before the curtain itself is raised and the pantomime begins (often a medley of tunes from the show itself). Music is also usually played in the brief breaks between scenes and again before the start of subsequent acts.

curtain-raiser *See* FOREPIECE.

custard pie scene *See* SLOSH SCENE.

cut-out An item of stage scenery consisting of a piece of painted board or fabric that is usually positioned in front of other flats to promote an illusion of depth. Mobile cut-outs (representing ships, clouds, etc.) were of particular value when used in conjunction with a moving DIORAMA and, when incorporating transparent fabric, were much used in the Victorian TRANSFORMATION SCENE.

D

Dainty, Billy (1927–86) English comedian, who was an enormously popular star of VARIETY and the pantomime after World War II. He made his pantomime debut at the age of 12 and gained early experience in such lowly roles as the back legs of a donkey. Subsequently he left drama college to establish a reputation as a singularly talented and energetic eccentric dancer with a large repertory of funny walks. These skills and his bluff seaside-postcard humour lent themselves readily to the pantomime and he excelled in the role of DAME, his most successful scenes including a hilarious 'striptease' routine. He continued to appear in the part of dame for 30 years and was last seen in the role in *ALADDIN* in 1986. Outside the pantomime he was also known for his memorable partnership with ROY HUDD in which they revived many old music hall routines.

Daisy The traditional name of the Cow in *JACK AND THE BEANSTALK*.

dame The comic female character (usually the hero's mother) whose presence dominates the modern pantomime and provides much of the best of its humour. Irascible, irrepressible in the face of adversity, quick to take offence, vulgar, vain, and probably the best loved of all characters in the pantomime, she has long been the province of male comedians.

The role was played by a man as long ago as 1731, when an actor by the name of Harper played the part of COOK in *DICK WHITTINGTON* at Southwark Fair. In 1806 Samuel Simmons played the dame in the famous production of *MOTHER GOOSE* in which JOSEPH GRIMALDI was much admired, although the practice only became universally accepted in the 1860s (by which time the female PRINCIPAL BOY was well established) with the success of various MUSIC HALL stars in such parts.

Nonetheless, the comic dame was a familiar sight to Regency audiences and Grimaldi himself appeared in a number of female roles during his career, among them the part of Queen Rondabellyana at COVENT GARDEN in 1812. The playing of female roles by men and boys was, of course, customary in early domestic English drama with women being forbidden from taking the stage until late in the 17th century. Among the most celebrated examples of early equivalents of the dame in the MYSTERY PLAYS of the Middle Ages, for instance, were the roles of Noah's Wife and Mac the Sheepstealer's Wife, two broad comic parts always played by men.

When they were finally permitted to appear, most actresses preferred to leave the less glamorous roles of elderly ladies to men, among whom were such actors as Samuel Foote and HENRY WOODWARD, who also excelled in the role of HARLEQUIN. In the HARLEQUINADE too it was common for males to appear in female roles, with CLOWN occasionally disguising himself as a comic old woman. Originally, the dame character could be synonymous with the BENEVOLENT AGENT, the supernatural figure (usually an old woman played by a man) who oversaw the action in the role of Fairy Godmother or similar and intervened to transform the cast into the characters of the harlequinade with a wave of her magic wand. The supernatural aspect of the character diminished however as the harlequinade declined and the dame emerged as a major comic figure in her own right. It became conventional for the dame role to be that of mother to the principal boy, although initially at least it was rare for both characters to be found on stage at the same time.

The most celebrated of all dames was DAN LENO, in whose hands each dame (clad in a distinctive bonnet and shawl but otherwise plainly dressed) became a fully-rounded comic character with her own distinctive traits. He first appeared as a pantomime dame in 1886, playing Dame Durden in *JACK AND THE BEANSTALK* at the SURREY THEATRE, and subsequently became part of theatre legend in such parts as WIDOW TWANKEY and MOTHER GOOSE.

Famous dames since his time have included (at DRURY LANE) HARRY RANDALL, WILKIE BARD, and GEORGE GRAVES, and (elsewhere) GEORGE CONQUEST, STANLEY AND BARRY LUPINO, FRED EMNEY, GEORGE ROBEY, G. S. Melvin, SHAUN GLENVILLE, Billy Danvers, DOUGLAS BYNG, CLARKSON ROSE, GEORGE LACY (who extended the dame's penchant for outrageous outfits), NAT JACKLEY, Sonnie Hale, Cyril Fletcher, and ARTHUR ASKEY.

Among notable dames of contemporary times have been DANNY LA RUE, Stanley Baxter, Les Dawson, Terry Scott, JACK TRIPP, and John Inman. Even the great tragedian SIR HENRY IRVING is reputed to have played the part of Cook in *THE SLEEPING BEAUTY*. Women have, however, sometimes played the role, even in relatively modern times – though (in deference to traditional notions about the 'gentler sex') female dames are never hit or subjected to the more physical slapstick humour of the SLOSH SCENE as their male counterparts are. Among the more successful of the female dames over the years have been NELLIE WALLACE, who appeared as dame throughout her career, and Iris Sadler, who was seen as Widow Twankey in London in 1940.

Modern dames fall into roughly three categories: such experienced performers as Jack Tripp preserve the tradition of the 'believable' dame created by Leno, while Danny La Rue is the most famous of the 'feminine' dames (playing the part as a camp drag role), and many lesser actors opt for the more two-dimensional 'over-the-top' dame with most of the humour deriving from the character's exaggerated costumes and make-up. *See also* CRUSOE, MRS; DAME TROT.

Dame Trot or **Dame Durden** The DAME in *JACK AND THE BEANSTALK*. One of the best of all dame parts, she is the doting and long-suffering mother of the hero Jack. Her name has varied over the years. When DAN LENO first appeared in the role of dame, on his pantomime debut at the

SURREY THEATRE in 1886, she was called Dame Durden, though a subsequent version starring Leno at DRURY LANE identifies her under the name Mrs. Simpson.

It is as Dame Trot, however, that modern audiences generally see her now. A 'trot' was an archaic nickname for an old hag and Dame Trot herself began life as an alternative 'Mother Hubbard' character associated with various nursery rhymes. She – and her 'comical cat' – was a favourite character of CHAPBOOKS of the early 19th century, but had first appeared in such publications at least 100 years earlier. It has been cogently argued that Betsey Trotwood, in Dickens's *David Copperfield*, is much indebted to pantomime's Dame Trot both for her name and for her distinctive comic traits. Notable Dame Trots of the 20th century have included SHAUN GLENVILLE, who played the part many times in the 1930s and 1940s.

dance The element of dance has always been of great importance in the pantomime. Indeed, JOHN WEAVER, whose ballets-pantomimes mark the origins of the modern pantomime, is also regarded as one of the founding fathers of the contemporary British ballet. Weaver's first interest was in the restoration of dance as a respectable art form in his own country and performers in his productions relied almost solely upon physical gesture and action to convey their meaning.

Dance remained of crucial importance for many years, with all theatres except the two PATENT THEATRES being formally prohibited from using spoken dialogue by the Licensing Act of 1737. As the decades passed, however, so other forms of communication – such as the signboards called FLAGS, limited verse, and other forms of mime – were introduced and eventually the modern pantomime in which the spoken word plays the key role developed. Highlights of the harlequinade in the early 19th century though still included graceful dances by Harlequin and Columbine and the action was often suspended for guest artistes to perform a speciality dance act.

The dance tradition is still strong in the modern pantomime and virtually every pantomime over the last hundred or more years has had at least one scene given over to dancing by nymphs, fairies, or other characters, who – in recent times – are often portrayed by pupils at local dance schools (who come somewhat cheaper than professional dancers). Eccentric dancing, at its extraordinary best when FREDERICK VOKES made appearances in the 1860s and 1870s, remains a popular feature of the modern pantomime, though usually confined to relatively modest displays by the DAME and the UGLY SISTERS and similar comic characters. Notable eccentric dancers in the pantomime in recent decades have included BILLY DAINTY.

Dandini In *CINDERELLA* the best friend of and valet to PRINCE CHARMING. Sometimes treated as a role for a female PRINCIPAL BOY though more often as a comic foil for the prince himself, Dandini arrived in the pantomime via Rossini's opera *La Cenerentola* (first performed in England at Covent Garden in 1820). J. S. GRIMALDI was the first to appear in pantomime under the name Dandini that same year, although the character was at this early stage in his development synonymous with the DANDY LOVER, who himself claimed descent from the *COMMEDIA DELL'ARTE*. A character by the name of Dandini had also made regular appearances in French plays in the 18th century.

dandizette *See* DANDY LOVER.

Dandy Lover or **Lover** A character of the HARLEQUINADE, descended from the Lover of the *COMMEDIA DELL'ARTE*, who rivals HARLEQUIN for the attentions of COLUMBINE. He was invariably played as an outrageous and ridiculous fop wearing parody versions of current men's fashions who though favoured by PANTALOON as a match for his daughter is doomed never to win her. The Dandy Lover of the English tradition is thought to have been influenced by the fops of Restoration drama and may also have absorbed some of the traits of the villains of melodrama. It has been suggested that his love of fine clothes is a reflection of the Paris mob's identification of elaborate evening dress with the hated aristocracy (the earliest melodramas having originated in France at the time of the French Revolution).

As Lover, he appeared in the English pantomime as early as the 1780s at COVENT GARDEN, when he courted Columbine in, for instance, the olio *Harlequin's Chaplet* (1789). It was not until 1807, however, that he appeared as 'Dandy Lover' in the full regalia of the contemporary fop, in Drury Lane's *Furibond; or, Harlequin Negro*. The redefined character quickly caught on and in J. R. PLANCHÉ's early pantomime *Rodolph the Wolf; or, Columbine Red Riding-Hood* (1818) he was promoted to principal comic character.

Writers and performers alike relished the opportunity to lampoon the dandies of their day (who included such luminaries as Beau Brummell, the Prince Regent, and the much-ridiculed amateur actor Robert 'Romeo' Coates) and poked fun at their mannerisms, clothes, and eating habits. The craze among London's dandies for driving carriages at high speed was a particular subject of derision and JOSEPH GRIMALDI himself received an ecstatic reception when he raced about the stage in a makeshift coach pulled by a pair of dogs.

The Dandy Lover's costume typically comprised a highly ornamented green coat with padded shoulders and high collar, a flamboyant cravat and cuffs, beribboned shoes, and a huge curved military hat topped with a cockade. Very often he would carry a lorgnette, through which he would peer disdainfully at the other characters. Similar attentions were also occasionally paid to the female version of the dandy, who were popularly known as **dandizettes**.

The Dandy Lover remained, though, an optional part and he was omitted from many harlequinades even at their height in the Regency theatre (he was rarely included before 1820 in pantomimes at Covent Garden, for instance, where Grimaldi as Clown reserved the right to poke fun at the dandies himself).

During the opening the actor playing the Dandy Lover usually appeared as the hero's rival suitor, vain, slow-witted, and ridiculous; in TOM DIBDIN'S *Harlequin and Humpo; or, Columbine by Candlelight* (1812), for instance, the Dandy Lover was played by the actor performing the role of Humpo prior to the TRANSFORMATION SCENE. During the harlequinade the Dandy Lover would join Pantaloon in a hectic pursuit of his beloved but highly reluctant Columbine and inevitably fell prey to all kinds of hilarious traps.

Noted performers of the role – who had to be fine acrobats and 'posture masters' – included CHARLES FARLEY, ANDREW DUCROW, James Parsloe, and William West. Few, though, equalled Grimaldi, who satirised the whims of the Regency fop in the 1820s in such roles as My Lord Humpy Dumpy in *Harlequin Munchausen* (1818). His son, J. S. GRIMALDI was also admired in the part.

The character, once the most popular target of good-natured satire in the pantomime, vanished from all but the Covent Garden pantomimes in the 1820s (being retained by Farley to counterbalance the loss of Grimaldi's Clown) and disappeared completely from the harlequinade after two last appearances at the Garden in 1833 and 1834. *See also* DANDINI.

dark scene The brief but climactic penultimate scene of the HARLEQUINADE, in which HARLEQUIN completes the task he has been set and wins COLUMBINE. These exciting final adventures were conventionally set in some gloomy and menacing cavern, forest, wilderness, or prison and are thought to have been much influenced by the 'Gothic' dramas popularised by such authors as Horace Walpole and Matthew Lewis in the late 18th century. One pantomime, seen in 1835, made use of the uncompleted Thames Tunnel as the setting for the dark scene. Typically Harlequin is so pleased to win Columbine that he forgets his magic SLAPSTICK, which PANTALOON then seizes. However, the situation is usually saved by the Good Fairy or other supernatural character (*see* BENEVOLENT AGENT), who reconciles the various parties and then transforms the scene in preparation for the glittering finale in a magnificent temple or palace. Scenery for the dark scene often recalled that of the opening, thus reuniting the harlequinade with the initial story, and was often plain and shadowy in deliberate contrast to the splendour of the concluding scene that followed it. Openings of mid-Victorian pantomimes would often begin with a similar dark scene in the course of which various allegorical figures representing good and evil (such as Superstition and Knowledge, for instance) would delineate the underlying moral of the ensuing story. When the harlequinade contracted in the mid-19th century, however, this opening dark scene was one of the episodes to be lost (AUGUSTUS HARRIS dropped it at Drury Lane in 1880). Modern pantomimes still make occasional use of such dark opening scenes, however, to provide a fitting setting for the first entrance of such villainous characters as ABANAZAR and King Rat. *See also* TRANSFORMATION SCENE.

d'Aulnoy, Madame *See* AULNOY, MARIE-CATHÉRINE LE JUMEL DE BARNEVILLE DE LA MOTTE, COMTESSE D'.

De Loutherbourg, Philippe Jacques (1740–1812) German artist and stage designer, who won acclaim as scene painter for the pantomimes and other productions staged by DAVID GARRICK at DRURY LANE in the late 18th century. De Loutherbourg (who was trained in Paris) joined Garrick at the theatre in 1773 and subsequently established himself as the leading scene painter of his day, introducing a series of major innovations.

His most important achievements included his emphasis on more naturalistic designs, backed up by more imaginative use of lighting (he placed dyed silks in front of the lamps to get coloured illumination of the stage area) and his own skill in painting illusionist views. He also rejected conventional wing-and-border scenery arrangements in order to explore the possibilities of perspective, invented new machines to produce realistic sound effects, and executed fully-detailed painted backcloths that were considered works of art in their own right.

He was particularly admired for his backdrops depicting rural landscapes, which were contributed for such pantomimes as *Harlequin Teague; or, the Giant's Causeway*, *The Wonders of Derbyshire; or, Harlequin in the Peak*, and *The Witch of the Lakes; or, Harlequin in the Hebrides*. Other admired scenic coups included volcanic eruptions and magnificent moonlit scenes.

Critics of the day were united in their praise of De Loutherbourg, calling him a genius, and he continued in his post after RICHARD BRINSLEY SHERIDAN (who immortalised the artist in his play *The Critic*) took over as manager of the theatre.

Delpini, Carlo Antonio (1740–1828) Italian actor, born in Rome, who was credited with 'inventing' the Regency pantomime after stressing the importance of character and scenic invention in contemporary productions. Trained in the conventions of the Italian *COMMEDIA DELL'ARTE*, Delpini specialised in the roles of PIERROT and CLOWN and effectively transformed them into central characters of the HARLEQUINADE. He made his debut at COVENT GARDEN in 1776 and subsequently enjoyed great success over many years there and at the HAYMARKET. He also assisted DAVID GARRICK at DRURY LANE and contributed the harlequinade for SHERIDAN's celebrated pantomime *ROBINSON CRUSOE* (1781).

Demon King The evil 'baddie' who pits his wits against Good Fairies, heroes, and heroines in a number of the most popular pantomimes. As baddies go, the Demon King is the most undilutedly wicked – and relished – of them all, threatening cast and audience alike. His every entrance, made by convention in a green spotlight from stage left (left being the devil's side) is invariably greeted with a storm of booing and hissing by audiences who know how to react when they see the man they love to hate.

Demonic characters became much more important in the pantomime in the early 19th century when writers were being influenced by the 'Gothic' drama then in vogue at a number of major theatres. In imitation of horror stories by such authors as Horace Walpole and Matthew 'Monk' Lewis, pantomime authors learnt to people their plots with numerous imps, sprites, goblins, and other demons and such was their popularity that they have never since disappeared.

Performers of the role, who relish the opportunity to indulge in this most menacing and rascally part have included two of the greatest tragedians ever to grace the English stage – EDMUND KEAN (who played a demon while still a child) and SIR HENRY IRVING (who once played the role in Edinburgh in the 1850s).

The Demon King has increasingly dominated the action in recent decades as a result of the proliferation of relatively undistinguished male PRINCIPAL BOYS in the 1950s and 1960s; to compensate for the often weak performances turned in by celebrity stars taken from the world of television and pop music, managements allowed the Demon King a greater share of the limelight and many leading performers now covet the role in preference to playing a 'goody'. Equivalents of the Demon King in various stories include King Rat in *DICK WHITTINGTON AND HIS CAT*, ABANAZAR in *ALADDIN AND HIS WONDERFUL LAMP*, and the wolf in *LITTLE RED RIDING HOOD*.

desert island *See ROBINSON CRUSOE.*

designer A member of the production team who, working alongside the DIRECTOR, oversees the design of lighting, scenery, costumes, and related technical aspects of a pantomime. Among the most distinguished early designers of the pantomime – whose efforts went far beyond anything seen today – may be counted PHILIPPE JACQUES DE LOUTHERBOURG and WILLIAM BEVERLEY.

Deulin, Nicola (Isaac Dowling; 1809–57) English actor, who was highly acclaimed in the role of CLOWN in the early 19th century. Deulin began his career playing HARLEQUIN at the Grecian Saloon in the City Road but subsequently triumphed as Clown, being described by many critics as one of Grimaldi's most able heirs. His relatively short career ended with his death from consumption at the age of 48.

dialogue Pantomime, in its early history, was entirely silent (but for an orchestral accompaniment). JOHN RICH's entertainments, for instance, relied upon the mime skills of himself and other members of the cast to convey meaning and it was many years before arrangers began to explore the possibilities of dialogue in a major way. This remained the case even after plots grew more ambitious, with stories from Classical mythology being used as a background for the comic adventures of Harlequin and his fellows.

The absence of dialogue from virtually all early pantomimes was also a reflection of the extraordinary rule laid down by the LICENSING ACT of 1737, which prohibited all theatres other than the PATENT THEATRES from presenting spoken drama. Legend has it that performers who inadvertently uttered so much as a single word during performances at the so-called MINOR THEATRES risked automatic fines by the theatre management.

Even the managements of the Patent Theatres proved reluctant to place much emphasis upon spoken lines. DAVID GARRICK, for instance, only took the revolutionary step of introducing a speaking Harlequin at DRURY LANE in the 1750s when he realised the impossibility of finding anyone capable of matching the mime skills of his rival John Rich at COVENT GARDEN. The experiment was not a success and it was many years before the idea was tried once again (hence the development of the bizarre convention that certain coloured patches on HARLEQUIN'S costume indicated particular emotions when pointed to).

Other factors that precluded the early introduction of dialogue were the use of the huge masks called BIG HEADS (which had the effect of muffling a performer's voice so that few in the audience could make out what he was saying) and the notoriously bad acoustics in the large rebuilt auditoria of both COVENT GARDEN and DRURY LANE.

The idea of the 'speaking' pantomime was revived, however, towards the end of the century when, in 1779, spoken lines were incorporated in Dibdin's *The Touchstone; or, Harlequin Traveller* at Covent Garden and subsequently many other managements ventured to explore the possibilities of speech, despite the restrictions laid down by the law (*see* BURLETTA). The extent to which the pantomime was vocal in the early 19th century is impossible to determine from existing records, although it seems that the pantomime at many leading venues relied on a combination of song, dance, physical gesture, painted placards (*see* FLAG), and brief bursts of rhymed or prose dialogue to explain the narrative where necessary.

Even the Patent Theatres, allowed by law to use as much dialogue as they liked, continued to make use of such devices as 'flags' and maintained a strong mime tradition (as in the case of the harlequinades featuring the taciturn though not entirely silent Clown Grimaldi at Covent Garden). OPENINGS when spoken were conventionally delivered in rhymed or blank verse, which was also used for the transformation and closing scenes – but there are also records from the period of considerable extracts or even whole pantomimes being delivered as prose at Patent Theatres and unlicensed venues alike.

Everything changed in 1843, when the legal restrictions on spoken dialogue were finally lifted. The case that led to this change was a remarkable one, with a theatre management taking an Italian actor to court for uttering the only English word he knew – "beefsteak" – after dropping a weight on his foot during a performance: the presiding judge and everyone else in the courtroom were reduced to a state of helpless mirth and the ruling was literally laughed out of court.

The lifting of the restrictions on spoken drama promoted the adoption of the 'speaking pantomime' at all venues, although the harlequinade (with the exception of a number of relatively garrulous Clowns) remained largely silent until its final demise in the 20th century. *See also* VERSE.

Dibdin, Charles (Isaac Mungo) (1768–1833) English actor, theatre manager, songwriter, and pantomime author, who oversaw the early triumphs of JOSEPH GRIMALDI at the SADLER'S WELLS THEATRE, of which he was the manager. He was the illegitimate son of the actor, playwright, and songwriter **Charles Dibdin** (1745–1814), whose pantomimes included *The Touchstone; or, Harlequin Traveller* (1779). Charles Dibdin the younger cast Grimaldi in the role of CLOWN for the first time in 1800 in his own pantomime *Peter Wilkins; or, Harlequin in the Flying World*. Grimaldi's success in the part encouraged Dibdin to dispense with the services of the ageing resident Clown BAPTISTE DUBOIS and to entrust the role to Grimaldi on a permanent basis; other notable performers in his pantomimes included JAMES BARNES and Thomas Ridgway.

Dibdin was especially acclaimed for his comic songs for pantomime, of which the two most successful were TIPPITY WITCHET, composed for the Sadler's Wells pantomime *Bang Up!, or, Harlequin Prime* (1810), and HOT CODLINS, both written for Grimaldi. Dibdin's pantomimes were also seen at other theatres than the one he managed, his *Harlequin Hoax*, for instance, proving a big hit in production at the LYCEUM THEATRE in 1814. He was also celebrated for his witty references to topical affairs of the day, which he took great pride in, his targets ranging from bare-knuckle fighting to the adulteration of food by corrupt shopkeepers.

As well as over 200 plays and pantomimes, Charles Dibdin also wrote an autobiography and a *History of London Theatre* (1826). After leaving the Wells he served as manager for a time of both ASTLEY'S AMPHITHEATRE and the SURREY THEATRE.

Dibdin, Thomas (John) (1771–1841) English actor, playwright, and songwriter, who was the author of many popular pantomimes in which JOSEPH GRIMALDI enjoyed great success. The illegitimate son of the actor and playwright Charles Dibdin and younger brother of CHARLES DIBDIN junior, he made his stage debut, as Cupid opposite Sarah Siddons as Venus, at the age of four at DRURY

LANE. Later he worked in the provinces and at SADLER'S WELLS (1794–97) as prompter before taking over the SURREY THEATRE (with a marked lack of success) in 1816 and briefly also controlling the HAYMARKET THEATRE.

Having known the young Grimaldi while at Sadler's Wells, he was instrumental in luring him finally to COVENT GARDEN in 1806. His plays included the nautical dramas *The Mouth of the Nile* (1798), *Naval Pillar* (1799), and *Nelson's Glory* (1805). The most successful of all his pantomimes, which included such titles as *Harlequin Harper; or, a Jump From Japan* (1813), was *MOTHER GOOSE* (1806), in which Covent Garden's new acquisition Grimaldi enjoyed his greatest triumph.

His collaboration with Grimaldi on this and other pantomimes had a profound impact upon the development of the pantomime in the 19th century and gave the genre new potential as a tool of mild social and political satire (as well as establishing the dominance of Clown over the harlequinade). He was also the author of around 2000 songs.

Dickens, Charles (John Huffam) (1812–70) English novelist, who was passionately interested in the theatre and a great defender of the pantomime in particular. Dickens was an enthusiastic amateur actor and presented performances with various friends in a private theatre in his Tavistock House home in London. He was himself admired as a performer of comic roles (as well as for his recitations of his own works) and wrote a number of farces and burlettas for the professional stage. His first experience of the theatre was, indeed, through the pantomime and he frequently recalled the thrill of seeing JOSEPH GRIMALDI in London productions in 1819 and 1820, when the future novelist was not quite ten years old; much later he was to devote himself to rewriting the *Memoirs of Joseph Grimaldi* and to contribute many articles on the genre to various publications.

Dickens lovingly described pantomime at the BRITANNIA THEATRE in *The Uncommercial Traveller* and several of his fictional characters (including David Copperfield) are depicted enjoying a visit to the pantomime. According to the US writer Edwin M. Eigner in *The Dickens Pantomime* the influence of the pantomime upon Dickens's work may have gone even deeper, with the great novelist actually basing many of his own characters on familiar pantomime creations (Wilkins Micawber, for instance, being derived fairly directly from the personality of CLOWN).

In structure too, his novels are thought to echo the traditional two-part framework of the pantomime, linked by the crucial transformation scene, while in terms of atmosphere critics have found direct parallels in Dickens's fiction for the DARK SCENES and absurd burlesques familiar to all contemporary pantomime audiences. This is not a new theory, as Eigner himself points out, and comparisons were being made between Dickens's fiction and the pantomime as early as 1834. Many years later George Bernard Shaw (no lover of the pantomime) was to summarise the whole of *Pickwick Papers* as an extended harlequinade.

It may also have been significant that Dickens numbered among his closest friends such stars of the pantomime as the scene designer CLARKSON STANFIELD, the pantomime reviewer George Augustus Sala, and the pantomime authors MARK LEMON and Gilbert á Beckett; he was also acquainted with such writers as J. R. Planché, Nelson Lee, J. B. Buckstone, Robert Brough, and E. L. Blanchard. For his own part, Dickens called the confusion and hilarity of the pantomime a mirror for reality and maintained the moral potential of the form.

Dick Whittington The central character in the pantomime *Dick Whittington and his Cat*, who was based on the historical figure Richard Whittington (d. 1423), who was three times elected Lord Mayor of London (in 1397, 1406, and 1419).

The real Dick Whittington was born into a wealthy family around 1350 at Pauntley Court in Gloucestershire. He moved to London in about 1379 and established himself as a trader in costly textiles, marrying Alice Fitzwaryn, whose father was a rich merchant by the name of Sir Ivo Fitzwaryn. Whittington was appointed an alderman and then sheriff in 1393, being raised to the office of Lord Mayor in 1397 by Richard II. He was duly re-elected to the post twice more and became a member of parliament in 1416.

He courted royal favour by making large loans to Henry IV and Henry V and was particularly known for his work for charity, which included financing an almshouse for the poor and the rebuilding of Newgate Gaol. There is no evidence, however, that he ever owned a cat or returned to London on hearing the city's bells (despite the stone marking the spot on Highgate Hill where he changed his mind about leaving).

Notable male performers in the role in recent years have included Tommy Steele, who triumphed in the part in the 1960s, and Cliff Richard. More usually, however, the part is treated as a role for a female principal boy (being played in recent times by such performers as Cilla Black, Anita Harris, and Lulu).

Dick Whittington and his Cat One of the most popular and enduring works in the pantomime canon, which is based on the body of legends surrounding the historical figure of Richard Whittington, three times Lord Mayor of London in the early 15th century. As a pantomime, the tale was first presented at Covent Garden in 1814, as *Dick Whittington; or, The Lord Mayor of London*. The cast of this first production included Joseph Grimaldi, who played the role of Dame Cecily Suet.

Of the many productions that followed over the years the most significant included T. L. Greenwood's version of 1852, seen at Sadler's Wells, that of 1891–92 at the Grand Theatre, Islington, in which Lottie Collins first sang Ta-ra-ra-boom-de-ay, and that seen at Drury Lane in 1908–09, in which Wilkie Bard introduced the song 'She Sells Sea Shells on the Sea Shore'.

As one of the standard texts of the 20th century pantomime, the tale has been produced countless times, even on ice. Recent versions include those by Betty Astell, Alan Brown, John Crocker and Eric Gilder, Verne Morgan, and David Wood. Part of an adaptation by John Morley was chosen for study under the National Curriculum in 1992.

Story Dick Whittington, the son of poor parents, sets off to London (where, he has heard, the streets are paved with gold) to make his fortune. He befriends a cat, which turns out to have magical powers, and falls in love with the daughter of Alderman Fitzwarren, in whose stores Dick and the cat are employed. All does not go well for Dick, however, and he is thrown out of the stores when he suspected of stealing his employer's money (or of some other crime). He decides to leave the city – but changes his mind after the bells of London (often personified as the Fairy of the Bells) bid him to "Turn again, Whittington" in a dream as he lies sleeping on Highgate Hill and persuade him that he is destined for great things (often the subject of a spectacular transformation scene, which ends the first act).

With the help of the cat, Dick drives a plague of rats from London and then sets sail on one of Fitzwarren's ships on a voyage of adventure to an exotic distant land – often Morocco or Barbary – where he and his cat have a final showdown with the evil King of Rats and his followers. Dick triumphs and is rewarded with great wealth and the hand of his employer's daughter and the Lord Mayorship. Other characters in the pantomime include the comical COOK. Many modern productions add a spectacular underwater scene when Dick's ship goes down in a storm.

Origins The adventures of the real DICK WHITTINGTON were first adapted for the stage in a lost play of around 1605, although the story had previously been kept alive in popular ballads. The writer Richard Johnson subsequently wrote another ballad around the same events and the story became one of the favourite tales published in CHAPBOOKS of succeeding centuries. There is no historical evidence for linking Whittington with a cat, but it remains unclear whether the cat was an invention of the chapbook writers or belonged originally to a much older legend. The role of the rats in the story is thought to symbolise the part they played in carrying the Black Death to London in the Middle Ages, when the disease was responsible for the deaths of one third of the English population. One of the earliest records of a dramatic entertainment telling the story of Whittington's life dates from 1668, when Samuel Pepys gave an account in his diary of a puppet show (which he enjoyed) on the subject.

diorama An elaborate painted backcloth, which was gradually unfurled across the stage to present an ever-changing panoramic view in numerous pantomimes of the mid-19th century. The moving diorama consisted of a very long canvas cloth (which could be as much as eight times as long as the width of the PROSCENIUM ARCH) that was wound onto two vertical cylinders, one in each WING. As one cylinder unwound so the other took up the slack, so that the portion of the diorama on view to the audience slowly changed as the cloth travelled across the stage.

The cloth itself was painted – often to a very high standard – to depict a continuous landscape, which was frequently based on a real location. Typical scenes depicted in such dioramas included views of rural England and of the Continent, affording audiences a sight of renowned places they were unlikely ever to see with their own eyes. Later, the diorama was used to depict an ever-increasing range of subjects, from the Royal Progress of George IV on a journey through Scotland to a series of landscapes based on the novels of Sir Walter Scott and scenes illustrating the contemporary political situation in the Middle East and the current conflict involving Great Britain, Greece, Turkey, and Russia.

The effect was first presented at COVENT GARDEN, when a moving diorama was used for a production of the pantomime *Harlequin and Friar Bacon; or, The Brazen Head* (1820). In this case, the cloth was decorated with a series of seascapes depicting a journey by Harlequin and Columbine across the Irish Sea, culminating in views of the docks of Dublin. The innovation was rapturously received and soon all the major theatres were taking up the idea, though not always under the same name (some managements preferring to call their own creations **panoramas** or **cosmoramas**).

It was DRURY LANE, however, that was to set the standard that other theatres would have to match when the management there realised the potential of this new scenic device. Just three years after the innovation was first attempted a diorama designed for the pantomime *Harlequin and the Flying Chest; or, Malek and The Princess Schirine* at Drury Lane cost the theatre the enormous sum of £1380, which was far greater than many other theatres spent on their entire productions.

The designer of this and many other similar scenes was the acknowledged master of the diorama, CLARKSON STANFIELD. Stanfield's diorama for *Harlequin and the Flying Chest* was very ambitious, presenting a series of views based on sketches made on location from a viewpoint overlooking Plymouth Sound and the newly-constructed breakwater there, complete with depictions of the quarries from which the stone for the breakwater came, of the harbour itself, and of various noble ships riding at anchor. Added drama was created by the use of various special effects and CUT-OUTS to suggest a ship in trouble during a storm and then a gradual improvement in the weather with the magical appearance of a rainbow. As a former Navy man, Stanfield was ideally placed to realise the potential of the diorama to depict journeys at sea and nautical scenes quickly established themselves as favourite subjects for such scenic invention. Stanfield was well rewarded for his efforts and in 1831 the Drury Lane management even paid his expenses to journey to Venice to make sketches from life for a diorama for *Harlequin and Little Thumb*.

A refinement of the system was the **aerial diorama**, in which the painted cloth was rolled slowly from one horizontal roller above the stage to another below it to suggest the illusion of flight. This development was particularly well-timed to take advantage of the current fashion for hot-air ballooning and was first used to add reality to a balloon flight from London to Paris of a terrified Clown and Pantaloon in *Harlequin and Poor Robin* at Covent Garden in 1823, with a cloth painted by members of the GRIEVE FAMILY. The scene was a major success and inspired numerous imitations over the next two decades or more. Such devices are still sometimes used to achieve such illusions as that of Jack climbing the beanstalk in *JACK AND THE BEANSTALK*.

Later dioramas seen at Covent Garden were the work of DAVID ROBERTS, formerly Stanfield's pupil, who was wisely recruited by the theatre to offer some competition to his erstwhile master. The moment when the diorama was set in motion became the most eagerly awaited event of the evening and by the 1830s much of the focus of the pantomime as a whole had switched from the comedy to the splendour of such scenic detail. Initially the diorama proved compatible with the comedy of the harlequinade but in time the performers were increasingly exiled from the stage while the diorama was being shown and the tone of the scene in which it appeared tended more and more towards the edifying and educational rather than the humorous, thus further weakening the already threatened status of the harlequinade itself.

Dioramas were even employed on occasion in the opening, where their use suggested a change in locale without the need for a break in the action (in most productions of *Dick Whittington* a diorama is still used to move the action from 'outside the store' to 'inside the store'). Some managements went to the extravagance of presenting more than one diorama in the course of an evening to satisfy the public's thirst for such scenes and on at least one occasion two such dioramas were put into operation at the same time. Such was the case with the 'double panorama' created for *Robinson Crusoe* at Drury Lane in 1881, which created the illusion of a boat ride down the Thames with the banks slipped slowly by on either side of the stage as a ship sailed down its course.

In an effort to outdo their rivals at other theatres artists experimented with different pigments and concentrated increasingly on the interplay between the painted canvas of the diorama and LIGHTING, thus providing an impetus for the raising of standards in both scene-painting and in lighting technology (which was to have implications throughout English theatre).

The earliest dioramas were relatively monochromatic and crudely executed compared with their successors, which attracted serious consideration by leading art critics of the day and led no less an author than J. R. PLANCHÉ to complain that his own contribution was being "painted out". The fashion for the diorama, beautiful though it often was, finally faded towards the end of the 19th century, when the comedy element of the pantomime reasserted itself.

director The person who is responsible for bringing together the various aspects of a production and ensuring that the final show is a success. The director (called 'producer' in the UK until a decision in 1956 favoured 'director') rules on such topics as casting, costume and set designs, and lighting as well as enjoying control during rehearsals and acting as general trouble-shooter.

The role is a relatively recent invention and previously such tasks were undertaken by a variety of theatre officials, who included stage managers, principal actors, prompters, and theatre managers. In the early 19th century pantomime productions were generally overseen by an **arranger**, who might combine the roles of author, choreographer, and musical director as well as working closely with the stage machinists and devisers of trickwork. Among those to fulfil the demanding role of arranger in the 19th century were such distinguished figures as the DIBDINS and CHARLES FARLEY.

Disney, Walt (Walter Elias Disney; 1901–66) US film-maker, whose many successful cartoons included several classic adaptations of popular pantomime stories. Disney began his career in cinema in the 1920s; subsequently he went on to develop a large number of original cartoon characters but also drew on a range of folk stories and fairytales.

His first full-length feature film was *Snow White and the Seven Dwarfs* (1937), which rapidly attained the status of a modern classic. Among the pantomime stories to receive the Disney treatment since then have been *Cinderella* (1950), *The Sleeping Beauty* (1958), and *Aladdin* (1993).

Critics of the Disney style of cartoon complain that the original stories are often sentimentalised, but in the case of the pantomime adaptations the Disney films remained reasonably close to the plots and atmosphere of their models and (in conjunction with the construction of fairy castles and other fanciful buildings at Disneyland and elsewhere) probably promoted the popularity of stage productions of the same stories. Certainly, the choice of such plots has consolidated the high position of the fairytale among the increasingly wide range of entertainments available to the young.

djinn *See* GENIE.

dog drama A minor theatrical genre of the 19th century that inspired numerous burlesque scenes featuring dogs in the contemporary pantomime. A parallel form of the EQUESTRIAN DRAMA, the dog drama featured canine performers in the lead roles of various popular stories. In most of these entertainments a simple melodramatic plot was constructed around a dog's known trick-performing ability, which ranged from pulling drowning children out of pools to playing dead.

Such pieces were staged with great success at DRURY LANE and elsewhere and inspired a number of imitative scenes in the pantomime before the fashion for such entertainments finally fell from favour. Pantomime managements frequently created opportunities for dogs to display their skills and JOSEPH GRIMALDI himself several times shared the limelight with a dog that was trained to pull a mock carriage. A full-scale hunt with a pack of real hounds was successfully staged at COVENT GARDEN in the course of *Harlequin and the Red Dwarf* in 1812 while at the same theatre in the Christmas entertainment of 1816 a dog played one of the main roles in *The Blind Beggar of Bethnal Green*, in which it was 'killed' bravely protecting its owner's daughter and then revived in time to see off Pantaloon and Clown in the harlequinade.

Acts featuring real dogs have disappeared from the pantomime in recent decades in response to increasing public reaction to the possibility of cruelty involved in their training (animal acts were dropped from children's television in 1970).

dogs Although dogs have never enjoyed the status of the pantomime CAT a number of canine characters have nonetheless distinguished themselves over the years. As well as appearing in scenes inspired by the DOG DRAMAS seen at many theatres in the early 19th century, dogs have participated in numerous acrobatic acts and parades.

The most memorable pantomime dogs have included a number of SKIN PARTS, of which the most remarkable was undoubtedly Tatters, the dog who befriends the lost children in some versions of *BABES IN THE WOOD*. In the 1894–95 production of the story seen at the LYCEUM THEATRE he was played with such heartrending realism by CHARLES LAURI that the original ending in which the dog died had to be changed in response to a public outcry that his death was too harrowing for younger members of the audience to witness.

Among other noteworthy pantomime dogs is the canine companion of Robinson Crusoe in various versions of his adventures.

Dottore, Il *See* *COMMEDIA DELL'ARTE*.

double harlequinade A harlequinade in which all the parts were doubled (and in some cases tripled) in an attempt to double the comic impact. The idea was tried as early as 1813, when CHARLES FARLEY doubled the number of performers in *The Swans; or, The Beauty of Bath* at COVENT GARDEN in an attempt to steal the limelight from a forthcoming spectacular at Drury Lane. Even more ambitious double harlequinades were seen on several occasions in the late

19th century, when such authors as E. L. BLANCHARD tried to reverse the decline in the harlequinade's popularity. The measure was not a success, however, and audiences and critics alike complained that doubling the characters simply doubled the boredom.

down-trap A TRAP through which a performer could appear to dive through the solid stage floor. The mouth of the trap was concealed by a mat, which sprung back into place after the performer had passed through. The performer himself would be caught in a blanket below the stage.

dress circle *See* CIRCLE.

dress rehearsal The final rehearsal before the opening night of a pantomime or other production. Members of the cast wear full costume and make-up and the show is run through as though before a real audience, only stopping if things go badly astray. According to theatrical superstition a bad dress rehearsal means a good first night.

droll or **drollery** A form of folktale in which the humour usually depends upon the innate stupidity of the central character. Similar to the fable, drolls differ in that there is no moral lesson to be drawn from them; the most famous examples have sometimes provided the basis for pantomimes, or characters in them – notably the story of *TOM THUMB*.

Druriolanus, Augustus *See* HARRIS, SIR AUGUSTUS HENRY GLOSSOP.

Drury Lane The oldest and most prestigious theatre in London, which was for many years famous for its spectacular pantomimes. Granted its charter by Charles II in 1662, the Theatre Royal, Drury Lane opened the following year under Thomas Killigrew and witnessed appearances by Nell Gwynn among others. After a fire in 1672, the theatre was rebuilt by Sir Christopher Wren and went on to host major plays by such playwrights as Sir John Dryden.

CHRISTOPHER RICH took over in 1693 but was eventually obliged to remove himself after his penny-pinching ways alienated him from the actors and the authorities alike. It was, however, under Rich that the theatre became a leading venue for performances of ITALIAN NIGHT SCENES in the early years of the 18th century. As early as 1677 the character of HARLEQUIN was seen on the stage at Drury Lane (in Edward Ravenscroft's *Scaramouch a Philosopher, Harlequin a Schoolboy, Bravo, Merchant and Magician*) but he only became a regular visitor there after 1700, when the Sieurs Alard from France presented their Italian Night Scenes at Rich's invitation. These lighthearted farces attracted huge audiences to the theatre, to the chagrin of 'serious' playwrights, although after Christopher Rich's departure the LINCOLN'S INN FIELDS THEATRE took the lead in presenting such shows under the management of JOHN RICH.

By 1716 Drury Lane (controlled by the distinguished 'Triumvirate' of Colley Cibber, Robert Wilks, and Thomas Doggett) and Lincoln's Inn were in fierce competition for audiences. The Italianate productions they flocked to see came to be called 'pantomimes' after the revival of the word by the Lane's dancing master, JOHN WEAVER, who selected it to describe his ballets-pantomimes (which he claimed were authentic recreations of an ancient Roman theatrical genre).

The management at Drury Lane preferred a more elevated tone in their entertainments loosely based on Roman mythology rather than the more knockabout style adopted by Rich at Lincoln's Inn Fields, but audiences began to shrink and when DAVID GARRICK – a co-patentee of Drury Lane from 1747 – found that even he could not rely upon being able to appear every night, he decided that the time had come to fight Rich with his own weapons. Accordingly he collaborated with the Harlequin performer HENRY WOODWARD on *Queen Mab* (1750), the success of which confirmed pantomime's place in the theatre's repertory and challenged Rich's reputation as the leading producer of pantomime in London. In 1759 Garrick staged his own pantomime, *Harlequin's Invasion*, in which Harlequin spoke for the first time (it having proved impossible to find a mime Harlequin to rival Rich); the experiment was not, however, judged a great success although it had considerable gimmick value at the time.

After Rich's death in 1761, Drury Lane asserted its role as the foremost pantomime venue in London. Notable names associated with the venue in the years that followed including the scene painter PHILIPPE JACQUES DE LOUTHERBOURG and the playwright RICHARD BRINSLEY SHERIDAN, who was manager in succession to Garrick. The theatre also witnessed the gradual replacement of Harlequin as the central comic character by the usurpers PIERROT and then CLOWN in the hands of CARLO DELPINI and JOSEPH GRIMALDI, who divided his early theatrical career between the Lane and SADLER'S WELLS.

Other milestones included the first production of *CINDERELLA*, which was seen at Drury Lane in 1804, one of the first appearances of a woman in the role of PRINCIPAL BOY (in 1819 in *JACK IN THE BEANSTALK; OR, HARLEQUIN AND THE OGRE*), the first productions to feature scenery painted by the great stage artist CLARKSON STANFIELD (in the 1820s), and the first of the 37 annual pantomimes written for the theatre by E. L. BLANCHARD (in 1852).

Characteristics of the Drury Lane pantomime in the early 19th century included relatively long OPENINGS and a great emphasis upon spectacle, with numerous magnificent processions and elaborate scenery. After a relatively lean period the theatre was saved from the threat of demolition by E. T. SMITH, who took over as manager in 1853 and over the next ten years presented magnificent pantomimes featuring scenery designed by WILLIAM BEVERLEY. Performers at the Lane under the management of Edmund Falconer and F. B. Chatterton in the 1860s included the remarkable VOKES FAMILY, who starred in every production between 1869 and 1879 (with a single break in 1873).

The appointment of AUGUSTUS HARRIS as manager in 1879, however, signalled a new era in the history of the pantomime: he dispensed with the Vokes troupe, radically re-edited Blanchard's scripts, and in the 1883 production of *CINDERELLA* dropped the harlequinade for the first time. A long series of spectacular shows starring major stars imported from the MUSIC HALL then followed and for many years the Drury Lane pantomimes were second to none, with such names as DAN LENO, who first appeared there in 1888 and subsequently every Christmas up to 1904, HARRY RANDALL, FRED EMNEY, WILKIE BARD, and GEORGE GRAVES all appearing on the theatre's bills. Harris's productions were legendary for their opulence, featuring casts running into several hundred, extravagant costumes, and magnificent scenery (though critics lamented the disappearance of the harlequinade and the sacrifice of plot to allow music hall stars full rein).

The tradition established under Harris continued under ARTHUR COLLINS (with the assistance of the writer J. HICKORY WOOD) after Harris's death in 1896, finally coming to an end in 1920, when the annual pantomime was elbowed out by the spectacular drama *The Garden of Allah* by Robert Hitchens. The previous year's Drury Lane pantomime was hastily relocated at COVENT GARDEN, but pantomime was doomed to disappear permanently from the Drury Lane repertory (after isolated revivals by the producer Julian Wylie in 1929 and in 1934) and its place was taken after World War II by musical comedy.

Dubois, John Baptiste (1762–1818) French actor, acrobat, and singer, who was the resident CLOWN at SADLER'S WELLS until 1801, when he was replaced by the great JOSEPH GRIMALDI. Having trained in the circus, Dubois made his debut at the Wells in 1787 and quickly won recognition as London's leading Clown, making many more appearances there and at DRURY LANE. He was particularly admired for his mime skills and attempted many innovations that foreshadowed the redevelopment of the role of Clown by his successor.

Ducrow, Andrew (1793–1842) English equestrian performer, who was the leading star at ASTLEY'S AMPHITHEATRE and appeared in pantomime at a variety of venues. Astley's talents in EQUESTRIAN DRAMA brought him a number of roles there and elsewhere in the EXTRAVAGANZAS of J. R. PLANCHÉ and in pantomime and he appeared with success at such leading venues as COVENT GARDEN and DRURY LANE. His most successful (mounted) roles in the pantomime included CLOWN and the DANDY LOVER, in which part he won acclaim in such productions as CHARLES FARLEY'S *Harlequin and Poor Robin* at Covent Garden in 1823. He acquired a share in the ownership of Astley's in 1825 but did not long survive the theatre's destruction by fire in 1841.

Duggan, Maggie (1860–1919) English actress, who rose to become one of the most popular PRINCIPAL BOYS of the late 19th century. Born into a poor family, she made a living as a street dancer and appeared in pantomime while still a child. Later she joined a dancing troupe and appeared in Berlin and elsewhere in comic opera, burlesque, and variety. She made her debut as principal boy in Liverpool and subsequently won recognition as one of the finest interpreters of the role in the provincial theatres. She retired in 1904.

dwarfs The little people of myth and legend, who have appeared in many pantomimes over the years, most notably in *SNOW WHITE AND THE SEVEN DWARFS*. According to various superstitions (of mostly Norse and Germanic origins), dwarfs live underground, are fully grown at three years old, may have backwards-facing feet, may be able to become invisible, love feasting when not at work at their forges, may be clairvoyant, are inclined to tease and steal, and are quick to take revenge if offended.

As children are usually cast in such roles on the stage dwarfs do not generally play a major part in the action. The fact that the dwarfs in *Snow White* are so amiable is largely due to the influence of the somewhat sentimental cartoon classic by WALT

DISNEY. It is thought possible that there are seven dwarfs because seven metals were known in ancient times. Other well-known stories about dwarfs that have enjoyed success as pantomimes include *Snow-White and Rose Red* and THE YELLOW DWARF (never performed now because of its prejudiced depiction of the once stereotypical wicked dwarf).

E

Elephant and Castle Theatre A theatre in Newington, London, which was once famous for its pantomimes. Built on the site of the Newington Butts Theatre first opened in 1576, the Elephant and Castle Theatre staged its first shows in 1872 and became a popular venue for both melodrama and pantomime. It was eventually converted into a cinema.

Ellar, Thomas (1780–1842) English actor, who was much admired as HARLEQUIN in the early 19th century. He established his reputation first as a dancer at the Crow Street Theatre in Dublin before being invited by CHARLES FARLEY to make his debut at COVENT GARDEN in 1813, playing the part of Second Harlequin in a DOUBLE HARLEQUINADE. Subsequently he took over the role of resident Harlequin at the theatre from JACK BOLOGNA in 1816 and continued to appear in the part for many years, appearing alongside such stars as JOSEPH GRIMALDI, JAMES BARNES, and TOM MATTHEWS.

He was particularly praised for his agility in executing countless dramatic leaps through concealed traps though he found such trickwork more demanding towards the end of his career in the 1830s. On one infamous occasion, during a performance of *Harlequin Munchausen* in 1818, he was badly injured when a stagehand he had offended failed to break his fall properly after one of his spectacular exits through a hidden trap. He suffered greatly in his last years and was reduced to dancing in the MUSIC HALL and playing guitar in the streets of London; he finally died in poverty, leaving his family destitute.

Emney, Fred (1865–1917) English comedian, who was one of the great stars of the DRURY LANE pantomimes. Unlike DAN LENO and other contemporaries in the Drury Lane shows, he became a star in pantomime before establishing himself as a popular turn in the MUSIC HALL, specialising in the role of DAME, who was usually presented by him in the form of the neighbourhood gossip. His comic songs included 'A Sister to assist 'er'. He was the father of the well-known comedian, also called Fred, a large man whose trademarks were a cigar and monocle, who played in pantomime in the 1930s.

entrances According to tradition, good and evil characters in the pantomime always enter from a particular side of the stage. This convention, inherited from medieval mystery plays, dictates that wicked characters enter (usually in a green spotlight) from stage left (the left side of the stage when looking out into the auditorium), while heroes enter (usually in a pink or white spotlight) from stage right. In the mystery plays themselves, the Angel Gabriel always entered from the right, while Mephistopheles came on from the left. The tradition is almost always followed in modern pantomimes, as most directors still insist that it is adhered to. The convention is thought to have originated in the biblical idea of the devil always sitting on the *sinister* (left) side of God; in pre-Christian society the left side was considered unlucky as the sun set in the west (the left side of the world according to ancient auguries).

equestrian drama A theatrical genre of the 18th and 19th centuries in which displays of horsemanship were central to the entertainment. Offered at such major venues as COVENT GARDEN, DRURY LANE, and at ASTLEY'S AMPHITHEATRE, the equestrian drama was a curiosity that enjoyed something of a vogue with London audiences and was thus bound to sound an echo sooner or later in the pantomime.

Around the beginning of the 19th century pantomimes featuring various animal acts, including horses, were quite common, though sometimes the 'animals' advertised were in fact played by actors (*see* SKIN PARTS). Attempts to stage equestrian versions of Shakespearean and other classic works leant themselves readily to parody and provided much fodder for the satirists of the pantomime stage.

Animal acts became a central attraction of the pantomime at even the most prestigious venues: thus it was that such productions as *BLUEBEARD*, staged at Covent Garden in the early 19th century, came complete with a 'troop of Horses', who gave a display at the close of the show – under the supervision of no less a personage than JOSEPH GRIMALDI himself. On another occasion Grimaldi scored a great hit when he appeared on a donkey (which he dubbed 'Neddy') to lampoon the 'gentleman jockeys' who liked to compete with professional riders at contemporary races.

Inspired by the success of such equestrian drama, some managements sought to make stars of other members of the animal kingdom. An attempt at Covent Garden in 1811 to present a real elephant among the cast of *Harlequin and Padmanaba*, another pantomime starring Grimaldi, did not inspire further imitations, however, after the elephant – called 'Chuny' – proved unpredictable when it came to making her entrances and exits. Other pantomimes featured a live llama (playing the part of a frightened stag in a spectacular hunting scene in *Harlequin and the Red Dwarf* in 1812) and various 'composite' beasts (or 'Nondescripts') in which performers impersonated bizarre mythological creatures that combined such features as wings and lion skins. *See also* DOG DRAMA.

Evans, Will (1875–1931) English comedian, who became one of the most celebrated performers in the DRURY LANE pantomime in the early 20th century. The son of the comedian Fred Evans (who appeared as DAME at DRURY LANE in 11 pantomimes), he established his reputation in the MUSIC HALL before appearing in pantomime, in which he employed his skill in SLAPSTICK comedy to great effect.

He acted in every Drury Lane pantomime between 1911 and 1919, often partnering WILKIE BARD who shared his fondness for the fast-disappearing HARLEQUINADE, which they both attempted to revive. He also formed a successful partnership with STANLEY LUPINO – their parts including the babes in *BABES IN THE WOOD* (1918) – and appeared with him in *CINDERELLA* a year later in what was to prove the last of the regular annual Drury Lane productions.

Outside pantomime, Evans was co-author of *Tons of Money*, the first of the classic Aldwych farces.

extravaganza A theatrical entertainment of the early 19th century that developed initially quite separately to the pantomime, but was eventually absorbed by it. The key features of the extravaganza included lavish costumes and sets, a strong musical element, a lighthearted satirical edge, scripts written in rhymed couplets or blank verse and larded with puns, and plots derived from mythology and folklore in which a happy ending was assured without the artificial interpolation of a harlequinade.

Among the most popular writers of such entertainments were J. R. PLANCHÉ, in whose works MADAME VESTRIS excelled in the role of PRINCIPAL BOY at both the OLYMPIC THEATRE and the LYCEUM THEATRE, and H. J. BYRON. The first of Planché's extravaganzas, *Olympic Revels*, was staged by Vestris in 1831 but billed as a BURLETTA in order to satisfy the requirements of the licensing authorities. It was not until 1833 that Planché first dared to add the word extravaganza to that of burletta (in the billing for his entertainment *High, Low, Jack, and the Game*).

The success of *Olympic Revels* and of *Olympic Devils* staged shortly afterwards encouraged Planché to lure audiences away from the traditional Christmas pantomime and the Olympic Theatre rapidly became the most popular venue in the capital. When the Olympic management transferred to COVENT GARDEN, however, the fact that the extravaganza did not come complete with a HARLEQUINADE meant that it was postponed until Easter. Nonetheless, managements responded to public enthusiasm for the genre and soon began to incorporate the essential features of the extravaganza in their pantomimes in order to reclaim their audiences, replacing the two or three simply staged scenes of the conventional OPENING with a full-scale extravaganza complete with spectacular scenery and effects, many of which drew heavily on English legend as source material.

One consequence of this and the resulting upgrading of the opening was that the status of the HARLEQUINADE, now considerably shortened in length and increasingly irrelevant to the action of the opening, was badly undermined. The relatively strong satirical element of the pantomime was also tempered (to the regret of many) as it did not sit easily with the harmonious charm of the typical extravaganza-style opening.

F

fairies The supernatural sprites whose intervention in many a pantomime plot leads ultimately to a happy conclusion. They include among their ranks the Fairy of the Bells of *Dick Whittington and his Cat*, the Vegetable Fairy of *Jack and the Beanstalk*, and the *Fairy Godmother* of *Cinderella*. Fairies have appeared in the pantomime since the beginning, when the emphasis was very much upon myth and magic.

The history of the fairy in English drama goes back to Shakespeare and beyond but received a major boost with the incorporation of the fairy-tales of Charles Perrault and others as the basis for pantomime openings towards the end of the 18th century. The Benevolent Agent, who worked the change from the opening to the harlequinade was often identified as a fairy and subsequently the transformation scenes of the Victorian pantomime were frequently adorned with a tableau of fairies sitting on flowers or hovering in the air.

In keeping with the high morality of the pantomime in the Victorian era, the assistance of the fairies is only made available to those who have performed some act of goodness, thus proving that they deserve such help. Not all fairies are good, of course, and Wicked Fairies abound in such tales as *The Sleeping Beauty* and *The Yellow Dwarf*. J. M. Barrie added extra detail to fairy mythology through the character of Tinker Bell in the children's play *Peter Pan*, warning that every time someone denied the existence of fairies a fairy died; Tinker Bell's own life is saved by the device of the audience clapping their hands and thus breaking the spell threatening her.

Fairy Godmother The good fairy in *Cinderella*, who protects Cinders after the girl shows her kindness while gathering sticks in a wood. Fairies have been linked with name-giving ceremonies since ancient times and a Fairy Godmother was introduced into the story of *Cinderella* by Charles Perrault – who perhaps significantly described a similar incident in another of his stories, entitled *The Fairies*. Her first appearance in the pantomime version of the tale, however, was somewhat delayed, the magical role she fulfilled being taken, for instance, by Venus in the initial production seen at Drury Lane in 1804.

In Rossini's influential comic opera *La Cenerentola* (1807) responsibility for the magical element in the tale rested with the Prince's tutor Alidoro but that same year the Fairy Godmother herself finally made her pantomime debut, at Covent Garden in *Harlequin and Cinderella; or, The*

LITTLE GLASS SLIPPER. The Fairy Godmother conventionally enters from stage right (*see* ENTRANCES) and (formerly at least) always blessed the 'goodies' with the wand in her right hand and cursed the 'baddies' with it in her left. According to another tradition the part is never turned into a comedy role in Scotland. The Fairy Godmother's magic always loses its power at midnight, the 'Witching Hour' when the forces of evil hold sway.

In the folklore of some countries the Fairy Godmother is identified as the ghost of Cinderella's own dead mother, who has returned to earth to protect her daughter, while in others Cinderella is assisted not by a fairy, but by some domestic animal such as a goat or cow (as in the versions known in Finland, Portugal, and other countries). Popular performers of the role in recent times have included such 'mature' actresses as Dame Anna Neagle, June Whitfield, Barbara Windsor, Dora Bryan, Fenella Fielding, Evelyn Laye, Peggy Mount, and Wendy Craig.

fairytales The folkloric stories from which many of the plots of the best known pantomimes were ultimately derived. In fact, few of the stories mention fairies and the term can refer to any fabulous tale of ancient origins. The oldest known fairytale, told in an Egyptian papyrus, dates from around 1250 BC. Psychologists have written extensively upon the origins of such folk mythology, interpreting it variously as an expression of fear and fascination with the unknown mysteries of nature and as a species of allegorical investigation into man's identity and the possibility of personal fulfilment – hence the particular relevance of the tales to the young. Common characters in the tales include witches, dwarfs, giants, ogres, princes and princesses, and talking animals.

The telling of fairytales was initially a purely oral tradition but collections of such stories were made as early as the 9th century AD. Important collections formed in subsequent centuries included the *ARABIAN NIGHTS ENTERTAINMENTS*. The fairytale enjoyed a revival in popularity in aristocratic French society in the late 17th century, when the telling of such stories became a favourite pastime of adults at the court of Louis XIV, and it was not long before this enthusiasm was communicated to English culture and theatre (at a time when the pantomime was beginning to emerge as a distinct dramatic genre).

The first person to set about committing these tales to paper in a serious fashion was MADAME D'AULNOY, whose first fairytale appeared in 1690. Other writers quickly followed suit, the most illustrious name being that of CHARLES PERRAULT, whose relatively simply written versions inspired many pantomime authors in later years. English translations of these tales appeared very soon after their publication in France and reached a wide readership through inexpensive CHAPBOOK adaptations, which appeared alongside such native English stories as *JACK AND THE BEANSTALK*.

Not everyone approved of these tales, however, and a number of educationalists criticised the stories on the grounds that they promoted superstition and lacked a defined moral purpose (modern psychologists, in contrast, argue that fairytales teach important lessons and actually contribute to healthy emotional development).

For a time in the early 19th century it was widely believed that the day of the fairytale was past, but new editions continued to appear and the stories were raised to new heights by such authors as the GRIMM BROTHERS – whose writings were first translated into English in 1823 – and HANS CHRISTIAN ANDERSEN, whose works arrived in Britain in thc 1840s.

Some fairytales (which are often known in a number of variant forms in different cultures) have never been adapted as pantomimes, while a great many more have long since disappeared from the stage after enjoying some popularity with Victorian audiences (for instance, *THE YELLOW DWARF*). Others, however, have remained perennial favourites: they include *SNOW WHITE AND THE SEVEN DWARFS*, *LITTLE RED RIDING HOOD*, *THE SLEEPING BEAUTY*, *THE BABES IN THE WOOD*, *PUSS IN BOOTS*, and that most popular of all stories *CINDERELLA*.

The majority of these tales were first seen as pantomimes between the years 1781 and 1832 (*ALADDIN AND HIS WONDERFUL LAMP*, for instance, was first performed as a pantomime in 1788). GEORGE COLMAN suggested that fairytales would make excellent subjects for pantomimes as far back as 1754 but it was many years before the fairytale came to dominate the pantomime, a development which owed a great deal to the EXTRAVAGANZAS of J. R. PLANCHÉ, who dramatised many fairytales in the 1830s and 1840s.

Most of the fairytales that form the basis of popular modern pantomimes have a long history, although J. M. Barrie's *Peter Pan* (1904) and Frank L. Baum's *The Wizard of Oz* (1900) represent rare examples of modern additions to the fairytale canon. The great age of the Victorian fairytale ended with the horrors of World War I, but such stories remain essential reading for all children 200 years after they were first adapted for the pantomime.

falling flap A hinged flap, of the type formerly much used to effect a rapid change of SCENERY as required by countless pantomimes. Such flaps, painted on both sides, were fitted to FLATS and other scenic items and when released allowed an almost instantaneous transformation in the setting. Sometimes such flaps were sprung so that they flapped upwards or sideways to reveal the new scene. They often also played a role in the transformation of various PROPERTIES, enabling boxes to turn into tables and windmills into giants, etc. (*see* TRICK-WORK).

fan effect *See* TRANSFORMATION SCENE.

Farley, Charles (1772–1859) English actor, pantomime arranger and writer, who as manager of COVENT GARDEN oversaw many of the most significant pantomime productions seen in London in the early 19th century. Among the famous productions in which he had a hand were the celebrated 1806 Covent Garden production of THOMAS DIBDIN's *Harlequin Mother Goose; or, the Golden Eggs*, in which Farley's close friend JOSEPH GRIMALDI appeared as CLOWN with great success, the 1813 production of *ALADDIN* also at Covent Garden, which starred Mrs. Charles Kemble as Aladdin and Grimaldi as Kasrac, and the 1822 version of his own *Harlequin and the Ogress; or, the Sleeping Beauty of the Wood*, which again starred Grimaldi.

Other pantomimes by his hand included *Harlequin in Asmodeus* (1810), *Harlequin and the Red Dwarf* (1812), *Harlequin and Fortunio; or, Shing-Moo and Thun-Ton* (1815), which saw the first performance by a female PRINCIPAL BOY, *Harlequin Munchausen; or, The Fountain of Love* (1818), *Harlequin and Friar Bacon* (1820), *Harlequin and Mother*

Bunch; or, The Yellow Dwarf (1821), *Harlequin Pat and Harlequin Bat; or, The Giant's Causeway* (1830), *Hop o' My Thumb and His Brothers; or, Harlequin and the Ogre* (1831), *Puss in Boots; or, Harlequin and the Miller's Son* (1832), and *Old Mother Hubbard and Her Dog; or, the Tales of the Nursery* (1833) – his last.

In collaboration with Grimaldi and the Dibdins, Farley sharpened the pantomime as a tool of satirical wit and raised the harlequinade, dominated by Clown, to its greatest heights. Although Grimaldi's genius was very much his own, Farley could claim some credit for his unparalleled success and coached his star in several of his roles. Other dramatic pieces by Farley's hand included successful farces, comic operas, melodramas, and various other theatrical entertainments. As an actor he played such roles as Lover at Covent Garden and sometimes appeared opposite Grimaldi himself.

Fatima (1) In some versions of *Aladdin*, the name under which Abanazar insinuates himself into the hero's household, disguised as a woman. In the original folktale Fatima was a holy woman who was killed by Abanazar's brother, who then entered Aladdin's house and was killed by him on being unmasked by the genie. (2) In *Bluebeard*, the original name of the last of Bluebeard's wives, who discovers the fate of his previous wives (her sisters).

Fawn, James (1851–1923) English comedian, who was one of the first stars of the music hall to establish a reputation as a performer in pantomime. Famous in the halls playing amiable drunkards and for his singing of such comic songs as 'It Must Have Been the Lobster, It Couldn't Have Been the Booze', he appeared in pantomime as early as 1874, when he scored a big hit with his song 'Tommy Make Room for your Uncle' in *The Children of the Wood* at the Adelphi Theatre.

Subsequently he enjoyed even greater success with the song 'If You Want to Know the Time Ask a Policeman' and was one of the music hall stars to be invited by Augustus Harris to take part in the Drury Lane pantomime of 1880, the first occasion that the Lane's pantomime was dominated by music hall performers. He went on to form a classic partnership in the Drury Lane shows with Arthur Roberts and also appeared in pantomime at the Surrey Theatre.

fee-fi-fo-fum The giant's cry in *Jack and the Beanstalk* when he thinks he can detect Jack's presence in his castle: "fee-fi-fo-fum, I smell the blood of an Englishman; be he live or be he dead, I'll grind his bones to make my bread". The verse is usually also included in productions of *Jack the Giant-Killer* and has been a feature of giant stories for hundreds of years (it was quoted by William Shakespeare in *King Lear*, indicating that it was widely known in his day).

flag A signboard carrying the words of a song, or other dialogue etc., that was an important tool of the pantomime in the days when venues other than the Patent Theatres were prevented from staging spoken drama by the Licensing Act of 1737. Such boards, which were lowered from the flies or carried on by the performers themselves, were commonly seen at the lesser theatres but were also frequently employed at both Covent Garden and Drury Lane to overcome the difficulties of poor acoustics or the problems imposed by the use of Big Heads, which muffled the voice. In the modern pantomime their use is generally restricted to the song sheet brought on for community SINGALONGS.

flat A wooden frame, usually rectangular and covered in fireproofed canvas or lightweight board, of the type used to construct most pantomime sets. Such flats, held in place by means of weights and braces, were first introduced as the basic constituent of theatre sets in the 17th century. Frequently joined together in pairs, flats were formerly often slotted into grooves running across the stage floor, which meant that they could be manoeuvred with a minimum of difficulty.

Fleshcreep *See JACK AND THE BEANSTALK.*

Flexmore, Richard (1825–60) English comedian, who enjoyed a brief but highly successful career in the role of CLOWN in the 1850s. Having served a hard apprenticeship in the MUSIC HALL, he won particular praise in the pantomime for his acrobatics and for his parodies of the Spanish dancers then very fashionable in London as well as for his lively sense of humour. He made his pantomime debut as Clown at the OLYMPIC THEATRE and subsequently appeared at the PRINCESS'S THEATRE and elsewhere, often in DOUBLE HARLEQUINADES.

His adoption as Clown of a new costume with tights and short frilled trunks was very influential and it became the standard Clown outfit used by all his successors. He died at the age of 34 as a result of the injuries he had received on stage during his short career. His post as principal Clown at COVENT GARDEN subsequently passed to HARRY PAYNE.

flies The area above the stage, which is fitted out with various catwalks and bars from which lighting equipment and items of scenery can be 'flown' (in other words, raised and lowered).

floodlight or **flood** A stage light that casts a broad diffuse beam, used for illuminating large areas uniformly.

flying ballet The manipulation of members of the cast suspended by wires through the air above the stage. Flying ballets were long one of the prime attractions of the pantomime, though such feats were previously perfected in the Classical theatre. In the late 19th century, when spectacle was everything, scores of performers might be hoisted into the air and enabled to 'fly' round the stage and even into the auditorium in the guise of fairies or nymphs. Noted practitioners of the flying ballet included GEORGE CONQUEST, who devised such scenes firstly for the Gaiety Theatre and subsequently at the GRECIAN THEATRE.

The first flying ballet at DRURY LANE was seen in 1878 and was such a success that performers continued to become airborne in pantomimes there over many years. Practical limitations required that the fliers (each anchored to a single stagehand) rarely weighed more than eight stone. The effect was less often seen in pantomime in the early 20th century, though the employment of flying techniques in J. M. Barrie's children's play *Peter Pan* represented a significant revival of the practice and such outfits as Kirby's Flying Ballet specialised in such scenes. The requirement that all performers in flying ballets should be very heavily insured has sadly meant the virtual disappearance of such displays in recent decades.

follow spot A large manually controlled spotlight that is used to cast a single bright beam at one character or spot on the stage.

footlight or **float** One of a row of lights placed at the front of the stage, at floor level, in order to illuminate performers and scenery from a low angle (thus cancelling out shadows cast by overhead lighting). Before the advent of electric lighting, these lights ran on gas and before that consisted of oil jars containing a lit floating wick (hence the term 'float') or simply of a row of candles.

Forde, Florrie (Florence Flanagan; 1876–1940) Australian actress, who was one of the most famous performers of the role of PRINCIPAL BOY in the early years of the 20th century. Born in Melbourne and blessed with both an impressively large voice and generous figure, she was nicknamed the 'Australian Marie Lloyd' and was very popular with pantomime audiences over a period of many years, appearing in Sydney from 1894 and making her debut in London in 1897. Highlights of her performances included renditions of such songs as 'Hold Your Hand Out, Naughty Boy', 'Oh, Oh, Antonio', 'Down at the Old Bull and Bush', and 'Sahara'. She remained one of the most popular performers in pantomime until the very end of her long career, numbering among her last successes her appearance in the MELVILLE BROTHERS production *The Forty Thieves* at the LYCEUM THEATRE in 1935–36.

forepiece or **curtain-raiser** A play or other entertainment formerly presented at the beginning of an evening's entertainment, prior to the pantomime itself. Pantomime was from the very start only one part of the conventional evening's programme, although later its popularity meant that it gradually took over the entire bill. Such forepieces included comedies and tragedies and were often intended to provide an element of 'moral improvement' for the often rowdy and ill-educated audiences the pantomime attracted in the late 18th century. (Less wealthy members of the audience could, however, opt to enter some theatres at nine o'clock and see just one full-length play).

It was DAVID GARRICK who made such presentations a traditional feature of the pantomime programme at DRURY LANE from 1759 on. On many occasions the pantomime has rubbed shoulders with such companion pieces as the tragedies of William Shakespeare himself, though the most popular of all the instructive dramas presented as forepieces were such melodramas as *Jane Shore* and *The London Merchant; or, The History of George Barnwell*, in which a young apprentice is duly hanged after murdering his uncle. It was a version of the history of George Barnwell that prefaced the classic 1806 COVENT GARDEN production of *MOTHER GOOSE*.

In time such uplifting moral entertainments were abandoned, though not before both those already mentioned had been burlesqued as pantomimes themselves. Successors of these two pieces included a rash of dramatisations of Harriet Beecher Stowe's anti-slavery novel *Uncle Tom's Cabin* in the 1850s, but audiences by then were less than patient with the high moralising tone and it was common for such forepieces to be ignored altogether or else disrupted by unruly behaviour (which was often partly attributable in the early days to the fact that in some of the larger houses the poor acoustics made the plot virtually impossible to follow). Such forepieces were dropped permanently before the end of the 19th century. *See also* AFTERPIECE.

Fox, George Washington Lafayette (1825–77) US actor, who enjoyed some success in pantomime in the theatres of New York in the late 19th century. Having made his theatrical debut in Boston at the age of seven, Fox moved to the National Theatre, New York in 1850 and then as manager to the famous BOWERY THEATRE, where he established a reputation as a leading star of pantomime, which enjoyed a brief vogue over the next few years. He managed the theatre until its destruction by fire in 1866 and then transferred to the Olympic Theatre, New York, where he consolidated his reputation in such productions as his own pantomime *HUMPTY-DUMPTY* (1868), which ran for over 1200 performances, and numerous BURLESQUES.

He was much acclaimed as CLOWN, to which role his skills as a mime artist were ideally suited and was hailed as the funniest performer ever to appear in pantomime in US theatrical history. His career ended in 1875, when he was committed to a lunatic asylum.

foyer The area through which an audience passes before entering the AUDITORIUM. Such facilities as the BOX OFFICE, refreshments counters, and cloakrooms are usually situated in the foyer area.

Fragson, Harry (Léon Vince Philippe Pott; 1869–1913) Anglo-French comedian and singer, who was one of the most popular pantomime stars of the 1900s. Having risen to fame in France as a café concert singer, Fragson established his reputation in the MUSIC HALL with such songs as 'Hullo, hullo, who's your lady friend?'. He was much acclaimed in pantomime at DRURY LANE, where he appeared as 'Dandigny' in *CINDERELLA* in 1905. His career ended tragically when he was shot dead by his insane father.

Friday *See* MAN FRIDAY.

Frog Prince, The Fairytale that was used as the basis for a number of pantomimes seen on the Victorian stage (though seldom revived since due to the problems presented by the need for a frog costume and the similarity between the tale and the better-known *BEAUTY AND THE BEAST*).

Story A princess drops a golden ball into a pond and strikes a deal with a frog to the effect that she will marry him if he will recover the ball. The frog fetches the ball but the princess refuses to honour her promise. When the king hears of the pact after the frog arrives at the palace, he obliges his daughter to share her food and bed with the frog. The princess spurns the frog at first but is eventually persuaded to kiss it, on which it is magically transformed into a prince, who had previously been turned into a frog by an evil witch. The two fall in love and live happily ever after.

Origins The story was popularised by a version written by the GRIMM BROTHERS, who discovered it in the Hesse region of Germany. A Scottish variant of the tale, in which the frog persuades the princess to chop off his head with an axe (upon which he becomes a prince once more), has also been documented.

front of house All the areas of the theatre except for the AUDITORIUM itself that are open to the public. The running of the FOYER area and bars etc. is usually entrusted to a front of house manager.

Funambules, Théâtre des A theatre on the Boulevard du Temple in Paris, which was an important venue for performances of the *COMMEDIA DELL'ARTE* in France. It began as a fairground BOOTH for acrobats and mime artists but was eventually replaced by a permanent theatre in 1813. It was at this theatre that the great French mime artist Jean-Gaspard Deburau further developed the character of PIERROT in the 1830s, transforming him into the melancholy lover who was to replace HARLEQUIN as the central character in the English HARLEQUINADE.

Productions at the theatre were notable for the use of elaborate scenery and complicated technical effects, which included full TRANSFORMATION SCENES and even real waterfalls. Deburau died in 1846, after which his son continued the tradition for a time, playing his father's roles. The theatre was finally demolished in 1860 during the rebuilding of Paris.

Fyffe, Will (1885–1947) Scottish singer and comedian, who became a star of MUSIC HALL and pantomime in the early 20th century, notably in the role of DAME. He was enormously popular in both comic sketches and singing such songs as 'I Belong to Glasgae'. He also appeared in melodrama and revue.

G

gallery The upper level of seating in an AUDITORIUM, overlooking the PIT. The gallery was traditionally occupied by the poorest sections of the audience and was the rowdiest part of the theatre. In the 18th and 19th centuries entertainments that failed to please those in the galleries (sometimes dubbed 'the gods' because they were so high up) were likely to be greeted with a hail of missiles (chiefly orange peel and nuts) and abuse. This lively tradition lasted at least until 1950, when bored gallery audiences were occasionally known to 'boo' pantomimes they did not like.

Garrick, David (1717–79) English actor and playwright, who exercised a major influence on the development of the pantomime as manager of DRURY LANE. Born in Hereford and educated at Lichfield, Garrick came to London with Dr Johnson in 1737 and subsequently established himself as one of the great English actors, becoming a joint patentee at Drury Lane in 1747 (after a brief stay at the LINCOLN'S INN FIELDS THEATRE under JOHN RICH).

The success Rich was then enjoying at Lincoln's Inn obliged Garrick to concede – much against his own inclinations – that pantomime would have to be given serious consideration at Drury Lane. He produced his first pantomime, *Queen Mab*, in 1750 and soon the two venues were engaged in a veritable 'pantomime war'.

Garrick's acquisition of HENRY WOODWARD, who had been trained in the role of HARLEQUIN by Rich himself, proved invaluable, although Garrick himself admitted that they would never find a performer to match the mime skills of Rich. Accordingly, in Garrick's pantomime *Harlequin's Invasion; or, A Christmas Gambol* (1759), written in collaboration with George Colman the elder, he introduced a talking Harlequin – the first time the character had spoken since APHRA BEHN'S *The Emperor of the Moon*. The production, in which Harlequin and his compatriots were put to flight by William Shakespeare, was a success but the experiment with Harlequin was controversial and henceforth he remained generally silent as before.

The production was also significant for Garrick's song 'Hearts of Oak', which struck an immediate chord with audiences very aware of the threat of Napoleonic France and became the first 'hit' song to come out of pantomime. It was also under Garrick that Drury Lane first became famous for the spectacular nature of its pantomimes with, in 1753, a real waterfall, and – from 1773 – sets designed by the brilliant theatre artist

PHILIPPE JACQUES DE LOUTHERBOURG. Garrick's achievements in the theatre earned him a permanent place in the nation's cultural history and eventual burial in Westminster Abbey.

gauze A very thin veil of material (usually painted) that is used for various scenic effects. The gauze was an invaluable tool of Victorian pantomime designers, who employed numerous gauzes in the great TRANSFORMATION SCENES for which many leading theatres of the time were famous. Often a whole series of coloured gauzes would be placed under highly dramatic lighting upon the stage. Gradually light would 'bleed through' these gauzes to reveal more gauzes behind as a magnificent panoramic view of paradise or some other similar landscape was slowly unfolded.

gel A filter of heat-resistant coloured plastic, which when placed in a spotlight beam changes the colour of the light cast. The earliest filters were made of gelatin, hence the name.

Genie A supernatural being of Oriental origins, who is able to make wishes come true. The most famous genies (originally, *djinn* or *jinnis* in Arabic) are those of the lamp and of the ring in the ever-popular pantomime *ALADDIN AND HIS WONDERFUL LAMP*.

Such genies populated several tales contained in the *ARABIAN NIGHTS ENTERTAINMENTS* and were readily absorbed into the English pantomime. Though they rarely appear outside the story of *Aladdin* now, they were formerly familiar figures in other tales; a Good Genie and an Evil Genie appeared on the stage as early as 1808, in a tale entitled *Kelaun and Guzzarat*.

Genies are conventionally humourless, awe-inspiring, dark-skinned, turbaned figures who display a fierce character but are bound, however reluctantly, to fulfil the desires of their master with the stock phrase "You command and I obey". They have been given a variety of names over the years, few less reverential than JOHN MORLEY's Genie of the Lamp Mazda (after the light bulb manufacturers). In the modern pantomime it is usual to have one genie of the traditional type (as played by the boxer Frank Bruno) and another of a more curvaceous variety (as performed by Britt Eckland and Eartha Kitt).

ghost glide A variety of TRAP, which allows a performer to appear to glide across the stage (he is in fact carried across on a wheeled platform running under the stage). One form of the ghost glide was called the **Corsican trap** after its initial use in Dion Boucicault's melodrama *The Corsican Brothers* (1852).

ghost scene Traditional scene that has been incorporated into a wide range of pantomimes and which remains one of the most effective standard comic interludes. The scene typically revolves around a terrified DAME who finds herself in a gloomy haunted bedroom, kitchen, or other chamber where she is hounded by mischievous spirits of various kinds (some apparently skeletons and others of the conventional sheet-clad variety).

The best examples of the scene make imaginative use of ingenious special effects, such as luminous costumes and concealed panels in the walls, and mix hilarity at the dame's confusion with the occasional genuinely startling surprise. Another device formerly used was 'Pepper's Ghost', an arrangement of mirrors that created the illusion of a ghost walking on the stage among real characters (actually a reflection of an actor walking in the pit). The scene has a long history and was familiar to pantomime audiences in the early 19th century, when JOSEPH GRIMALDI enjoyed great success in it (hence the informal name 'Joey-Joey' which is sometimes applied to scenes of this kind).

Giant Roc *See SINBAD THE SAILOR.*

giants Huge and usually hostile ogres feature in a number of popular pantomime plots. The best-known giant in the contemporary pantomime is the ogre who pursues Jack down the beanstalk in *JACK AND THE BEANSTALK* after the latter has robbed him of the singing harp and other treasures.

The problems of presenting a realistic giant on stage are obvious but many pantomimes in the past have been celebrated for their ingenuity in persuading spectators of the giant's authenticity. Audiences are generally disappointed if the giant is only a 'huge' offstage voice and various productions have seen the part played by all manner of stiltwalkers and other performers wearing colossal papier-maché heads and bodies. The shadow of the giant as the beanstalk fell in the famous DRURY LANE version of the 1890s blotted out the stage lights; when they came up again the 'body' filled virtually the entire stage.

Among other pantomimes to present similar giants is the now rarely-performed *JACK THE GIANT-KILLER*, in which the hero overcomes several such creatures (including the Cornish Giant who lives on St. Michael's Mount) by various ingenious methods.

According to the mythology of several cultures a race of giants were the earliest inhabitants of the earth, though one tradition differs from another when it comes to the details of cannibalism and so forth. Psychologists have suggested that the fascination children have for giants – and their delight when they are outwitted – derives from their identification of such figures with their own parents.

Gilbert, Sir W(illiam) S(chwenk) (1836–1911) English author, who is best known for the comic operas he wrote in collaboration with the composer Sir Arthur Sullivan, but who also had a hand in no less than three pantomimes. Gilbert's linguistic humour was admirably suited to the pantomime although he only enjoyed mixed success with *Harlequin Cock-Robin and Jenny Wren; or, Fortunatus and the Water of Life, The Three Bears, The Three Gifts, The Three Wishes, and The Little Man who Woo'd the Little Maid* (1867), which was his single solo contribution to the genre.

Written for the LYCEUM THEATRE, the production (which was much beset with technical difficulties) was particularly notable for the provocative casting of a notorious London prostitute in the role of PRINCIPAL BOY. Gilbert also collaborated on another two pantomimes, but felt constrained by the compromises and conventions the Victorian pantomime demanded of the writer and resented the interference of theatre managements in his scripts. He even went so far to poke fun at the genre in one of his famous *Bab Ballads* (1869) and in 1904 devised a burlesque transformation scene for *The Fairy's Dilemma*.

gingerbread house The witch's cottage in *HANSEL AND GRETEL* that the two starving children begin to eat until caught by the witch herself. According to the original tale the house is made of bread and cakes, with windows of clear sugar. The concept of such edible houses was not new and reference to such a building was made as far back as the 14th century, in a poem about an abbey made of cakes and meat that was constructed some distance off the Spanish coast.

glass slipper In *CINDERELLA*, the shoe lost by Cinders as she runs from the ball when the clock strikes midnight. Although the Cinderella story is of ancient origin, the glass slipper first appeared in the version included in *TALES OF MOTHER GOOSE* by CHARLES PERRAULT, who describes a *pantoufle de verre*. There has been considerable debate over the years about Perrault's glass slipper and many critics have suggested that it arrived through confusion with the French *pantoufle de vair* (fur slipper). It seems more probable, however, that Perrault saw the advantage of a glass slipper (that could not be stretched or otherwise tampered with) and deliberately preferred it to the velvet, satin, or silk slipper of earlier versions.

According to Chinese legend, it was a golden slipper; other traditions have the prince identifying Cinderella by the ring she wears. Perhaps significantly in ancient China (where the first versions of the story were written) a small foot was considered an indication of great beauty and virtue (the reasoning behind the barbaric practice of binding girls' feet so that they would remain underdeveloped and small).

Glenville, Shaun (1884–1968) Irish-born comedian, who emerged as one of the most accomplished of pantomime DAMES of the 1930s and 1940s. Married to DOROTHY WARD, Glenville (whose mother was manager of the Abbey Theatre, Dublin) made his stage debut as a baby and subsequently established himself as a star of variety both in London and in the provinces (as well as appearing with success in the USA). In the pantomime he was hilarious in such roles as DAME TROT, which he played on numerous occasions, MOTHER GOOSE, MRS CRUSOE, the Queen in *THE QUEEN OF HEARTS*, and the dame in *PUSS IN BOOTS* – although he also played BUTTONS in *CINDERELLA* in 1928.

Glover, Jimmy (James Mackay; 1861–1931) Irish-born composer, arranger, conductor, manager, journalist, and author, who was for many years director of music at DRURY LANE. Born in Dublin, Glover took the post at Drury Lane in 1893 at the invitation of AUGUSTUS HARRIS and subsequently arranged the music for the classic Drury Lane pantomimes until the tradition ended in 1920, his many successes including the score for *THE BABES IN THE WOOD* in 1897. Among his best known songs were 'Dearie, Dearie' (1896) and 'Archibald, Certainly Not' (1909). He finally resigned from his post at the theatre in 1923. His adventures working alongside such great stars as DAN LENO and HERBERT CAMPBELL were recorded in his three volumes of autobiography.

gobo A shaped filter, which when attached to a spotlight casts a particular pattern on the floor suggesting, for example, sunlight pouring through leaves or the bars of a cell window.

gods *See* GALLERY.

Golden Goose, The A fairytale about a goose with golden feathers, which has in the past been adapted several times as a pantomime.

Story In the original tale, the hero is rewarded for his kindness towards an old man by the gift of a goose whose feathers are made of gold. The goose brings its owner great good fortune, but those who try to steal the goose find they are unable to let go of the creature and are obliged to form an ever-increasing procession behind it. In the meantime the king has announced that he will give the hand of his daughter in marriage to anyone who can make her laugh (which she has never done). Many try but all fail until the hero arrives with his entourage of gormless thieves. The princess laughs at the sight and the two are betrothed (although the young man has to call on supernatural aid to perform a further three difficult tasks before the marriage can go ahead).

Origins The myth of the Golden Goose was told in detail in *The Golden Goose* by the GRIMM BROTHERS, but is an ancient folkloric tale of both European and Indian origins.

Goldilocks and the Three Bears Fairytale about a young girl who stumbles upon the house of three bears, which continues to be adapted as a pantomime to the present day. The story was regularly staged in Victorian times under such titles as *Harlequin and the Three Bears; or, Little Silver Hair and the Fairies* and in 1867 was the subject of W. S. GILBERT's main contribution to the genre. More recent versions have included one seen at the Wimbledon Theatre in 1992.

Story Goldilocks, a young girl, happens upon a small house deep in the forest. She goes inside and finds breakfast prepared. Feeling hungry, she sits at the table, choosing the smallest of three chairs (which she then breaks). One bowl of porridge is too hot, another too cold, but the last is just right and she eats it all. She then feels tired and goes upstairs: one of the beds is too hard, another too soft, but she falls asleep quite happily in the third. The house in fact belongs to three bears, who now return home. The smallest of the three bears is horrified to find someone has eaten his breakfast and broken his chair – and is now sleeping in his bed. When Goldilocks awakes to find the three bears around her bed she flees from the house in terror.

The original folktale is usually much altered and expanded in its pantomime form with all manner of devices being employed to introduce the DAME and other conventional characters. One of the more successful of these is to have the three bears joining the circus, which is managed with some incompetence by the dame herself – as in the popular version by JOHN MORLEY. The bears make the circus a success, incurring the wrath of a rival circus owner, who attempts to poison all three of them but is eventually thwarted. Stock features of all pantomime versions of the story include the song 'The Teddy Bears' Picnic'.

Origins The tale of Goldilocks is thought to have had its origins in an ancient Scottish folktale about a vixen that is eaten after trespassing in a bears' den (a salutatory lesson for the young about the dangers of breaking the laws protecting another's privacy and property). It became popular after it was re-told by Robert Southey in his miscellany *The Doctor* (1837), while another notable version was that included in the collection compiled by the GRIMM BROTHERS, which added the forest location and the nap in the bed. Many early versions – including Southey's – identified the trespasser in the bears' house as an old woman (who tumbles out of the window after being discovered), but subsequent writers preferred to describe her as a young girl, variously called Silverhair, Silverlocks, and finally Goldilocks.

John Rich as Harlequin (without his mask), 1753

Joe Grimaldi as Clown in *Mother Goose*, c. 1806

Above Grimaldi, as Clown, squares up to a man made of vegetables in *Harlequin and Asmodeus*, 1810

Below Grimaldi as the Bold Dragoon in *Harlequin and the Red Dwarf; or, The Adamant Rock*, Covent Garden, 1812

Harlequinade (with Pantaloon, Harlequin, Columbine, a dwarf acrobat and James Huline as Clown), *The King of the Castle; or, Harlequin Prince Diamond and Princess Brighteyes*, Princess's Theatre, 1856

Poster for *Bluebeard*, Covent Garden, 1860

George Conquest being shot from a Dragon's mouth and appearing as the Octopus in *Grim Goblin* at the Grecian Theatre, 1876

Charles Lauri as Puss, Drury Lane, 1887

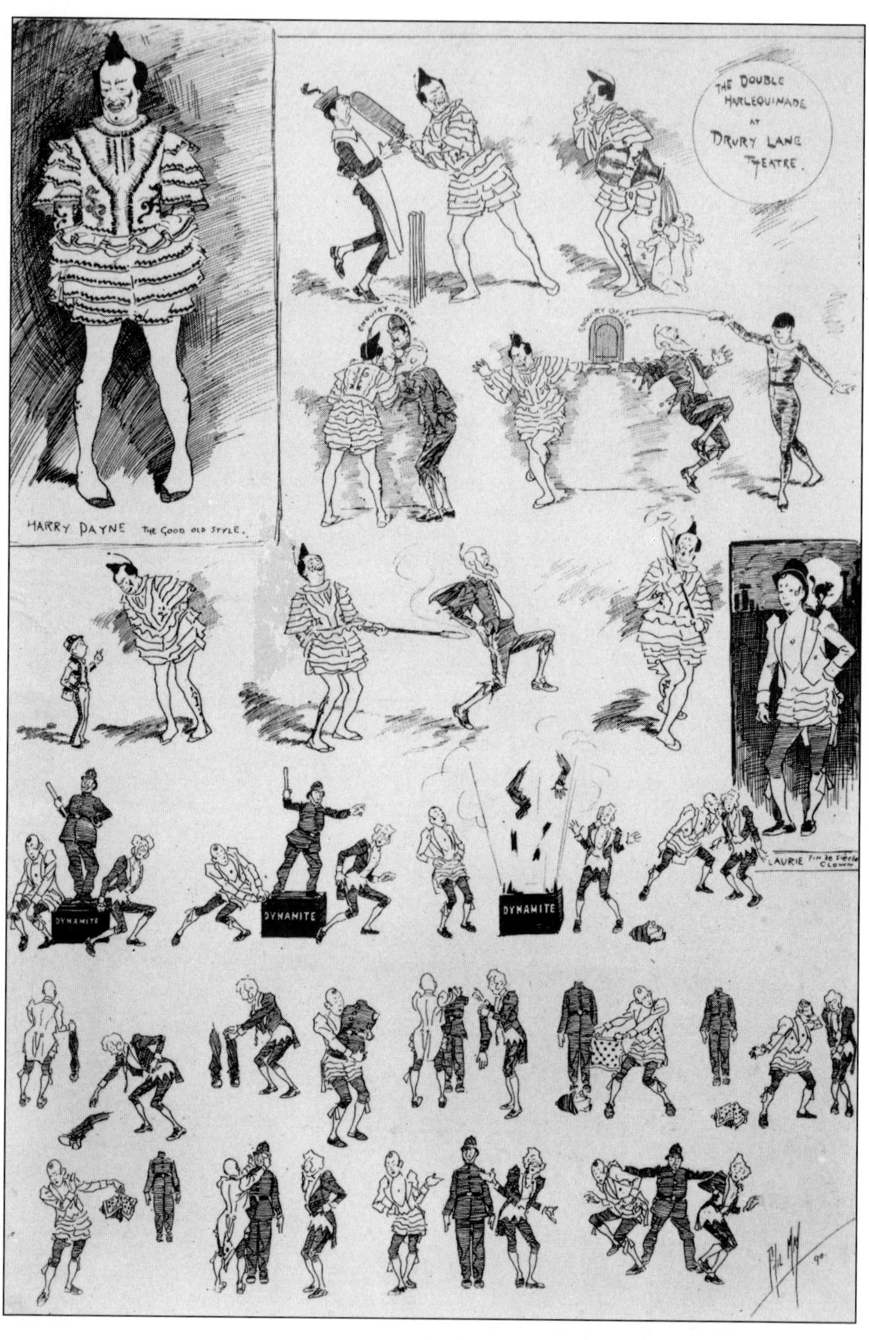

Harry Payne as Clown in *The Double Harlequinade* at Drury Lane, 1890

Above The cast in *Queen of Hearts*, Drury Lane, 1892

Left Dan Leno as Idle Jack in *Dick Whittington*, Drury Lane, 1894

Preparing for *The Forty Thieves*, Drury Lane, 1898

Above Set for *The Sleeping Beauty*, Drury Lane, 1900

Right Star trap, showing the mechanisms below the stage

Poster for *Cinderella*, Drury Lane, 1895

Vesta Tilley as Dick Whittington, Prince of Wales' Theatre, c. 1900

SOME FAMOUS PANTOMIME DAMES

George Robey

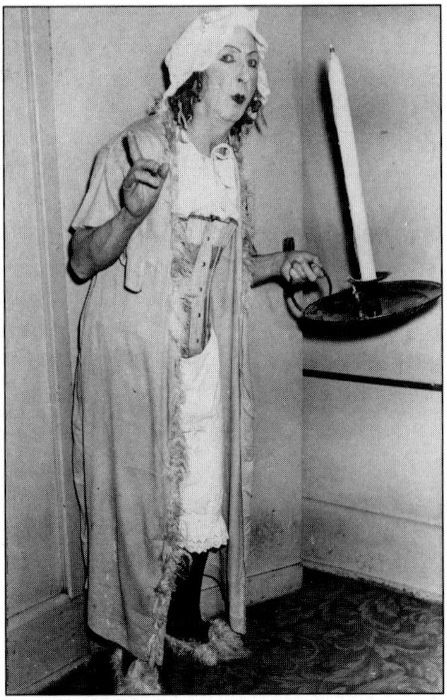

Douglas Byng

Jack Tripp

Les Dawson

Arthur Askey as Widow Twankey in *Aladdin and the Wonderful Lamp*, London Palladium, 1964

TWO OF THE MOST POPULAR PERFORMERS OF CONTEMPORARY PANTOMIME

Cilla Black

Roy Hudd

Goody Two-Shoes Fairytale that was once regularly used as the basis of pantomime plots, though less frequently in the 20th century. The tale was staged as a pantomime at SADLER'S WELLS in 1803 and subsequently established itself as one of the most popular pantomime plots on the Victorian stage. Notable pantomime versions of the story included the 1862 production of E. L. BLANCHARD's *Little Goody Two-Shoes; or, Harlequin and Cock Robin* at DRURY LANE, with a cast that included the acclaimed comedian TOM MATTHEWS as Little Boy Blue's rival suitor Peter Gripe and LYDIA THOMPSON in the title role (which was transformed into Harlequin in the harlequinade). Rare revivals of the story in the 20th century have included a version staged by EMILE LITTLER in 1944.

Story The heroine Margery and her brother Tommy are orphans without a penny to their name (Margery herself has only one shoe). A fairy cobbler takes pity on them, however, and makes for Margery a pair of new shoes. With the fairy's help Margery goes on to win fame and fortune and distinguishes herself for her many acts of kindness and generosity (in the original story she becomes a teacher and is tried as a witch before finally being reunited with Tommy, marrying a rich widower, and acquiring the estate of the wicked local squire).

Origins The story of Goody Two-Shoes was popularised by John Newbery's version published in 1765, which is actually thought to have written by Oliver Goldsmith, who was then working for Newbery. According to a popular tradition, Goldsmith was inspired to write the story after meeting a young girl as she rushed out of one of London's 'Ragged Schools' for the poor: she proudly showed him a pair of shoes she had been given as a reward for being a good girl and thus provided the writer with the germ from which his tale was to grow. The story was widely read in CHAPBOOKS and became a favourite with children everywhere. The pantomime version is, however, more closely linked to a revision of the story written by 'Lady Kathleen' in 1914, in which the role played by the fairies is more prominent than in the original.

Goose In *MOTHER GOOSE*, the goose that lays golden eggs, thus transforming the financial affairs of MOTHER GOOSE and her family. In most versions of the tale the goose is named Priscilla, as she was in the celebrated 1902 production starring DAN LENO (Ann Priscilla Mary May being the name of Mother Goose's grandmother).

The goose occupies an important position in ancient folklore, figuring prominently in many cultures, including those of ancient Egypt, Rome (in the story of the geese alerting the guard at the Capitol to an attack), and China. Celebrated modern performers of the role, which is considered one of the most demanding of the SKIN PARTS because of the uncomfortable position the actor has to adopt in the costume, have included Kay Lyell, Gerry Lee, and Barbara Newman – though FRED CONQUEST, who played the part in the early 20th century, remains more closely identified with the role than any other. Conquest not only constructed his Goose costume himself (using 11 strings to operate the various parts of the Goose's body) but also spent many hours studying the behaviour of geese and making sketches of their movements.

Properly made goose costumes, which are based on a wicker frame, can cost well over £1000. It is an occupational hazard of the role that if a performer wearing a full goose costume accidentally falls over it is impossible for him to regain his feet without assistance.

Grand Theatre, Islington A theatre in Islington, London, which was once famous for its pantomimes. Opened in 1870 as a music hall, it was burnt to the ground in 1883 and was further damaged by fire in 1887 and 1900. As the **Islington Empire**, it hosted touring shows, variety, and pantomime from 1908. The pantomimes were especially celebrated (from 1891) for the performances of HARRY RANDALL, one of the most admired dames of his day. His debut there in *DICK WHITTINGTON* was also distinguished by the performance of LOTTIE COLLINS singing her show-stopping number TA-RA-RA-BOOM-DE-AY. The tradition came to an end in 1932, when the theatre was converted into a cinema.

Grandma *See LITTLE RED RIDING HOOD.*

Grand Transformation *See* TRANSFORMATION SCENE.

Gratiano *See COMMEDIA DELL'ARTE.*

Graves, George (1876–1949) English comedian, who was one of the successors to DAN LENO in the celebrated DRURY LANE pantomimes of the early 20th century. Graves made his Drury Lane debut in 1909 as Abanazar in *ALADDIN* and subsequently made many appearances as DAME, his performances enriched by his robust sense of humour. His greatest successes included his performances as dame in *JACK AND THE BEANSTALK* at Drury Lane in 1910–11 and as the Duke of Monte Blanco in the three *SLEEPING BEAUTY* pantomimes that were staged at the theatre between 1912 and 1914.

grave trap A rectangular body-length TRAP in the middle of the stage, so-called after its introduction in the gravediggers' scene in *Hamlet*. Such traps, which opened downwards, were routinely employed in the pantomime until their use was prohibited in the mid-20th century (a change enacted after ARTHUR ASKEY was badly injured after falling through an unsecured grave trap).

Gray, 'Monsewer' Eddie (1897–1969) English comedian, who was a star of pantomime both before and after World War II and achieved national fame as one of the Crazy Gang. Among his successful pantomime appearances were several in the 1930s under the management of the MELVILLE BROTHERS at the LYCEUM THEATRE, where he shared the bill with fellow Crazy Gang members NAUGHTON AND GOLD.

Grecian Theatre Former theatre in the City Road, Shoreditch, London, which was home to a celebrated series of pantomimes in the latter half of the 19th century. Opened in 1830 as a concert hall (called the **Grecian Saloon**), it subsequently staged serious classical drama before eventually diversifying with pantomime and ballet under the management of BENJAMIN CONQUEST, who reopened it in 1851, and subsequently of his son GEORGE CONQUEST, who established it as one of the most popular pantomime venues in the capital.

Pantomimes staged there under the Conquest management were generally outside the usual run-of-the-mill repertory presented elsewhere and were for many years the work of George Conquest and H. Spry. Vast audiences of anything up to 1700 flocked to see Conquest himself and thrilled at the spectacular CHASE

SCENES for which the theatre was much celebrated.

Stars who made their debuts there included such significant names as HERBERT CAMPBELL, HARRY NICHOLLS, and G. H. MACDERMOTT. The last pantomime staged at the Grecian by the Conquests before they moved to the SURREY THEATRE was typically original, bearing the title *Hokee-Pokee the Fiend of the Fungus Forest*. The theatre was rebuilt in 1876, sold by Conquest in 1879, and in 1880 became the property of the Salvation Army, who eventually demolished it.

Greenwood, T(homas) L(ongden) (1806–79) English author, who was one of the foremost writers of pantomimes for the early Victorian stage. Greenwood was descended from a long line of theatrical scenic artists who had worked mainly at the SADLER'S WELLS THEATRE. Accordingly the young T. L. Greenwood also joined the staff at Sadler's Wells, in time rising to assistant manager and resident writer and then becoming joint-manager (1843–59) alongside Samuel Phelps.

His pantomimes for the theatre were well-received and were especially notable for their allegorical OPENINGS; typical products of his pen included *Whittington and His Cat; or, Old Dame Fortune, and Harlequin Lord Mayor of London* (1852). Many of the pantomimes he worked on were the result of collaborations with E. L. BLANCHARD, with whom Greenwood was paired as the **Brothers Grinn**. Greenwood eventually retired from theatre management in 1859 but continued to write for the pantomime.

Grieve, John Henderson (1770–1845) English artist, who was the senior member of a family of noted set painters who worked on the first DIORAMAS to be seen in the pantomime in the early 19th century. Having established a reputation for his work at COVENT GARDEN under the management of Charles Kemble, J. H. Grieve, together with his sons Thomas Grieve (1799–1882) and William Grieve (1800–44), enjoyed enormous success with his presentation of a moving diorama depicting a sea-crossing from Wales to Ireland in the pantomime of 1820, thus inaugurating an era in scene design that was to have a profound effect upon the Victorian pantomime.

Although they worked with a relatively restricted palette, the Grieves attracted great interest with their beautiful designs, which quickly persuaded rival theatre managements to recruit artists to execute dioramas for their own productions. Among the most ambitious dioramas created by the Grieves was the very first aerial diorama, in which they rendered views 'enjoyed' by a terrified Clown and Pantaloon (Grimaldi and Bologna) during a hot-air balloon flight (for *Harlequin and Cock Robin* at Covent Garden in 1823). Others included a nautical sequence executed for Covent Garden's *PUSS IN BOOTS* in 1832; this depicted a series of seascapes following the voyage of a steam frigate from Calais to Antwerp.

Thomas's son Thomas Walford Grieve (1841–82) continued in the family tradition and, like William Grieve (who later defected to Drury Lane), was ranked alongside CLARKSON STANFIELD himself. Over 700 designs executed by the various members of the family survive.

Griffiths brothers English comedy double act that was very popular both in MUSIC HALL and in pantomime at DRURY LANE in the 1890s, being considered by many to have been the finest specialists in SKIN PARTS. **Frederick George Griffiths** (1856–1940) made his pantomime debut in *Hi-Diddle-Diddle* in 1861 and subsequently won acclaim in music hall and the circus both in the UK and in the USA before teaming up with his brother **Joe Griffiths** (1853–1901) in 1877.

The brothers were well-known for their clowning in their 'burlesque kangaroo boxing match' and similar acts and appeared regularly under the management of AUGUSTUS HARRIS. Their roles included the CHINESE POLICEMEN in *ALADDIN*, Mr. and Mrs. Wolf in *Little Bo-Peep, Little Red Riding Hood and Hop o' My Thumb*, a comic wrestling lion, Daisy the Cow, and – most popular of all – their 'Blondin Donkey' (which performed a mock tightrope act). The brothers were also admired for their comedy skills in the harlequinade. When Joe died his place in the act was taken by his son Fred. Fred senior finally retired in 1937, at the age of 81.

Grimaldi, Giuseppe (*c.* 1710–88) Italian-born actor, who was the father of the celebrated pantomime star JOSEPH GRIMALDI. Giuseppe Grimaldi began his career as a dancer at fairs in Italy and France and settled in England in 1759, playing PANTALOON at COVENT GARDEN. Somewhat bizarrely, he also held the post of dentist to Queen Charlotte, although he gave up this alternative career soon after his arrival in England.

Subsequently he transferred to DRURY LANE to appear in a ballet called *The Miller* and became DAVID GARRICK's ballet-master, winning particular acclaim at the theatre as HARLEQUIN and (at the age of 71) as CLOWN. His performances as Clown, in which he brought to the part some of the comic business usually associated with Harlequin, prepared the way for his son's recreation of the role.

Giuseppe Grimaldi – the son of a dancer nicknamed 'Iron Legs' – was often himself nicknamed 'Old Grim' (a reference to his unruly and sometimes morbid nature). He was already in his sixties when Joseph was born to the cockney chorus-girl Rebecca Brooker, his 25-year-old mistress (one of several). The older Grimaldi proved a difficult father to live with. He beat his son regularly (even on stage) and finally left his family virtually nothing when he died. He was detested by many and lived an unprincipled life that caused his family considerable suffering. Nonetheless he immersed his son in the business of the theatre, appearing alongside him (with Joseph dressed as a miniature version of his father) as soon as the infant could walk.

Grimaldi, Joseph (1778–1837) British comedian, who remains the most influential single figure in the history of the pantomime. The pantomime was transformed by Grimaldi between 1806 and 1823, during which years he made the role of CLOWN central to the harlequinade for the first time.

Born in London, Grimaldi was the illegitimate son of GIUSEPPE GRIMALDI, and Rebecca Brooker, who were both connected with DRURY LANE. Grimaldi suffered a harsh childhood at the hands of his father, with frequent beatings, and was forced into a stage career almost as soon as he could walk. Joe made his debut in 1781 at the age of two years, four months and at the age of three narrowly escaped death when impersonating a monkey on stage at SADLER'S WELLS, being hurled into the pit when the chain by which his father was swinging him through the air broke without warning (fortunately he was safely caught by a spectator).

Subsequently he made frequent appearances as fairies and dwarfs and in other minor roles throughout his childhood at both Drury Lane and Sadler's Wells and gradually learnt the basic skills upon which he later came to rely. He pursued a hectic life in which he endeavoured to fulfil his commitments at the two theatres (to compensate for his low salary) and enjoyed his first hit at the age of 16, when he played the hag Morad in *The Talisman of Orosmanes; or, Harlequin Made Happy* at Sadler's Wells.

Six years later he won acclaim as Clown at Sadler's Wells, in CHARLES DIBDIN's *Peter Wilkins; or, Harlequin in the Flying World* (1800) and his career blossomed. His performance was especially enhanced by his choice of a more flamboyant costume than was customary in the role and his adoption of distinctive white facial make-up, with two red half-moons painted on his cheeks – an innovation that became a permanent feature of the clown in the theatre, variety, and the circus.

He quickly replaced the ageing BAPTISTE DUBOIS as the resident Clown at Sadler's Wells and became the theatre's main attraction. In 1806, however, he broke with the Drury Lane management and offered his services instead to COVENT GARDEN, where he made a well-received debut under the management of CHARLES FARLEY in the challenging part of Orson in *Valentine and Orson*.

Christmas that year witnessed his greatest success to date playing Clown (the SQUIRE prior to the HARLEQUINADE) in TOM DIBDIN's *Harlequin Mother Goose; or, The Golden Egg*. The relatively modest production of the pantomime allowed Grimaldi's comic talent to take centre stage and – although Grimaldi himself thought Dibdin's script unexceptional – the piece enjoyed unparalleled success, scenes from it being toured all over the country.

Grimaldi maintained his links with Covent Garden and Sadler's Wells for another 17 years, transforming the pantomime with his inventive but subtle gags ridiculing all manner of pomposity and pretension. Audiences flocked to see Grimaldi's comic depiction of Clown as an amoral rogue, in which his skills as a dancer, mime, acrobat, and actor were all brought into play. As for TRICKWORK, he had no equal; the Lord Chancellor himself was said to have seen Grimaldi in *Mother Goose* on no less than nine occasions, so fascinated was he by the dexterity with which the great performer stole some fish in the shop scene of the harlequinade.

His most famous ploys involved the thieving of a long string of sausages, assaulting a policeman with a RED-HOT POKER, executing a parody of the dagger scene from *Macbeth* (in *Harlequin and Fortunio*), and trying to find the neck of a bottle of wine in the dark with the aid of a nightwatchman's lantern. Celebrated examples of his ingenuity (or TRICKS OF CONSTRUCTION) included a famous scene in which he concocted his own version of a hussar's uniform out of kitchen utensils and a lady's muff and another in which he assembled a figure made entirely of vegetables (in *Harlequin Asmodeus; or, Cupid on Crutches* in 1810).

Among other highlights of his performances were his songs, which included TIPPITY WITCHET, 'Me and my Neddy' (which he first sang in 1806), and 'An Oyster Crossed in Love' (from the 1815 production of *Harlequin and Fortunio*), as well as the great favourite HOT CODLINS. His cry of "Here we are again!" became the catchphrase of clowns everywhere, who worked tirelessly to imitate his brilliant handling of trick props and acrobatic feats.

Grimaldi's brilliance was not confined to the part of Clown, however; among his many other hugely successful comic roles were such parts as My Lord Humpy Dandy, the Regency fop in *Harlequin Munchausen* (1818) and various DAMES. He also exercised his prodigious talent outside the pantomime, numbering among his other roles that of Bob Acres in SHERIDAN'S *The Rivals*, in which part he appeared many times with great success.

Unfortunately, the great man was exceedingly accident-prone. He broke a collar-bone at the age of just five when he fell 40 feet through a trapdoor and among other mishaps once suffered serious injury when his stocking caught fire after the pistol he was brandishing accidentally went off: typically, though in great pain, he still managed to complete the scene before stumbling off the stage (the audience remained unaware of his agony and laughed uproariously as the clown's boot swelled with the heat).

By 1824 Grimaldi was a virtual cripple as a result of the injuries he had received on stage and – after his last pantomime, *Harlequin and the Ogress* – he had to retire, though aged only 45. He made two farewell appearances in 1828, one at Sadler's Wells and another at Drury Lane; for the latter he was carried on stage and enacted one final scene in the role of Clown (including the song 'Hot Codlins') seated on a chair, but still succeeded in bringing the house down. His second wife (his first died after a year of marriage) died shortly afterwards and the tragic decline of his son was another cause of grief in his retirement.

The great man himself, called 'the Garrick of Clowns' and 'the Michel-angelo of buffoonery', finally died at the age of 59 on 21 May 1837. His grave at St. James's Chapel in Pentonville is the scene of an annual pilgrimage by English clowns, who parade there in full costume and make-up. His memoirs, written in the last year before his death, were subsequently edited by CHARLES DICKENS and form an invaluable record of his life and career.

It is a curious fact that Grimaldi's prowess in the role of Clown may have contributed to the decline of the harlequinade as a whole; after his retirement no one could be found to match his achievements and – for this and other reasons – the emphasis switched increasingly to the opening. *See also* JOEY.

Grimaldi, Joseph Samuel William (1802–1832) English comedian, the son of the celebrated JOSEPH GRIMALDI, who was for a time expected to inherit his father's position as one of the great figures in the English pantomime.

The son of Grimaldi by his second wife, the actress Mary Bristow, the younger Joseph showed an early enthusiasm for the stage and made his debut at SADLER'S WELLS in 1815, playing Clowny-Chip (a miniature version of his father's Clown) in *Harlequin and Fortunio*. He was very well received and Grimaldi himself believed his son would duplicate his own great success. The two performers played alongside each other on numerous occasions afterwards and when Grimaldi senior became ill in 1823 the younger Joseph (whose past successes included a number of appearances in the role of DANDY LOVER) took over his part in *Harlequin and Padmanaba*, to much acclaim (critics praised his nimbleness of foot and cleverness although they also found that, as yet, he lacked his father's confident and relaxed comic style).

Upon his father's forced retirement the younger Grimaldi was invited to play Clown in *Harlequin and Poor Robin; or, the House that Jack Built* at Covent Garden. The pantomime played to packed houses and the young man's future seemed secure. His popularity went to his head, however, and he became estranged from his family as he recklessly indulged in increasingly extravagant and debauched behaviour. He was dropped from the bills of the leading theatres and gradually sank into alcoholism and insanity (possibly the result of a head injury sustained in a scuffle with police).

His death came shortly after his 30th birthday, in the dingy surroundings of a room above a public house in the Tottenham Court Road; he spent his last days standing on his bed and loudly rattling through all his pantomime parts, complete with actions. His unhappy life was subsequently commemorated in the 'Stroller's Tale' in the *Pickwick Papers* by CHARLES DICKENS.

Grimm brothers The German philologists and folklorists **Jakob Ludwig Karl Grimm** (1785–1863) and **Wilhelm Karl Grimm** (1786–1859), whose *Household Tales* (popularly called 'Grimm's Fairy Tales') provided much source material for pantomime plots.

Dedicated pioneers of the study of folklore, the Grimm brothers wrote numerous scholarly works – including Jakob's *Deutsches Grammatik* (1819–37), in which he formulated Grimm's Law concerning consonant changes in Indo-European languages, and a new German dictionary – but remain best known for their collected fairytales. They collected about 200 such stories in all from neighbours and friends around Germany, publishing their first compilation in 1812 and a second volume in 1814 and adding a volume of local German legends (1816–18). Contributors of tales to their famous collection included an old soldier, the old nurse to the family next door, and Katharina Viehmann, a tailor's wife who sold eggs, who furnished the brothers with versions of 20 tales they had not heard.

Notable among the stories that were to blossom as plots for the pantomime were *HANSEL AND GRETEL*, *THE FROG PRINCE*, *SNOW WHITE AND THE SEVEN DWARFS*, *RUMPELSTILTSKIN*, *THE GOLDEN GOOSE*, and *Snow-White and Rose-Red*. The first English translations of the Grimm brothers' tales appeared in the 1820s and greatly promoted the fairytale's popularity (despite reservations over some of the more gruesome scenes).

grotesque Descriptive term often used to refer to HARLEQUIN and his confederates in the early history of the pantomime. The word was commonly heard in disparaging comments about the comic characters of the HARLEQUINADE, who were considered crude and unsophisticated by such critics as JOHN WEAVER, who used the term in advertising his piece *The Shipwreck; or, Perseus and Andromeda* (1717). According to Weaver the term was suggested to him by the exaggerated and conventionalised gestures and distorted movements employed by performers of the ITALIAN NIGHT SCENES. The term soon lost its disparaging connotation and was used simply as a technical term to denote the comic business and characters of the pantomime.

groundrow A long low section of freestanding scenery used in conjunction with other FLATS and scenic details. They were once commonly used to suggest waves and were often employed in the pantomime as essential components of the DIORAMA and the TRANSFORMATION SCENE.

Gulliver's Travels The classic satirical novel published in 1726 by Jonathan Swift (1667–1745), which was once frequently adapted as a pantomime. Early pantomime adaptations included CHARLES FARLEY's *Harlequin Gulliver; or, The Flying Island*, which was staged at COVENT GARDEN in 1817 and was followed by further productions at many leading venues. Modern adaptations of the novel usually take the form of children's plays.

Story Lemuel Gulliver is brought by shipwreck to a succession of extraordinary lands, which in various ways are exaggerated parallels of real society. In Lilliput the inhabitants are just six inches tall and inclined to go to war over the issue of which end a boiled egg should be broken at; in Brobdingnag they are all giants; Laputa is populated with a race of mad scientists and inventors; and the fourth country is populated by a race of reasonable horses, called Houyhnhnms, and the loathsome Yahoos. Most pantomime versions played down the satirical element of the original novel and exploited the tale's considerable potential for spectacle, concentrating especially upon Gulliver's adventures in Lilliput.

Origins Swift's novel was an instant success and inspired numerous adaptations and imitations as well as abridged versions published in journals and CHAPBOOKS. The story continues to be read by both adults and children.

H

Hansel and Gretel A fairytale that has been regularly adapted as a pantomime since the mid-19th century. The tale also inspired a children's opera by Engelbert Humperdinck (1893). Recent productions include one staged at the COLISEUM THEATRE in 1992.

Story Hansel and Gretel are the children of a poor woodcutter who is persuaded by his wife, the children's WICKED STEPMOTHER, to abandon his offspring in the forest as there is not enough food for them all. Hansel overhears the plot and leaves a trail of pebbles behind them as they go into the woods. They return safely home by following the trail but the next day Hansel is unable to find any more pebbles and has to use breadcrumbs for his trail instead. The birds eat the breadcrumbs and the children are lost.

Hansel and Gretel then happen upon a GINGERBREAD HOUSE, which is actually the home of an evil WITCH. The witch catches them eating pieces of gingerbread broken off her house and takes them in. She then locks Hansel in a cage so that he may be fattened up for her to eat and forces Gretel to perform the household chores. The witch is short-sighted and when she commands Hansel to put out his finger for her to see if he is fat enough to eat yet, he fools her by poking a thin bone through the bars of the cage.

Eventually, however, the witch loses patience and prepares to cook the boy. She orders Gretel to crawl into the stove to see if it is hot enough but Gretel asks if she will show her how: the witch does so and Gretel locks her inside. The children help themselves to the witch's treasure and return home, where their father is overjoyed to see them and forces the stepmother to leave. As in the case of other pantomimes based on folkloric sources the usual cast including DAME and SKIN PARTS are introduced by various ingenious means.

Origins The familiar pantomime plot is a fairly faithful interpretation of the fairytale told by the GRIMM BROTHERS in their *Household Tales*. This in turn was passed down from ancient northern European legend, although other versions (possibly descended from the European tale or of independent origin) are to be found in the mythologies of India, Japan, Africa, the Americas, and the peoples of the Pacific. One variant from Jamaica has the children being guided to the gingerbread house by the witch herself in the guise of a bird.

Harlequin The central character of the HARLEQUINADE, who was descended from the ARLECCHINO figure of the *COMMEDIA DELL'ARTE* tradition. The comic antics of Harlequin were central to the success of the ITALIAN NIGHT SCENES in the early 18th century, although the character had previously made occasional appearances on the English stage in plays by native authors. John Day introduced the figure of Harlequin in his *The Travailes of the Three English Brothers* as early as 1607, while later he also appeared in plays by APHRA BEHN, WILLIAM MOUNTFORD, and EDWARD RAVENSCROFT.

It was JOHN RICH who transformed the character into the great popular favourite of the early pantomime, playing the role under the pseudonym Lun. In Rich's productions Harlequin – the "speckled wizard" in a parti-coloured costume – became a mystical figure with magical powers, conducting spectacular TRANSFORMATION SCENES with his magic bat or SLAPSTICK, which had replaced the wooden sword of Arlecchino, and executing ingenious tricks and acrobatic feats with elegant ease.

Of particular note were the increasingly imaginative ways in which the figure of Harlequin was first revealed to the audience, pantomimists vying with one another for the most spectacular effects. In different productions he emerged from lakes, furnaces, mounds of earth, and – in one of Rich's most celebrated scenes – from an egg.

Rich's unsurpassed Harlequin acted in dumb show, but in 1759, in a production by DAVID GARRICK, HENRY WOODWARD spoke in the role after it was realised that it would be impossible to find another actor to equal the mime performances of Rich; in subsequent productions, though, he generally remained silent.

Another performer in the part, JAMES BYRNE, transformed Harlequin visually in 1800 when he created for him his distinctive close-fitting one-piece costume decorated with coloured diamond-shaped patches and spangles (which by Victorian times could amount to almost 50,000 in number on a single outfit). Each coloured patch on the suit had a particular significance and at key moments Harlequin would strike one of a small range of set poses ('attitudes') and point with the tip of his bat to one of the patches to indicate a particular emotion; yellow signified jealousy, blue love, scarlet anger, and mauve fidelity. When he pointed to a black patch he was understood by the audience to be invisible to the other characters of the harlequinade. This device was particularly useful as a way of getting round the restrictions placed on DIALOGUE at the majority of theatres.

Performers of the role had to be fine acrobats and dancers, but were not necessarily distinguished actors; among those admired as Harlequin were Thomas Ridgway, the daredevil acrobat JACK BOLOGNA, TOM ELLAR, the great tragedian EDMUND KEAN, Wilson Barrett, who was best known for his unrivalled prowess as an actor of Victorian melodrama, and Fred Payne, who was described as the last great performer of the role.

By Payne's time, however, the spirit of mischief that had once enlivened the role had long since passed to other characters (firstly to PIERROT and then to CLOWN) and Harlequin had become a rather lacklustre hero-figure with few redeeming traits. The part diminished still further as the harlequinade shrank and finally disappeared altogether. The process was somewhat hastened as Pantaloon's battles with Clown overshadowed the pursuit of Harlequin and Columbine and Harlequin participated less and less in the central slapstick comedy except as 'straight man'.

By the mid-19th century he was reduced to executing series of hair-raising leaps through concealed traps in an attempt to impress bored audiences. Spectacular vaults through clock faces, hoops of fire, and shop windows, however, failed to restore Harlequin to popular favour, despite publicity advertising his death-defying efforts. Young audiences not acquainted with the background from which Harlequin came were also perplexed by the lack of motive given for lengthy chase sequences and by the fact that on occasion he apparently changed sex, with several actresses taking the part from the 1830s onwards (although male performers generally stood in to perform the acrobatics). His memory is now preserved in the many reproductions of his image in china and in occasional revivals of the old-fashioned pantomime on the amateur and professional stage.

Harlequina Female counterpart to HARLEQUIN, who was sometimes introduced into HARLEQUINADES of the mid-19th century. She appeared in the DOUBLE HARLEQUINADES devised by E. L. BLANCHARD and others, in which every character was duplicated in a futile attempt to revive flagging popular interest in this part of the pantomime. Her role in the plot was usually fairly insignificant and she was generally included purely for the sake of extra spectacle, often being picturesquely costumed in the style of the popular paintings of the French artist Antoine Watteau. Quite where she stood in relation to Harlequin and Columbine was never explained.

harlequinade (1) Theatrical entertainment depicting the comic adventures of HARLEQUIN, which was for many years an indispensable component of the English pantomime. Derived from the Italian *COMMEDIA DELL'ARTE*, the harlequinade developed out of the ITALIAN NIGHT SCENES, which were seen in London in the early 18th century.

JOHN RICH established the harlequinade as a comic counterpart to the telling of a story from mythology or folklore and his success in the role of Harlequin confirmed the unique appeal of the genre. For a long time the harlequinade, seen in separate episodes, was quite unconnected to the main action and most pantomimes had 'double' titles, as in the case of *PUSS IN BOOTS; OR, HARLEQUIN AND THE MILLER'S SONS*, *Old Mother Hubbard and Her Dog; or, Harlequin and the Tales of the Nursery*, and *Conrad and Medora; or, Harlequin Corsair and the Little Fairy at the Bottom of the Sea*.

Eventually the harlequinade was separated out from the OPENING, which preceded it, and a link was established between the two parts through the TRANSFORMATION SCENE, in which the main characters of the opening were identified as the familiar figures of the harlequinade. The action of the harlequinade revolved around the romantic intrigues of Harlequin and COLUMBINE, against the opposition of Columbine's father PANTALOON, who was not only the butt of Harlequin's humour but often also the victim of the schemings of CLOWN.

In most harlequinades Harlequin was set a difficult task to perform by the Good Fairy or other supernatural figure (*see* BENEVOLENT AGENT) who also effected the transformation scene. Harlequin and Columbine then set out on their quest, pursued by Pantaloon and Clown (and sometimes also the DANDY LOVER, who was favoured by Pantaloon as his daughter's suitor). In order to slow down their pursuers Harlequin used his magic SLAPSTICK to throw up various obstacles in their path, with spectacular and comic results. All the characters were reconciled after the climactic DARK SCENE and then magically transported to a magnificent 'Bower of Bliss' or other paradise for a grand finale.

Practical joking and elaborate TRICKS OF CONSTRUCTION involving specially-prepared stage equipment and sleights of hand were an essential part of the entertainment, the most spectacular effects being cued by Harlequin's slapstick. Characters would be hurled through windows, flattened in doorways, squeezed through mangles, and exposed to a thousand other comic hazards to the enormous enjoyment of packed houses. This hectic action would be punctuated with graceful dances by Harlequin and Columbine, songs, and other extraneous interludes of all kinds.

During the course of these extended CHASE SCENES characters would visit such outlandish places as hell and the bottom of the sea as well as careering through shops and farmyards. The humour was generally conservative, with much fun being had at the expense of innovations of every kind, from the latest fashions in clothing to the newest technological breakthroughs in transport and industry.

As the years went by the harlequinade grew increasingly ambitious, with added emphasis being placed on the elements of magic and spectacle and the comic focus being transferred gradually to PIERROT and Clown, in which role JOSEPH GRIMALDI excelled. Grimaldi's enormous success in *MOTHER GOOSE* in 1806 set the pattern for the contemporary harlequinade and an experiment to do away with it altogether in *Jack the Giant Killer* at the LYCEUM THEATRE two years later was doomed to failure; it was another 50 years before any leading management ventured to repeat the idea.

The harlequinade reached a peak in length and in popularity around 1815, when audiences sat with varying degrees of impatience through the opening and were then treated to a harlequinade that might last as long as two hours. It was at this time that the harlequinade also assumed a distinct satirical air, making comedy out of such affairs of the day as the progress of the Napoleonic War and the dandyism fad. By the 1830s, however, with Grimaldi in retirement and managements unable to find anyone to maintain Clown as the central comic figure as he had done, the satiric thrust weakened and the emphasis switched to spectacular scenic effects (anticipated by the popularity of the DIORAMA). The harlequinade shrank under pressure from the opening (newly transformed by the influence of the EXTRAVAGANZA and the universal adoption of the 'speaking opening'), which expanded and took on a new comic character until the harlequinade was largely superfluous (many treated the start of the harlequinade as a signal to put on their coats and leave).

The advent of the female PRINCIPAL BOY also undermined the conventions of the harlequinade with Harlequin no longer being played by the same performer who had played the hero in the opening (females being adjudged incapable of performing the acrobatics required of Harlequin). It has also been suggested that the often violent comedy of the harlequinade (which involved the maltreatment of babies and the flouting of authority) was out of place in a society that set increasing store on family life and Christian values.

Calls for the complete abandonment of the harlequinade were heard as early as 1846 and by the 1880s the harlequinade rarely lasted more than three scenes, though such venues as the GRECIAN THEATRE and the SURREY THEATRE defended its status. Better terms were offered to the more accomplished actors in the main part of the entertainment than to those in the harlequinade and attempts to redouble the appeal of the harlequinade by doubling – and even tripling – the characters involved in it did not reverse the trend (*see* DOUBLE HARLEQUINADE).

The writing was on the wall when the DRURY LANE pantomime of 1883 dropped the harlequinade – once the heart and soul of the pantomime itself – altogether. Since the 1930s, when the MELVILLE BROTHERS always incorporated brief harlequinades in their pantomimes, the tradition has only been revived on an occasional basis.

(2) A children's picture book, which retold the basic plot of one of the most popular 18th and 19th century pantomimes. The pages of such books could be folded so that new figures appeared against the same background.

Harris, Sir Augustus Henry Glossop (1852–96) English theatre manager, whose spectacular pantomimes at DRURY LANE earned him the nickname 'Father of Modern Pantomime'. Otherwise dubbed 'Augustus Druriolanus' and less reverently 'Gusarris', he was the son of the theatre manager Augustus Glossop Harris (1825–73) and took over at Drury Lane in 1879, becoming at the age of 28 the youngest manager in the theatre's history.

Harris rapidly set about revitalising the Drury Lane pantomime, which had become rather set in its ways after 28 consecutive productions of the scripts of E. L. BLANCHARD, in which the VOKES FAMILY had enjoyed a monopoly of all the major parts for ten years. The Vokes family were persuaded to move to COVENT GARDEN and a freer approach was adopted to Blanchard's text, much to the writer's disgust.

Harris also opened a new era in the history of the pantomime by taking the controversial step of inviting leading singers and comedians from the MUSIC HALL to participate in the long series of pantomimes that he subsequently staged at the theatre, correctly assuming that they would bring a new energy and range of skills to his stage (although they sometimes swamped the pantomimes in which they appeared). The first major music hall star to be engaged by Harris was G. H. MACDERMOTT, who appeared in *ROBINSON CRUSOE* in 1881.

Among the many music hall stars to follow the most celebrated included DAN LENO, who appeared at Drury Lane every Christmas between 1888 and 1903 after Harris had seen him in *SINBAD AND THE LITTLE OLD MAN OF THE SEA* at the rival SURREY THEATRE. Others were MARIE LLOYD, HERBERT CAMPBELL, who was paired by Harris with Leno to form one of the greatest comic partnerships in the history of pantomime, and LITTLE TICH.

Between 1879 and his death in 1896 Harris's productions dominated the late Victorian pantomime and established the future pattern of the genre, enshrining the convention of the female PRINCIPAL BOY and witnessing the development of the DAME as a fully-rounded comic character in the hands of Leno. Other innovations taken up in his productions included the upgrading of the pantomime as the sole entertainment on the evening's programme (previously it had been nominally at least only an AFTERPIECE).

Harris's reign is usually recalled,

however, for the lavishness with which he staged his productions, which represented the high point of pantomime spectacle. Under Harris's direction the conventional TRANSFORMATION SCENE was replaced with huge processions of fabulously-costumed characters (including on one occasion every English monarch since the Norman Conquest and on another characters from all the most important plays of William Shakespeare) and no expense was spared when it came to costumes and sets. It was common for casts of over 500 people to be presented on stage at the same time (as they were in one scene of *Sinbad the Sailor*), and each year designers at the Lane were exhorted to exceed all their previous efforts.

Many critics lamented the damage done to the old-fashioned pantomime of earlier times (in particular through the brash humour of the music hall stars), but audiences flocked to the Lane to see Harris's opulent productions and no other management could match him for sheer visual spectacle, which remains unsurpassed to this day. Harris himself died at the early age of 44, largely as a result of overwork but the Lane's reputation as a prestigious pantomime house was maintained and indeed increased by his successor ARTHUR COLLINS.

Harris was knighted not in recognition of his unique contribution to the pantomime as might be expected but in acknowledgement of his office as Sheriff of the City of London at the time that the capital was visited by the Emperor of Prussia.

Haymarket A theatre in London, which was once famous for its pantomime tradition. Built in 1720, the Haymarket was managed in its early history by such distinguished theatrical figures as Henry Fielding, Samuel Foote, and George Colman the Younger. It was as a result of an unfortunate accident to Foote (in which the manager lost a leg after a wager in which the Duke of York and others bet that Foote could not ride a wild horse) that the Duke of York arranged a royal patent for the theatre, which allowed the venue to open in the summer months.

Pantomime was staged here regularly in the early 19th century. Among the most notable productions was the celebrated *MOTHER GOOSE* of 1808, a revival of the great COVENT GARDEN success of 1806, which was moved to the Haymarket after the former theatre had been burnt down that year. It was in the pantomime *Dr. Hocus-Pocus; or, Harlequin Washed White* staged at the Haymarket in 1814 that an early experiment was made with spoken rather than sung or chanted dialogue in the OPENING – an innovation that was not generally accepted until 20 years later.

MADAME VESTRIS excelled in EXTRAVAGANZAS at the rebuilt Haymarket in the 1830s and the theatre – managed by J. B. BUCKSTONE – became one of the most popular venues for pantomime in the Victorian era, when the magnificent scenery seen there won many admirers (an 1860 production of *Queen Ladybird*, for instance, included real fountains and pools). Subsequently the theatre enjoyed success with plays by Oscar Wilde, Terence Rattigan, and many others although pantomime disappeared from its bills.

here we are again! The traditional cry of the clowns on making their entrance. The first to utter it was the great JOSEPH GRIMALDI, the most celebrated performer ever to appear as CLOWN. *See also* CATCHPHRASES; JOEY.

Herring, Paul (1800–78) English actor, who was one of the most accomplished of JOSEPH GRIMALDI's successors in the role of CLOWN. Herring modelled his humour closely upon Grimaldi's and was much admired for his agility as Clown, making anything up to 40 appearances in a single day and night early in his career. Later in life he appeared as PANTALOON and finally in minor roles as comic old men and women until his death at the age of 78.

Hill, Jenny (Jane Woodley; 1848–96) English actress and singer, who was hugely successful in both the MUSIC HALL and the pantomime billed as 'The Vital Spark'. She made her stage debut in pantomime at the age of seven and rapidly built up a reputation with her lively wit, singing such songs as 'The Boy I Love Sits Up in the Gallery'. She was one of the first music hall stars to make a mark in the pantomime and subsequently appeared many times, notably as PRINCIPAL BOY, before her early death at the age of 48.

Hop o' My Thumb A fairytale, which provided the plot for a perennially successful pantomime of the 19th century. Early versions included CHARLES FARLEY'S 1831 COVENT GARDEN version *Hop o' My Thumb and His Brothers; or, Harlequin and the Ogre*, in which ELIZABETH POOLE (one of the earliest female performers to appear as PRINCIPAL BOY) took the title role.

In the 1840s General Tom Thumb played the main part in *Hop o' My Thumb; or, The Ogre and his Seven League Boots* under the Keeley management at the LYCEUM THEATRE and was so successful that he was requested to perform the role before Queen Victoria herself. Another version in 1866 saw the last appearance of the celebrated clown TOM MATTHEWS. The most famous production of the tale was that seen at DRURY LANE in 1892 under the title *Little Bo-Peep, Little Red Riding-Hood and Hop o' My Thumb*. LITTLE TICH played the role of Hop o' My Thumb, while DAN LENO played Daddy Thumb and HERBERT CAMPBELL appeared as his wife Goody Thumb.

Story Hop o' My Thumb is the youngest of the seven sons of a poor peasant and is no taller than his father's thumb. When their parents tearfully decide they can no longer feed their family, the children are abandoned in the woods – but Hop o' My Thumb lays a trail of pebbles and leads them all back home. A second time the trail of breadcrumbs that Hop o' My Thumb lays is eaten by birds and the children are lost. They arrive at the house of an ogre, whose wife tries – in vain – to hide them. Hop o' My Thumb, however, manages to disguise his brothers as the ogre's daughters and the ogre kills his own offspring by mistake. The boys escape but are pursued by the ogre in his seven-league boots. When the ogre stops to take a rest, Hop o' My Thumb removes his magic boots and puts them on himself. He then steals the ogre's treasure and returns to his parents, who are overjoyed that he is safe.

Origins The tale was included in the *MOTHER GOOSE* stories of CHARLES PERRAULT in 1697 and appeared in translation in England in 1729. Some elements of the story can be found in similar tales dating back to the 17th century and bear more than a passing resemblance to the events in *HANSEL AND GRETEL*. In early pantomime productions of the story links were made between the poverty of Tom's family and the Poor Laws that caused great misery in contemporary rural English society.

Hot Codlins Risqué comic song by CHARLES DIBDIN that was one of the best-loved features of the pantomime act of JOSEPH GRIMALDI. Such was the popularity of 'Hot Codlins' that the great CLOWN was obliged to include it in every performance in which he appeared.

The song, first heard in the SADLER'S WELLS pantomime *The Talking Bird; or, Harlequin Perizade* in 1819, depicted the condition of an old lady who makes her living by selling baked apples (codlins) in the streets of London, but who is mercilessly teased by local urchins and also has a fatal weakness for gin. Audiences quickly learnt to sing the climactic word 'gin' as Grimaldi stared back at them with open-mouthed shock and as time went by enthusiastic spectators sang much of the rest of the song in unison with their idol.

Even after Grimaldi's second farewell appearance in 1828 (during which he sang the song for the last time), audiences continued to demand 'Hot Codlins' from his successors, many of whom resented having to revive the old favourite year after year. Some managements felt obliged to warn spectators in advance that pressure for impromptu delivery of such songs would be resisted by the performers. Later, Victorian audiences found the open references to gin drinking less attractive and TOM MATTHEWS for one took to singing it in a version that omitted all mention of alcohol. GEORGE LUPINO is thought to have been the last person to sing it in pantomime, including it in a HARLEQUINADE seen in Birmingham as late as 1926.

House That Jack Built, The A nursery rhyme that was formerly regularly adapted as a pantomime. Early versions included a production that was staged at the OLYMPIC THEATRE in 1821 (as *The House that Jack Built; or, Harlequin Tattered and Torn*) and, in 1823, COVENT GARDEN'S *Harlequin and Poor Robin; or, The House that Jack Built*, in which the young but doomed J. S. GRIMALDI enjoyed success in his famous father's role as Clown. Notable productions after that date included a version entitled *The House That Jack Built; or, Old Mother Hubbard and Her Wonderful Dog* by E. L. BLANCHARD (1861), which included a burlesque of the witches' scene from *Macbeth* and with typical ingenuity combined the Jack legend with the nursery rhyme about Old Mother Hubbard.

Story The original nursery rhyme is a chant that slowly builds up with each verse repeating the one before but with an extra line added. Jack of the title builds a house and various animals bite, kick, and otherwise assault each other in a cumulative round of comic violence. Pantomime versions veered greatly from this original model and presented a variety of plots based on the central character. The 1823 version seen at Covent Garden, for instance, followed the progress of Jack's courtship of Rosebud, daughter of Gaffer Gander, who opposes the match and orders Rosebud to marry the local squire. Jack seeks the aid of Poor Robin, a penniless old man, and the plot culminates in the harlequinade, when the lovers are finally united.

Origins The earliest printed versions of the nursery rhyme date back to the mid-18th century and various scholars have attempted to make a link with a similar Hebrew chant. Another theory has it that the various animals represent such historical figures as John Bull, William the Conqueror, and Henry II. The rhyme was a popular subject of many CHAPBOOKS of the 18th and 19th centuries and was adapted by several writers as a satire upon contemporary figures – the most famous of these was William Hone's 'The Political House that Jack Built' (1820), in which the targets included the Prince Regent; it subsequently became the most popular satirical pamphlet of the century and ran to 52 editions in the first year alone.

Howerd, Frankie (1921–92) English comedian, who was a popular star of pantomime from the 1950s onwards. Howerd excelled in such roles as IDLE JACK and SIMPLE SIMON in *JACK AND THE BEANSTALK* and was equally popular with adults and children. He was particularly loved for his apparently spontaneous – and often slightly risqué – asides to the audience; highlights of his performances included conversations with various animal characters, notably the Cow in *JACK AND THE BEANSTALK*.

Hudd, Roy (1936–) English actor, who has enjoyed a long career in pantomime in a variety of roles. He first appeared in a double comedy act in 1957 and subsequently established himself as a popular performer of music hall, light comedy, and other entertainments both in the theatre and on television and radio. He made his first appearance in pantomime in 1959 (at the Empire Theatre, Leeds) and has since earned a reputation as one of the most reliable and much-loved performers of such roles as IDLE JACK. As well as acting in pantomime, he has also directed his own pantomime scripts – among them, *BABES IN THE WOOD* (1993).

Humpty-Dumpty A nursery rhyme that has been adapted as a pantomime on many occasions since the early 19th century. Early pantomime versions of the story included a production staged at SADLER'S WELLS in 1831, scenes from which included one lampooning the electoral abuses in the news that year. The 1868 production of the story at the LYCEUM THEATRE was notable for the fact that it featured the first appearance of the celebrated VOKES FAMILY. That same year the pantomime was staged with such success by GEORGE L. FOX in the USA that subsequently all US pantomimes were popularly known as 'Humpty-Dumpties' for many years.

The spectacular DRURY LANE version of 1891 starred MARIE LLOYD as Princess Allfair, DAN LENO as the Queen of Hearts, GEORGE LUPINO as Twirley Whirley, and LITTLE TICH in the title role. A second distinguished production at the Lane in 1903 (with a script by J. HICKORY WOOD) saw the last appearances in pantomime of both Leno and HERBERT CAMPBELL, who died during the course of 1904.

Although the story is irregularly given on the contemporary stage it remained one of the most popular pantomimes until at least the 1950s; in 1943 a version staged at the Coliseum starring PAT KIRKWOOD attracted audiences of 122,000 in the first month of its run. Another in 1945, staged by Francis Laidler at the Grand Theatre, Leeds, ran for a remarkable five months. Recent reworkings of the story include versions by JOHN MORLEY, John Crocker and Eric Gilder, and Norman Robbins. Unusual productions have included one which featured a fully mechanised version of the children's character Orville the Duck.

Story Pantomime versions of the original story necessarily embellish the original rhyme with extra details and characters (usually taken from other well-known nursery rhymes such as that of Old King Cole). At some point, however, the central event of Humpty-Dumpty – an animated egg – falling off a wall and subsequently being tended to by "all the king's horses and all the king's men" is included, if only briefly.

Origins The nursery rhyme that forms the basis of the pantomime is of obscure origins and no records exist of it before the early 19th century. One theory has it that Humpty-Dumpty himself was originally meant to represent Richard III; others have suggested that the original rhyme was made up as a riddle, the answer to which was 'an egg'. In the late 17th century a 'Humpty Dumpty' was an ale and brandy punch, while a few decades later the phrase was being used as an insulting description of a short or unattractive person. Most enterprising of all is the theory that links the name Humpty-Dumpty to a siege tower or cannon used in the siege of Gloucester in 1643 (as in Richard Rodney Bennett's opera *All the King's Men*); this link dates, however, only to 1956. It is unclear how the name Humpty-Dumpty first became linked to an egg, but when Lewis Carroll depicted the character as an egg in *Through the Looking-Glass* he was clearly drawing on a well-established tradition. Similar egg characters featured in the folklore of Denmark, Finland, and Germany in the 19th century.

hunting scene Traditional opening scene in *CINDERELLA*, in which PRINCE CHARMING appears for the first time while out hunting with the royal entourage. This royal scene has its roots in the fairytales of CHARLES PERRAULT, who had close links with the court of the French king Louis XV through his brother, who was the king's chief architect. Louis was an enthusiastic huntsman and enjoyed the chase virtually every day of the week. Although many other aspects of the story have altered over the years this scene has remained ever since – although in recent years the prince's interest in bloodsports has led to Cinders herself being presented on occasion as an anti-hunting lobbyist who persuades the prince into letting the fox go.

I

ice The performance of pantomimes on ice is a postwar phenomenon that has enjoyed some popularity. Such ice shows depend upon the element of visual spectacle and first captured the headlines back in the 1930s, when huge ice spectaculars were staged with massive casts at such venues as the COLISEUM. Later similar shows were staged at the vast Wembley Empire Pool (for example, *Dick Whittington on Ice* in 1968) and Olympia and elsewhere. The need for large audiences to fill such venues, however, has been a factor against regular revivals of such ice spectaculars. Few performers relish the thought of such shows, as the huge spaces involved and awkward acoustics make communication with the audience difficult; the Carioli brothers can be counted among the few who – through the use of comic exploding cars and other spectacular visual gags – have successfully overcome these formidable obstacles.

Idle Jack The hero's best friend and sidekick in *DICK WHITTINGTON AND HIS CAT*. An equivalent of WISHEE-WASHEE in *ALADDIN* and Tinbad the Tailor in *SINBAD THE SAILOR*, Idle Jack has long been the province of the male comedian, being played over the years by such notable figures as DAN LENO and in more recent times by such comedians as Jimmy Tarbuck, Ken Dodd, FRANKIE HOWERD, and Max Boyce.

Immortals The supernatural characters of the pantomime. In the early days these included the gods, goddesses, nymphs, and sprites who governed the action of the pantomime OPENING and oversaw the changeover to the HARLEQUINADE that took place in the TRANSFORMATION SCENE (*see* BENEVOLENT AGENT). In the modern pantomime the descendants of these figures include the FAIRIES, witches, and sorcerers who influence the plot with their powers of magic. By convention such characters always spoke in rhymed couplets – and continued to do so after the rest of the cast had adopted prose in the late 19th century. Even now, many current scripts have supernatural characters delivering some, if not all, of their lines in verse. *See also* ENTRANCES.

impresario A promoter of theatrical productions, who organises the financial backing and undertakes many of the managerial tasks that need to be fulfilled. Famous impresarios connected with the pantomime include the many noted theatre managers who helped to shape the development of the genre in the 18th and 19th centuries. In the 20th century the golden age of these 'Pantomime Kings' was between the 1920s and the 1960s, when the most celebrated included such names as JULIAN WYLIE, Francis Laidler, Tom Arnold and EMILE AND PRINCE LITTLER, all of whom would be involved in as many as a dozen or more productions each season. Notable organisations connected with the performance of pantomime throughout the UK in the 20th century have included Howard and Wyndham and, more recently, Triumph Productions and Paul Elliott.

improvisation The performance of a play or other theatrical production without the use of a written script. Improvisation was a key feature of the *COMMEDIA DELL'ARTE*, in which the actors had only a rough scenario (a skeleton plot) and their own funds of gags and bits of 'business' to rely upon. Such skills were also invaluable in the English harlequinade although they decreased in importance with the increased use of dialogue in the early 19th century. Subsequently DAN LENO was one of the very few performers who was allowed to improvise his own material during performance. The nature of SLAPSTICK comedy means that there remains some good scope for off-the-cuff topical remarks and actions by the stars in the modern pantomime, though the rest of the cast stick to their scripts. Similar techniques were employed in performances of the English MYSTERY PLAYS.

Irving, Sir Henry (John Henry Brodribb; 1838–1905) English actor-manager, who remains one of the most revered actors ever to have appeared on the English stage. Celebrated for his unsurpassed performances in such roles as Mathias in *The Bells* and in some of the most demanding roles in Shakespeare, he became the first theatrical knight and was finally honoured with burial in Westminster Abbey, his reputation secure for all time. Irving is not usually recalled for his interest in the pantomime, yet accounts exist of his appearances in at least three pantomimes staged in Edinburgh at a relatively early stage in his career. According to these, he played the Demon (suitably enough) in *PUSS IN BOOTS*, the WOLF in *LITTLE BO-PEEP*, and – most remarkably of all – the role of COOK in *THE SLEEPING BEAUTY*.

Italian Night Scenes A form of dance entertainment that became popular as AFTERPIECES at the leading London theatres in the early 18th century, through which the conventions of the *COMMEDIA DELL'ARTE* were transmitted to the English stage (*see* HARLEQUINADE).

The Italian Night Scenes consisted of slapstick comedies in which the characters told their story exclusively through mime-dance rather than dialogue. The characters themselves were taken from the French version of the *commedia dell'arte* (*see* COMÉDIE-ITALIENNE) although the setting in which they appeared – usually a tavern or fair – was English. Scenery was elaborate and particular emphasis was placed on special effects. Plots were simple: typically a comical misunderstanding between the characters would lead to a slapstick brawl. The accent was firmly on knockabout farce and dance, which was then enjoying a vogue in London society.

Visiting performers from France had presented such **ballets-pantomimes** in London over a period of several years, among them the popular Sieurs Alard who appeared at DRURY LANE at the invitation of CHRISTOPHER RICH, but it was some time before such prestigious figures as JOHN WEAVER could be persuaded to countenance such performances, which many considered crude and beneath contempt. The Italian Night Scenes did, however, draw large audiences, who delighted in the clowning of HARLEQUIN and his confederates and from 1715 they were a regular feature of the bill at the LINCOLN'S INN FIELDS THEATRE, obliging other theatres to follow suit.

Weaver himself eventually incorporated characters from the Italian Night Scenes in his productions for the first time in *The Tavern Bilkers* (which is thought to have been first performed some time after 1702) and soon these redefined Italian Night Scenes were being called by the title he had revived himself from Classical theatre – pantomime.

J

Jack The hero of *JACK AND THE BEANSTALK* and *JACK THE GIANT-KILLER*. Jack is the atypical folkloric hero – lazy, unscrupulous, sharp-witted, and essentially warm-hearted. Known in the folklore of other cultures under such names as Juan, Jean, and Hans, Jack is one of the most memorable hero characters of the pantomime, providing a perfect foil to the DAME (who is often identified as his mother). He is thought to have been derived from a hero of Cornish legend or alternatively from Coroneus, the Trojan who accompanied Brutus to England. Research has also linked the Jack of English legend to an East Anglian peasant who bravely fought a seven-foot Viking in pre-Conquest times. Performers of the role, which is usually treated as a part for a female PRINCIPAL BOY, have included Marie Burke, CILLA BLACK, and Helen Shapiro. The first woman to appear in the role (and indeed the first female to take the part of principal boy who can be identified with any certainty) was ELIZA POVEY, who interpreted it in a version of the story seen at DRURY LANE in 1819.

Jack and Jill Nursery rhyme that was formerly much used as a basis for pantomime plots. Early pantomime productions included one staged at the LYCEUM THEATRE back in 1812, with such additional characters as 'Watty Wildgoose' (who was transformed into the DANDY LOVER in the harlequinade). E. L. BLANCHARD wrote a version in 1854 and the composer Richard Wagner was enthusiastic about a production of the story he saw at the ADELPHI THEATRE in 1855. EMILE LITTLER enjoyed considerable success with the tale in a pantomime he toured widely in the 1940s and 1950s.

Story The original nursery rhyme about Jack and Jill may have had only one verse but by the early 19th century it had grown to 15 stanzas, in the course of which the pair go through a number of adventures besides the best known episode in which they tumble down a hill while fetching a pail of water. Conveniently for pantomimists, the nursery rhyme includes a 'Dame Gill', who scolds them for their misdeeds. Pantomime adaptations of the tale were very loose and all manner of subplots were added to bring in the usual pantomime characters. In the version that Wagner saw, for instance, the nursery rhyme about Jack and Jill was combined with the stories of the Goose that laid the golden eggs, Little Red Riding Hood, and Cinderella among other tales.

Origins The earliest printed versions of the nursery rhyme date from the 18th century, but it is thought possible that it is somewhat older and, according to some folklorists, may recall some obscure ritual ceremony or myth. The rhyme was often printed in the CHAPBOOKS of the 18th and 19th centuries.

Jack and the Beanstalk Perennially popular tale that has provided some of the best parts and most dramatic spectacles ever seen in the English pantomime tradition. The story was first seen as a pantomime in 1819, at DRURY LANE, as *Jack and the Beanstalk; or, Harlequin and the Ogre* by CHARLES DIBDIN the younger; subsequent productions of note included E. L. BLANCHARD's Drury Lane version of 1859, which began imaginatively high up in the sky above Earth, the SURREY THEATRE production of 1886 in which DAN LENO made his pantomime debut, and a further Drury Lane production in 1899, which created a sensation with its climactic scene in which the British Army (played by children in full uniform) marched out of the dead giant's pockets in tribute to the nation's forces then engaged in the Boer War in south Africa. This last version culminated in a spectacular pageant of Shakespearean heroines (who emerged from huge books in the giant's library) and views depicting the gods and goddesses on Olympus.

The pantomime remains one of the most regularly performed stories in the modern tradition. Among the most effective scenes in the story are the early episodes in which Jack parts with his mother's cow (which when played by such performers as DOROTHY WARD has been known to reduce audiences to tears) and the climactic felling of the BEANSTALK. Among the many modern retellings of the story are versions by such noted pantomime writers as Ronald Parr, David Cregan, John Crocker and Eric Gilder, Verne Morgan, and JOHN MORLEY.

Story JACK is the lazy son of a poor widow (the DAME role), who is obliged to send Jack to market with their only cow (usually called Daisy) in order to raise a little money. On the way to market Jack, seeing his opportunity to save himself a lengthy journey, exchanges the cow with a stranger for a handful of BEANS and returns home. His mother is furious and throws the beans out of the window. Next day Jack discovers that the beans have sprouted into a huge beanstalk that reaches up to the clouds. Jack climbs the beanstalk and arrives at the giant BLUNDERBORE's castle. (In some early versions of the tale when Jack reaches the top of the beanstalk he meets a fairy, who appoints him avenger of all the victims the giant has killed, thus justifying Jack's theft of the giant's treasures).

The cannibal giant thinks he smells Jack's presence (*see* FEE-FI-FO-FUM) but the giant's wife conceals Jack from him and prepares a gargantuan supper. The giant falls asleep after the meal and Jack steals the giant's little red hen that lays golden eggs before returning home. The following day Jack climbs back up the beanstalk and this time steals the giant's bags of gold before leaving. On the third day he snatches the giant's magic singing harp, but the harp cries out and the giant wakes. Jack climbs down the beanstalk with the giant in hot pursuit and at the bottom chops the beanstalk down so that the giant falls to his death, leaving Jack and his mother to live happily ever after.

Modern versions of the story often embellish the basic plot with such additional characters as a wicked witch as well as the giant's henchman Fleshcreep and the Vegetable Fairy (standard figures introduced by John Morley).

Origins The basic plot of the pantomime was taken from the well-known English fairytale, which is one of the so-called 'Jack' cycle of stories of English and Irish origins and dates at least from the early 18th century (one manuscript version appeared in 1807). Similar tales can be found in the mythologies of other European countries, although the beanstalk element is not common to all of them. In one of the versions told in the USA, Jack steals a gun, a knife, and a coverlet from the giant.

Jack the Giant Killer Well-known fairytale that was formerly frequently used as a basis for pantomime plots. The story was first adapted for the stage by DAVID GARRICK, who presented it in the form of a Christmas play in 1773. Pantomime adaptations of the tale date back to the early 19th century, with, for instance, the LYCEUM THEATRE staging a version of it in 1809. It has, however, been dropped from the list of tales that are regularly revived for the modern pantomime (partly because of its similarity to the better-known *JACK AND THE BEANSTALK*).

Story JACK, the lazy son of a Cornish farmer, pits himself against a local giant named Cormoran, wishing to seize the ogre's vast treasure. He sets about the task with great ingenuity, trapping him in a pit he has dug. He is hailed as 'Jack the Giant Killer' and is asked by King Arthur to undertake further giant-killing deeds. The giant BLUNDERBORE, however, succeeds in capturing Jack and locks him up in a cell overlooking a courtyard. When Jack hears Blunderbore talking beneath his window (sometimes to himself as Blunderbore has two heads in some versions) he lets down a rope and succeeds in strangling the giant (or giants).

Another giant invites him to stay the night in his castle but attempts to kill his guest as he lies sleeping. Jack, however, has placed a log in the bed and at breakfast complains only of flea-bites. He challenges the giant to an eating contest, stuffing great mounds of porridge into a bag concealed in his shirt; he then relieves the pressure by slitting the bag open. The giant does the same and kills himself. His severest test comes against a giant who owns a cloak of invisibility, a cap of wisdom, an irresistible sword, and some SEVEN-LEAGUE BOOTS. Jack pretends to warn the giant of an approaching army and receives in return the various magic talismans. Subsequently he uses the seven-league boots and other magical objects to defeat the remaining giants in the land before returning home a hero and being made a knight of the Round Table.

Origins The pantomime plot draws on that of the famous English fairytale, one of a series revolving around the mythical Jack. Some of the giant-killing episodes have parallels in the mythology of Scandinavia and other cultures and it is thought probable that this familiar compilation of them was put together in the late 17th century. It was a favourite story in the CHAPBOOKS of the 18th and 19th centuries.

Jackley, George (1885–1950) English comedian, who was especially renowned for his performances as DAME and in other comic roles at such leading pantomime venues as the LYCEUM THEATRE. He was the leading comic star to appear under the management of the MELVILLE BROTHERS at the theatre in the interwar years and numbered among his many successes such parts as Will Atkins in ROBINSON CRUSOE, IDLE JACK, and the BARON. His son **Nat Jackley** was also highly acclaimed as dame.

Jefferini (Jeffreys; fl. 1840s) English comedian, also owner of a well-known gambling den, who won acclaim in the role of CLOWN in the 1840s. He learnt the business of playing Clown as a pupil of TOM MATTHEWS and made the most of his height (although his long legs added extra hazard to the daring leaps he was required to execute and he suffered greatly from the injuries he received in the course of his career). He specialised in comic monologues and jokes, as a result of which he was often described as a 'noisy' Clown. Among many other productions, he appeared as Clown in *Harlequin King Alfred the Great* (1846), the first pantomime by E. L. BLANCHARD.

Jim Crow Fictional character created by the US vaudeville entertainer Thomas Dartmouth Rice (1808–60), who became a popular figure in English pantomime in the early 19th century. Jim Crow, as presented by Rice in black make-up, was an archetypal 'yankee niggar' who drew huge crowds nightly to the ADELPHI and SURREY theatres in London. Such was the popularity of Jim Crow's comic patter and singing that numerous pantomime managers inserted imitation Jim Crows in their productions for nearly half a century after Rice's departure for the USA in 1836. Typical offerings featuring the character included the Adelphi's *Cowardy, Cowardy, Custard; or, Harlequin Jim Crow and the Magic Mustard Pot* (1836).

jinni *See* GENIE.

Joey The traditional name of all clowns, in honour of JOSEPH GRIMALDI, who is acknowledged to have been the greatest performer ever to play the role of CLOWN. The comic business of the pantomime is sometimes referred to as 'Joey-Joey' in his memory.

jokes Many of the jokes heard in the modern pantomime have been included in scripts for years. Since dialogue became acceptable in the 18th century, pantomimes have been recognised as repositories of the nation's favourite quips.

The oldest datable joke refers to the opening of the Great Exhibition at the Crystal Palace in 1851 and is still found in most modern versions of *CINDERELLA*: as the GLASS SLIPPER is brought on one of the UGLY SISTERS remarks "I will now get my foot into the crystal slipper", to which the other retorts "You couldn't get your foot into the Crystal Palace".

There are many examples of these so-called 'good-bad' jokes that audiences everywhere love to scorn. Another of the best known exchanges from *Cinderella* runs: "My teeth are like stars" to which comes the reply "Yes, they come out at night". Another, from *SINBAD THE SAILOR* goes: "The Mosque is on fire" – to which comes the instant response "Holy Smoke!" Other well-established chestnuts include the King's (or Queen's) reaction on learning that they have just been asleep for a hundred years (in *THE SLEEPING BEAUTY*): "In that case I must go and put the cat out." Many jokes are interchangeable and have appeared at one time or another in all the best known stories (as is the case with the question and answer routine "Why don't you grow up, stupid?" – "I have grown up stupid"). Countless Buttons have presented the love of their life with a piece of string to which is attached a bunch of carrots (with the explanation that it is an 'eighteen-carrot' necklace). Many a dame, on being told to say 'Your Grace' on being introduced to a handsome emperor or king, has responded with "For what I am about to receive may the Lord make me truly thankful".

Such writers as E. L. BLANCHARD delighted in inventing the most excruciatingly corny witticisms and in Blanchard's case even incorporating them in playbills and programmes. In the programme for his *JACK AND THE BEANSTALK*, for instance, the actors playing the various months of the year were listed as "Messrs Slippy, Drippy, Nippy, Showery, Flowery, Bowery, Hoppy, Croppy, Poppy, Wheezy, Sneezy, and Freezy". Other writers have also made jokes out of their characters' names; recent examples of joke names include the oriental Rhum Baba, the bailiffs Sage and Onions, and the harem keeper Tuffazell. In some versions of *Cinderella* the Ugly Sisters have a horse called 'Miniature' ("One miniature on, next miniature you're off).

Jokes in the contemporary pantomime are generally fairly innocuous, but there was a period in the 1960s and 1970s when a certain amount of 'blue' material was used (particularly in that part of a RUN after the school holidays were over and there were fewer youngsters in the audience). This tendency to include more risqué material backfired, however, and rather than luring larger audiences it offended many and threatened theatre profits; as a result such material was expunged and the pantomime's reputation for wholesome family entertainment was gradually restored. *See also* PUNS.

juvenile drama *See* TOY THEATRE.

K

Kasrac *See* ABANAZAR; *ALADDIN AND HIS WONDERFUL LAMP.*

Kean, Edmund (*c.* 1789–1833) English actor, who was the most admired tragedian of his time, winning particular fame in the great tragic roles of Shakespeare. Kean is usually remembered for his sensational success playing such villainous parts as Richard III, Shylock, and Macbeth, but at an early stage in his career also attracted attention playing the role of HARLEQUIN in the pantomime. While still a child he appeared as a demon in pantomime at DRURY LANE; subsequently, as a relatively unknown strolling player he played Harlequin in *MOTHER GOOSE* to packed houses around the country.

Keeley, Mary Ann (Mary Ann Goward; 1806–99) English actress and theatre manager, who was one of the most popular performers of burlesque (among other productions) at the LYCEUM THEATRE, the HAYMARKET THEATRE, COVENT GARDEN, the ADELPHI THEATRE, and the OLYMPIC THEATRE.

She made her debut at the Lyceum and later excelled under MADAME VESTRIS at the Olympic, where she often appeared alongside her husband, **Robert Keeley** (1793–1869). Together the Keeleys were managers of the Lyceum from 1844 until 1847, in which role they oversaw the production of numerous successful burlesques and similar entertainments.

Noted members of the company they formed at the Lyceum included the beautiful actress Louisa Fairbrother, one of the most admired early female performers of the role of PRINCIPAL BOY, and the midget General Tom Thumb. Successful works that were presented under the Keeley management included burlesques by J. R. PLANCHÉ, Charles Dance, Albert Smith, and MARK LEMON.

King, Hetty (1883–1972) English actress, who was much admired in the role of PRINCIPAL BOY. She began as an established star of the MUSIC HALL, specialising in male impersonation; subsequently she applied her skills in this regard to such pantomime roles as ALADDIN, in which part many considered her unsurpassed. Highlights of her act included her song 'All the Nice Girls Love a Sailor'.

King Rat *See DICK WHITTINGTON AND HIS CAT.*

Kirkwood, Pat (1921–) English actress, who emerged as a star of variety and pantomime in the 1940s. She made her debut as a stage entertainer at an early age and established herself as a popular PRINCIPAL BOY in the pantomime in the late 1930s. Her success in *HUMPTY-DUMPTY* at the Coliseum in 1943 brought her to the attention of US cinema magnates and for several years afterwards she concentrated upon her film career in Hollywood (her films included *After the Ball* (1957), in which she starred in the life story of VESTA TILLEY). Subseqently she returned to the stage and appeared in further pantomime roles.

kiss The most famous kiss in pantomime is undoubtedly that bestowed upon the sleeping princess in *THE SLEEPING BEAUTY*. In fact, this kiss was an invention of the pantomime. In CHARLES PERRAULT's original story the princess conveniently wakes up as the prince kneels beside her bed; however, in an earlier Italian variant of the tale she only wakes as she gives birth to twins nine months after she has been raped while asleep by the king who discovers her. Elsewhere, Snow White is similarly woken by a kiss from an adoring prince and in the *FROG PRINCE* the spell under which the prince has become a frog is broken with a kiss.

L

Lacy, George (1904–) English comedian, who was widely considered the best performer to succeed DAN LENO in the role of DAME. Skilled as a dancer and a master of comedy, he made his stage debut at the age of 12 and first played a dame while only 24 years old, making him one of the youngest men ever to appear in the part on the professional stage (he was still appearing in the part in the 1980s). He was most popular in the role of MOTHER GOOSE, which he first performed in 1930 (in Leeds) and once played for 11 years in succession. Audiences applauded his skills at repartee and his hugely funny and never offensive imitation of feminine airs and graces. He is credited with being the first dame to specialise in outrageously extravagant costumes, wearing a new outfit for virtually every scene; among the most remarkable of these was one decorated as a snooker table, complete with cues, balls, and pockets.

lamp *See ALADDIN AND HIS WONDERFUL LAMP.*

Lane, Lupino (Henry George Lupino; 1892–1959) English comedian and singer, who was one of the famous LUPINO FAMILY connected with the pantomime for 200 years. He took his stage name from that of his great-aunt Sara Lane, who held the lease of the BRITANNIA THEATRE, Hoxton, and began his career as a MUSIC HALL comedian. He made regular appearances in pantomime as well as in musical comedy, most notably in *Me and My Girl* (1937), in which he created the 'Lambeth Walk'.

Lane, Sam (1804–71) English theatre manager, who built the BRITANNIA THEATRE in Hoxton, London, and made it one of the most celebrated pantomime venues in the city. As well as his pantomimes, which were renowned for their originality, he also staged melodramas and comedies. After his death the theatre passed to his widow, **Sara Lane** (1823–99), who carried on the tradition and also starred as PRINCIPAL BOY in the pantomimes herself from 1856 to 1878, after which she continued to appear in other roles. She was a hugely popular figure and was widely known by her nickname 'the Queen of Hoxton'.

La Rue, Danny (Daniel Patrick Carroll; 1928–) English female impersonator, born in Ireland, who has played some of the most glamorous DAMES seen in pantomime since World War II. He established himself as perhaps the best known female impersonator in the country through his performances in revue, cabaret, and on television back in the 1960s and has continued to repeat his highly polished routines in pantomime, always depicting the dame as an essentially glamorous role (somewhat against the time-honoured tradition of very obviously masculine dames). The pantomimes in which he has appeared have ranged from *Queen Passionella and the Sleeping Beauty* (1968) to *ALADDIN AND HIS WONDERFUL LAMP* (1992).

Lauder, Sir Harry (Hugh MacLennan; 1870–1950) Scottish singer and comedian, who began his working life as a coalminer before becoming a MUSIC HALL star overnight in 1900 when he made his debut at Gatti's and subsequently winning acclaim as a popular performer in pantomime. Dressed in a kilt and carrying a distinctive knobbly walking stick, he was hugely famous for his rendition of such songs as 'Roamin' in the Gloamin' ' and 'Keep Right on to the End of the Road'; he first sang another favourite, 'I Love a Lassie', in pantomime in Glasgow in 1905. His most successful pantomime roles included that of BUTTONS, in which he was reckoned one of the most effective of his time.

laundry scene The traditional CHASE SCENE in *ALADDIN*, in which ALADDIN himself is pursued through his mother's laundry by the two CHINESE POLICEMEN. The scene, which evolved largely in the 1890s, became a stock feature of *Aladdin* and commonly features the spectacular use of TRAPS let into the scenery, through which the hero, the policemen, and sometimes WIDOW TWANKEY herself propel themselves – to the endless delight of children in the audience.

Lauri, Charles (fl. 1890s) English actor, who was considered second only to the great GEORGE CONQUEST as a performer of SKIN PARTS. The son of the celebrated CLOWN Charles Lauri (1833–89), he played his first skin part at the age of six, when he appeared in pantomime in Birmingham as a cat. Subsequently he won acclaim in a diverse range of roles, which included bears, wolves, ostriches, kangaroos, frogs, and an ibis (a role in which he first 'flew' in 1891) as well as the more usual animal characters.

He was particularly popular in the role of the CAT in *CINDERELLA*, to the extent that in the 1893–94 version of the story staged at the LYCEUM THEATRE the Cat took the place of BUTTONS. The highlight of his performance in the role was his customary (and highly perilous) stroll round the dress circle balcony during the interval, when he would shake hands with many children in the audience.

His interpretation as the dying dog Tatters in a version of *BABES IN THE WOOD* entitled *Santa Claus* at the Lyceum in 1894 was so heart-rending that critics demanded that the character should be spared (as indeed he was in subsequent performances).

lazzi A humorous comment or bit of comic 'business' that was interpolated into the main action at the will of performers in the *COMMEDIA DELL'ARTE*. The ability to enliven a performance by such improvised embellishments was highly prized and was an essential feature of the Italian tradition from which the harlequinade ultimately developed. Examples of famous *lazzi* that became traditional in the harlequinade included Harlequin trying to catch an imaginary fly. Others ranged from obscene gestures to tumbles and mock fights. *See also* BURLA; IMPROVISATION.

Lee, (Richard) Nelson (1806–72) English author and theatre manager, who was one of E. L. BLANCHARD'S leading rivals as a writer of pantomimes in the mid-19th century. Lee was born at Kew, acquiring the name Nelson in honour of the great admiral whose magnificent funeral was in preparation at the time of his birth (Lee's father, a naval officer, was among those involved in the ceremony).

He made his theatrical debut as a juggler and magician, later touring widely with Richardson's Show. This enterprise included pantomime in its repertory as well as melodrama and music (all often combined in one show). Lee accumulated much experience as an actor with the company, playing all of the harlequinade roles (with the single exception of Columbine) and writing many of the troupe's pantomimes himself.

He eventually moved into management at a series of London theatres, initially at the SURREY THEATRE, where several of his pantomimes were staged. He transferred to the ADELPHI THEATRE in 1834 and subsequently to Richardson's Travelling Theatre, SADLER'S WELLS, the Marylebone Theatre, the STANDARD THEATRE, the City of London Theatre, where he remained for several years, and Crystal Palace.

Throughout his career he consolidated his reputation as a writer of pantomimes with an elevated moral and literary tone and by the time of his death could claim the authorship of over 200 such works. Among the most successful of these were such pieces as *The Forty Thieves; or, Harlequin Ali Baba and the Robbers' Cave*, *Red Rufus; or, Harlequin Fact, Fiction, and Fancy*, and *Romeo and Juliet; or, Harlequin Queen Mab and the World of Dreams*, in which Lee burlesqued Shakespeare's plot.

Lemon, Mark (1809–70) English pantomime writer and journalist, whose pantomimes were among the most successful presented on the Victorian stage. The first editor of *Punch*, he was a close friend of the novelist and pantomime enthusiast CHARLES DICKENS and appeared in the latter's amateur (but excellent) theatrical productions. His fairytales included *The Three Sisters* (1868) and *Tinikin's Transformations* (1869).

Leno, Dan (George Galvin; 1860–1904) English comedian and singer, who became the most celebrated of all performers to play the central role of the DAME in English pantomime.

Leno (who took his stage name from that of his stepfather) was born in London, the son of two minor MUSIC HALL performers, and began his extraordinary career at the age of four, billed as 'Little George, the Infant Wonder, Contortionist and Posturer'. An accident led to him switching from tumbling to dancing and the singing of comic songs and in 1880 he won the title of Clog-Dancing Champion of the World in a competition in Leeds. Among early admirers was CHARLES DICKENS, who is supposed to have seen him on tour in Belfast at the age of nine and speculated there and then that he had a great future ahead of him.

Back in London, Leno rapidly built up a reputation as one of the most popular entertainers in the halls with an act based on comic songs and monologues perfectly suited to his wistful yet irrepressibly mischievous air. Audiences flocked to marvel at his hilarious character studies, of which the most celebrated included a recruiting sergeant, a shopwalker, a fireman, a railway guard, and the immortal Mrs. Kelly (who shared several traits in common with the dames Leno was later to develop).

It was GEORGE CONQUEST who heard Leno singing 'Fetching in the Milk for the Twins' and went on to sign him to appear (as Dame Durden in *Jack and the Beanstalk*) at the Surrey Theatre for the 1886–87 season. Leno was so successful in this pantomime and the following year as Tinpanz the Tailor in *Sinbad the Sailor* that Augustus Harris decided to engage him to appear at Drury Lane.

Leno first appeared in pantomime at the Lane in 1888 playing the wicked aunt in *Babes in the Wood*, after which he appeared there every Christmas until his death 16 years later. He won particular acclaim in such roles as Mother Goose (specially rewritten for him by J. Hickory Wood), Widow Twankey, Sister Anne in *Bluebeard*, the Baroness, and Dame Trot. With the assistance of first Harris and then his successor Arthur Collins, he effectively created the modern pantomime dame familiar to contemporary audiences, transforming her into a fully-developed realistic comic personality and taking the greatest care over his characterisation so that each new dame took on her own individual personality.

His other roles included Daddy Thumb in *Little Bo-Peep* (1892), in a cast including Marie Lloyd as Little Red Riding-Hood, Idle Jack in *Dick Whittington*, Mr. Lombard Streete in *Beauty and the Beast*, Reggie (one of the babes) in *The Babes in the Wood*, Abdallah in *The Forty Thieves*, and Queen Ravia in *The Sleeping Beauty and the Beast* (1900).

In some of his best performances he formed a brilliant partnership with the oversized comedian Herbert Campbell, who was perfectly suited as a foil to Leno's small frame and quick wit. Highlights of his performances in the pantomime included his singing of various inventive comic songs (among which was 'Young men taken in and done for').

He was idolised by London audiences and was even summoned to Sandringham to perform before Edward VII in 1901, thus acquiring the nickname 'The King's Jester'; he also performed his music hall act on tour in New York in 1897. The pressures of fame took their toll, however, and in 1903 Leno suffered a nervous breakdown. He died insane in 1904, just months after his final appearance in *Humpty-Dumpty* (Campbell having died just three months before). Enormous crowds attended Leno's funeral and he is still considered, with Joseph Grimaldi, the finest of all pantomime performers.

Leslie, Fanny (1857–1935) English actress, who was one of the most popular principal boys of the late Victorian pantomime. She began her career as a dancer at the Metropolitan, Edgware Road and subsequently enjoyed great success both in burlesque and as principal boy under the management of Augustus Harris at Drury Lane, where she appeared alongside such acclaimed performers as Dan Leno and Herbert Campbell. Her best-known songs included 'Where the Ocean Meets the Sky' and 'Pretty Polly on a Tin Gee-Gee'.

Licensing Act (1737) The act of parliament that reserved for the two Patent Theatres (Covent Garden and Drury Lane and subsequently in the summer months only, the Haymarket) the exclusive right to stage spoken drama in London. The Lyceum Theatre was permitted to present English opera and musical productions, while the Adelphi Theatre and the Olympic Theatre were allowed to stage burlettas alone; all the remaining theatres in London were restricted to 'music and dancing', which as the years passed came to include pantomime and ballet among other entertainments.

One of the effects of the act was to promote productions of pantomime, which was then silent, at various theatres both inside and outside London. Over the next few years producers of such entertainments proved themselves ingenious in their attempts to get round the restrictions of the act by disguising performances of spoken drama as musical plays etc. Their efforts were, however, frequently obstructed by the stringent enforcement of the Act by the Examiner of Plays, to whom all plays had to be submitted and by whom they must be approved before they could be performed.

The act was finally replaced in 1843 by the more liberal **Theatre Regulation Act**, which allowed all theatres to stage any type of entertainment, though from 1851 subject to approval of the script by the Examiner of Plays at the Lord Chamberlain's office. As a result many music halls became full-scale theatres and many new venues where pantomimes could be performed were opened.

lighting Illumination of the stage and auditorium was largely by candles, knots of burning tarred rope, and oil lamps before the introduction of gas lighting in the 19th century (first seen at the LYCEUM THEATRE in 1817). Nonetheless, despite the restrictions such means of lighting imposed, theatrical productions of the 18th century witnessed significant advances in the theory of stage lighting and the pantomime in particular was notable for experimentation with various light effects.

One of the most influential early innovators in the use of lighting for the pantomime was the scenic artist PHILIPPE JACQUES DE LOUTHERBOURG, who worked on the pantomimes staged by DAVID GARRICK at DRURY LANE in the 1770s. He sought a new realism in his scenic designs and experimented with coloured lighting, placing squares of dyed silk in front of the lamps to colour the beam. He also explored the possibility of moving lighting effects, startling audiences with panoramas of scudding clouds achieved with the use of pivoted silk screens.

By the early 19th century lighting techniques were fairly sophisticated and were designed in conjunction with the scenery to achieve the maximum possible effect – although it was not until later in the century that it became the custom for lighting in the auditorium to be dimmed during a performance (an innovation introduced by SIR HENRY IRVING and his lighting technician Bram Stoker, who is better known as the author of *Dracula*).

The arrival of gas and subsequently electricity revolutionised stage lighting and made possible an even wider variety of dramatic effects. Gas lighting was wonderfully atmospheric, revealing the scenery in a misty glow and Irving for one resisted the inevitable changeover to electricity (which had the advantage of being more controllable and much less dangerous). More recently the armoury of the lighting technician has been further improved with the addition of ultraviolet (often used to pick out the luminous costumes of performers playing ghosts and skeletons) and even laser technology. The complex lighting rig of the contemporary theatre is usually computerised and thus far more easily adjusted than it was in previous centuries. *See also* LIMELIGHT; STROBE.

limelight A form of theatre lighting in which the light generated by a piece of heated lime was directed as a beam at the stage. Developed in the early 19th century, limelight was first seen on the English stage in 1826, when Charles Macready experimented with it in his production of the pantomime *Peeping Tom of Coventry* at COVENT GARDEN. It proved a distinct advance on earlier more primitive forms of lighting and provided a much more brilliant beam that had been possible previously. The distinctive greenish glow of the light cast did, however, mean that a green costume rendered the wearer almost invisible.

Lincoln's Inn Fields Theatre A former theatre in Portugal Street, London, which has a unique position in British theatre history as the birthplace of the pantomime, for it was here that JOHN RICH staged the first such entertainments in the early 18th century.

Opened in 1656 as Lisle's tennis court, the building was turned into a theatre in 1661 by Sir William Davenant, who installed London's first PROSCENIUM ARCH there. Classic plays by such authors as John Dryden and William Shakespeare were presented there until 1671, when the resident company left and Thomas Killigrew took over. In 1675 the building again became a tennis court, reopening as a theatre in 1695 to house a company including such great names as Anne Bracegirdle and Thomas Betterton.

CHRISTOPHER RICH began the restoration of the then deserted theatre after arriving in 1714; when he died shortly afterwards (little lamented on account of his treacherous and penny-pinching ways) his sons John and Christopher Rich completed the work but were faced with a monumental struggle to restore the theatre's fortunes. Appearances by John Rich in serious drama were not a success and gossip had it that members of the theatre's company had been arrested for debt and removed from the stage in mid performance.

Salvation came through Rich's decision to pander to the contemporary taste for all things Italian (catered for at Drury Lane by masques and dances on Roman mythological themes) by presenting performances of ITALIAN NIGHT SCENES with increasing regularity, with great success. Rich himself found his true niche as a performer in the role of HARLEQUIN and began a career that was to make his theatre the best-attended venue in London. It was one of these productions that was first billed as a 'pantomime' in 1717.

Subsequent entertainments included the pantomime *The Magician; or, Harlequin a Director* (1721), among many others, as well as plays by George Farquhar and John Gay. The commercial breakthrough Rich needed came in 1723 with his pantomime *The Necromancer; or, Harlequin Doctor Faustus*, which enjoyed a run of several weeks (a rare event indeed at that time). Rich's fortune was established and his reputation continued to grow with an enormously successful series of pantomimes through the 1720s.

The unparalleled success in 1728 of Gay's *The Beggar's Opera*, which was said to have made "Gay rich and Rich gay", provided Rich with the funds to build a brand new theatre at COVENT GARDEN and he finally left Lincoln's Inn Fields in 1732 in order to move into his new base. The Lincoln's Inn Fields Theatre eventually closed in 1744, after which it was put to a variety of uses (including the storage of china) before demolition in 1848. The site of the building is now occupied by the Royal College of Surgeons.

lion comique A comic character of the MUSIC HALL tradition who made many appearances in the Victorian pantomime. The lion comique was a cheerful, dissipated, young gentleman-about-town who would charm the audience with such suave comic songs as 'Champagne Charlie'. The character was first seen in the music halls around 1865 and subsequently many times in musical interludes in various pantomime plots. The most famous lions comique included such performers as George Leybourne, Alfred Vance, and G. H. MACDERMOTT, although many female comedians also excelled in the role.

Little Bo-Peep Nursery rhyme that has long been used as the basis for popular pantomimes. Early pantomime versions included that staged at the ADELPHI THEATRE in 1831 under the title *Harlequin and Little Bo-Peep*.

One of the most famous productions of all was that seen at DRURY LANE – as *Little Bo-Peep, Little Red Riding-Hood and Hop o' My Thumb* – in 1892, when the cast included the great music hall singer MARIE LLOYD, who appeared in the role of Little Red Riding-Hood, LITTLE TICH as Hop o' My Thumb, DAN LENO as Daddy Thumb, and MARIE LOFTUS as Bo-Peep herself. This production culminated in a magnificent pageant in which the characters of virtually every well-known nursery rhyme were paraded on the stage.

Story The simple nursery rhyme original does no more than tell the story of Little Bo-Peep losing her sheep, which finally come home of their own accord 'carrying their tails behind them'. Pantomimists of the 19th century exercised considerable licence to turn this sketchy episode into a full-scale OPENING with the required number of characters, usually by combining a number of other widely known nursery rhymes. Bo-Peep and her sheep come in handy for the plot of *LITTLE RED RIDING-HOOD*.

Origins As a nursery rhyme, the tale of Little Bo-Peep probably does not predate the early 19th century, although the name 'Bo-Peep' has featured in children's games since at least Elizabethan times.

Little Jack Horner Nursery rhyme of English origins that has in the past been adapted many times as a pantomime. One of the earliest pantomime versions of the tale was that seen at DRURY LANE in 1816, under the title *Harlequin Horner*.

Story According to the original ballad, Little Jack Horner is only 13 inches high but with the aid of a coat that makes him invisible and some bagpipes that can make people dance against their will he always gets his own back on those who cheat or otherwise mistreat him. After various adventures he finally kills a giant, wins the hand of a knight's daughter, and is raised to the rank of squire. The 1816 version made great play upon the theme of charity to the poor, with the Horners (with the exception of the kindly Jack) being roundly condemned by the Genius of the Sun after failing to give food to a starving woman; when the harlequinade began Jack became Harlequin and the woman Columbine.

Origins The story of Little Jack Horner (which may have been influenced by that of *TOM THUMB*) is thought to have its roots in historical fact, being inspired by an incident in the history of the Horner family of Mells Manor in Somerset. According to legend, Jack Horner was a humble steward to the Abbot of Glastonbury who was despatched to London with a pie containing the deeds of twelve manors as a gift for Henry VIII. Before delivering the pie Jack removed one of the deeds – for Mells Manor – to keep for himself ('he put in his thumb and pulled out a plum'). The Horner family, still in residence at Mells, contest the story's accuracy, but do not deny that the family did indeed acquire Mells under Henry VIII. The story became legend as a nursery rhyme and also as a popular ballad (first printed in 1763) and was frequently retold in the CHAPBOOKS circulated in the 18th and 19th centuries.

Little Miss Muffet Nursery rhyme about a small girl frightened by a spider that has several times been adapted as a pantomime in the past. Not one of the most popular story-lines, the tale (embellished with additional characters and subplots) continues to be revived on an occasional basis.

Story The original rhyme offers only a skeleton plot, with Little Miss Muffet being frightened off by a huge spider while sitting down to eat her 'curds and whey'. Typical pantomime versions of the story have Little Miss Muffet being carried off by the spider and subsequently rescued by Boy Blue (who may well turn out to be a prince).

Origins The nursery rhyme is linked with the historical figure of Thomas Muffet (1553–1604), a poet and physician interested in the study of insects, who wrote an account of silkworms in verse. The earliest written versions of the rhyme date back, however, to only 1805 (though it may be descended ultimately from the Cushion Dance ritual associated with May Day festivities).

Littler, Prince and Emile English impresarios, who established themselves as the most successful impresarios in English theatre after World War II. Prince Littler (1901–73) and his brother Emile Littler (1903–85) emerged as leading pantomime producers in London's West End in the 1930s, their greatest successes including *JACK AND THE BEANSTALK* at DRURY LANE in 1936 and *HUMPTY-DUMPTY* at the Coliseum in 1943.

Over the next 20 years they presented many notable pantomimes (often written by themselves) and musical comedies and came to control half of the theatres in the West End and many touring companies. They were pioneers of pantomimes built around major stars from outside the theatre and customarily advertised their productions with the words "All-Star". Emile (who presided over the Coliseum and the Palace Theatre for many years) retired in 1973, the year of his brother's death, and was knighted in 1974.

Notable stars who made their pantomime debuts under the Littlers included DOUGLAS BYNG and Stanley Holloway.

Little Red Riding Hood A well-known fairytale that has long been a popular pantomime subject. GEORGE COLMAN the elder had suggested the story of Little Red Riding Hood as a possible pantomime plot as early as 1754, but the earliest pantomime version was not staged until 1803, when CHARLES DIBDIN staged *Red Riding Hood; or, The Wolf Robber* at SADLER'S WELLS.

Subsequently the story provided the basic plot for one of J. R. PLANCHÉ's first pantomimes, *Rodolph the Wolf; or, Columbine Red Riding-Hood* (1818) – an early 'speaking' pantomime that did not meet with success. Perhaps the most famous production of the tale was that seen under the title *Little Bo-Peep, Little Red Riding-Hood and Hop o' My Thumb* at DRURY LANE in 1892, when MARIE LLOYD played Little Red Riding Hood.

In 1938 the story was chosen for the last pantomime staged at Covent Garden (the casting of revue star

Nelson Keys was not a success, however, and the production did not prosper). Adaptations by contemporary pantomime writers include those by David Cregan and by John Crocker and Eric Gilder.

Story Little Red Riding Hood, so-called because she wears a bright red cape, is on an errand to her grandmother (the DAME role) who lives deep in the forest. A Wolf sees her coming and hastens ahead to her grandmother's house, where he eats (or locks up) the grandmother and then disguises himself in her clothes and occupies her bed. Little Red Riding Hood, who has dallied on the way against all advice, arrives and is impressed with the size of grandmother's big ears ("all the better to hear you with"), big eyes ("all the better to see you with"), and big teeth ("all the better to eat you with"). The Wolf is about to devour Little Red Riding Hood when a woodsman (often played by a PRINCIPAL BOY) bursts in and kills the Wolf with his axe.

In the original fairytale accounts of the story, Little Red Riding Hood is often swallowed (like her grandmother) and is rescued when the woodsman cuts the Wolf's belly open. In most pantomime versions both grandmother and little girl – and indeed the Wolf (who may be persuaded to become a vegetarian or otherwise mend his ways) – escape unharmed. Additional characters customarily introduced in pantomime adaptations include Forest Fairies, Squires, Princes, and an assortment of wizards and witches. *See also* CLOAK.

Origins The plot of the popular pantomime is derived from versions by the GRIMM BROTHERS and by CHARLES PERRAULT, although the tale may date back to Roman times; a similar story involving a little girl wearing a red cap who is devoured by a pack of wolves appeared in France as early as 1023. In both the Grimm brothers' and Perrault's versions, however, Little Red Riding Hood (or Little Red Cap) is actually eaten by the Wolf – although in the Grimm brothers version she is then rescued alive. The original fairytale was known in various versions in several European and African countries, sometimes being confused with the tale of *The Three Little Pigs*. In English folklore, the tale of Little Red Riding Hood has been linked to the legendary adventures of the mistress of a smuggler operating in the Winchester area in the 18th century, who was in the habit of concealing bottles of brandy and other contraband goods under a voluminous red cape.

Little Tich (Harry Relph; 1867–1928) English comedian, just four feet tall, who became one of the great stars of MUSIC HALL and BURLESQUE and was subsequently very popular for his appearances in pantomime (in which he made his debut in Glasgow in 1885). He included impersonation, eccentric dancing in huge boots, and various songs in his act and proved a major attraction in the celebrated DRURY LANE pantomimes of the 1890s, appearing alongside such performers as MARIE LLOYD, DAN LENO, and HERBERT CAMPBELL every year between 1891 and 1894. His roles included Hop o' My Thumb, Humpty-Dumpty, and MAN FRIDAY.

Lloyd, Marie (Matilda Alice Victoria Wood; 1870–1922) English singer, who emerged as one of the greatest of all MUSIC HALL stars in the 1880s and subsequently became a popular actress in pantomime at DRURY LANE and elsewhere.

Famous for her rousing songs – which included 'The Boy I Love Sits Up in the Gallery' and 'A Little of

What You Fancy Does You Good' – and for her irrepressible bawdy humour, 'Our Marie' made her first Drury Lane appearance in 1891, starring alongside DAN LENO and LITTLE TICH. Subsequently she appeared twice more for the management of AUGUSTUS HARRIS and also in the provinces.

Her Drury Lane roles were Princess Allfair in *HUMPTY-DUMPTY* (1891), in which she appeared with Leno, GEORGE LUPINO, and Little Tich, Little Red Riding Hood in *LITTLE BO-PEEP, LITTLE RED RIDING-HOOD AND HOP O' MY THUMB* (1892), again with Little Tich and Dan Leno, and Polly Perkins in *ROBINSON CRUSOE* (1893), alongside Ada Blanche, Leno, HERBERT CAMPBELL, and Little Tich.

Audiences flocked to see her, although her somewhat risqué comedy did not particularly suit her to the role of PRINCIPAL GIRL in which she appeared. Before she became a household name, she often appeared on the halls and in pantomime with her two sisters Alice and Grace, as the Lloyd Sisters.

Loftus, Marie (1857–1940) English actress, who became a major star of the MUSIC HALL and subsequently one of the leading performers in pantomime at DRURY LANE under the management of AUGUSTUS HARRIS. She specialised in the role of PRINCIPAL GIRL, her most successful parts including Little Bo-Peep in *Little Bo-Peep, Little Red Riding-Hood and Hop o' My Thumb* in 1892, when she appeared alongside DAN LENO, HERBERT CAMPBELL, and LITTLE TICH. She was the mother of the actress Cissie Loftus.

London Palladium A theatre in Argyll Street, London, which became famous for its annual pantomime after World War II. Opened in 1910 as the Palladium and seating over 2000 spectators, it soon acquired a reputation for lavish revues and variety shows. Early successes included *Peter Pan*, which was seen on an annual basis between 1930 and 1938. Renamed the London Palladium in 1934, it became the home of the Crazy Gang and since World War II has presented a mixed programme of revues, variety shows, and musicals, as well as being widely recognised as the most prestigious West End home of the pantomime.

Notable productions there have included *HUMPTY-DUMPTY* (1951), with Norman Evans and Terry-Thomas, the 1954 version of *MOTHER GOOSE* starring Peter Sellers, Richard Hearne, and Max Bygraves, *ALADDIN* (1956), featuring NORMAN WISDOM and Sonnie Hale, *JACK AND THE BEANSTALK* (1968), *DICK WHITTINGTON* (1969), starring TOMMY STEELE, and *CINDERELLA* (1972), with Ronnie Corbett, Terry Scott, and Julian Orchard. ARTHUR ASKEY was also among the most popular of the Palladium's stars.

The *Aladdin* production of 1956 was especially significant in that Wisdom's success as PRINCIPAL BOY launched an era lasting about 15 years in which male performers generally monopolised the role at the Palladium; it was CILLA BLACK who restored the old tradition of the female principal boy when she took the part there in 1971. In 1982 the Palladium witnessed the last pantomime appearance of Dame Anna Neagle, in *Cinderella*.

Lover *See* DANDY LOVER.

Loves of Mars and Venus, The A *ballet-pantomime* presented by JOHN WEAVER at DRURY LANE in 1717. An AFTERPIECE in which dancers performed 'in character', the piece remains significant in the history of theatre as the first entertainment to be billed as a 'pantomime'. The cast of Weaver's piece included the figures of Mars and Venus, the three Graces, four followers of Mars, and four Cyclops (played by the comedians in the troupe); the character of Vulcan was portrayed by Weaver himself.

Lun *See* RICH, JOHN.

Lupino family English theatrical family, which enjoyed an almost uninterrupted association with the pantomime from its inception to the present century. Members of the Lupino family claimed descent from a line of Italian puppeteers and were first seen on the English stage shortly after the Restoration.

George Estcourt Lupino (1710–87) performed in the profoundly influential productions of JOHN RICH and his son, **Thomas Frederick Lupino** (1749–1845), worked on pantomime scenery at COVENT GARDEN and elsewhere (as did his son in turn). Another Lupino was a noted pupil of JOSEPH GRIMALDI and succeeding members of the family were subsequently closely linked with the role of CLOWN.

In 1887 no less than six members of the family played in a pantomime at Newcastle; in 1940 another five appeared together in pantomime at the Nottingham Theatre Royal. **George Hook Lupino** (1820–1902) distinguished himself in the role of HARLEQUIN, while his son **George Lupino** (1853–1932) was much acclaimed in the classic DRURY LANE pantomimes of the 1890s, when he acted alongside such stars as DAN LENO and LITTLE TICH. **Arthur Lupino** (1864–1908) created the role of Nana in *Peter Pan* in 1904, while **Henry Charles Lupino** (1865–1925) married into the Lane family connected with the BRITANNIA THEATRE.

George's son **Barry Lupino** (1882–1962) made his stage debut while still a baby and later became resident comedian at the Britannia Theatre and won acclaim in musical comedy and pantomime, writing over 50 scripts for the pantomimes in which he appeared, most memorably in the role of DAME (in which he made his last appearance, in *MOTHER GOOSE*, with great success in 1937). This last pantomime was notable for its incorporation of tricks using TRAPS, many of which dated all the way back to the Grimaldi era.

George's other son, **Stanley Lupino** (1893–1942), also made his debut as a child and later became a star of variety and musical comedy; he was particularly admired for his skill as an acrobat and starred in pantomimes at Drury Lane under ARTHUR COLLINS. Later in his career he also appeared in a number of Hollywood films, as did his daughter **Ida Lupino**. *See also* LANE, LUPINO.

Lyceum Theatre A theatre in Wellington Street, London, that was once famous for its pantomimes. Opened in 1771 as a concert hall and later as a circus venue, the theatre became one of the most important early homes of the pantomime. Notable early productions included, in 1809, the second version ever staged of *CINDERELLA* and, in 1814, Dibdin's *Harlequin Hoax*, in which the young Fanny Kelly – later to be hailed as one of the great actresses of her day – enjoyed much success.

The building housed the DRURY LANE company (1809–12) while the latter theatre was being rebuilt after a fire and also staged opera as well as straight drama. In 1817 the Lyceum became the first theatre in London to be lit by gas, but it was itself destroyed by fire in 1830 and subsequently rebuilt (as the Royal Lyceum and Opera House), after which it prospered as one of the venues used to stage the spectacular EXTRAVAGANZAS of MADAME VESTRIS and her husband CHARLES MATHEWS, who shared the management of the theatre. It was for the Lyceum's production of Planché's *The Island of Jewels* in 1849 that WILLIAM BEVERLEY designed his first TRANSFORMATION SCENE, which caused a sensation.

Other notable productions under the management of E. T. SMITH in the 1860s included W. S. GILBERT'S pantomime *Harlequin Cock-Robin and Jenny Wren; or, Fortunatus and the Water of Life, The Three Bears, The Three Gifts, The Three Wishes, and The Little Man who Woo'd the Little Maid* (1867), which, though spectacular, was plagued with technical problems on the first night and was not an outstanding success. In 1869, in the Lyceum production of *HUMPTY-DUMPTY*, the VOKES FAMILY made their celebrated stage debut.

Even greater times followed in the 1870s with productions starring the great actor SIR HENRY IRVING in Shakespeare and in such melodramas as *The Bells*. Irving's management (1878–99) elevated the Lyceum (with its superb scenery and costumes in correct period style) to the status of England's national theatre and he continued to appear there, often opposite Ellen Terry, until 1902.

During the 1890s Oscar Barrett staged further acclaimed pantomimes, the best of which included a version of *CINDERELLA* starring ELLALINE TERRISS as Cinders; other highlights of the production included the triumph of CHARLES LAURI as a stray cat who befriends the forlorn Cinders (usurping the role usually taken by BUTTONS).

Pantomime, melodrama, and MUSIC HALL dominated the theatre's programme for the next 30 years (with a pantomime being staged every Christmas between 1908 and 1939, with the single exception of 1917–18 when it was replaced by a popular war drama). In the early years of the 20th century the Lyceum (rebuilt once more in 1904) was second only to Drury Lane for its pantomimes and when the Lane's long pantomime tradition was broken in 1920 the Lyceum was unrivalled as London's foremost pantomime venue.

From 1910 the theatre's pantomimes were written by the MELVILLE BROTHERS, who had taken over the management in 1909. Their productions – which included numerous melodramas as well as three classic versions of *Cinderella* (1915, 1918, and 1921) among many other pantomimes – enjoyed long runs and made the brothers rich. Among the performers to appear in these cheerful and lavish shows were CLARKSON ROSE, GEORGE JACKLEY, and NAUGHTON AND GOLD. Another was the young Ninette de Valois, who was eventually to found the Royal Ballet and who gained early experience as a stage dancer in pantomime at the Lyceum between 1914 and 1919.

It all came to an end, however, with plans for the theatre's demolition to make way for a road improvement scheme and the theatre closed in 1939 with farewell performances starring John Gielgud in such classic roles as Hamlet. The last Lyceum pantomime, *THE QUEEN OF HEARTS*, was one of the most successful ever staged at the venue. Subsequently the plan to improve the roads around the theatre was dropped and the Lyceum became (1945) a dance hall; in the late 1980s it was suggested as a possible future venue for leading British ballet companies – an idea still under consideration.

M

Maccus A comic character of the ancient Roman ATELLANA, who may have been an early prototype of the comic figures upon which the *COMMEDIA DELL'ARTE* depended. He was a dim-witted, greedy peasant and anticipated the development of such characters as ARLECCHINO, although a direct link has not been proved. His hooked nose and hunched back were centuries later inherited by the English puppet character Punch.

Macdermott, G. H. (Gilbert Hastings Farrell; 1845–1901) English singer and actor, billed as 'The Great Macdermott', who was the first great star of the MUSIC HALL to be engaged for pantomime. Famous in the music hall for such rousing songs as 'We Don't To Fight But By Jingo! If We Do', he went to sea and was a bricklayer's labourer before he launched a new career in the theatre, working as stage manager and actor at the GRECIAN THEATRE and then establishing himself as a singer in the halls.

Although other music hall performers, including JENNY HILL, HARRY RANDALL, and NELLY POWER had already appeared in pantomime in the provinces, it was Macdermott's success in *BLUEBEARD* (1871) and subsequent pantomimes that spearheaded the 'invasion' that quickly followed. He brought great energy, a strong stage presence, and a fine singing voice to the parts he played and continued to enjoy good reviews throughout his pantomime career, which included appearances in the DRURY LANE pantomimes of the 1880s under the famed theatre manager AUGUSTUS HARRIS.

Among his most popular pantomime songs was 'You Are Always Sure to Fetch Them with a Wst, Wst, Wst', which he first sang in the early 1880s; the song was criticised by many who resented the use of music hall stars in the pantomime and was considered by them to represent all that was coarse and vulgar in the halls themselves. After his retirement from the stage, Macdermott became a theatrical agent and ran several halls. His daughter Ouida Macdermott was also popular in pantomime, in the role of PRINCIPAL BOY.

magic carpet *See ALADDIN AND HIS WONDERFUL LAMP.*

Maid Marian *See* ROBIN HOOD.

make-up The wearing of special stage cosmetics either to alter one's appearance or to compensate for the effect of bright stage lighting. The building of huge new auditoria such as those at COVENT GARDEN and DRURY LANE added a further purpose to the use of stage make-up, as the exaggeration of an actor's features made it easier for members of the audience seated a considerable distance away to register his facial expressions.

Among the actors to realise this need and the possibilities it offered for comic invention was the great Clown JOSEPH GRIMALDI, who remains one of the most important figures in the development of stage make-up in the 19th century. Grimaldi derived much of the humour of his act from his physical appearance, contriving costumes out of miscellanous household items and paying particular attention to the make-up he wore as Clown. He adopted a whitened face, red painted cheeks, and outrageous hairstyle (in his case a blue cockscomb) and inspired his successors in the role to develop the standardised Clown make-up associated with the character to this very day. Every clown has his own unique 'face', a miniature copy of which is painted onto an eggshell and preserved as a permanent record.

The development of greasepaint (by Ludwig Leichner) in the late 19th century was another significant step forward (welcomed by many performers who risked serious illness through the use of paints containing white lead) and subsequently water-based and even fluorescent stage make-up has also been introduced. In the contemporary pantomime, players continue to wear relatively heavy make-up to compensate for the use of dramatic strongly-coloured lighting. Dames in particular apply heavy make-up for comic effect.

Man Friday The native companion of the hero in *ROBINSON CRUSOE*. Unlike the majority of the other characters who accompany Crusoe on his desert island in the pantomime version, Man Friday did appear in the original novel (1719) by Daniel Defoe. On the first occasion that the pantomime was performed, in a version by RICHARD BRINSLEY SHERIDAN at DRURY LANE in 1781, the role was played by GIUSEPPE GRIMALDI; after the TRANSFORMATION SCENE Man Friday – driven to the brink of suicide by the treatment meted out to him by Pantaloon – was transformed by a magician into HARLEQUIN with one touch of a magic wand.

Performers of the role over the years have included LITTLE TICH, who appeared in the role in the Lane's version of 1893. The actor playing Man Friday in a version entitled *Robinson Crusoe; or, Friday Turned Boxer* seen at Birmingham towards the end of the 18th century was obliged to go through a sparring match with the celebrated boxer Daniel Mendoza as part of the entertainment.

masks A variety of masks have traditionally been used in the pantomime over the years. The use of half-masks for most of the characters of the HARLEQUINADE originated in their use in the *COMMEDIA DELL'ARTE*, although the use of the mask already had a long history in the indigenous English theatre, being used in court MASQUES and various forms of folk theatre as far back as medieval times. The *PANTOMIMI* of ancient Rome wore masks (perhaps in imitation of even earlier ritualistic theatre) and the advantages of such disguises were recognised long before the modern pantomime developed.

Masks have generally been used in the theatre to heighten personality and promote instant recognition of a character; in Brechtian theatre they are also used as a tool of the so-called alienation effect, encouraging audiences to concentrate upon the meaning of what they are seeing without being distracted by the humanity of the characters themselves.

In the harlequinade new conventions surrounding their use were born; when John Rich put his mask on as Harlequin, for instance, audiences accepted at once that he was thus deemed to be invisible to the other characters on the stage. Masks are still used in the pantomime, chiefly as a means of disguise by various Demon Kings, though only giants and other monsters and animal characters are expected to retain them throughout a performance. *See also* Big Heads.

masque A form of ceremonial musical drama that was popular at royal courts throughout Europe in the 16th and 17th centuries and which has since been recognised as one of the remoter ancestors of the English pantomime. Distantly descended from the pageants and plays of medieval times, the masque – popularised by the Italians (who named it the bergamasque after the town of Bergamo where the tradition originated) – developed as a ritualised dance entertainment in which the participants (who often included royalties themselves) wore masks and dressed as mythological or allegorical figures.

In the later history of the masque, when such playwrights as Ben Jonson, Inigo Jones, John Milton, and William Davenant contributed highly literary scripts, the genre was notable for the sophistication of the scenery and technical effects employed. In particular, the use of the tableau and often highly elaborate transformation scenes anticipated the incorporation of such techniques into the pantomime itself.

The legacy left by the masque also included the proscenium arch, changeable scenery, and various developments in stage machinery. In England such masques continued to be performed under the Stuarts but disappeared from the national theatre with the fall of the monarchy under Cromwell.

Mathews, Charles James (1803–78) English actor and theatre manager, who with his wife Madame Vestris enjoyed great success in the extravaganzas of J. R. Planché. The son of the distinguished actor and comedian Charles Mathews (1776–1835), he succeeded his father as manager of the Adelphi Theatre in 1835 and at the same time launched a new career as an actor (having previously trained as an architect).

He made his debut with Vestris's company at the Olympic Theatre that same year and played a major part in Planché's influential extravaganzas, ultimately marrying Vestris herself in 1838. After a tour of the USA, they assumed the management (1839–42) of Covent Garden, where Mathews won acclaim in the plays of Dion Boucicault, but their efforts were not rewarded with financial success and their reign ended in bankruptcy (and a period of imprisonment for debt).

Subsequently they were admired in performance at Drury Lane and at the Haymarket Theatre before taking over the management of the Lyceum Theatre in 1847. This venture also ended in financial disaster (largely because of the lavishness with which they staged their shows) and in a brief spell in gaol. Mathews retired from management in 1855 and, after the death of his wife a year later, married the actress Lizzie Davenport after a second US tour.

matinée A theatrical performance that takes place in the afternoon, usually for the benefit of children for whom an evening performance would be too late. The matinée is of particular relevance to the pantomime, which has been aimed at a younger audience for well over a hundred years and such performances generally coincide exactly with the period of the Christmas school holiday. Virtually all pantomime runs include regular matinée performances and such performances are often the first to be sold out.

The very first matinée performance was presented back in 1843 at the Olympic Theatre, New York. Although popular with children and theatre managements, matinées are less beloved by performers and stage crews, who have to cope with large, excitable juvenile audiences and usually enjoy only a brief break after the show before having to begin all over again for the evening performance. Matinée audiences are noted for their noisy and often disruptive behaviour, making the business of being heard above the din a particularly exacting one.

Matthews, Tom (1806–89) English comedian, who succeeded JOSEPH GRIMALDI as the most acclaimed CLOWN of his day. A pupil and assistant of Grimaldi himself, Matthews made his debut at the Olympic Theatre and first appeared as Clown at SADLER'S WELLS in *The Hag of the Forest* in 1829; subsequently he filled the post of principal clown at DRURY LANE for nearly 40 years, winning acclaim for his straightforward slapstick humour (he never danced or performed the acrobatics traditionally demanded of the part).

As the emphasis was placed more on the OPENING than on the HARLEQUINADE in the 1830s and 1840s so Matthews appeared exclusively in the opening and another actor took his place as Clown after the transformation scene. He finally retired to Brighton in 1865, after a last appearance in *HOP O' MY THUMB*; or, *HARLEQUIN OGRE OF THE SEVEN-LEAGUED BOOTS*.

Mayne, Clarice (1886–1966) English singer, who was a popular star of the music hall and the pantomime from the Edwardian period onwards. She was particularly acclaimed for her rendition of songs written for her by her husband James W. Tate and enjoyed her greatest success with the rousing 'Joshu-ah'. She was very popular in pantomime in the role of PRINCIPAL BOY.

melodrama Genre of 19th century drama, which was with pantomime the most popular form of theatrical entertainment for many years. The relationship between melodrama, which evolved in France at the end of the 18th century (during the upheaval of the French Revolution), and pantomime is very close.

Many noted pantomime writers, including J. B. BUCKSTONE and the Dibdins, wrote for both forms of theatre and frequently the two genres shared the same plots and characters (as in the case of *BLUEBEARD*, which began life as a melodrama in 1811 and was subsequently adapted as a pantomime by CHARLES DIBDIN the younger, as *Harlequin and Bluebeard*).

The villains of pantomime were particularly influenced by the development of the melodrama, in which the wickedness of evil squires and barons was given full rein (*see also* DANDY LOVER). Such characters survived the demise of melodrama towards the end of the 19th century (with audiences tiring of their implausibility and naivety) by absorption into the pantomime, where their ranting and raving found an eager audience and promoted the growth of such larger-than-life characters as the dame.

Most analyses of melodrama conclude that its essence relies upon the subordination of character to plot (unlike true tragedy), hence the extremism and outlandish nature of such entertainments. The Victorian melodrama was notable for its employment of highly atmospheric lighting and other technical effects and productions were often very spectacular; in the early days music also played a major role. Later, however, the musical content diminished and the emphasis was upon sensationalism of all kinds, with characters indulging in much high rhetoric.

Among the most lurid and successful English melodramas (the fare of many a crowded penny gaff theatre) were such classics as *The Bells* (1871) by Leopold Lewis, which provided SIR HENRY IRVING with his most famous role, *The Corsican Brothers* (1852) by Dion Boucicault, and *Lady Audley's Secret* (1863) by C. H. Hazlewood. *See also* NAUTICAL DRAMA.

Melville brothers The English theatre managers and authors **Walter Melville** (1875–1937) and **Frederick Melville** (1879–1938), who wrote and staged a series of highly successful pantomimes at the LYCEUM THEATRE, which they managed from 1909 until 1938.

The brothers – as much loved for their eccentricity as for their kindnesses as employers – were descended from a theatrical family and had a third brother, Andrew Melville (d. 1938), who wrote several successful plays (some of which were staged at the Lyceum). Their spectacular pantomimes, of which the first was seen in 1910, rivalled those at DRURY LANE in terms of popularity and made the Melville brothers' fortunes.

Their productions were cheerful, glittering shows in which the fairytale plots were faithfully delivered. Stars of the Melville brothers pantomimes (all of which were hits) included the popular CLARKSON ROSE as DAME and such comedians as GEORGE JACKLEY and NAUGHTON AND GOLD.

Other productions presented at the theatre included a number of immensely successful melodramas, many by the hands of the brothers themselves. Walter's death ended the great partnership though Frederick continued to manage the theatre for another 14 months (it is thought his own death was hastened by grief over the loss of his brother). The last Melville pantomime at the Lyceum was *THE QUEEN OF HEARTS* (1938) – a production famous for the spectacular collapsing House of Cards – after which the theatre was forced to close.

Merson, Billy (William Henry Thompson; 1881–1947) English comedian and singer, who established himself as a star of MUSIC HALL with his wide range of comic characters and songs, which anticipated his success in pantomime. He made his debut in Birmingham in 1900 and later appeared under many guises, including that of the acrobatic clown Ping-Pong. His many songs included the celebrated 'The Spaniard That Blighted my Life', which he composed himself. His greatest successes in the pantomime included his appearances in *PUSS IN BOOTS* in 1924. He also appeared in musical comedy and revue.

Minor Theatres Formerly, those theatres that did not enjoy the privileges of a royal patent (*see* PATENT THEATRES). The Minor Theatres were constrained by the LICENSING ACT of 1737 from presenting spoken drama, although enterprising arrangers found many loopholes through which they could still present various 'romances', 'spectacles', 'burlettas', and 'extravaganzas' in which a certain amount of dialogue was included (*see also* FLAG). As the years passed the pressure for a relaxation of the rules governing the Minor Theatres grew with such notable contemporary figures as the playwright Edward Bulwer-Lytton spearheading campaigns for change. The distinction between the Minor Theatres and the Patent Theatres became largely meaningless after a change in the law in 1843, after which all theatres enjoyed the same rights to present spoken drama. This encouraged the opening of a great many new theatres and the performance of more ambitious 'speaking' pantomimes at a wide range of venues.

mirror A magic talking mirror plays a major role in the pantomime *SNOW WHITE AND THE SEVEN DWARFS*, in which it informs Snow White's WICKED STEPMOTHER that she is not "the most beautiful of them all". As a result of this the Wicked Stepmother plans the death of Snow White, who is named by the mirror the fairest in the land.

Mirrors have a long history as magical objects and many ancient peoples feared that a reflection in a mirror could be captured by evil spirits. In medieval times some sorcerers practised catoptromancy, the science of using mirrors to foretell the future, and were consulted by every class of subject, from humble peasants to members of royal families. Such 'scrying' reached a peak in Elizabethan times, when mirrors were used by magicians, alchemists, and all manner of prophets; the most famous of them all was the mirror of Dr. John Dee (who was later immortalised as the model for Christopher Marlowe's *Dr. Faustus* – a story that was itself rendered as a pantomime).

In the 17th century many people wore a small mirror in their hats as it was believed that mirrors provided protection against evil. The crystal balls used by gypsy soothsayers are probably derived from similar superstitions. Even in modern times it is still thought unlucky to break a mirror and that seven years of bad luck will follow such an accident (the cinema also preserves the belief that a vampire has no reflection).

Momus The god of clowns, who was frequently introduced as a character in the HARLEQUINADE. Descended from the Greek god of ridicule, Momus was sometimes used as an alternative name for a clown.

Morgiana *See ALI BABA AND THE FORTY THIEVES.*

Morley, John (1924–) English actor and author, who is the best known pantomime writer of modern times. Nicknamed the 'King of Panto', Morley wrote his first pantomime – *DICK WHITTINGTON AND HIS KIT* – in 1944 for performance by the Coldstream Guards, with whom he was then serving in Palestine. Subsequently he wrote pantomimes for the Footlights Club in Cambridge and for all the leading pantomime venues in the country as well as for amateur companies (there are approximately 200 amateur productions of his pantomimes each year).

By the 1980s he had written around 200 pantomimes, many of them tailored for the needs of particular performers (among them ARTHUR ASKEY, DANNY LA RUE, Terry Scott, and Basil Brush). They have included such titles as *ALADDIN AND HIS WONDERFUL LAMP*, which enjoyed a record-breaking run at the Theatre Royal, Nottingham in 1980–81, *DICK WHITTINGTON*, which was selected for study under the National Curriculum in 1992, *GOLDILOCKS AND THE THREE BEARS*, *JACK AND THE BEANSTALK*, in which he introduced the standard characters Fleshcreep (the Giant's henchman) and the Vegetable Fairy, *Robinson Crusoe*, and *Sinbad the Sailor*.

He has also written a version of *Pinocchio*, as a family entertainment, and an updated stage adaptation of *The Wind in the Willows*, among many other pieces. His pantomimes have been seen as far afield as Botswana, Hong Kong, and the USA; he has also had several performed on television and radio. As an actor he appeared in 14 West End musical comedies.

Mother Bunch A legendary equivalent of Mother Goose who was formerly presented as the authoress of various fairytales and nursery rhymes. The tales of Mother Bunch were a popular feature of the chapbooks of the 18th and 19th centuries, although the name was familiar in earlier centuries. The original Mother Bunch is thought to have been a well-known London ale-wife in the 16th century. A number of early pantomimes incorporated her name in the title and even introduced her as a character on stage. *See also* Aulnoy, Marie-Cathérine le Jumel de Barneville de la Motte, Comtesse d'.

Mother Goose The dame in the pantomime *Mother Goose*, who is considered one of the best comic characters in the whole pantomime tradition. French fairytales of the 17th century were sometimes called 'Mother Goose tales' and Mother Goose – an old peasant woman – was frequently presented as the teller of these ancient tales and superstitions.

Mystery surrounds the identity of the original Mother Goose, whose stories include many of the best known nursery rhymes and fairytales. Some researchers have even traced her back to Queen Goosefoot, mother of Charlemagne the Great. She is particularly closely associated with the nursery rhyme in the USA (where attempts were made to prove that the real Mother Goose was one Elizabeth Goose, a member of the Goose or Vergoose family of English extraction who settled in Boston in the middle of the 17th century).

Having been credited as the 'author' of Charles Perrault's fairytales (translated in 1729), Mother Goose made her first appearance in the pantomime in the celebrated 1806 version of *Mother Goose* by Thomas Dibdin. Dibdin (as in all early versions of the tale) depicted her as a benevolent mystical figure who was capable of such magical feats as raising the Squire's long-dead wife from the grave in order to teach him a lesson; ultimately she magically transformed the characters of the opening into the figures of the harlequinade. In terms of appearance, she had much in common with Old Mother Hubbard (who appeared a few years later), being played as an old crone with a hooked nose and long chin.

It was not until the early 20th century that Mother Goose became the rollicking dame of the modern pantomime tradition, largely as a result of the appearance in the role of Dan Leno, who transformed her in a celebrated production at Drury Lane in 1902. Leno introduced the famous 'beautification scene' and turned Mother Goose into a plausible sympathetic figure through the subtlety and acuteness of his characterization (with the collaboration of scriptwriter J. Hickory Wood and theatre manager Arthur Collins).

Other outstanding performers of the part included Wilkie Bard, who was the first to play the role after Leno, and George Lacy, who applied both his skill as a dancer and his talent as a comedian to the part.

More recent exponents of the role have included Stanley Baxter, who was particularly celebrated for his hilarious transformation from an old crone to a glamorous creature on the lines of Marlene Dietrich.

Mother Goose Ever-popular pantomime that has kept its place as one of the most regularly performed pantomimes for nearly 200 years. The most celebrated early pantomime production of the story dates back to 1806, when JOSEPH GRIMALDI played the SQUIRE and CLOWN to great acclaim in THOMAS DIBDIN's *Harlequin and Mother Goose; or, the Golden Egg* at COVENT GARDEN.

This famous production (described as the most successful pantomime of the 19th century) was unusually plain in design and setting, allowing Grimaldi's brilliance to take centre stage; it ran for 92 nights and scenes from it were subsequently seen throughout the country. It was revived at the theatre a year later and again in 1808 at the HAYMARKET. A version of it was also toured (without success) to the BOWERY THEATRE in New York in 1831 and this is sometimes claimed to be the first pantomime ever performed in the USA (in fact, DAVID GARRICK's *Harlequin's Invasion* had been seen together with *ROBINSON CRUSOE* at the John Street Theatre, New York as early as 1786).

The success of the piece established Clown as the central character of the HARLEQUINADE and confirmed the English country village as a popular setting for future pantomimes. It shared little, however, in common with the version familiar to contemporary audiences, with 15 of the 20 or so scenes being devoted to the harlequinade.

The most effective scenes of the modern pantomime include the 'beautification' of the dame – a comic episode that was first seen in the 1902 landmark version written by J. HICKORY WOOD for DAN LENO at DRURY LANE; other members of the cast in this historic production included HERBERT CAMPBELL as IDLE JACK, FRED EMNEY as the Mayor of Tapham, and ARTHUR CONQUEST as the Golden Goose. Highlights of this version included Leno's hilarious first entrance as dame, venting his wrath upon some motorists who have just caused his cart of (live) geese to overturn.

More recent versions of the tale have included those by such writers as Betty Astell, Verne Morgan, Ron Hall, Norman Robbins, and JOHN MORLEY.

Story Mother Goose is forced to auction off her possessions to fend off the Squire and his bailiffs. Her fortunes change, however, when (sometimes courtesy of a good fairy) she comes into possession of a goose, usually called Priscilla, that lays golden eggs for her and makes her rich. The DEMON KING (who is sometimes identified as the 'Demon Discontent' after his contention that there is not a single man or woman in the world who is contented with his lot) tempts Mother Goose – usually with the Squire as his henchman – to part with the goose, offering her the chance to exchange her new-found happiness for great beauty.

Mother Goose agrees and is transformed at the Waterfall of Beauty (or similarly-named pool or lake) into what she considers a more ravishing figure (an ideal opportunity for a comical strip-tease). No-one (including her own son COLIN) recognises or likes the transformed dame, however, and she soon concludes that riches and beauty are not everything and comes to regret the deal; after various adventures she manages to revert to the much-loved character she once was – and retrieves Priscilla.

Origins *Mother Goose* is possibly the oldest of all the pantomime stories, being descended ultimately from a Greek legend that concerned a goose that laid golden eggs. The plot of the modern pantomime, however, is largely the invention of J. Hickory Wood, as devised in collaboration with Leno in 1902.

Mother Goose, Tales of A collection of fairytales published by CHARLES PERRAULT in 1697 (translated into English around 1729), from which the plots of several pantomimes were derived. It was through Perrault that many of the stories were first introduced to England and it was through his collection that the name MOTHER GOOSE became familiar. The stories became more widely known in England in the 1760s when a further edition, issued by John Newbery, appeared under the title *Mother Goose's Melody*.

Perrault's collection of stories included *BLUEBEARD*, *PUSS IN BOOTS*, *CINDERELLA*, *HOP O' MY THUMB*, *THE SLEEPING BEAUTY*, and *LITTLE RED RIDING HOOD*. Each tale was followed by a rhymed moral. When it came to publication, Perrault sought to protect his literary reputation by releasing the collection under the name of his son, Perrault Darmancour.

Most of the tales had been published in various Italian versions a century before although it is thought that Perrault himself learnt them through the oral French tradition. Newbery's translation (on which the poet, playwright, and essayist Oliver Goldsmith may have collaborated) contained 51 nursery rhymes (many of which had never before been committed to paper) alongside 'songs and lullabies' by William Shakespeare. The publication was extensively copied by other publishers throughout England and the USA (where Perrault's stories were known by 1795) and thus promoted the public's familiarity with the tales upon which many pantomimes were to be based.

Mother Hubbard *See OLD MOTHER HUBBARD.*

Mountford, William (1664–92) English playwright and actor, whose most successful play was the first English drama to incorporate figures from the *COMMEDIA DELL'ARTE*. His farcical version of Christopher Marlowe's tragedy *Doctor Faustus*, as *The Life and Death of Doctor Faustus, made into a Farce* (1685), included scenes in which Harlequin and Scaramouche indulge in the slapstick comedy familiar to audiences of the *commedia dell'arte* and marked a significant stage in the absorption of the Italian tradition, which was to prove crucial in the early development of the pantomime. Mountford himself acted at DRURY LANE and won acclaim in aristocratic roles in the plays of William Wycherley among others. He was murdered at the instigation of a Captain Hill, his rival for the love of the actress Anne Bracegirdle. *See also* BEHN, APHRA.

music *See* SONGS.

musical comedy A theatrical genre, in which a strong dramatic (though often fairly unchallenging and lighthearted) story is blended with a fully orchestrated musical element. These typically large-scale lavishly-staged shows were first presented in the second half of the 19th century, when they developed from the comic operas of Gilbert and Sullivan, among others. In the latter half of the 20th century they all but banished pantomime from the West End stage (in the 1992–93 season there was not a single production of pantomime in the West End largely because of the rival demands of the musicals, which are not confined to a limited Christmas season as the pantomime is).

Over the years several devisers of musical comedies have attempted to profit by plundering pantomime plots, with varying degrees of success. The results have included such shows as *CHU-CHIN-CHOW*, *Princess Charming*, *Mr Whittington*, *The House That Jack Built*, and *Mr Cinders*. Many stars of the pantomime have also distinguished themselves in musical comedy.

music hall Popular form of theatrical entertainment that enjoyed a tremendous vogue in the late 19th and early 20th centuries and provided many of the stars of the late Victorian and Edwardian pantomime. The music hall had its roots in the song-and-supper rooms and taproom concert halls that were a feature of nightlife both in London and in other major cities throughout the country as far back as the early 19th century.

The music hall tradition gradually evolved as a series of 'turns' presented by a wide range of entertainers who included singers, comedians, magicians, dancers, and circus performers, all of whom performed with varying degrees of professionalism. The complete show was presided over by a chairman, who kept order and announced the acts. Audiences were allowed to drink and smoke and though the music hall acquired a somewhat dubious reputation for rowdiness and vulgarity and hardly qualified as 'family entertainment', it became immensely popular with all classes.

Such venues as the Canterbury Music Hall, opened in 1852, the Holborn Empire, opened in 1857, and the London Pavilion, opened in 1861, attracted large crowds and made stars of such performers as SIR HARRY LAUDER, DAN LENO, LITTLE TICH, MARIE LLOYD, GEORGE ROBEY, and NELLIE WALLACE, all of whom were to appear with great success in pantomime.

Minor music hall performers appeared in pantomime as SPECIALITY ACTS throughout the century but the influence of the halls only began to have a major effect upon the pantomime in the 1860s when such leading artists as JENNY HILL, HARRY RANDALL, NELLY POWER, and Bessie Bonehill joined pantomime casts. It was the success of G. H. MACDERMOTT – who first appeared in pantomime at DRURY LANE in 1871 at the invitation of AUGUSTUS HARRIS – that signalled the start of a major invasion of music hall performers. Such artists soon dominated the Lane's bills; Harris's version of *LITTLE BO-PEEP, LITTLE RED RIDING-HOOD AND HOP O' MY THUMB* in 1892, for instance, featured Leno, Lloyd, Little Tich, HERBERT CAMPBELL, ADA BLANCHE, Arthur Williams, and MARIE LOFTUS – all music hall stars.

All types of acts were imported from the halls as well as individual comics and singers and it was quite common for the action of a pantomime to be interrupted for a spectacular display of acrobatics or a trapeze act, although many members of the audience came to resent these interruptions. Opponents of the so-called 'invasion' attacked such performers as Marie Lloyd for vulgarity and coarseness and feared a debasing of the pantomime, which had developed until then as a family entertainment with no little artistic merit. E. L. BLANCHARD, who saw his highly literary scripts mangled to accommodate these new stars, was among those who resisted the invasion when it first gathered pace in the 1860s.

Nonetheless, the sheer popularity of the music hall stars did for a time sweep all objections aside and by the late 1880s all the major London venues were building casts around leading music hall performers, who were eager to appear before new audiences (many of whom would not dream of entering a music hall). Some concessions were eventually made in the 1890s, when even Augustus Harris began to apprcciate that the predominance of such spirited comedians was obstructing the progress of the plot and more attention was paid to getting a good balance between comedy, spectacle, and fairytale.

In the long term the invasion resulted in a realignment of the pantomime: the elegant rhymed scripts of Blanchard and his predecessors suddenly looked old-fashioned and dull and future writers for the genre provided more exuberant texts in which the comedy was distinctly livelier and adapted to the comic style of the music hall guests. Many classic music hall songs are still regularly heard in the contemporary pantomime (in, for instance, the pantomimes of Alan Brown) and many gags and comedy routines seen today were first played in the halls at the turn of the century. *See also* VARIETY.

mystery plays or **miracle plays** English medieval theatrical tradition that was in some respects a distant ancestor of the pantomime. Based on biblical stories, mystery plays were presented by trade or craft guilds at such important religious centres as Chester, York, and Wakefield as part of the celebration of certain church festivals. The performers acted on small platform stages and scripts were often enlivened with much coarse humour. This indigenous dramatic tradition is thought to have had some impact upon the early development of the pantomime, chiefly through the impersonation by men of various comic old women (anticipating the development of the pantomime DAME). The convention that the FAIRY GODMOTHER should enter from the right while the DEMON KING comes on from the left is also a legacy of the ancient mystery play, in which the Angel Gabriel (an equivalent of the pantomime's BENEVOLENT AGENT) came on from the right while Mephistopheles (an ancestor of the Demon King) entered from the left.

N

Naughton and Gold The popular English comedy act that comprised Charlie Naughton (1887–1976) and Jimmy Gold (James McConigal; 1886–1967), who are usually remembered as two of the seven comedians who made up the Crazy Gang. Before World War II Naughton and Gold delighted pantomime audiences (who often included members of the Royal family) at the LYCEUM THEATRE (and subsequently elsewhere) with their comic antics. They were virtually unrivalled as masters of such slapstick scenes as 'papering the parlour' (which involved the misuse of much wallpaper and paste) and making cakes in the Palace kitchen.

nautical drama A theatrical genre of the early 18th century, which provided much inspiration for writers of BURLESQUE and pantomime. In an age when the British Navy was proudly declared to be the most powerful in the world, audiences flocked to melodramas telling the heroic adventures of typical 'Jolly Jack Tars'. The most successful example of the genre was Douglas Jerrold's *Black Ey'd Susan* (1829), which enjoyed an enormous vogue in numerous productions and adaptations. Within a year of its first performance at the SURREY THEATRE – the leading home of such drama – the story was being burlesqued in pantomime at DRURY LANE, as *Davy Jones; or, Harlequin and Mother Carey's Chickens* by William Barrymore.

In fact, similar burlesque versions had been seen even before Jerrold's play had reached the stage, both the play and the parodies deriving ultimately from a well-known popular ballad. In the pantomime version, the sailor-hero of the ballad was transformed into Harlequin, his beloved to Columbine, and her father – the Old Commodore – to Pantaloon; the climax of the story took place appropriately in the Palace of Neptune. *See also* AWKWARD SQUAD.

Nervo and Knox The English comedians Jimmie Nervo (James Holloway; 1897–1975) and Teddy Knox (Albert Edward Cromwell-Knox; 1896–1974), who formed a popular comedy double act in the 1930s. Best known for their appearances as part of the Crazy Gang before and after World War II, Nervo and Knox were also highly successful pantomime performers, executing hilarious slapstick scenes and often pairing up with fellow-Crazy Gang members NAUGHTON AND GOLD.

Nicholls, Harry (1852–1926) English comedian, who was immensely popular in pantomime at DRURY LANE and elsewhere in the late 19th century. One of the most popular imports from the MUSIC HALL, he enjoyed particular success in partnership with HERBERT CAMPBELL at the GRECIAN THEATRE in 1875 and subsequently at Drury Lane. Nicholls was especially admired for the topical duets he wrote for Campbell and himself to sing, adding extra verses based on items in the evening papers each night. He also contributed as a writer to a number of the celebrated pantomimes seen at the Lane. His most famous roles included the Queen in *PUSS IN BOOTS* and one of the babes in *BABES IN THE WOOD*.

night scenes *See* ITALIAN NIGHT SCENES.

Nurse The traditional role of the DAME in *THE SLEEPING BEAUTY* (and sometimes other pantomimes). The Nurse is usually an irrepressible, bossy, incompetent who cares for her royal charge with an alarming recklessness. She is, however, immensely endearing and is broken-hearted when Beauty falls victim to the Wicked Fairy's curse. The character was first played by a man around 1860 (when a Nurse figured in a production of *THE BABES IN THE WOOD*). She may be loosely descended from the mythical 'Nurse Lovechild' of English folklore, who – like MOTHER GOOSE and other similar figures – is credited with the authorship of various nursery rhymes. *See also* BATHING THE BABY.

nursery rhymes Many nursery rhymes have been adapted as the basis of famous pantomime plots over the years. These include such perennial favourites as *HUMPTY-DUMPTY*, *JACK AND JILL*, and *LITTLE JACK HORNER*, among many others. Less well-known pantomimes based on nursery rhymes have included *Sing a Song of Sixpence*, *Little Miss Muffet*, *The Grand Old Duke of York*, *Hickory Dickory Dock*, *Baa, Baa, Black Sheep*, and *Twinkle, Twinkle, Little Star; or, Harlequin Jack Frost*, a somewhat improbable pantomime of 1870.

The nursery rhyme has a long history with most being widely known by the middle of the 18th century and some dating back to medieval times. The first serious collections were made in the early 19th century and these provided valuable source material for pantomimists looking for new plots. Particularly attractive to the arrangers were the groups of rhymes and fairytales associated with such mythical figures as MOTHER GOOSE, MOTHER BUNCH, OLD MOTHER HUBBARD, and TOM THUMB.

Where the nursery rhymes were too short to do anything more than provide a skeleton plot writers often combined several rhymes or interpolated characters and events from a range of other sources, including of course ones of their own invention. Though most nursery rhymes are now preserved through their repetition to the young, many did not begin life as children's verses but were satirical comments upon contemporary politics or social conditions or were otherwise descended from pagan ceremonies, mummers' plays, or popular ballads.

O

ogre A monstrous creature, sometimes a GIANT, who preys on the good in numerous fairytales and pantomimes. It is thought that CHARLES PERRAULT coined the word 'ogre' in his *TALES OF MOTHER GOOSE* in 1697, possibly borrowing it from the Italian word *orco* (demon). Ogres have a wide range of characteristics, which may include sharp claws, great strength, and a taste for human flesh. The most well-known ogres in the pantomime include that in *HOP O' MY THUMB*.

Oh yes it is *See* AUDIENCE PARTICIPATION.

oil jars *See ALI BABA AND THE FORTY THIEVES*.

Old Bowery Theatre *See* BOWERY THEATRE.

Old King Cole Nursery rhyme about a jovial monarch, which has often been adapted for use in the pantomime. The story of the "merry old soul" and his pipe and his fiddlers three has surfaced regularly in the pantomime, though usually only in a minor way, sometimes as a song. As a full-length pantomime the plot is usually expanded through the loss of King Cole's pipe and subsequent attempts to retrieve it. Complete pantomimes built upon the original rhyme in recent years include a version, subtitled *King Cole in Space*, by Verne Morgan. Performers of the central role over the years have included CLARKSON ROSE. One theory has it that the original Old King Cole was the 3rd-century ruler after whom Colchester was named, another that he was a wealthy merchant called Colebrook who lived in the Reading area, and yet another that he was the legendary father of the giant Fyn M'Coule.

Old Man of the Sea The demon in *SINBAD THE SAILOR* who refuses to be dislodged after climbing onto Sinbad's shoulders. Sinbad finally rids himself of the burden by getting the Old Man of the Sea so drunk that he falls off. Alternatively, a non-alcoholic version of the episode has the Old Man of the Sea boasting that no-one knows his secret rhyme about his long beard, which Sinbad must repeat in order to free himself (the audience discover what the rhyme is and shout it out, thus freeing Sinbad). The character has also made appearances in other pantomimes, among them *ROBINSON CRUSOE*. Legend has it that the original Old Man of the Sea was in fact one of the hairy apes of Formosa (now Taiwan).

Old Mother Hubbard Nursery rhyme about a comical old woman and her dog, which was used as the basis of popular pantomimes in the 19th century and is still occasionally revived. Early pantomime versions of the tale included CHARLES FARLEY'S *Old Mother Hubbard and Her Dog*, which was seen at COVENT GARDEN in 1833; one of the more unusual scenes of this version featured a full-scale brawl between a party of sailors and a group of clergymen and others belonging to the Temperance Society (the sailors won). More recent adaptations of the rhyme include a family musical by DAVID WOOD. Among recent productions was one seen at the Queen's Theatre, Hornchurch in 1992.

Story Old Mother Hubbard leaves her home on a series of errands and each time returns to find her dog in some comical situation (for instance, riding a goat). Pantomime versions of this sketchy plot have exercised considerable licence to turn it into a full pantomime story with the usual large cast of characters. Customarily, Old Mother Hubbard is turned out of her house by bailiffs at the beginning of the tale and goes through various adventures with her brood of children (all based on nursery rhyme characters) before settling into a new home in the huge boot of another original rhyme.

Origins The well-known rhyme about Old Mother Hubbard and her dog was first printed in 1805 and is thought to have been the work of Sarah Catherine Martin (1768–1826), who may well have intended it as a political satire. The original rhyme was fairly lengthy and ran to several verses (and also boasted a sequel by the same author). Old Mother Hubbard herself is a folkloric figure of older origins, being mentioned in the works of Edmund Spenser in the 16th century (she may have acquired her dog through association with Saint Hubert, patron saint of hunting and of dogs). In appearance, she was traditionally played as an old crone with a hooked nose and chin (as was MOTHER GOOSE).

Old Vic Theatre A theatre in the Waterloo Road, London, which was formerly famous for its pantomimes. Opened in 1816 as the Royal Coburg Theatre, it became a popular venue for MELODRAMA and pantomime after the control of the theatres was relaxed in the Act of 1843, after which such shows continued to be produced there throughout the 19th century. Other early productions included plays starring the great actor EDMUND KEAN. Pantomime audiences here were among the most vocal anywhere in London. The theatre was renamed the Royal Victoria Theatre in 1833 and the New Victoria Palace in 1871.

Emma Cons, a member of the Temperance Society, reopened it in 1880 as the Royal Victoria Hall and Coffee Tavern; as the Old Vic, it became celebrated for its Shakespearean productions after Lilian Baylis took over in 1912. The programme was varied with ballet in the 1930s and the theatre consolidated its reputation as a home of serious drama with further acclaimed Shakespearean productions. Bombed in World War II, the theatre reopened in 1950; in 1963 the resident company was reorganised as the National Theatre company, winning great praise before moving to a new home in 1976. The theatre changed hands in 1982 and now stages large-scale musicals as well as Shakespearean and other dramas.

olio A selection of miscellaneous scenes from a number of different productions that are cobbled together to make an evening's entertainment. Pantomime olios were regularly presented on tour in the provinces in the early 19th century, with such leading stars as JOSEPH GRIMALDI appearing over and over again in some of his most celebrated scenes (he was still presenting episodes from the celebrated 1806 production of *MOTHER GOOSE* 16 years later). Such compilations were, however, also presented – especially as benefit performances – from time to time at even the most prestigious venues; the COVENT GARDEN management, for instance, presented an olio comprising scenes taken from ten successful pantomimes under the title *Harlequin's Chaplet* as early as 1789.

Olympic Theatre (1) A theatre in the Strand, London, which prospered in the 1830s with a series of EXTRAVAGANZAS written by J. R. PLANCHÉ that were to have a profound influence upon the development of the pantomime. The original Olympic was erected by Philip Astley in 1806, using timber taken from a French sailing ship, and was used initially as a venue for circus entertainments. It was renamed the Little Drury Lane Theatre in 1813 and staged plays until objections from the management of DRURY LANE nearby caused the licence to be withdrawn.

In 1830 the theatre (situated in one of the most disreputable areas of London) was taken over by MADAME VESTRIS and renamed the Olympic, promising (as stipulated by the licence) a programme of BURLETTA and other light entertainment. Success came immediately with *Olympic Revels; or, Prometheus and Pandora*, after which the partnership of Vestris and Planché went from strength to strength, until the theatre was the most popular venue in the city (causing producers of pantomimes elsewhere to set about the wholesale imitation of the productions seen there). Madame Vestris appeared in many of the shows herself, to wild acclaim, and gathered a fine company of players around her before finally leaving with her husband CHARLES MATHEWS to manage COVENT GARDEN in 1839.

Fire destroyed the theatre in 1849; it was rebuilt as a venue for romantic drama and was finally demolished in 1904.

(2) A theatre in New York, which opened originally in 1837 and hosted a variety of spectacular entertainments and burlesques, which included several pieces by J. R. PLANCHÉ. After destruction by fire in 1854 a second Olympic Theatre opened in 1856. It was here that the US actor George L. Fox enjoyed success in the 1860s in such entertainments as the pantomime *HUMPTY-DUMPTY*, which established a new record run for a US pantomime. The theatre was finally closed and demolished in 1880.

opening In the early history of pantomime, the name given to the first, fantastical, part of the entertainment, in which the story of some myth or folktale was recounted. Sources for these tales originally included Classical mythology and folklore but were subsequently widened to take in stories based on FAIRY-TALES, NURSERY RHYMES, and popular literature (with, for instance, plots based on such classics as *Don Quixote*, Samuel Johnson's novel *Rasselas*, William Combes's satirical poem *Doctor Syntax in Search of the Picturesque*, and Jonathan Swift's *GULLIVER'S TRAVELS*).

Burlesque versions of operas and other theatrical productions were also commonplace. Among the most successful of these were plots borrowed from Douglas Jerrold's NAUTICAL DRAMA *Black Ey'd Susan* and Carl Maria von Weber's opera *Der Freischütz* (the key features of which included a demon, a magic bullet, and a DARK SCENE that took place in the Wolf's Glen).

Typically, the plot of the opening would concern the opposition of a prince or country squire to the marriage of his daughter to a poor suitor, wanting her to marry instead some elderly acquaintance of few charms. The opening built up to a climax – the lovers' fortunes seeming doomed forever – at which point the characters involved were magically turned by the BENEVOLENT AGENT into the familiar figures of the HARLEQUINADE, in which guise they settled their differences in a series of knockabout slapstick scenes. Characters in the opening were often disguised by BIG HEADS, which were dramatically discarded during the TRANSFORMATION SCENE when the performers revealed themselves in the roles of Harlequin and his comrades.

In the very early days of the pantomime, the opening – which included chanted lines and songs but little spoken dialogue other than rhymed couplets – was broken up into a series of scenes interspersed with the comic business conducted by Harlequin and his colleagues, which bore no relation at all to the plot of the opening itself. In time, however, the two parts were separated in the cause of coherence (as in the 1781 DRURY LANE version of SHERIDAN's *ROBINSON CRUSOE* – the first time the two parts were distinguished), but it was the concluding harlequinade that remained the most important part of the entertainment.

For many years the opening simply provided an excuse for the knockabout part of the entertainment to commence (the celebrated 1806 production of *MOTHER GOOSE* at COVENT GARDEN, for instance, devoted just five of the 20 or so scenes to the opening). In 1817 the Drury Lane management experimented with a pantomime which brought the harlequinade and the opening back together, but it was not a success and the two parts remained separate. An early experiment with spoken dialogue in the opening was attempted at the HAYMARKET in 1814, with *Dr. Hocus-Pocus; or, Harlequin Washed White*, but it was not until the 1830s that the 'speaking opening' was widely adopted in imitation of the BURLESQUE and EXTRAVAGANZA, finally being sanctioned universally in 1843 with changes in the law governing the use of dialogue outside the Patent Theatres.

In the hands of such writers as E. L. BLANCHARD – nicknamed 'The Prince of Openings' – the opening was elevated to an admired art form, with highly poetic language and spectacular sets depicting often supernatural realms. One of the characteristics of the Blanchard pantomime was the 'dark' scene with which the opening began: against a sinister subdued background characters representing good and evil confronted one another and announced the underlying themes of the entertainment to follow. Various figures symbolic of Progress, Science, or Industry would often appear in these scenes to celebrate the great age of Victorian enterprise and argue the worth of education and other forms of self-improvement. Other figures such as Alcohol and Idleness, conversely, illustrated the dangers of various kinds of immoral behaviour.

Under the influence of the extravaganza, plots became more fully rounded and no longer depended upon the harlequinade for a resolution. As the restyled opening expanded, so it absorbed the comic role hitherto filled by the harlequinade, until ultimately the opening (much changed in character from its early days) became synonymous with the pantomime itself.

Open Sesame The magic formula by which the hero gains entrance to the robbers' cave in *ALI BABA*. Such formulae are a feature of many ancient folkloric tales, although sometimes it is not a cave but a tree, rock, or flower that opens up. The pantomime has made the formula so well known that it is now often quoted when any stuck door, locked safe, etc. is opened. Sesame, the French name for an oil-producing plant widely grown in the countries of the Middle East, itself has considerable significance in the folklore of eastern countries, enabling the dead to bypass hell in the Hindu religion. The GRIMM BROTHERS gave the magic formula as 'Semsi mountain, open up' in their version of the tale, but it is unknown which variation is of older parentage.

orchestra The sunken, usually semicircular, area in front of the stage in most large theatres where the musicians sit.

P

Palladium *See* LONDON PALLADIUM.

panorama *See* DIORAMA.

Pantaloon A masked character of the HARLEQUINADE, who was frequently the butt of HARLEQUIN's practical jokes and schemes. Pantaloon, a wily but gullible and money-grabbing old man and usually the father of COLUMBINE, began life as **Pantalone** in the *COMMEDIA DELL'ARTE* tradition in Italy. He was then portrayed as a grasping Venetian Jew, wearing a distinctive red cap (all Jews in Venice were obliged to wear such a cap), who jealously attempted to foil his daughter's suitors but was not above lusting after other young women himself. In times of perplexity he sought the advice of the pompous Il Dottore, but this invariably failed to protect him from the tricks and ploys of the other characters (including eventually his own servant, CLOWN) who coveted both his daughter and his wealth.

On the English stage his prime role came to be that of 'straight man' to Clown, whose antics (in the hands of JOSEPH GRIMALDI) gradually replaced the pursuit of Harlequin and Columbine as the comic heart of the harlequinade. In the early pantomime tradition an actor playing a baron, king, or other similar father figure would be 'revealed' as Pantaloon in the TRANSFORMATION SCENE.

Unlike some of the other roles in his harlequinade, Pantaloon demanded the best efforts of performers who were not only capable of all the usual physical feats, but were also excellent character actors who helped to clarify the plot. Famous English Pantaloons included Richard Norman and JAMES BARNES, who distinguished themselves in the part in the heyday of the harlequinade in the early 18th century. Later Pantaloons were criticized for sacrificing character to agility as they strove to outdo each other as acrobats and performers of TRICKWORK.

pantomime Originally, a theatrical entertainment in which meaning is conveyed entirely without DIALOGUE, through gestures and bodily actions. The term was first used in relation to the *PANTOMIMUS* tradition of Classical Greek and Roman theatre (otherwise unconnected with the modern British pantomime) and in most other countries outside the UK the word is taken to mean the sort of mime entertainment of which such performers as Jean-Louis Barrault and Marcel Marceau have proved master exponents.

In England, it was John Weaver who revived the word to describe the ballet-style entertainments he presented in the early 18th century and John Rich who developed the central idea of combining a mythological or folkloric story with a harlequinade and thus established the pattern of what was to prove a distinctive new form of theatre in which mime as such was to play a decreasing role.

pantomimus The sole performer in the ancient Roman pantomime (which was itself descended from an older Greek tradition). The link between the Roman pantomime (actually the name of the performer rather than that of the entertainment itself) and the modern variety is tenuous in the extreme, but in certain basic aspects the art of the *pantomimus* (a word which came from the Greek phrase *pantos mimos* – 'I imitate everything') was coincidentally an antecedent of the more familiar form of entertainment that developed in the 18th century.

The *pantomimus* was a resourceful performer who presented a one-man show in which he demonstrated his skills as a dancer, actor, and mime, telling a story to a musical accompaniment; he was often backed by a chorus. He wore a number of masks, one for each role that he played, and relied entirely upon mime gestures to convey meaning and emotion. Leading performers were noted for their agility and mastery of physical gestures and the best of them could expect to be rewarded with vast sums of money for their efforts.

The material performed in such entertainments ranged from tragedies to bawdy comedies that were often criticised for their scurrilous humour. The *ballets-pantomimes* seen in France in the 18th century and the Italian Night Scenes staged in London by John Weaver purported to revive the ancient Roman pantomime, though they were very different in form from their professed model, sharing in common little more than the fact that dance was an important part of the entertainment.

Acclaimed *pantomimi* of the Roman Empire included Bathyllus, Paris, who was murdered on the orders of Emperor Nero when his skills provoked the ruler's jealousy, and Pylades. Such was the popularity of the *pantomimi* that decrees were issued under Tiberius forbidding the Roman nobility from mixing in the street with these entertainers, who were originally regarded as lying at the very bottom of the social ladder. The growth of Christianity also militated against support for the increasingly indecent performances of the *pantomimi* and they disappeared permanently as the Empire collapsed, with no attempt being made at even the loosest revival of their art until the Renaissance. *See also* BACCHANALIA.

parodies The parodying of other forms of theatre has long been one of the standard jokes in the pantomime. Such parodies were particularly celebrated in the early 19th century, when the contemporary theatre was swamped by a succession of increasingly bizarre theatrical entertainments, which pantomimists were quick to lampoon. The EQUESTRIAN DRAMA, in which real horses played leading roles, was a rich source of humour for the pantomime, as was the DOG DRAMA and other similar entertainments featuring other species in principal roles. Thus, the pantomime *The White Cat* introduced an elephant in a mock performance of Shakespeare, while performers of SKIN PARTS appeared regularly in such roles as 'Nondescripts' – hilarious animals made up of bits of different species (among them the 'cameleopard').

The conventions of MELODRAMA in particular lent themselves to parody, which was achieved in the pantomime by the simple ruse of casting a man in the role of heroine. The 'legitimate' drama was not immune either and JOSEPH GRIMALDI himself appeared as CLOWN performing the 'dagger scene' from William Shakespeare's *Macbeth*. Other pantomimes lampooned the NAUTICAL DRAMA, opera, and popular romances.

Just as the pantomime mimicked other dramatic forms, however, so too has the pantomime itself inspired various parodies over the years, extending right back to the earliest history of the genre. Many of these parodies were published anonymously. Typical of early attacks on the pantomime delivered in the form of a parody was the uncredited *Dido and Aeneas; or, Harlequin, a Butler, a Pimp, a Minister of State, Generalissimo, and Lord High Admiral, dead and alive again, and at last crown'd King of Carthage by Dido* from the early 18th century. As well as having fun at the expense of the pantomimist's love of long titles, the piece also lampooned the contemporary taste for all things Italian at the expense of native English art.

Among the writers who actually admitted to being the authors of celebrated burlesques of the pantomime was the novelist and playwright Henry Fielding, who in 1736 penned *Tumble-Down Dick; or, Phaeton in the Suds*, which parodied the productions of JOHN RICH through a satirical depiction of one of his pantomime rehearsals. A similar line was taken in a pantomime of 1815 staged at the OLYMPIC THEATRE, which parodied itself under the title *Broad Grins; or, Harlequin Mag and Harlequin Tag* and sent up the business of rehearsing the harlequinade.

George Bernard Shaw's *You Never Can Tell* (1910) incorporated the figures of Harlequin and Columbine in the last act, while much more recently the conventions and characters of pantomime were ingeniously employed to explore Victorian values and hypocrisy in relation to the opium trade that flourished under the Empire in *Poppy* (1982) by Peter Nichols. The conventions of the pantomime were also employed by playwrights Caryl Churchill in *Cloud Nine* (1979) and by Louise Page in *Beauty and the Beast* (1985), while both Cheryl Moch – in *Cinderella, The Real True Story* (1987) – and the Gay Sweatshop company – in *Jingle Ball* (1976) – controversially explored the possibilities presented by a lesbian Cinders. A Black version of *Cinderella* was also seen in London in 1976 under the title *I Gotta Shoe*.

Other modern parodies have included a number of 'adult' pantomimes masquerading under such titles as *Red Hot Cinders*, *Don't Put Your Dick on the Stage*, *Mrs Whittington*, and *Sinderella* (written by comedian Jim Davidson). *See also* BURLESQUE; CRITICS; SATIRE.

Pasquino One of the minor characters of the *COMMEDIA DELL'ARTE*. A satirical valet, he was one of the *ZANNI* and reappeared as Pasquin in the COMÉDIE-ITALIENNE but did not survive the integration of the *commedia dell'arte* tradition into the English theatre.

Patent Theatres The London theatres that operate under the terms of a royal patent, which formerly allowed them the exclusive right to present spoken drama in London. The two Patent Theatres are DRURY LANE and COVENT GARDEN, both of which were granted Letters Patent by Charles II in 1662 – although the HAYMARKET also acquired a limited patent that covered the summer months only.

The patents were actually given to individuals connected with the theatres (namely Thomas Killigrew and William Davenant) and this provided a loophole that led to the unscrupulous CHRISTOPHER RICH for one claiming rights for his LINCOLN'S INN FIELDS THEATRE (where Davenant had been manager at the time he received the patent).

The two leading theatres, which generally opened between September and June, guarded their valuable patents jealously and all other venues were obliged to disguise their dramatic productions as essentially musical entertainments (*see* BURLETTA). Other theatres were finally able to enjoy the same rights as the Patent Theatres after 1843, when the rules governing London's theatres were relaxed (although both Drury Lane and Covent Garden still operate formally at least under the terms of their original patents). *See also* LICENSING ACT.

Paulo, Redigé (1787–1835) English comedian, who was popular in the role of CLOWN in the early 19th century. He was the son of two rope-dancers at SADLER'S WELLS but spent most of his career connected with DRURY LANE. Appointed resident Clown at the Lane in 1815, he emerged as one of JOSEPH GRIMALDI's leading rivals in the role, standing in for him when the latter quarrelled with the Wells management in 1817. He continued to appear in the part until shortly before his death and is credited with having introduced the tufted 'Red Indian' hairstyle and tights that became accepted features of the costume of Clown in the 19th century. Paulo is reputed to have died after an accident while playing HARLEQUIN after leaping through a window find that a safety carpet had not been prepared to break his fall.

Payne, Harry (1830–95) English comedian, who was much admired in the role of CLOWN. Dubbed 'the last of the great Clowns at Drury Lane', he was one of the leading stars to appear in the DRURY LANE pantomimes of the 1880s. He was the son of the actor W. H. PAYNE and first appeared in the role of HARLEQUIN at COVENT GARDEN. He changed to the part of Clown in 1859 when RICHARD FLEXMORE was taken ill during a performance of *LITTLE RED RIDING HOOD*, his brother Fred Payne inheriting his old role of Harlequin. Harry Payne continued to appear as Clown at the theatre until 1870, subsequently appearing at the SURREY THEATRE and the STANDARD THEATRE and then becoming resident Clown at Drury Lane in 1883. Much of his act was based on the traditional routines made famous by JOSEPH GRIMALDI. After his death he was succeeded by WHIMSICAL WALKER.

Payne, W. H. (1804–78) English actor, who was dubbed the 'King of Pantomime' for his performances as CLOWN at COVENT GARDEN in the mid-Victorian era. Payne made his pantomime debut in London in 1825 and quickly established a reputation for his hilarious playing of barons, villains, and sorcerers as well as Clown. He was particularly admired for his skill as a mime artist (though he was equally successful later in his career as a talking Clown) and for his irrepressible humour, which enlivened his performances into his old age. His two sons were similarly successful, HARRY PAYNE as Clown and Fred Payne as Harlequin.

Pedrolino *See* PIERROT.

penny plain, tuppence coloured *See* TOY THEATRE.

Perrault, Charles (1628–1703) French poet and author – possibly in collaboration with his son, Pierre Perrault Darmancour (1678–1700) – of *TALES OF MOTHER GOOSE* (1697), which provided the source material for several famous pantomimes. The tradition of the MOTHER GOOSE character being a fount of fairytales existed before Perrault picked up the idea for the title of his collection of eight tales with accompanying moral lessons, which quickly won a wide readership and acceptance as the standard form of these stories.

Perrault, the son of a Parisian barrister, was the first author to attempt anything approaching a comprehensive collection of such tales, which had hitherto been kept alive largely through the oral tradition. He inspired many imitators, but few matched his expressive but succinct style. He was well-connected with the French aristocracy, his brother having designed the Louvre, and his writings quickly won a wide and influential readership. A revival of interest in his writings in the early 19th century came at a time when pantomimists in England were eager for folkloric material for their scripts.

Notable among the stories they borrowed from his writings were such future pantomimes as *BLUEBEARD*, *CINDERELLA*, *HOP O' MY THUMB*, *LITTLE RED RIDING HOOD*, *PUSS IN BOOTS*, and *THE SLEEPING BEAUTY*. The versions of these tales staged in the modern pantomime tradition remain very much the stories as Perrault himself told them, though without quite the same bloodthirstiness.

Pied Piper of Hamelin, The Narrative poem by Robert Browning (1812–89), which continues to be adapted as a popular pantomime to the present day. Written in 1842 for the amusement of Willie Macready (son of the great actor William Macready) the poem enjoyed a very wide readership and inevitably attracted the attention of the pantomimists.

Notable productions in the late 20th century include one seen in Coventry, which featured the talents of Ken Dodd, Beryl Reid, and Frankie Vaughan. Recent reworkings of the poem for the pantomime stage include one by DAVID WOOD (in collaboration with Dave and Toni Arthur), which brought the story right up to date, with the Pied Piper returning to contemporary Hamelin. The tale was also the subject of a remarkable production at the National Theatre in 1987, in an adaptation by Adrian Mitchell.

Story The town of Hamelin, near Hanover, is overrun with rats (usually at the command of the evil Rat King). Various efforts to rid the town of the rat plague (by eccentric inventors, magicians, etc.) all fail until the mysterious Pied Piper arrives. When he plays his magic pipe the rats are entranced and follow him down to the River Weser, where they are all drowned.

Subsequently (either because the townsfolk refuse to pay the Pied Piper for his services, as in Browning's poem, or more usually because of the further machinations of the Rat King) the Pied Piper bewitches the children of Hamelin and leads them into a nearby hill. Just one crippled child is left behind.

Browning's poem ends here, but the pantomime generally takes the story further, with the townsfolk finding their way into the hill and confronting the Rat King in his lair. The Rat King is vanquished and all are reunited.

Origins Browning's poem was based on a legend of ancient origins, the earliest recorded version of it dating back to around 1450 and claiming to recall events that took place in

1284. In this original version the Pied Piper's music lures Hamelin's children out through the East Gate of the town and they are never seen again.

Various theorists have linked the tale to the Children's Crusade of 1212 (during which many children from France and Germany left on a doomed mission to the Holy Land) and alternatively to a bloody feud between the Hamelin area and a neighbouring region that cost many young lives in 1260. It is more likely, however, that the tale was a reworking of even older legends and the details of the mysterious stranger wreaking a terrible revenge after a slight and his use of a magic pipe are common features of several old folktales. Early translations of the story into English included that in James Howell's *Familiar Letters* (1645–55).

Pierrot A character of the HARLEQUINADE, who was descended from **Pedrolino**, one of the *ZANNI* of the *COMMEDIA DELL'ARTE*. Pedrolino was a simple, honest, servant in the original Italian tradition, but in French hands he was subtly changed in the 17th century into a stereotypical pathetic lover who wore a distinctive flowing white costume, with white face make-up.

Pierrot figured in several of the most famous early pantomimes, including several presented by JOHN RICH, among them *The Jealous Doctor* (1717) and *The Necromancer; or Harlequin Doctor Faustus* (1723). The popularity of Pierrot in the early English pantomime was largely a result of the appearances made by CARLO DELPINI in the role, although his subsequent transformation into an overtly sentimental figure was completed by the French pantomimist Jean-Gaspard Deburau (Jan Kaspar Dvorak; 1796–1846), who appeared in the role many times at the THÉÂTRE DES FUNAMBULES in Paris in the early 19th century.

Thus redefined, Pierrot became one of the dominant characters in the harlequinade, usurping the role of HARLEQUIN himself. In the hands of JOSEPH GRIMALDI, however, the character CLOWN subsequently stole the limelight from Pierrot and assumed his place. After the harlequinade went out of fashion the image of the melancholy Pierrot was perpetuated in the white costumes of English seaside concert parties for many years and by popular Pierrot dolls and pictures, while in France he received a new lease of life through the work of the mime artist Marcel Marceau (1923–) and his character Bip.

pirates *See ROBINSON CRUSOE.*

pit The central and rear area of seating at ground level. Seats in the pit are generally the cheapest in the house and in former times the pit often witnessed much unruly behaviour among packed pantomime audiences (though the rowdiest sections of the audience were usually to be found in the GALLERY). In the modern theatre the seats in this area of the auditorium are more usually referred to as the back stalls.

Planché, J(ames) R(obinson) (1796–1880) English author and theatrical designer, of Huguenot descent, whose many EXTRAVAGANZAS, BURLESQUES, and MELODRAMAS written between the 1820s and the 1870s had an enormous influence upon the development of the Victorian pantomime. After success with his first burlesque – *Amoroso, King of Little Britain* – in 1818, Planché established his reputation with the melodrama *The Vampire; or, the Bride of the Isles* (1820). Subsequently he proved an innovator in matters of costume, designing historically accurate outfits for the cast of a celebrated production of *King John* in 1823.

As a writer of pantomimes, Planché was active as early as 1818, when his speaking pantomime *Rodolph the Wolf; or, Columbine Red Riding-Hood* was staged (with scant success) at the OLYMPIC THEATRE in London. His most popular work, however, was to be the series of extravaganzas he wrote for MADAME VESTRIS in the 1830s.

He had previously met Vestris when they were both involved in a production of an opera at COVENT GARDEN in 1826, but it was not until 1830 that she invited him to provide an extravaganza with which to open her management of the Olympic. The resulting entertainment, *Olympic Revels*, which was billed as a 'burlesque burletta', was a great success and Planché quickly embarked on a sequel, *Olympic Devils; or, Orpheus and Eurydice*, which proved even more popular (Vestris showing her legs to great effect in the role of Orpheus).

A long series of similar shows followed, making the Olympic the most prosperous venue in London. These original entertainments, most of which drew on mythology and folklore for their subject matter and usually featured Vestris herself as PRINCIPAL BOY, were much admired for their music, elaborate presentation, and witty rhymed dialogue and soon threatened to eclipse the conventional pantomime.

Pantomime arrangers and authors of the 1840s and 1850s learnt to imitate the new drama created by Planché and in time the conventional OPENING was remodelled after his pieces, putting new pressure on the already fading HARLEQUINADE. Planché himself refused to call his plays pantomimes and they were usually billed as BURLETTAS (as dictated under the terms of the theatre's licence) although they fell more accurately into the category of extravaganza.

Typical works included such entertainments as *The Deep, Deep Sea; or, Perseus and Andromeda* (1833), *The New Planet* (1847), in which the author lamented the passing of the great days of the Regency pantomime, and *The Island of Jewels* (1849), for which WILLIAM BEVERLEY designed his first TRANSFORMATION SCENE. Such was the success of Beverley's scenery and special effects for this latter piece that Planché complained that all else was being sacrificed for technical effects and that his own contribution was being "painted out".

Riquet with the Tuft (1836), which featured such characters as CINDERELLA, Jack the Giant Killer, the UGLY SISTERS, Little Red Riding Hood, and other folkloric figures, was especially significant as it marked the first time Planché had turned to fairytales (as collected by MADAME D'AULNOY and CHARLES PERRAULT) rather than Classical mythology as a source. Subsequently he presented extravaganzas based on the stories of *PUSS IN BOOTS*, *BLUEBEARD*, and *BEAUTY AND THE BEAST*, among others.

Planché continued to write his charming extravaganzas for the Olympic after Vestris left and in the 1850s FREDERICK ROBSON was particularly well received in such extravaganzas as *The Discreet Princess* (1855). The success of such pieces – which were described as pantomimes without the harlequinade and vulgarity of the conventional genre – marked a sea change in the pantomime itself as managers awoke to the fact that deprived of the talents of such performers as the now-retired JOSEPH GRIMALDI audiences were hungry for something new – exactly the sort of spell-binding spectacle Planché was offering. The author himself also contributed libretti for several operas and was director of music at Vauxhall Gardens.

Plautus, Titus Maccius (*c*. 254 BC–184 BC) Roman playwright, whose comedies had some impact upon the development of the *COMMEDIA DELL'ARTE* many centuries after his death. Little is known of Plautus's life but around 21 of his 150 plays survive. His comedies were lively, bawdy, and farcical and profoundly influenced the growth of European comedy in the 17th and 18th centuries through the plays of such writers as Molière and Shakespeare.

The outrageous humour of his works had a particular effect upon the *commedia dell'arte*, in which his comic character Miles Gloriosus, a cowardly soldier, was redefined as Il Capitano. It is thought possible that some comic routines still seen in the pantomime today may have originated in his plays. The Stephen Sondheim musical *A Funny Thing Happened on the Way to the Forum* was based on his works.

playbill A theatre programme or poster giving details of a particular production. Playbills are among the oldest surviving relics of the early pantomime, the earliest such sheets dating back to 1737, when they were produced for both COVENT GARDEN and DRURY LANE. Notable theatre artists formerly included the design of playbills in their contributions to a production and writers were also expected to complete such bills (some of the wittiest were put together by E. L. BLANCHARD for his own pantomimes).

Player's Theatre Club Theatre in Villiers Street, London, which is one of the few professional venues in London still known for its pantomimes. Founded in 1927 as Playroom Six, the club reopened under its permanent name in 1936 in King Street, Covent Garden, and established a reputation for revivals of Victorian pantomime with its wealth of puns and its rhymed couplets, BURLESQUE, and MUSIC HALL. The club moved to a new home beneath the railway arches in Villiers Street in 1946, eventually transferring to the Duchess Theatre in Catherine Street in 1987 and shortly afterwards to a new theatre below Charing Cross railway station.

plots Pantomime writers have drawn on a bewilderingly wide range of sources for their plots over the 300-year history of the genre. In the earliest days of the pantomime, when the emphasis was firmly upon the relatively plotless HARLEQUINADE element of the entertainment, a basic narrative was related in the OPENING, with which the evening began.

Typically, 18th-century arrangers plundered Classical mythology for their opening scenes, which built up to a climactic confrontation that would then be resolved in the harlequinade. Towards the end of the 18th century, however, writers began to range more widely, adapting popular novels (notably Defoe's *ROBINSON CRUSOE*, Swift's *GULLIVER'S TRAVELS*, and even Samuel Johnson's *Rasselas*) and making their first forays into English folklore.

Other plots were composed largely from the writers' imaginations with borrowings from well-known history, Shakespeare, and contemporary science. The 19th century saw writers raid popular CHAPBOOKS for their nursery rhymes, ballads, and folktales (including many adaptations of stories from elsewhere in Europe) and absorb the fairytales collected by such influential writers as the GRIMM BROTHERS and HANS CHRISTIAN ANDERSEN.

Many original plots also continued to be presented; among the more bizarre titles in the early Victorian period, for instance, were *King Humming Top and the Land of Toys*, *Harlequin Columbus; or, The Old World and the New*, *Harlequin King Ugly Mug and My Lady Lee of Old London Bridge*, *Harlequin King Richard III; or, The Magic Arrow and the Battle of Bosworth Field*, *Old Woman Tossed in a Blanket*, and *Lindley Murray's Grammar; or, Harlequin A.E.I.O.U. and Y.*

Eventually the fairytale emerged as the predominant source of pantomime plots, although certain nursery rhyme stories and other plots of diverse origin have maintained their place in the contemporary pantomime canon (which at its widest includes a number of pieces more correctly described as 'Christmas plays'). The number of pantomimes regularly seen has diminished somewhat in recent decades, the most popular stories to fall by the wayside since Victorian times including *The White Cat*, *Riquet with the Tuft*, *The Fair One with the Golden Locks*, and *Bluebeard*.

Writers continue to experiment. Alongside more familiar stories, recent pantomimes have included plots based on the adventures of the glove puppets Sooty and Sweep (*see* television) and those of Punch and Judy. The 'Big Six' of recent decades, however, are *Cinderella*, *Aladdin and his Wonderful Lamp*, *Jack and the Beanstalk*, *Dick Whittington and his Cat*, *The Babes in the Wood*, and *Mother Goose* (which in very recent times has been increasingly rivalled by *Snow White and the Seven Dwarfs*).

Polichinelle A character of the Comédie-Italienne, who was a French interpretation of Pulcinella from the *commedia dell'arte*. Essentially the same character in appearance, the French version – who appeared both as a character on the stage and as a puppet – was markedly more cunning than his Italian model and may have contributed to the development of the English Harlequin and Clown. Although he played a relatively small role in the harlequinade itself he found a permanent place in the English theatrical tradition as the puppet character Punch in the popular Punch and Judy show.

Poole, Elizabeth (1820–1906) English actress, who was one of the first female performers to win acclaim in the role of principal boy. After making her debut in a male role in 1829 (as a dandy in *Jack in the Box; or, Harlequin and the Princess of the Hidden Island* at Drury Lane), she went on to play principal boy three times for Charles Farley at Covent Garden, playing Hop o' My Thumb in the pantomime of the same name (1831), Josselin the Miller's Son in *Puss in Boots* (1832), and Cupid in *Old Mother Hubbard and her Dog; or, Harlequin and the Tales of the Nursery* (1838).

She was particularly admired for her youthful good looks and as a singer of comic songs, although her role in the harlequinade was played by a male stand-in. Her success was to prove a factor in the gradual expansion of the opening in the 1830s, which was to signal the start of the decline of the harlequinade.

Povey, Eliza (1804–61) English actress, who is thought to have been one of the first (if not the very first) female performers to take the role of principal boy in the English pantomime. Records exist to the effect that she played the male hero of *Jack and the Beanstalk; or, Harlequin and*

THE OGRE at DRURY LANE as early as 1819, although another performer (JACK BOLOGNA) took her place as HARLEQUIN after the TRANSFORMATION SCENE in deference to the prevailing opinion that female performers were unsuited to the acrobatic demands of the role.

Power, Nelly (1853–87) English actress, who enjoyed a highly successful, if brief, career in the MUSIC HALL and the pantomime. Her songs included 'The boy I love is up in the gallery' (which MARIE LLOYD later adopted, without Power's permission). She made her debut, as a spirited PRINCIPAL BOY, in the 1860s, becoming one of the very first music hall stars to make an impact upon the Victorian pantomime and subsequently appeared at the SURREY THEATRE and in the spectacular shows staged by AUGUSTUS HARRIS at DRURY LANE. Her most successful roles included that of Sinbad (which she played in 1863).

Prince Charming The prince who falls in love with Cinders after dancing with her at the royal ball in *CINDERELLA*. Often treated as a PRINCIPAL BOY role, the prince is one of the few characters to have been included in the earliest versions of the story. Over the years he has variously been called Bountiful, Caramel, Elegant, Evergreen, Exquisite, Ferdinand, Floridor, Lovesick Lackadaisy, Paragon, Par Excellence, Peerless, Plenteous, Poppet, Poppetti, Prettihop, Primrose, Roderick, Rudolph, and Vanilla among other names.

The name Prince Charming was a translation of *Le Roi Charmant*, the name used in MADAME D'AULNOY's fairytale *The Blue Bird*, which was included in her celebrated collection of fairytales in 1697. As Charming he first appeared as Don Charmante as far back as the 17th century in a play by APHRA BEHN, while much later MADAME VESTRIS played a King Charming in 1850. He was first identified under the full title Prince Charming at Wakefield in 1880, although it was not until 1915, when he was thus called in the LYCEUM THEATRE's production of the story, that other variants were generally dropped.

In the days of the HARLEQUINADE, the performer playing Prince Charming was usually transformed into HARLEQUIN. Famous performers of the role have included Madge Elliott, Marie Burke, and Evelyn Laye; more recent interpreters have included comedienne Aimi Macdonald.

Princess's Theatre A former theatre in Oxford Street, London, which was one of the leading venues for pantomime in the 19th century. The theatre opened as a concert hall in 1840 and was subsequently used for opera, drama, and pantomime. Among the many famous performers to appear there were William MacReady, Fanny Kemble, and SIR HENRY IRVING, who acted there under the management of AUGUSTUS HARRIS.

Pantomime productions at the theatre were especially notable for the performances of the Clowns RICHARD FLEXMORE and Watty Hildyard and for the quality of the scenic designs. The most remarkable of the pantomimes seen at the venue was probably the 1856 production of *ALADDIN AND HIS WONDERFUL LAMP*, in which male performers took the roles of both Aladdin and the princess. The theatre was rebuilt in 1880 as a venue for straight drama and melodrama but failed to prosper and closed in 1902, finally being demolished in 1931.

principal boy The ostensibly male hero of all pantomime plots, who is usually by convention played by an actress. Such actresses are most definitely not male impersonators and retain their femininity in the role, generally wearing flattering costumes showing off their legs – to which they draw enthusiastic attention by giving them an occasional hearty slap – despite the fact that the character they play is generally of the strapping, undaunted, even chauvinistic, masculine variety. The principal boy is jaunty, unruly, unflinching in the business of vanquishing giants and demons and ultimately always successful in his love for the PRINCIPAL GIRL.

Although such 'breeches parts' were known to the earlier theatre (the Romans indulged in such cross-dressing during the rituals associated with the BACCHANALIA, while HARLEQUIN was sometimes played by a woman in the 18th century and again during the GRIMALDI era), it was not until the mid-19th century that the custom became a characteristic feature of the pantomime. Even then managers proved reluctant to cast women in roles that carried with them a certain amount of physical danger (true of most parts in the harlequinade at least) and male stand-ins took over when the knockabout began.

After a female played a male role in CHARLES FARLEY's operatic version of *ALADDIN* in 1813 the breeches role finally came to the pantomime in 1815, when such a part was written into the opening of *Harlequin and Fortunio*, again by Farley. The first female principal boy known by name is ELIZA POVEY, who appeared in the role of JACK in *JACK AND THE BEANSTALK; OR, HARLEQUIN AND THE OGRE* at DRURY LANE in 1819; a male stand-in took her place when it came to climbing the beanstalk itself and acting in the harlequinade. Subsequently, ELIZABETH POOLE played several principal boy roles in the 1830s, although she – like Povey before her – was still very young and accordingly played the hero as little more than a child.

The idea of more mature principal boys was promoted by opera and by the appearances of MADAME VESTRIS in male roles in the EXTRAVAGANZAS of J. R. PLANCHÉ; she first played a principal boy role in what was essentially a pantomime story in 1837, when she appeared as Ralph in *PUSS IN BOOTS* and it was she who established the long-cherished tradition of the slapped thigh.

Audiences responded well to the innovation and female principal boys were seen with increasing regularity in the 1850s and 1860s (though they remained skirted to the knee for some years). One consequence of this was the hastening of the decline of the HARLEQUINADE, which made less and less sense now Harlequin was no longer played by the same (male) performer who appeared as the hero in the opening.

It is uncertain which actress has the best claim to being the first to play a fully-fledged adult principal boy in the pantomime, though some critics have suggested it was a Miss Saunders, who played a prince at the Marylebone Theatre in 1847 or else a Miss Ellington, who played such a role at the LYCEUM THEATRE in 1852. Other contenders for the honour include MADAME CÉLESTE, who first played such a part in 1855. These pioneers were quickly followed by many more actresses, among whom LYDIA THOMPSON was probably the first to establish herself as a specialist in such parts in the pantomime.

The tradition was given the official seal of approval in the Drury Lane productions of AUGUSTUS HARRIS – in which ADA BLANCHE played the part every year between 1892 and 1897. Other celebrated principal boys presented by Harris included HARRIET VERNON, who was much admired for her shapely figure (Victorian principal boys were generally rather more 'strapping' figures than the more slimlined heroes of later generations). Nevertheless, the Drury Lane management has figured amongst those who have experimented with males in the role since then, presenting male principal boys every year between 1912 and 1915, when stars of operetta took such roles as the Prince in *THE SLEEPING BEAUTY*.

More recently there was a spate of male principal boys in the late 1950s and 1960s, when NORMAN WISDOM, Edmund Hockridge, Frankie Vaughan, Cliff Richard, TOMMY STEELE, Jimmy Tarbuck, and Edward Woodward were amongst the comedians, rock and roll singers, and balladeers to play the part on the London stage. For a period of several years it seemed the days of the female principal boy were over for good (despite the fact that the provincial theatres remained loyal to the old tradition), but CILLA BLACK's success in the role at the LONDON PALLADIUM in 1971 reversed the trend.

Among the most famous of all principal boys have been VESTA TILLEY, FLORRIE FORDE, Sara Lane, FANNY LESLIE, NELLY POWER, DOROTHY WARD, who appeared in such roles over a period of 50 years, Maggie Duggan, Nellie Stewart, Queenie Leighton, Phyllis Dare, Gwladys Stanley, Madge Elliott, CLARICE MAYNE, FAY COMPTON, Anne Ziegler, Jill Esmond, Evelyn Laye, Binnie Hale, PAT KIRKWOOD, and Anita Harris.

On the amateur stage notable principal boys have included no less a personage than the future Elizabeth II, who performed the role in three performances at Windsor in 1936. Perhaps the most notorious principal boy of all was Mabel Gray, a well-known prostitute who appeared in the role at the LYCEUM THEATRE in 1867.

Traditionally it is the principal boy who speaks the closing couplet of any pantomime, though never until the first actual performance for fear that speaking the final lines in rehearsal will bring bad luck (*see* SUPERSTITIONS). Many actresses find the part unappealing as it carries with it little opportunity for comic byplay, although principal boys of the last 20 years have been allowed the odd joke or two.

principal girl The heroine who provides the romantic interest in numerous pantomimes, opposite the PRINCIPAL BOY. The part ranges from that of one of the many princesses who populate the pantomime – in which the actress is often required to do no more than look pretty and perhaps to join in love duets with the principal boy – to the central role in *CINDERELLA*.

The chief attributes of actresses playing the principal girl include a sweet disposition and an ability to win over the audience's sympathy, a melodic singing voice, and a pretty face. Notable principal girls of the past have varied from LOTTIE COLLINS and MARIE LLOYD (whose robust humour did not suit the role particularly well) in the late 19th century to Twiggy, Mary Hopkin, and Clodagh Rodgers in the 1970s and Dana and model Linda Lusardi in the 1990s.

producer The person who takes responsibility for various managerial and financial matters associated with a theatrical production. Before 1956, the term 'producer' was synonymous with DIRECTOR, but since then the producer has been less closely involved with the actual rehearsing and performing of a production. *See also* ARRANGER.

prologue Traditional opening scene before the main plot gets underway, in which the supernatural forces representing good and evil in the pantomime confront one another. Pantomimes of the 19th century always began with such a prologue, with fairies and demons as well as more abstract characters (such as Industry and Idleness) vowing to defeat each other. Such scenes remain useful in that they introduce the idea of magic and conflict and get the audience in the right frame of mind for the fantastical scenes that are to follow – as well as underlining the moral lesson that can be learnt from the story to come. Following the convention concerning the entrances of such 'Immortals' the 'goody' appears from stage right in a pink spotlight, while the 'baddy' comes on from stage left in a green spotlight. *See also* OPENING.

prompter The person whose duty it is to follow the action in a copy of the script and to give the correct line when a performer has forgotten it. In the past the prompter's duties could be much wider, including overseeing rehearsals and even contributing as a writer of scripts and deviser of stage business (TOM DIBDIN, for instance, was prompter at DRURY LANE).

properties or **props** Any of the various items of equipment used on stage during a performance other than the scenery, costumes, and various technical devices. Personal properties (or hand-props) include things carried on by the performers themselves, usually kept on a 'props table' in the WINGS when not in use, where they remain the responsibility of the STAGE MANAGER. The nature of the pantomime often dictates the use of a huge variety of props, many of which rely upon the ingenuity of stage carpenters. Over the years these have ranged from a realistic serpent capable of wriggling across the stage, a working windmill, and a fire-breathing dragon (all created for the pantomimes of JOHN RICH in the early 18th century) to countless versions of Cinderella's coach and real (or exploding) cars (as seen in a number of early 20th-century shows). *See also* TRICKS OF CONSTRUCTION.

proscenium arch The high opening that divides the main stage area from the auditorium. Descended from the acting space of Classical Greek theatre, which bore the same name, the proscenium arch was the characteristic structural feature of virtually every theatre built in the UK between the 17th and 19th centuries. The arch acts as a frame for the action that takes place on the stage and was often very elaborate in design, just as a picture frame might be. In many theatres built in the 20th century, however, designers have rejected the formal proscenium arch in favour of more flexible staging arrangements.

It is generally acknowledged that pantomime works best in a traditional proscenium arrangement as more naturalistic staging methods undermine the essentially non-naturalistic character of the genre, although many touring groups and amateur companies have made a success of pantomimes using a wide range of staging techniques. The presence of a proscenium arch also enables a curtain or other frontcloth to be hung and therefore permits the use of the

CARPENTER'S SCENE, which takes place downstage while scenery is changed upstage of the cloth.

provincial theatres Although many of the most significant advances in the history of the pantomime are associated with productions seen in London, it would be wrong to ignore the role of the provincial theatres in the development of the genre. Among cities with a distinguished history of productions going back almost to the birth of the pantomime are Manchester, Glasgow, Birmingham, Bristol, Bradford, Liverpool, York, and Newcastle, among many others.

Manchester, for example, saw its first pantomime back in 1743, when *Harlequin's Vagaries* was staged there; subsequently pantomimes were regularly staged at the Theatre Royal, Manchester from 1846 to 1920 and the city became one of the customary stopping places for productions on tour from London – including, in the early days, those created by JOHN RICH.

Birmingham's first pantomime was seen in 1840 and the city has since been blessed with an unbroken run of pantomimes (with the exception of the years 1900–03, when rebuilding of the Theatre Royal took place); back in the 1880s as many as six professional pantomimes were staged in the city simultaneously. In the 20th century the city's Alexandra Theatre was also famed for its pantomimes, many of them being presented under the direction of Leon and Derek Salberg.

So successful were the pantomimes staged by Wilson Barrett at the Grand Theatre, Leeds in the 1870s that special 'pantomime trains' were put on to bring audiences from as far away as Manchester and London itself. Productions at the Tyne Theatre, Newcastle were for some years distinguished by the presence of the celebrated manager AUGUSTUS HARRIS, before he went on to even greater fame in London.

North of the border, both Glasgow and Edinburgh have strong traditions of pantomime that extend to the present day (notably in the case of the Citizens' Theatre, Glasgow and the Prince's Theatre, Glasgow, which staged many pantomimes based on less well-known plots), while many of the finest pantomimes staged in London were regularly toured across the Irish Sea to Dublin.

Many London productions were staged as they had been seen in the capital (complete with original casts), although scripts (and even titles) would often be altered to include references to local people, places, and events. JOSEPH GRIMALDI himself was among the stars to make several tours of the provinces, often presenting a medley of scenes from past triumphs (*see* OLIO); among his favourite venues were Worcester, Edinburgh, and Liverpool. Some subsequent stars, indeed, spent most of their career in the provinces out of choice – among them the great MUSIC HALL performer VESTA TILLEY, who resisted many attempts to lure her to London on a regular basis.

In the golden years of the late Victorian pantomime London productions were rivalled for spectacle by several provincial theatres, to the extent that performers struggled to distract the audience's attention from the lavish scenery and spectacular effects. A version of *CINDERELLA* staged at the Alexandra Theatre, Liverpool in 1885, for instance, excited much interest with its depiction of a fox hunt and 'Swan Ballet' sequence.

Pantomime 'circuits' were well established by the mid-20th century with touring productions being mounted by such respected managements as that of Howard and Wyndham (J. B. Howard and F. W. Wyndham) and by succeeding generations of 'Panto Kings' (such as JULIAN WYLIE, PRINCE AND EMILE LITTLER, Tom Arnold, Francis Laidler, Duncan Weldon at Triumph Productions, and Paul Elliott), who presented as many as 20 pantomime productions around the country in a single season.

In the 1930s approximately 300 professional pantomimes were staged throughout the UK each year, and even in the 1990s, in the face of rising costs, the total of professional shows is over 200 annually. Not only have standards of production in the provinces kept pace with those in London over the years, but the pantomime outside the capital has been somewhat sheltered from some of the short-lived crazes that have distorted London's shows. Thus, for instance, the provincial theatres largely maintained the cherished convention of the female PRINCIPAL BOY in the 1950s and 1960s, when many London managements were casting male pop stars in the role.

Provincial strongholds of the contemporary pantomime range from Aberdeen in the north, Belfast and Cardiff in the west, and Norwich in the east to Chipping Norton, Northampton, Chichester, Bristol, Windsor, and Plymouth in the central and south UK.

Pulcinella One of the *ZANNI* characters of the *COMMEDIA DELL'ARTE*, who was eventually transformed into Punch of the English Punch and Judy show, by way of the COMÉDIE-ITALIENNE (*see* POLICHINELLE). Pulcinella was usually played as a mischievous but dim-witted and cowardly peasant from Acerra and may well have borrowed some of his traits from the character MACCUS of the ancient Roman ATELLANA. It has been suggested that the character was created by the actor Silvio Fiorillo and then further developed by Andrea Calcese (d. 1656).

Like other characters in the *commedia dell'arte* Pulcinella was easily recognized by his costume, which consisted of a baggy white shirt and trousers and a peaked hat. In his mockery of the other characters he had much in common with HARLEQUIN. The character was not included among the few who dominated the English HARLEQUINADE but had by that time already been adopted by English puppeteers who refashioned him as Punch, complete with hooked nose and hunched back (possibly derived from Maccus).

pumpkin The transformation of a pumpkin into a magnificent coach in *CINDERELLA* remains one of the most famous scenes in the whole of the pantomime tradition and is perhaps the single most enduring image of the genre as a whole. Treated by succeeding generations of pantomime technicians as an opportunity to display their skills, the transformation has long been one of the highlights of the story and a climax to the first act. As well as various magical effects, the transformation is not considered complete by many children unless Cinders' magnificent carriage is pulled by at least one real pony.

It was CHARLES PERRAULT who first described the magical transformation of a pumpkin into Cinderella's coach in his version of the story, which was translated into English in 1729. His choice of a pumpkin may have been suggested by a detail from an earlier, parallel, Italian tale about one Zezolla, who is prepared to go to a royal feast by fairies who sprinkle on her skin drops of 'pumpkin water' (a cosmetic oil). Many centuries earlier the pumpkin itself had some ritual significance for Druids and it is still closely associated with the 'magical' festivities of Halloween.

pun A humorous play on words, in which one word is deliberately confused with another for comic effect. The golden age of the pantomime pun was the mid-19th century, when such writers as J. R. PLANCHÉ, MARK LEMON, William Brough and his brother Robert William Brough, Robert Reece (who explained that red hair was 'hair-red-itary'), Gilbert à Beckett, and SIR FRANCIS BURNAND were among those who made audiences squirm with delight at their linguistic daring.

The prince of punsters was, however, H. J. BYRON, whose many 'gems' included such feats as translating the motto 'Honi Soit Qui Mal Y Pense' as 'On his walk he madly puns'. No modern pantomime would be considered complete without a litany of excruciating puns. Examples of puns of relatively recent coinage include the incompetent FAIRY GODMOTHER's lament about her age: 'I've passed my spell-by date!' and the Ugly Sisters' jibe that Cinderella has not cleaned the windows – and she's the "biggest pane" of the lot. Slave girls trying to kill rats "to no avail" are advised by Sultans "Then get one" while cats spotted in chemists have been dismissed as "Puss in Boots" more than once. *See also* JOKES.

Punch *See* PULCINELLA.

puppets Puppets have been used in the pantomime many times in the past and the two theatrical genres share much the same origins. There are accounts of puppet plays being staged in England as early as the 14th century and such entertainments – generally incorporating the use of glove puppets – grew increasingly popular, with adaptations of stories from the Bible, Shakespeare, and Marlowe or plots based on contemporary events (such as the Gunpowder Plot).

After the Restoration the genre was transformed under the influence of the *COMMEDIA DELL'ARTE*, which also gave birth to the HARLEQUINADE. PULCINELLA became Punch in the uniquely English Punch and Judy show and puppeteers turned to the CHAPBOOKS for many of their plots, which included such stories as *DICK WHITTINGTON AND HIS CAT* and other tales also adopted by the pantomimists.

Puppet scenes were interpolated into pantomimes as a novelty on a fairly regular basis and today puppet versions of entire pantomimes are often presented. Scenes featuring puppets in the pantomime received a boost some years back when fluorescent rod puppets were first developed (enabling the black-clothed puppeteers to remain unseen).

Puss in Boots English fairytale, which has remained in the pantomime canon over a period of nearly 200 years. Only rarely has the story not met with success, although records exist of a disastrous early production staged at COVENT GARDEN (as *The Marquis of Carabas; or, Puss in Boots*) in 1818: even with JOSEPH GRIMALDI playing Fairy Grimalkin this early rendition failed to find favour with the audience, who began to boo, pull up seats, and tear up the curtain until the management promised to end the production's run.

More successful early productions included *Puss in Boots; or, Harlequin and the Miller's Son* staged by CHARLES FARLEY at Covent Garden in 1832, in which ELIZA POVEY won acclaim in the part of the Miller's Son (making her one of the first female performers to excel in the role of PRINCIPAL BOY). MADAME VESTRIS also appeared as principal boy with success in 1838 in an influential version written by J. R. PLANCHÉ and Charles Dance, confirming the place of women performers in such parts.

Popular productions of the story in the 20th century have included two versions presented at the LYCEUM THEATRE (in 1929–30 and 1936–37) and more recently one written by Alan Brown.

Story When a poor young man receives no more than a cat for an inheritance, he thinks he will benefit little by it, but the Cat – which can talk when it is wearing a pair of enchanted boots – proves to be of immense value, having various magic powers that he places at his master's disposal. These powers enable the Cat to deceive the royal family into thinking his master is a dispossessed prince (in the original folktale the Marquis de Carabas) and, by his nonchalant attitude to his master's few gold coins, that he is also very rich.

When the Cat learns that the royal party will pass close to a certain river, he persuades his master to bathe in the water and then tells the royal party that his master is drowning and has lost all his fine clothes. By royal command the hero is rescued and clothed from the royal wardrobe; he, meanwhile, falls instantly in love with the princess. As the young man travels in the royal coach the Cat runs ahead, persuading shepherds by the roadside to tell the king that the flocks they tend belong to the young man.

To complete the deception the Cat then tricks an ogre into changing into a mouse, which he then devours, so that the young hero may pretend that the ogre's magnificent castle is his own. The young man wins the princess, wealth, and the castle for good and the Cat is transformed into a young prince, who reveals he was trapped in a cat's body by a spell. Pantomime versions of the tale have in the past adopted a wide variety of devices to introduce such conventional characters as the DAME.

Origins The pantomime story draws on a number of ancient legends, but is generally faithful to the version recorded by CHARLES PERRAULT. Perrault based his plot on one given in *The Delightful Nights*, a compilation of folktales by the Italian writer Gianfrancesco Straparola (*c.* 1480–1557), which was published in 1534. In variants around the world the cat is sometimes a fox, a jackal, or a monkey.

Q

Queen of Hearts, The Nursery rhyme that was regularly seen as a pantomime until the middle of the 20th century. Productions of the story were presented at the LYCEUM THEATRE on several occasions by the MELVILLE BROTHERS, who won acclaim for the spectacular collapse during a storm of the House of Cards in the productions seen in 1927, 1933 (when it was the first pantomime seen by the future Elizabeth II), and 1938.

Blanche Tomlin and Dorothy Seacombe won particular acclaim in the roles of principal girl and principal boy in the version of 1927. Other notable productions included one in Birmingham in 1922, which similarly won acclaim for a collapsing House of Cards and also featured a remarkable disintegrating castle, and another staged by JULIAN WYLIE at DRURY LANE in the 1930s.

The story is still occasionally adapted for the modern stage (in 1972, for instance, at the Palace Theatre, Manchester); recent adaptations include one by Betty Astell and another by John Crocker and Eric Gilder.

Story The original nursery rhyme consists of a number of short verses, each dealing with one of the royal characters in a standard deck of cards (the most famous being the opening verse about the Queen of Hearts herself and the villainous Knave of Hearts). Pantomimists have approached this basic premise in a wide variety of ways, tacking on all manner of subplots taken from other nursery rhymes and fairytales in order to introduce a complete pantomime cast.

Origins The rhyme was first printed in 1728, although it is thought that the first verse at least is much older. Charles Lamb developed the rhyme in his picture book *The King and Queen of Hearts* (1805), which told the full story of the theft of a plate of tarts by the Knave of Hearts.

R

Randall, Harry (1860–1932) English comedian and singer, who was one of the most popular DAMES to star in the celebrated DRURY LANE pantomimes of the early 20th century. He made his pantomime debut at the age of 11 and subsequently built up a reputation as an interpreter of the role of dame while at the Grand Theatre, Islington, where he first appeared – in *DICK WHITTINGTON* – in 1891; he went on to perform in every pantomime there annually until 1901, taking such roles as Old Mother Hubbard (in which he made his debut as dame) and Mrs Crusoe. In 1903 he played Little Mary in *HUMPTY-DUMPTY*, which was to be DAN LENO's last pantomime. When Leno died his close friend Randall was the natural choice as his successor and he remained the leading dame at the Lane until his retirement in 1913 (following a nervous breakdown).

rats *See DICK WHITTINGTON AND HIS CAT*; *PIED PIPER OF HAMELIN, THE.*

Ravenscroft, Edward (1643–1707) English playwright, whose many comedies reflected the growing influence of the Italian *COMMEDIA DELL'ARTE* upon the English stage. Writing in the years following the Restoration, when companies from abroad were once more welcome in England, Ravenscroft was the author of such successful farces as *The Careless Lovers* (1673), one of several plays based on the plays of Molière, and *The London Cuckolds* (1681), which was performed annually on Lord Mayor's Day at both DRURY LANE and COVENT GARDEN over a period of 70 years.

His incorporation of characters from the *commedia dell'arte* in *Scaramouche a Philosopher* (1677) promoted the familiarity of English audiences with the genre and, it has been argued, helped to pave the way for the early development of the pantomime itself (as did the plays of his contemporary APHRA BEHN). *See also* SCHOOLROOM SCENE.

red-hot poker *See* CLOWN.

Red Riding Hood *See LITTLE RED RIDING HOOD.*

Reeve, Ada (Adelaide Mary Isaacs; 1874–1966) English actress and singer, who was much admired in PRINCIPAL BOY roles in the late Victorian pantomime. She made her pantomime debut in 1878 and subsequently became a star of musical comedy and melodrama as well as straight drama on both sides of the Atlantic. Her most successful parts included

ALADDIN, in which she appeared in 1899 in full British army khaki uniform (in response to the outbreak of the Boer War that year).

rehearsal One of a series of meetings at which the director and cast gradually get a show ready for performance. Initial rehearsals are usually taken up with readings of the script and basic blocking of the performers' movements around the stage; subsequently attention is paid to details of performances and to all the technical matters arising, culminating in a DRESS REHEARSAL at which all the various aspects of a production are brought together.

The rising cost of putting on a professional pantomime has led to a reduction in the amount of time given over to rehearsals in recent years (sometimes with the consequence of a distinct lowering of performance standards – especially when inexperienced CELEBRITY STARS have been recruited). Whereas in 1950 a major pantomime might be rehearsed for over a month, equivalent productions today may be presented after only eight days or so preparation (though two weeks is a normal rehearsal time in most towns). Artistes are paid 'rehearsal salaries' in these weeks before the opening night.

Rich, Christopher (d. 1714) English theatre manager, who is remembered as one of the most notorious managers in theatrical history but who also played a key role in popularising the ITALIAN NIGHT SCENES that were to influence the early development of the pantomime. Rich began his controversial career as a lawyer but in 1690 bought a share of the management of DRURY LANE; by 1693 he was not only manager of the theatre but also holder of its Royal Patent, giving him complete control over all its activities.

Abetted by the theatre's treasurer Zachary Baggs, Rich lined his own pocket by systematically reducing expenditure at every turn, paying the smallest of salaries and refusing to devote anything more than the most minor sums to the theatre's productions. For years he presided over a company constantly on the verge of rebellion against his tyrannical regime. His masterstroke as a manager came around 1700 when he invited visiting companies from France to present their Italian Night Scenes at the theatre, among them the popular Sieurs Alard. These productions were a considerable success, bringing large crowds to Drury Lane – although some critics were appalled to see such 'low-brow' entertainment usurping the place of more serious drama.

Ultimately Rich's unscrupulous methods proved his downfall: his actors complained to the Lord Chamberlain, who imposed a 'Silence Order' on Rich, which effectively meant that he would have to relinquish his position (finally achieved after soldiers physically removed him from the building). Rich determined to rebuild his empire at the deserted LINCOLN'S INN FIELDS THEATRE and set about the restoration of the building. He died, however, before this work was complete, leaving his son JOHN RICH to assume control of the theatre and, inspired by his father's success, to present further mime entertainments, which were translated in his hands into the first true pantomimes.

Rich, John (1681–1761) English actor and theatre manager, who is often described as the father of the pantomime. The son of the widely-despised theatre manager CHRISTOPHER RICH, John Rich inherited (with his brother) control of the LINCOLN'S INN FIELDS THEATRE on his father's death.

Although eccentric and impatient with his actors, he was somewhat less resented than his notorious father, who had swindled backers and cast alike out of their money. Having completed the restoration of the theatre, John Rich – remembering his father's success with ITALIAN NIGHT SCENES – set about the Herculean task of rivalling the success of the management at DRURY LANE by staging similar productions that would attract mass audiences and a veritable 'pantomime war' developed between the two venues.

Under Rich's direction and following the example set by the *ballets-pantomimes* of JOHN WEAVER (in which Rich appeared), Lincoln's Inn took to presenting novel two-part entertainments in which serious scenes depicting a story taken from Ovid or some other Classical author were combined with unconnected comic episodes featuring the characters of the *COMMEDIA DELL'ARTE*. These productions were distinguished by their incorporation of music, dance, magic, elaborate TRICKS OF CONSTRUCTION and transformations, various imaginative technical effects, and not least by the acting of Rich himself (under the stagename **Lun**) in the role of HARLEQUIN.

Rich had always had pretensions as an actor, but had failed in straight drama largely due to his ill-educated manner and slow delivery. The silent role of Harlequin was thus very appealing to him and within a few years he was being hailed as the finest performer of the part anywhere in Europe. Rich was assisted at the theatre by John Weaver himself, who joined him in 1717, and it was from Weaver that Rich borrowed the term 'pantomime' to describe his innovative productions (Weaver had previously used it to describe his own *ballets-pantomimes*, which he claimed were an accurate imitation of the pantomimes seen in ancient Rome).

The first Rich production actually to be billed as a 'pantomime' was *Harlequin Sorcerer* (1717); it was an immediate success, attracting enthusiastic audiences, and proved to be the first of a long series of equally successful productions that Rich continued to present until shortly before his death over 40 years later. Remarkably, hardly one of these subsequent productions was a failure and it was this record that established the place of the pantomime in the national theatre.

Among the most significant of Rich's early productions was *The Magician; or, Harlequin a Director*, which opened on 16 March 1721. The script of this pantomime came complete with topical references (to the South Sea Bubble financial scandal) and mute HARLEQUINADE and surpassed all his previous successes. Even greater commercial success followed in 1723 with the pantomime *The Necromancer; or Harlequin Executed*, which was based on the legend of Doctor Faustus (a story tackled at Drury Lane almost simultaneously, though with much less success) and created a sensation, playing to packed houses for weeks on end.

Rich himself wrote the comic scenes and (being a skilled deviser of stage illusions) organised the tricks of construction while Lewis Theobald wrote the narrative sequences. Rich also interested himself in details of the scenery and other technical matters and made various innovations in backstage practice that were to have a major impact upon the improvement of standards throughout contemporary English theatre (these included the curtailing of the old tradition that allowed privileged members of the public to wander freely behind the scenes and even walk onto the stage during a performance).

Rich's productions were important not only in the early history of the pantomime, but also in the development of ballet and straight drama, encouraging David Garrick, for instance, to promote a more naturalistic style of acting. The popularity of such entertainments as *The Rape of Proserpine; with, the Birth and Adventures of Harlequin* (1723) and *Harlequin a Sorcerer; with the Loves of Pluto and Proserpine* (1725) – two of his biggest successes (both with music written by the respected composer Johann Ernst Galliard) – established the pantomime as a regular feature in the programmes of the London theatres, despite the protests of many (including Garrick, COLLEY CIBBER, and Alexander Pope) who feared that 'serious' theatre would thereby be eclipsed.

Spectacular stage effects in *The Rape of Proserpine* included a flying chariot drawn by dragons, an earthquake, an erupting volcano, a giant, and a raging fire. In time Rich outgrew the Lincoln's Inn Field Theatre and subsequently presented his hugely popular productions at his new theatre at COVENT GARDEN, which he built with the profits from *The Beggar's Opera* and opened in 1732. His arrival at the new theatre was a much-publicised event and became the subject of William Hogarth's celebrated picture 'Rich's Triumphant Entry', in which Rich is somewhat satirically presented approaching his new home with his retinue in the manner of an all-conquering Roman emperor. Rather than attempt many new pantomimes here, he concentrated over the next 20 years or so on producing ever more spectacular versions of the entertainments with which he had established his reputation at Lincoln's Inn.

Notable pantomimes presented under Rich's management included *The Royal Chace; or Merlin's Cave*, *Harlequin Skeleton*, and *Harlequin Everywhere*, in which elements of Classical mythology were entwined with traditional British folklore. Individual scenes that were cherished in the public's memory long after Rich's death included scenes in which he pretended to catch a butterfly and that in which he played Harlequin emerging from a giant egg, which he revived many times before astounded audiences.

His numerous admirers included George II who, like several others of Rich's most distinguished patrons, belonged to the Sublime Society of Beefsteaks, which Rich founded in 1735. After Rich's death it was universally agreed that no-one would ever be found to match his performances as Harlequin, though some performers were billed as the 'Ghost of Lun'. More importantly, perhaps, his combination of mythological narrative with the antics of the harlequinade was to set a pattern for pantomime that, although frequently adjusted, was to remain the basic structure of the genre until the harlequinade itself fell from favour at the end of the 19th century.

rise-and-sink One of the spectacular means by which pantomime sets were transformed almost instantaneously back in the 19th century. The effect relied upon the rapid removal of the upper half of a set of flats or other (often collapsible) scenic item by drawing it up into the FLIES while the lower half was carried down by a SLOTE into the cellar, revealing new scenery standing immediately behind.

Records exist of the 'rise-and-sink' being employed in pantomime by CHARLES DIBDIN the younger as far back as 1800. Typical of the use made of the rise-and-sink was Dibdin's much-admired trick by which a post-chaise carrying Pantaloon was transformed at the touch of Harlequin's bat into a humble wheelbarrow, the two halves of the post-chaise separating and vanishing from view in the merest instant, to the great consternation and embarrassment of the occupant.

Roberts, Arthur (1852–1933) English comedian and singer, who was one of the first MUSIC HALL stars to appear in pantomime. Specialising in the role of the debonair man about town and offering a distinctly risqué line of humour, he was invited by AUGUSTUS HARRIS to play one of the lead parts in *MOTHER GOOSE* at DRURY LANE in 1880, the first major production to be dominated by music hall performers. He was rapturously received in the comic role of Doctor Syntax, which was ideally suited to his quickfire humour, and continued to star at the Lane for another three years, often alongside fellow-comedian JAMES FAWN.

Roberts, David (1796–1864) English artist, who was much acclaimed in the early 19th century for his DIORAMAS. Roberts began as an apprentice to the great scene painter CLARKSON STANFIELD at DRURY LANE but was subsequently hired around 1827 by the rival management at COVENT GARDEN, where he strove to match the achievements of his teacher with mixed success.

His first diorama executed for the theatre was a series of seascapes for *Harlequin and Number Nip* (1827), which included views of the Battle of Navarino and was compared favourably by some critics with the productions of Stanfield himself. Later works included a diorama somewhat irrelevantly illustrating the 'Eastern Question', for *Harlequin and Little Red Riding Hood* (1828), and – equally irrelevantly – another depicting a polar expedition, for *Harlequin and Cock Robin* (1829). Like his former master, Roberts's work in the theatre brought him fame and wealth as well as election to the Royal Academy.

Robey, Sir George (Edward) (George Edward Wade; 1869–1954) English comedian and singer, who was one of the most popular stars of MUSIC HALL and pantomime. Nicknamed the 'Prime Minister of Mirth', he made his West End debut in 1891 at the Oxford Music Hall and enjoyed enormous success in such comic roles as the Mayor of Mudcumdyke and Daisy Dilwater, the raising of his pronounced eyebrows conveying all kinds of innuendo in even the most innocent lines.

He made his first appearance in pantomime in 1899 playing one of the babes in *BABES IN THE WOOD* and subsequently graduated to the role of DAME, in which he was again hugely popular. He made most of his pantomime appearances in the provinces but did appear on the London stage in 1921. Many of the songs he had made famous in the music hall surfaced in his pantomime act – among them thc suggestive 'Archibald, Certainly Not'. His other acclaimed roles in the theatre ranged from parts in revue to Falstaff.

Robin Hood Legendary English hero, who has been associated with the English pantomime since the mid-19th century. Possibly based on a real-life outlawed adventurer of the 12th century, Robin Hood was a familiar figure of the traditional May Day revels and Morris dances and also of the court MASQUES of Tudor England (though it is thought that originally he was descended from the mythical 'Green Man' of the pre-Christian era). Accounts of his life as a fugitive in Sherwood Forest and his opposition to the tyranny of the evil Sheriff of Nottingham were first written down around 1490 and were widely known through the many ballads sung about him and his merry band.

Plays were written about Robin Hood and his men in the 16th and 17th centuries and in 1741 the story of the outlaw of Sherwood inspired an opera, by Thomas Arne, while William Shield wrote another one in 1784. Robin finally made his pantomime debut in 1795 in *Merry Sherwood; or, Harlequin Forester* and pantomime adaptations of the legends surrounding his name continue to inspire occasional pantomimes, which treat the legends with varying degrees of respect.

It was, however, as an incidental character in *THE BABES IN THE WOOD* that he was to achieve lasting popularity. Among the first pantomimes to introduce Robin Hood and his band of Merry Men as the rescuers of the babes was *The Babes in the Wood*, seen in 1860, in which Robin was played by a woman. Press reaction to this combining of the two legends was mixed (critics pointing out that Robin Hood if he had existed at all had lived 200 years after the babes), but Robin's appearance in the story soon became obligatory.

The part of Robin himself continues to be played by both male and female performers, the most notable of whom have included HARRIET VERNON, FAY COMPTON, and more recently Edward Woodward, who was admired in the role at the LONDON PALLADIUM in 1972.

Robinson Crusoe The central character in the pantomime *ROBINSON CRUSOE*, which was based on the novel (1719) of the same name by Daniel Defoe. The Crusoe of Defoe's novel was inspired by the Scottish sailor Alexander Selkirk (1676–1721), who was stranded on the desert island of Mas-a-Tierra, one of the Juan Fernandez group off Chile, between 1704 and 1709 after he quarrelled with his captain. On his return to England Selkirk made the most of his adventures and became a minor celebrity of his day, telling his story to anyone prepared to pay, including Defoe. Defoe gave his fictional version of Selkirk the name Robinson Crusoe after noticing it on a gravestone while in hiding after the Monmouth Rebellion. Selkirk himself eventually joined the Royal Navy and was buried at sea off Africa after he died of a fever.

In the pantomime the part is often treated as a role for a female PRINCIPAL BOY, though in the very first version of the story (in 1781) the role was played by the acclaimed Italian actor CARLO DELPINI. Delpini's male successors include the singer Engelbert Humperdinck, who played the part at the LONDON PALLADIUM in the 1960s and pop singer David Essex; the most accomplished female Crusoes have included VESTA TILLEY.

Robinson Crusoe Enduringly popular pantomime, which was derived from the famous novel (1719) written by Daniel Defoe. The success of Defoe's novel created something of a fashion for stories concerning desert islands and shipwrecked mariners forced to rely upon their own wits to survive.

As a pantomime, the theme was first taken up in 1781, when RICHARD BRINSLEY SHERIDAN's *Robinson Crusoe; or, Harlequin Friday* was presented at DRURY LANE. Sheridan's pantomime was enormously successful, enjoying a long run of 38 nights. Significant features of the production included the separation of the OPENING and the HARLEQUINADE into two distinct halves for the first time (the harlequinade forming the last act of the entertainment and being linked to the first part by a TRANSFORMATION SCENE), the interpolation of characters from the harlequinade into the main plot (Pantaloon and Pierrot, for instance, were rescued from cannibals by Crusoe and Friday), scenery by DE LOUTHERBOURG, and the playing of GIUSEPPE GRIMALDI as Harlequin Friday. The harlequinade itself concluded with a spectacular dance in a magnificent temple dedicated to Venus.

Just five years later, in 1786, the production was seen – with DAVID GARRICK's *Harlequin's Invasion* – at the John Street Theatre, New York, making it the first pantomime to be seen in the USA. The popularity of the tale was subsequently confirmed by numerous successful revivals all around the country (a version staged at Newcastle in 1878 lasted ten and a half weeks) and by regular productions in London, of which the most admired included Drury Lane's 1881 production of a script written by E. L. BLANCHARD; critics considered the production a triumph although the author himself complained that the cast had taken so many liberties with his text that he regarded his payment as compensation for the damage done to his literary reputation.

Another notable (though relatively unsuccessful) production followed at Drury Lane in 1893, by which time stars from the music hall were heading the bills at all the major theatres (this was the only pantomime with which AUGUSTUS HARRIS actually lost money). The cast included MARIE LLOYD as Polly Perkins, ADA BLANCHE as Crusoe himself, DAN LENO as Mrs. Crusoe, HERBERT CAMPBELL as Will Atkins, and LITTLE TICH as MAN FRIDAY.

Several contemporary pantomimists have also written versions of the story, among them one by JOHN MORLEY, in which Crusoe pits his wits against the Demon Oylslick, the pirate band of the wicked Blackpatch, and a tribe of cannibals led by Queen Wotta Woppa.

Story Robinson Crusoe has been shipwrecked on a desert island and goes through various adventures, including a brush with cannibals, before he is finally rescued. Sheridan's version followed the original novel fairly faithfully, only departing from the book towards the end in order to introduce the obligatory harlequinade (with Friday being transformed into Harlequin and winning the hand of Columbine). In later versions Crusoe often falls in love with a native princess and searches for buried treasure – all embellishments of Defoe's original.

Mrs Crusoe, Polly Perkins, Neptune, the pirates Blackbeard and Will Atkins (who bears some resemblance to PANTALOON), and all the other characters usually seen in modern productions of the story are additional characters created by the writers of various pantomime versions. Other companions to the shipwrecked mariner in the pantomime story have included over the years his dog, his cat, his parrot, his goat, and the OLD MAN OF THE SEA.

Origins Defoe's novel was based on the experiences of the marooned Scottish sailor Alexander Selkirk and how he rescued Man Friday from the cannibals and taught him Christianity (*see* ROBINSON CRUSOE).

Robson, Frederick (Thomas Brownbill; 1821–64) English actor, who became the leading star in BURLESQUE, pantomime, and other entertainments at the OLYMPIC THEATRE in the 1850s. Despite the fact that he was only five feet tall, Robson enjoyed enormous success both in comedy and tragedy at the theatre and was particularly successful in such burlesques as *THE YELLOW DWARF* (1854), which was written by J. R. PLANCHÉ with him in mind for the title role. Robson found the strain of acting very great, however, and gradually succumbed to his addiction to alcohol, which contributed to his early death.

roll-out A concealed opening in a FLAT through which a performer can make a sudden surprise entrance. Such roll-outs, in which the hole was hidden by a flap of canvas, were a common feature of the HARLEQUINADE when used in combination with a variety of TRAPS.

rose Roses have long had significance in the folklore of many countries, being associated with Venus and Cupid, among many other mythological figures. The most significant rose in the pantomime is that plucked from the Beast's garden at the start of *THE BEAUTY AND THE BEAST*; as a consequence of this rash action Beauty is obliged to go and live with the Beast. In some versions of *THE SLEEPING BEAUTY* the Prince who eventually wins Beauty's hand offers her only a rose, whereas her other suitors offer her jewels.

Rose, Clarkson (1890–1968) English comedian, who became a star of concert parties before achieving wider fame as a performer in the role of DAME in pantomime. Tall and stately, he was particularly associated with the pantomimes presented by the MELVILLE BROTHERS at the LYCEUM THEATRE in which his comic talents took centre stage.

Rumpelstiltzkin A fairytale that continues to be adapted on an occasional basis as a pantomime plot (though less often now than previously). Recent adaptations of the tale include a version by Norman Robbins.

Story A miller is so proud of his beautiful daughter that one day he is overheard boasting that she could even spin flax into gold. News of the claim reaches the king, who demands that the girl must perform the miracle for him or perish. She is locked in a room with a spinning-wheel, where she is visited in her distress by the dwarf Rumpelstiltzkin, who agrees to help her. A deal is struck and the dwarf spins the flax into gold. The girl is betrothed to the king (or his son) but Rumpelstiltzkin demands that she fulfil the bargain she has struck, to the effect that she will give him her first child when it is born.

When the dwarf comes to claim his reward he is begged not to take the child. Rumpelstiltzkin agrees to the request on condition that the new queen guesses his name within three days. Subsequently the dwarf is overheard gleefully singing his own name; when the queen correctly tells the dwarf what his name is he dies in a rage (falling through the floorboards as they are smashed by his stamping feet).

Origins The pantomime plot was derived from the fairytale version included by the GRIMM BROTHERS in their *Household Tales*. The original folktale was common to several European traditions, although sometimes under different titles (including

Tom-Tit-Tot in England, where it may have been first told).

run An unbroken series of performances of a single production, which may on occasion be extended in response to heavy public demand. Such runs were once rare as productions were different on successive nights, but the pantomime's popularity changed this practice and several of JOHN RICH's pantomimes in the early 18th century ran for many nights. Pantomime runs gradually lengthened into a matter of weeks and runs of 40 days were quite usual for the pantomimes featuring the great JOSEPH GRIMALDI in the early 19th century. With as many as 3000 people seeing each performance, this meant that about one-eighth of the whole of the population of London witnessed each of his stage roles.

A new record was created in 1806, when THOMAS DIBDIN's *MOTHER GOOSE* ran for 111 nights at COVENT GARDEN. In 1842 the BRITANNIA THEATRE's *The Old Woman of Threadneedle Street* ran for 26 weeks, a record that lasted for over 100 years.

The trend for longer and longer runs continued and in the 20th century it became quite common for pantomimes to occupy theatres for two or three months at a time. This trend was reversed, however, in the 1980s when rising costs obliged theatre managements to end most runs after a period of four to six weeks (most pantomimes now begin and end more or less with the school holidays).

Inevitably, pantomimes nearing the end of a long run are sometimes perceived to be tired-looking and lacking the spontaneity of the first performances. The run does, however, offer performers themselves a substantial amount of work in what might otherwise be a lean season. The record for any pantomime run to date is held by JOHN MORLEY for his *ALADDIN AND HIS WONDERFUL LAMP*, which ran from December 1980 to April 1981 at the Theatre Royal, Nottingham. AMATEUR PANTOMIMES, in contrast, rarely run for more than a week, most of the cast having daytime jobs to fulfil.

S

Sadler's Wells Theatre A theatre in Finsbury, north-east London, which began life as a concert hall in 1683 but was later rebuilt (in 1765) as a theatre and became famous for its pantomimes starring JOSEPH GRIMALDI in the role of CLOWN. The theatre is situated over a spring that was once the heart of a fashionable spa resort (it now lies under the back row of the stalls).

The theatre did not hold a royal patent and operated as a MINOR THEATRE between Easter Monday and October until the rules were changed in 1843. In the early years of the 19th century the theatre was in a sorry financial state and only the introduction of a series of DOG DRAMAS saved it from closing for good. Better times were to follow, however, as its great Clown became established as the biggest box office draw in the capital.

Grimaldi made his stage debut at the theatre in 1781 aged only two years old (alongside his father) and subsequently worked in many capacities both in front of the tabs and backstage, learning the theatre craft. He appeared there (with the support of the theatre's manager CHARLES DIBDIN) every summer between 1781 and 1823, with the exception of a single year (1816) when he did not appear due to an argument with the management (public protests ensured his return the next year).

It was in the Sadler's Wells pantomime *Peter Wilkins; or, Harlequin in the Flying World* that Grimaldi first adopted the distinctive white make-up that was to become a hallmark of his Clown. A more lamentable event in the theatre's history occurred in 1807, when a false fire alarm led to a panic in which 18 people lost their lives. Dibdin's pantomimes drew large crowds who came both to see such stars as Grimaldi and also to marvel at the spectacular effects on display (the theatre was even fitted out with massive water tanks in 1803 so that full-scale AQUATIC DRAMAS could be staged).

The theatre was fortunate in having not only the talents of Grimaldi to call upon, but also those of the popular Harlequins Thomas Ridgway and JACK BOLOGNA and the Pantaloon JAMES BARNES. Consequently pantomimes staged at Sadler's Wells had noticeably shorter OPENINGS (as the stars were somewhat hampered by the wearing of the conventional BIG HEADS, which rendered them effectively anonymous) but a tradition of outstanding harlequinades which depended upon the clowning of its stars rather than upon the element of spectacle (technical effects were necessarily constrained by the lack of cellar space under the stage, where the water tanks were positioned).

Grimaldi's emotional farewell at the theatre in 1828 played to the customary packed house and for a time it seemed his son would match, if not even surpass, his father's achievements (hopes that were doomed to disappointment). Subsequent successes, many of which were celebrated for their 'hits' lampooning contemporary fads and personalities, included pantomimes written by the theatre's manager T. L. GREENWOOD in the 1840s and 1850s and such spectacular entertainments as *Harlequin and the Yellow Dwarf; or, the Enchanted Orange Tree and the King of the Gold Mines* (1851), which recreated scenes inspired by the Californian gold rush.

The theatre eventually closed in 1878, reopened a year later as a home of MELODRAMA, became a MUSIC HALL in 1891, and was finally closed in 1906 and demolished. The rebuilt theatre has confined itself to productions of opera and ballet since the 1930s and was the home of the internationally acclaimed Sadler's Wells Ballet (later renamed the Royal Ballet).

Sanger's Grand National Amphitheatre *See* ASTLEY'S AMPHITHEATRE.

Santley, Kate (1837–1923) US actress, who graduated from the MUSIC HALL to become a star of opera bouffe and of the pantomime at DRURY LANE. She was one of the first performers to bridge the gap between the music hall and the pantomime, appearing at the invitation of AUGUSTUS HARRIS in the Drury Lane pantomime of 1880 at the head of the company.

satire Pantomime has always had a mild satirical air, which has on occasion invested a harmless comic feast with a distinctive cutting edge. The tradition goes back to the very beginning of pantomime history, with topical references being made in comic songs in the productions of JOHN RICH. His *The Magician, or, Harlequin a Director*, for instance, included songs voicing public speculation about the South Sea Bubble financial disaster, reserving particular venom for a man named Knight, the treasurer of the South Sea Company who had recently fled London for France.

Later the attentions of the Examiner of Plays made political comment risky, although pantomimists still managed to keep alive a tradition of poking fun at such foreign rulers as Napoleon, who was considered an acceptable target in the early 19th century. As writers of pantomimes drew on an increasingly wide range of sources for their plots in the 18th century – basing their stories on everything from nursery rhymes (some of which were in any case politically or historically inspired) to broadsides – so they found more and more opportunities to glean relatively innocent humour from references to various events and personalities familiar to their audiences.

Satirical comments upon affairs of the day were at their most biting in the early years of the 19th century when JOSEPH GRIMALDI and his confederates had enormous success poking fun at all manners of social, artistic, and political fads. Instances included Grimaldi's hilarious sending-up of the Regency fop in several pantomimes and the many barbs directed at the British military's mixed success against Napoleonic France (*see* AWKWARD SQUAD). At a time when no other form of theatre could hope to make such comments without censure, the pantomime gleefully lambasted virtually anything or anybody who came within legitimate range, getting away with it by keeping the comedy always to the fore.

Often the pantomime was to prove a voice – albeit a restrained and somewhat reactionary one – for the national conscience, highlighting the sorry plight of the needy under the infamous Poor Laws, for instance, and voicing the doubts many had about the new technology associated with the Industrial Revolution. Among political issues touched on in the pantomime during this period were such matters of public concern as the repeal of the slave trade (through such figures as Man Friday), the disturbances caused by machine-smashing Luddites, and Catholic Emancipation, though references to these matters were generally indirect.

When politicians were mentioned by name – which was rare indeed – it was usually to praise them, in reflection of their current popularity with the electorate. Over the years, national crises, wars, elections, inventions, scandals – including the recurring theme of the quality of bread after interference by unscrupulous bakers – and sporting events have all furnished the pantomimists with material, as have such political issues as the state of education, the old age pension, and the poll tax. More usually, though, pantomime writers have found that concentrating on less weighty affairs offers the best scope for humour and have focused their attention on satirising day-to-day eccentricities and public foibles.

Some affairs of the day almost beg to be sent up in the pantomime, as was the case with *Harlequin and George Barnwell* (1834), which poked fun at the architects who had competed to produce the winning design for the new Houses of Parliament. Similarly, in 1846 every major pantomime in London had something to say about a controversial naked statue of the Duke of Wellington that had recently been erected on Marble Arch.

The pantomime has never been a great respecter of authority (as evidenced by the anti-social antics of CLOWN) and over the years fun has been had at the expense of all manner of representatives of the establishment, from watchmen and huntsmen to the Duke already mentioned. The attentions of the Examiner of Plays in former times meant that comments reflecting upon the monarchy and the government of the day or upon religious authorities were unwise, but the light-hearted nature of the genre and the scattershot approach adopted with such a wide range of targets getting a light peppering, meant that writers and performers were allowed greater licence than their contemporaries in other forms of drama. Few people took such satirical comments seriously and the satire was in any case rarely consistent.

Thus, while Grimaldi might have great fun at the expense of army recruiting methods he was equally likely to whip up the audience's enthusiasm with sincere renditions of nationalistic songs calculated to appeal to the spectators' patriotism. During the Napoleonic Wars, John Bull and Britannia were frequent visitors to the pantomime stage and many pantomimes capitalized upon the popularity of the Royal Navy, which had proved its superiority over the French navy many times. References to current fads and fashions were similarly harmless and played purely for laughs.

After the Grimaldi era such satirical comments virtually disappeared from the pantomime, proving incompatible with the telling of charming fairytales as perfected in the extravaganza (which the pantomime eventually absorbed). Nonetheless, audiences relished the occasional innocent 'hits' and 'raps' delivered at the expense of contemporary figures and the tradition experienced something of a revival with the incorporation of stars from the MUSIC HALL, where little was sacred.

The hilarious 'topical duets' that were an indispensable feature of the DRURY LANE pantomimes starring DAN LENO and HERBERT CAMPBELL were enormously popular, with references being made to items of news in the latest papers, which were cleverly inserted into prepared songs. Particular targets of these satirical duets included the leadership of the Liberal Party, who were mercilessly lampooned in *The Forty Thieves* in 1898 at a point when the party was split over a leadership crisis.

The contemporary pantomime continues to maintain a faintly satirical air, chiefly through the jokes delivered by dames and other characters at the cost of political figures, royalty, pop stars, modern art, etc. In recent years victims of many a dame's wit have included such nationally known figures as Arthur Scargill, Margaret Thatcher, Edwina Currie, and virtually every member of the royal family. *See also* PARODIES; TOPICALITY.

Scapino A stock character of the *COMMEDIA DELL'ARTE*, who was one of the most popular *ZANNI* roles. Scapino, usually dressed in green and white, was a cowardly rascal who was subsequently transformed into the equally immoral **Scapin** of the COMÉDIE-ITALIENNE; he was not, however, included among the figures that became central to the English HARLEQUINADE.

Scaramouche A stock character of the HARLEQUINADE, who was descended from **Scaramuccia** in the *COMMEDIA DELL'ARTE*. He was variously played as a boastful soldier like Il Capitano or as a valet and participated in the traditional knockabout antics as one of the *ZANNI*. The greatest performer in the role was Tiberio Fiorillo (1608–94), who played it in London and Paris as well as in his native Italy. Among his most notable successors were GIUSEPPE GRIMALDI and his celebrated son.

Like HARLEQUIN, Scaramouche was familiar to English audiences long before the development of the pantomime and appeared in a play of English origins as early at 1685 (in a farce based on Christopher Marlowe's tragedy *Doctor Faustus* by WILLIAM MOUNTFORD). Favourite scenes featuring Scaramouche as seen in the immensely popular pantomimes of JOHN RICH included one in which he used his own leg as a rifle when out hunting duck.

scenario The brief plot synopsis on which performances of the *COMMEDIA DELL'ARTE* were traditionally based. Such scenarios provided outlines of the action involving the main characters but no dialogue and little in the way of detail about the slapstick elements of the performance, these being left to the improvisational skills of the actors themselves. The same was true of the HARLEQUINADE for much of its history, meaning that accurate reconstructions of the genre are problematic, whereas the OPENING was completely scripted. Even today performers exercise a greater degree of licence in matters of dialogue and comic business than would be tolerated in virtually any other form of drama. *See also* BURLA; LAZZO.

scene One of the parts into which an ACT is divided. In the pantomime, which is famous for presenting a rich variety of exotic and often spectacular settings, it was once not uncommon for each succeeding scene to transport the audience to a totally new location (requiring a large number of scenic designs). In the early 19th century it was customary for there to be 18 such scenes, although some pantomimes had as few as 12 and others as many as 22. The cost involved in having so many settings has led to a reduction in the number of locations presented in the contemporary pantomime, which now rarely exceed half-a-dozen.

scenery The painted backcloths, FLATS, and various stage structures etc. upon which the pantomime has long depended for much of its spectacle. Ingenious scenic effects were a feature of the genre from the very beginning, with JOHN RICH setting the standard with the most elaborate TRICKS OF CONSTRUCTION and varied settings designed to please the eye.

As the pattern of OPENING followed by HARLEQUINADE became established the concluding scene that followed the DARK SCENE became the most ambitious in terms of scenery. As the Benevolent Agent restored the fortunes of Harlequin and Columbine and transported them from the gloomy cavern or ruin in which the Dark Scene had taken place so the scenery would magically transform itself into a glittering paradise or similar landscape.

In many respects designers of the earliest pantomimes were influenced by the theatre of Renaissance Italy and the *COMMEDIA DELL'ARTE* and in the early days pantomime designers presented somewhat sombre Continental and Classical settings exclusively. By the end of the 18th century, however, scene painters were beginning to develop the more colourful techniques that were to blossom several decades later and many venues prided themselves upon their lavish pantomime sets.

Imaginative designers produced scenery depicting a wider and wider range of foreign lands; THOMAS DIBDIN's *Harlequin Quicksilver; or, the Gnome and the Devil* (1804), for instance, was set in Spain, while Dibdin's *Harlequin's Magnet; or, the Scandinavian Sorcerer* (1805), moved through Russia, Siberia, and Tartary. At much the same time artists began to experiment with domestic English settings, as in COVENT GARDEN's innovative *MOTHER GOOSE* (1806), in which the scenery was unusually plain in contrast with other pantomimes of the day, and the rural English setting that was to become traditional for many pantomimes was presented. In some respects the choice of setting reflected changes in public taste, with pantomime scenery of the late 18th century, for instance, being heavily influenced by the Gothic Revival and subsequently by the fashion for the 'picturesque' (which inspired numerous sets featuring views of ruined castles and pastoral landscapes). Sets depicting London were also frequently seen because devisers of the comedy of the harlequinade found an urban setting more fertile ground for their brand of humour. The taste for all things oriental at the beginning of the 18th century was equally influential, inspiring sets depicting Chinese temples, bazaars, and court scenes as English artists imagined them to be.

Often the rendering of the scenery had value as a tool of public education – or even satire – with, for instance, many backcloths being painted to depict typical landscapes of newly-industrialised Britain in the early 19th century.

Technically the pantomime set consisted of the same components (flats, borders, wings, and backcloths) that were familiar in other forms of theatre, but the special needs of the pantomime soon pushed the imagination of the pantomime designer beyond the limits dictated elsewhere. Great advances in the technique of scene decoration and the use of lighting to show sets to their best effect were made in the 1820s with the development of the genuinely beautiful DIORAMA, which prompted respected artists to explore the use of new pigments and to adopt a much more varied range of colours than they had previously used. More attention was paid to getting the illusion of perspective right and standards of artwork rose dramatically at all the leading theatres, who placed new importance on the recruitment of established artists to work on their pantomime sets.

The Victorian pantomime witnessed the most glorious era in terms of stage effects and scenic invention and visual spectacle became the most important element of all (*see* TRANSFORMATION SCENE). By 1850 the stage carpenter and his assistants (who also often operated the various mechanical devices during performances) were among the most important figures connected with the pantomime and the success of productions depended largely upon their competence, being even more important than the success of the comedy of the pantomime.

It was not uncommon for work on pantomime sets to begin six months before the first performance, such was the complexity of the scenery itself. Enormous sums of money were spent on such stage decoration, which far outweighed the sums dedicated to sets for other types of drama. The public's thirst for new scenes meant that pantomime sets were rarely recycled, although pieces from them would often find further use in other forms of theatre. Many famous artists worked on pantomime sets for the major London theatres, the most celebrated including George Lambert, who contributed designs for John Rich, PHILIPPE JACQUES DE LOUTHERBOURG, who executed much admired scenes for DAVID GARRICK's productions at DRURY LANE, WILLIAM BEVERLEY, whose designs adorned the extravaganzas of J. R. PLANCHÉ, and CLARKSON STANFIELD, who was particularly noted for his mastery of the diorama.

Pantomime scenery of the 19th century was as spectacular and inventive as any in world theatre and even critics such as George Bernard Shaw had to concede that the popularity of the genre had preserved many scenic traditions and skills that would otherwise have been lost. The tradition of elaborate scenic design in the pantomime continued into the 20th century, but financial considerations in recent decades have meant that rarely do modern sets approach those of the previous century.

In the professional theatre pantomime sets (now made largely of canvas rather than more expensive wood) are often recycled from other shows or previous pantomimes and writers are even asked to construct their scripts so that existing scenery can be used and new settings kept to a minimum. Some sets last many years, though damage is often done in scenery stores by rats, who have a particular taste for the fire-resistant 'size' with which the canvas is coated.

Amateur companies generally make a considerable amount of new scenery each year (frequently having limited storage space for old scenery) but are often confined to a single basic set for the entire production (scene changes comprising the exchange of various scenic details around the stage). *See also* AQUATIC DRAMA.

schoolroom scene Formerly, one of the most frequently-presented traditional scenes of the pantomime, which originated as a comedy routine in the *COMMEDIA DELL'ARTE*. In it, HARLEQUIN (or one of his descendants) demonstrates his inability to come to terms with even the most elementary lessons, to the fury of the teacher, who eventually resorts to hitting him with a cane in an attempt to make him understand. The scene was first transmitted to the English theatre in the 17th century, when EDWARD RAVENSCROFT included it in his *Scaramouch a Philosopher, Harlequin a Schoolboy, Bravo, Merchant and Magician* (1677), which was based on a compilation of scenes from the comedies of Molière. The scene is still revived from time to time in *BABES IN THE WOOD*, through the adventures of the comical babes at the local village school.

seven-league boots *See HOP O' MY THUMB.*

Sheridan, Richard Brinsley (1751–1816) English playwright, theatre manager, and politician, born in Ireland, who is usually remembered for such brilliant comedies of manners as *The Rivals* (1775) and *The School for Scandal* (1777).

Having acquired DAVID GARRICK's share in the management of DRURY LANE in 1776, Sheridan pursued his great career as a playwright with comedies, BURLESQUES, and other entertainments to be staged at the theatre. In 1779 he is thought to have contributed a scene to the pantomime *Harlequin Fortunatus; or, the Wishing Cup* and two years later he was credited as author of the very first pantomime version of Daniel Defoe's novel *Robinson Crusoe*.

ROBINSON CRUSOE; OR, HARLEQUIN FRIDAY (1781) – which is sometimes claimed to have been the work of Sheridan's wife or of other members of his family – was well received (although Horace Walpole was moved to regret the changes wrought by Sheridan and other contemporary pantomimists and longed for a return to the pantomimes of JOHN RICH's day).

Inspired by Sheridan, pantomimists have continued to render new versions of Defoe's story to this day and the pantomime remains one of the most popular in the modern canon. Sheridan's adaptation was especially important for its linkage of the characters of the harlequinade with the story told in Defoe's narrative, with such characters as Pantaloon (who torments the unfortunate Man Friday) sharing Crusoe's island. Prior to 1781 the action of the harlequinade had borne no relation to the narrative and Sheridan's innovation marked a major development in the development of the pantomime, promoting coherence and inspiring many other pantomimists to follow suit (culminating in the identification of the characters of the opening with their equivalents in the harlequinade via the TRANSFORMATION SCENE).

As proprietor of the Lane, Sheridan showed considerable generosity to the young JOSEPH GRIMALDI after the death of his father in 1788.

sightline The limit of the stage area that can be seen by every member of the audience regardless of where they are sitting in the auditorium.

Simple Simon Nursery rhyme character who often appears as a secondary character in pantomime, for instance in versions of *JACK AND THE BEANSTALK*. Comical and slow-witted, he is generally introduced as the best friend (or even brother) of the PRINCIPAL BOY and is an equivalent of such familiar figures as BUTTONS and WISHEE-WASHEE. The nursery rhyme about Simple Simon was first printed in the 18th century and was expanded to as many as 15 verses cataloguing his comic misadventures (which include mistaking mustard for honey). The role is often taken by popular comedians, the best of whom have included NORMAN WISDOM, FRANKIE HOWERD, Des O'Connor, ROY HUDD, and Jim Davidson.

Sinbad the Sailor One of the popular tales from the *ARABIAN NIGHTS ENTERTAINMENTS* that was frequently adapted as a pantomime on the Victorian stage and is still regularly seen in the contemporary theatre. The first pantomime version of the tale was staged at DRURY LANE in 1814 as *The Valley of the Diamonds; or, Harlequin Sinbad*.

Notable among subsequent 19th century versions of the tale was *Sinbad the Sailor; or, Harlequin and the Fairies of the Diamond Valley* (1876), which was the result of a collaboration between E. L. BLANCHARD and T. L. GREENWOOD. Another version seen at the same theatre in 1882 must rank as one of the most spectacular productions ever staged, with a cast of hundreds (including an army of children dressed as British soldiers returning in triumph after Sir Garnet Wolseley's campaign in Egypt that year), a procession featuring every English monarch since the Norman Conquest, and magnificent scenery.

Subsequently, DAN LENO's success in the role of Tinpanz the Tailor in *Sinbad and the Little Old Man of the Sea; or, the Tinker, the Tailor, the Soldier, the Sailor, the Apothecary, Ploughboy, Gentleman and Thief* at the SURREY THEATRE in 1886 led directly to him being engaged to appear at Drury Lane, where he was to enjoy his greatest triumphs. More recent versions of the tale include those by John Crocker and Eric Gilder and by JOHN MORLEY and Paul Reakes, among others.

Story The plot of the original tale (which is often treated very loosely in pantomime versions) traces the penniless Sinbad's rise to fame and wealth through a series of adventures and charts the contrasting fortunes of his brother. In the pantomime he sets sail from Baghdad to bring back a lovely Eastern princess, who has been kidnapped by a sorcerer. Aided (and as often comically obstructed) by a crew that includes his own mother (the DAME role) and the dim-witted Tinbad the Tailor, he discovers the fabulous Valley of Diamonds (usually in the last scene of the first act) and variously battles with pirates, slave traders, and the sorcerer himself before rescuing the princess (who often becomes his wife). Among Sinbad's most fearsome foes is the OLD MAN OF THE SEA, a demon who gets on Sinbad's back and refuses to climb down again, and the Giant Roc (an enormous vicious bird).

Origins Historians claim that Sinbad was modelled on a real adventurer, who lived in 12th-century Persia, but in many respects the story seems to be indebted to a number of legends shared by several cultures and echoes the story of Odysseus. Equivalents of the Old Man of the Sea are found in the mythology of many regions of Africa and Asia. The tale was first translated into English in 1712 and was enthusiastically taken up by the CHAPBOOKS.

singalong That indispensable part of the evening's entertainment when the audience are invited to join the cast in singing either some familiar tune or a new song, the words of which are usually brought on to the stage and displayed on a large board (the 'song sheet'). The singalong in the pantomime dates back at least to JOSEPH GRIMALDI's rendering of HOT

CODLINS, in which the audience delighted to take part. Whatever its origins, the singalong was an accepted feature of all pantomimes by the 1860s and was subsequently much boosted by the arrival of singers from the MUSIC HALL who were well-skilled in whipping up enthusiasm for such songs. It is the convention in the contemporary pantomime for the audience to be split into two halves, which are then encouraged to outsing each other.

singing harp *See* *JACK AND THE BEANSTALK*.

skeleton scene *See* GHOST SCENE.

skin part A role in which a suitably disguised performer, usually a specialist in such parts, plays an animal character. Animal characters have figured in the pantomime since its earliest days, with such parts being one of the chief attractions of the productions of JOHN RICH among others. Rich himself played dogs and other animal characters many times during his career.

However, it was not until the early 19th century that animals, real and otherwise, became an essential feature of the action under the influence of such eccentric theatrical genres as the DOG DRAMA and the EQUESTRIAN DRAMA. Alongside real llamas, elephants, and donkeys, the pantomime was populated increasingly by animal impersonators. (It has been argued that this development was in part a response to the philosophical ideas of Rousseau and his contemporaries, which held that animals had individual identities just as humans did).

In 1824 the management of the LYCEUM THEATRE presented the celebrated French animal impersonator Charles-François Mazurier in the role of a monkey in *Monkey Island; or, Harlequin and the Loadstone Rock* and soon other actors were establishing themselves in similar ape disguises. CHARLES DIBDIN promoted the role of the animal impersonator in such pantomimes as *Walooka and Noomahee; or, The Ape of the Island* (1825) and it became quite common for the actor playing such a role to be transformed into the star part of CLOWN when the harlequinade began.

Along with the popular cats, dogs, horses, and cows, performers appeared as all manner of other species – including some which never existed in real life (weird combinations of different animals that were dubbed 'Nondescripts'). Although children have often been cast in such SKIN PARTS as the GOOSE, the COW, and the pantomime Horse, which are often non-speaking roles, many famous performers have also excelled in them. JOSEPH GRIMALDI, for instance, played a monkey at SADLER'S WELLS at the age of three, while no less a personage than SIR HENRY IRVING was much admired at the age of 19 playing the leader of a pack of wolves in *LITTLE BO-PEEP* at the Theatre Royal, Edinburgh in the 1850s.

Other noted performers specialised in such skin parts and made them one of the prime attractions of the pantomime. Of these the most accomplished was GEORGE CONQUEST, who won great acclaim in such roles at the GRECIAN THEATRE and subsequently also at the SURREY THEATRE. His many varied impersonations ranged from the usual cow to those of an octopus, a parrot, a porcupine, and even a spider crab, which he played with great success in *Spitz-Spitz, the Spider Crab* at the Grecian Theatre in 1875. His sons FRED CONQUEST and ARTHUR CONQUEST continued the family tradition, distinguishing themselves in the parts of Goose and 'Daphne the Chimpanzee' respectively.

Another famous player of skin parts was CHARLES LAURI, whose achievements included performances as such animals as bears, ostriches, kangaroos, and frogs as well as the more conventional CAT, in which role he was particularly successful in *CINDERELLA* at the LYCEUM THEATRE in 1893. Others have included the GRIFFITHS BROTHERS, who won acclaim in such roles in the 1880s, and more recently such duos as Desmond and Marks, June and Paul Kidd, and Peter Dayson and David Brody. The Pender troupe, a stilt-walking act that often tackled skin parts, were popular in the early years of the century (the stilts were particularly useful when it came to playing such creatures as ostriches). Among their members was the young Archie Leach, later to find fame in the US cinema under the name Cary Grant – epitomising the tradition of famous stars who began their careers 'as the back end of the pantomime horse', considered the most humble of all roles on the stage.

Typically all the great performers of animal roles made their own costumes, which were often highly complex and difficult to manoeuvre. On other occasions, the animal characters have been completely mechanised and operated by remote control from offstage, although this necessarily limits the participation of the animal concerned in the action taking place. *See also* CAMEL; DOGS.

slapstick The traditional boisterous and usually physical comedy from which much of the popular appeal of the pantomime is derived. Every good pantomime has at least one scene devoted almost entirely to visual comedy of this kind, as well as numerous opportunities elsewhere for a swift kick or 'pratfall'.

Classic slapstick scenes in the modern pantomime repertory include the LAUNDRY SCENE from *ALADDIN* and the make-up scene from *CINDERELLA*, in which the preparations of the UGLY SISTERS to go to the ball culminate in them flinging mudpacks and wet flannels etc. at each other (*see* SLOSH SCENE). The usual PROPS for such clowning range from planks and ladders to shaving-foam pies.

The original slapstick was the bat wielded by HARLEQUIN – a gift from the gods via the BENEVOLENT AGENT. From the earliest days of the pantomime its appearance signalled to the audience that the fun of the HARLEQUINADE was about to begin. The bat consisted of two strips of wood bound together, which, when struck against a firm object – usually some part of the anatomy of another character or some apparently solid item of scenery – made a convincing slapping noise without injuring the victim (it was not unheard of for performers to place a little gunpowder between the two wooden strips in order to create an even more dramatic effect). The noise produced by the bat was crucial in that it provided a cue for the stage crew to enact some specially prepared stage illusion or transformation; the crack of the bat had to be sufficiently loud to be heard above the noise of the action on stage, the hubbub of the audience, and the sound of the orchestra.

The slapstick itself disappeared with the harlequinade, but the term remains to denote any instance of the energetic physical comedy that has long been considered an indispensable ingredient of any successful pantomime. *See also* TRICKS OF CONSTRUCTION.

Sleeping Beauty, The One of the most enduringly popular of all pantomime stories, which was first dramatised at

DRURY LANE in 1806, as *The Sleeping Beauty, a Grand Legendary Melo-Drama*. Subsequently the story was seen as a pantomime starring JOSEPH GRIMALDI in 1822 (as *Harlequin and the Ogress; or, the Sleeping Beauty of the Wood* by CHARLES FARLEY).

Among the most celebrated productions that followed over the years was an extravaganza by J. R. PLANCHÉ, which was presented at COVENT GARDEN in 1840, and J. HICKORY WOOD's version staged at Drury Lane in 1900 starring DAN LENO and HERBERT CAMPBELL (as Queen Ravia and King Screwdolph), which was toured to the USA a year later. Subsequently the version staged at the Lane in 1912 was a great success, with GEORGE GRAVES and stars from musical comedy playing some of the leading roles (with famous male singers playing the PRINCIPAL BOY). Further versions of the story were given at the theatre in 1913 (as *The Sleeping Beauty Re-Awakened*) and in 1914 (as *The Sleeping Beauty Beautified*); it was also presented at the theatre in 1929 after the regular Drury Lane pantomime had ended.

Between the wars the story was successfully staged at a number of leading venues, with Dick Tubb winning particular acclaim in the role of Queen Guinevere in the version seen at the LYCEUM THEATRE in 1932 (where the pantomime had also been seen in the 1926–27 season). A production at the LONDON PALLADIUM in the 1950s was notable for its casting of a man, Edmund Hockridge, as the Prince (against the traditional convention of the female principal boy). Another version of 1967, *Queen Passionella and the Sleeping Beauty*, established DANNY LA RUE as a leading pantomime star. Most leading contemporary pantomimists include a version of the tale in their repertoire. Other interpretations of the fairytale have included a ballet composed by Tchaikovsky (1890) and a cartoon version by WALT DISNEY (1958).

Story The Sleeping Beauty is Rose, the daughter of a king and queen who are so delighted after her birth that they hold a great feast to which everyone is invited with the accidental exception of one particular wicked fairy. This fairy (often called Carabosse) vows revenge for the insult and prophesies that one day the princess will prick her finger and die. The Good Fairy, however, modifies the curse so that the princess will simply fall into a sleep lasting 100 years.

Elaborate precautions (usually supervised by an incompetent DAME) are taken to prevent this happening, with every thorn being removed from the palace roses, but to no avail. At the age of 15, the princess meets an old woman (in most versions of the tale the wicked fairy in disguise) using a spinning wheel in one of the ancient towers of the castle. The princess picks up the spindle and pricks her finger: at once she and everyone in the castle fall into a profound sleep. An impenetrable briar hedge springs up and the castle and everyone in it is forgotten.

After 100 years, a brave prince fights his way through the hedge and finds the princess, whom he wakes with a KISS. The spell is lifted and everyone lives happily ever after (early versions of the tale go further, describing how the prince and princess marry in secret and have to overpower the prince's mother, an ogress, who wants to eat her daughter-in-law and her two newly-born children).

Origins The immediate sources for the plot of the familiar pantomime include *The Little Briar Rose* by the GRIMM BROTHERS and another version published in 1696 by CHARLES PERRAULT, which was based on Persian folklore, although the story was also known in many other cultures in numerous variant forms. The earliest written version of the tale dates back to the 14th-century French romance *Perceforest*, in which the sleeping Zellandine is raped by the prince, Troylus, who discovers her. The crucial shared elements between these varying traditions include the magic sleep, the witch's revenge, and the breaking of the spell with a kiss. The story was first translated into English in 1729 and was later taken up in the popular CHAPBOOKS of the period.

slosh scene Stock comedy scene of the traditional pantomime, in which much fun is had with shaving-foam pies, reams of wallpaper, wallpaper paste, pastry, and other ammunition and props (such as exploding gas cookers). Slosh scenes hark back to the knockabout comedy routines of the HARLEQUINADE – they were a feature of the early pantomimes staged by JOHN RICH – and before that to the *COMMEDIA DELL'ARTE* although modern versions of such horseplay are modest in comparison to the finely-timed comic antics of performers in previous centuries.

Perhaps the most frequently seen example of the scene is that in which the UGLY SISTERS prepare to go to the ball in *CINDERELLA*; this rapidly declines into comic mayhem as talcum powder, mudpacks, and so forth are hurled about until every character on the stage is covered with mess. Other settings for such scenes include the dame's kitchen in various stories and the laundry in *ALADDIN AND HIS WONDERFUL LAMP*, in both of which there are ample supplies of such 'weapons' as buckets of water and flour, dough, and raw eggs.

Noted exponents of the scene over the years have included such comedy teams as NAUGHTON AND GOLD, who got the scene off to a fine art in pantomimes at the LYCEUM THEATRE in the 1930s, and more recently Morecambe and Wise (who learnt their trade in provincial pantomime), the Carioli brothers (famous for their exploding car), and ROY HUDD and JACK TRIPP.

slote or **sloat** A stage mechanism that allowed scenery to rise onto the stage through slots (also called slotes) cut in the stage floor. Employing a sophisticated arrangement of counterweights and rails, the slote system was developed in the Victorian theatre from earlier versions operating in a similar fashion and was much used in the spectacular productions of that era (*see* RISE-AND-SINK). The equivalent in the USA was known as a **hoist**.

slow trap A powered TRAP that can be used to raise members of the cast as well as various items of scenery up to the stage or lower them from it. Such traps are usually relatively small and square or rectangular and take different names according to the different areas of the stage where they are situated.

SM *See* STAGE MANAGER.

Smith, E(dward) T(yrell) (1804–77) English theatre manager, who oversaw many of the most admired pantomimes of the Victorian era at both DRURY LANE and the LYCEUM THEATRE. Smith entered theatrical management in 1850, when he took over the Marylebone Theatre and moved to the Lane in 1852 at a point when the theatre was experiencing a relatively poor spell.

Though combining the management of thc Lanc with that of several other venues in the city, he went on to revive the theatre's reputation as home of the best pantomimes in London, largely through his collaboration with the scene designer WILLIAM BEVERLEY, whose TRANSFORMATION SCENES created a sensation (the idea for these scenes came to Smith while he and Beverley were watching a joint of mutton roasting on a spit).

Smith was also responsible for the first productions at the Lane of the pantomimes of E. L. BLANCHARD. He left the Lane in 1862 after a disappointing season and subsequently became lessee of the Lyceum, where his pantomimes included W. S. GILBERT's *Harlequin Cock Robin* and productions starring the VOKES FAMILY.

Snow White and the Seven Dwarfs A fairytale that is included in the half-dozen most regularly performed pantomimes of the latter half of the 20th century (though it often takes the form of a children's play rather than a pantomime proper). Its popularity reflects the success enjoyed by the celebrated WALT DISNEY cartoon version of 1937, which established certain conventions about the characters of the dwarfs and provided a model for such details as Snow White's costume. Among the best-known actresses to appear as Snow White herself is Dana, who has appeared in the part many times.

Story Snow White is a beautiful young princess with skin as white as snow, rosy red cheeks, and black hair. The Queen, her WICKED STEPMOTHER, is intensely jealous of her beauty and, when her magic mirror names Snow White rather then herself as "the most beautiful of all", she orders Snow White's murder. Snow White is spared, however, by the man commanded to kill her and is instead abandoned in a deep forest while the henchman takes back a deer's heart as proof that he has fulfilled the Wicked Queen's wishes.

Snow White stumbles upon a small cottage, where she finds a table laid for seven people. She helps herself to food and drink and then falls asleep in one of the seven beds in the house. The occupiers of the house are seven dwarfs who work in the gold mines. The dwarfs (sometimes played by midgets, though often also by children) allow Snow White to stay with them in exchange for doing the housework and she settles down to a happy life with them.

Meanwhile the Queen learns from the mirror that Snow White is still alive and so she arrives at the cottage while the dwarfs are away, disguised as an old pedlar. She gives Snow White a lace, which she offers to help tie. She pulls the lace as tight as she can and Snow White drops, seemingly dead. The dwarfs revive her, however, and the Queen returns once more and this time gives Snow White a poisoned comb. Again Snow White is revived by the dwarfs but the Queen is undeterred and returns to offer Snow White a bite from a poisoned apple. The green side the Wicked Stepmother bites is safe but when Snow White bites into the red side she falls into a deep sleep from which no one can wake her. The dwarfs seal her in a glass coffin and lose hope of ever restoring her to life.

A handsome prince arrives at the cottage, however, and succeeds in waking Snow White when the piece of poisoned apple falls from her lips as he lifts her up. The pair marry and the Wicked Stepmother is suitably punished (early versions of the story have her dying after being forced to put on a pair of red-hot slippers that make her dance to death). Diverting variations of the basic story in recent pantomime versions have included one in which the Wicked Stepmother having changed herself into the old crone finds herself unable to change back.

Origins The pantomime is based upon the fairytale collected by the GRIMM BROTHERS, which was first translated into English in the 1820s.

Their version had its roots in a number of ancient legends shared by virtually all European cultural traditions.

songs The pantomime has always incorporated a strong musical element and the modern entertainment would be incomplete without the rendition of a dozen or so familiar tunes from the 'Top Ten' or specially-written songs, which might vary from sentimental ballads to rousing SINGALONGS. In the earliest years, when there was no DIALOGUE at all, the entire entertainment was delivered with a musical accompaniment, while from 1737 the LICENSING ACT dictated how much music had to be included before a production qualified as a BURLETTA and could thus be presented at one of the MINOR THEATRES. Managements quickly learnt to turn the act to their advantage, presenting all manner of serious dramas through the device of incorporating musical interludes into them and songwriters were in heavy demand.

Many a pantomime is remembered for the quality of its songs, some of which became great popular favourites that long outlived the productions in which they were first rendered. In the early days of the pantomime, most songs were specially written (by such arrangers as the Dibdins). Later, however, specially written songs were largely replaced by tunes that everyone knew (though sometimes with new lyrics). Subsequently the fashion swung back in favour of specially-written songs, the words and music for which would then be on sale after the show.

Probably the first song to become a universal hit was 'Hearts of Oak', written by DAVID GARRICK to a tune composed by William Boyce and first heard in the course of Garrick's *Harlequin's Invasion* (1759). The song admirably suited the patriotic sentiments of the age and acquired a life of its own quite independent to the pantomime from which it came.

Subsequently JOSEPH GRIMALDI had enormous success with such comic songs as HOT CODLINS and TIPPITY WITCHET, most of which were the work of CHARLES DIBDIN (set to music by such composers as William Reeve, William Ware, and John Whitaker).

Later in the 19th century the import of stars of the MUSIC HALL had a major impact and soon pantomime audiences were singing along with such rousing numbers as 'The Old Bull and Bush' and 'Let's All Go Down the Strand', regardless of any relevance such classics might or might not have to the script in progress. Among the most memorable songs of the late Victorian and Edwardian pantomime that are still occasionally heard today are the comic tongue-twisters made famous by WILKIE BARD and others, among them such classics as 'She Sells Sea Shells on the Sea Shore', and such enduring standards as TA-RA-RA-BOOM-DE-AY, which was originally sung by LOTTIE COLLINS in 1891.

The topical duets of HERBERT CAMPBELL and HARRY NICHOLLS were a major attraction of the pantomimes at Drury Lane at the end of the last century and no performers since have equalled the success they enjoyed with their tuneful reflections upon contemporary events and persons in the news. Subsequently the cheerful singalong numbers of the music hall were gradually replaced by more sophisticated and sentimental ballads, which often aped the songs of 'crooners' and balladeers of US origins.

The contemporary pantomime continues to mimic current musical fashions and it is now quite usual for pantomimes to incorporate songs from the year's pop charts, which may or may not be relevant to the story being told. Examples of totally irrelevant numbers being incorporated in the pantomime include 'My Yiddisher Momma', which was once included for the enjoyment of a largely Jewish audience in a production of *ALADDIN* at the Golders Green Hippodrome (Aladdin commanding the Genie to produce someone to sing the song before taking him to his Princess).

Typical of the more successful panto songs of recent decades has been 'Dream the Impossible Dream', which has attached itself to *DICK WHITTINGTON*, as well as hit singles by groups ranging from the Beatles and Abba to Boy George and Right Said Fred. The Adam and the Ants single 'Goody Two Shoes' was a natural for inclusion in pantomimes a few years ago, while the Beverley Sisters song 'Sisters' has provided a signature tune for many pairs of Ugly Sisters and numerous dames have rendered their own versions of the song 'There is Nothing Like a Dame'.

sound effects Sound effects in the contemporary pantomime are sometimes achieved through the use of recordings, which allow a wider range of sounds to be employed with greater realism. Before the advent of recorded sound, however, stage crews employed such devices as the rain machine (a revolving drum containing dried peas or marbles) and the thundersheet (a large piece of flexible board that is shaken to produce an imitation of thunder) to get the desired effect. Some of these devices are still occasionally used and most managements prefer 'live' sound effects as they are more easily controlled.

Musicians are often responsible for providing incidental sound effects, which include the blowing of the Swanee Whistle (a whistle with a slide attachment that alters the pitch of the note to produce a comical 'swooping' sound) and the striking of drums and cymbals to produce the 'Big Crash' that accompanies slapstick falls and tumbles on the stage. The use of synthesizers in many theatres allows one operator to produce a huge range of sounds, varying from howling gales, explosions, and earthquakes to echo effects, which are of great value for scenes set in dungeons, caves, and giant's castles.

speaking opening *See* DIALOGUE; OPENING.

speciality act A self-contained novelty act of the type that has been incorporated into pantomime productions since the earliest history of the genre. Interludes featuring acrobats, contortionists, tightrope walkers, jugglers, bird impersonators, trick cyclists, performing dogs, conjurors, and other skilled entertainers date back to the 18th century, when bizarre speciality acts included impromptu boxing matches and dancing dogs (seen in the pantomimes of JOHN RICH), although they reached a peak in the 19th century.

Sometimes an attempt was made to integrate such acts into the plot of the pantomime; equally often, however, lack of rehearsal time meant that they were presented exactly as they were given outside the pantomime and bore no relation whatever to the main thrust of the story.

The tradition fell from favour in the 1920s and 1930s when audiences demanded the restoration of the fairytale plots that had previously been much disrupted by such acts and such interludes are a rarity in the modern pantomime. Among the most famous speciality acts over the years have been those presented by such performers as PAUL CINQUEVALLI, whose skill as a juggler earned him a place in the casts at DRURY LANE alongside DAN LENO, and in more recent times Emerson and Jane, who create the illusion of a flying carpet, and the long-established comedy dance troupe Wilson, Keppel, and Betty, who are famous for their cod Egyptian dance. Speciality acts based on animals have fallen from favour in recent years because of public doubts about the training methods used to teach the animals their tricks. *See also* CELEBRITY STARS; FLYING BALLET; MUSIC HALL.

spill and pelt *See* CHASE SCENE.

spinning wheel *See* *SLEEPING BEAUTY, THE*.

spotlight An electrical lighting unit casting a bright sharp beam, which is the main component of most modern lighting systems. Modern lighting rigs can include a great many spotlights, which may carry such accessories as colour-wheels and gobos to provide a lighting technician with a wide range of effects to choose from. It is conventional in the pantomime for villains to enter in a green spotlight, while fairies enter in a pink spotlight. *See also* LIMELIGHT.

Squire One of the central characters in *MOTHER GOOSE* and other pantomimes. The squire is variously played as an evil villain, who plots the downfall of the hero and his friends, or as a gullible but lovable rascal who is duped by the DEMON KING into assisting him with his wicked designs but is finally redeemed by falling in love with the DAME or otherwise demonstrating that he has a 'heart of gold' beneath his menacing exterior. It has been argued that his presence in the pantomime is a legacy of pre-industrial British society, when the squire wielded considerable power over local rural communities. One of the most celebrated performers to appear in the role of the Squire was JOSEPH GRIMALDI, who – wearing a ridiculous hat and forever sliding off his comical horse – played Squire Bugle (Master of the Epping Hunt) in the classic 1806 version of *Mother Goose* seen at COVENT GARDEN and subsequently on tour throughout the country.

stage crew The various technical staff of a theatre, who oversee the operation of lighting, sound, and special effects and also manipulate the scenery, among a wide variety of other tasks. Stage crews at major venues may run to more than a dozen members and are directed by a STAGE MANAGER.

stage door The entrance at the back or side of a theatre through which members of the cast and other personnel enter and leave the building. In the pantomime, as in other forms of popular theatre, excited groups of children and other members of the audience frequently gather here at the end of a show to catch a last glimpse of the performers. Access to the backstage area of the theatre is usually controlled by a doorkeeper, who remains at his post throughout the evening.

stage manager or **SM** The senior member of the STAGE CREW, who oversees all aspects of activity backstage during a performance. In the modern theatre he (or she) is entirely subservient to the DIRECTOR, although formerly the stage manager often combined the roles of director, impresario, and even leading actor (as well as being on occasion the owner of the theatre), directing rehearsals and fulfilling the role of general organiser. Now in charge of props, scene changes, lighting, calling the cast to the stage, and related matters, he is usually helped by an assistant stage manager (ASM).

stalls The area of seating on the ground floor of the auditorium. Until the late 19th century the stalls were generally referred to as 'the pit'.

Standard Theatre A former theatre in Shoreditch, London, which was famous for its pantomimes. The theatre opened in 1835 as part of the Royal Standard Public House and Pleasure Garden and presented circus entertainments as well as plays and concerts under the capable management of John Douglass. It was rebuilt after a fire in 1866 and then became a prestigious theatrical venue (as the New Standard Theatre) under the management of Richard Douglass, who established a respected company there and also staged spectacular pantomimes, which were particularly notable for their scenery. In 1888 Andrew Melville, father of the MELVILLE BROTHERS, took the theatre over and presented a similar programme until 1907, when the theatre became the Olympia Music Hall. Ultimately the building was converted into a cinema (in 1926) and was destroyed by bombs in World War II.

Stanfield, Clarkson (1793–1867) English artist, who was the most admired scene painter of the 19th century and who created some of the most effective pantomime sets ever seen. Stanfield, the son of an actor, was born in Sunderland and spent some years (1808–15) in the Royal Navy until an accident forced him to seek another occupation in 1815. Having already contributed as a scene designer to theatrical productions on board ship, he found similar employment on shore firstly in Edinburgh and later at the Coburg Theatre (later renamed the Old Vic). Subsequently he was taken on at DRURY LANE, where he executed much of his best work.

He was particularly admired for his depiction of water and for his mastery of the DIORAMA, which was ideally suited to his talents. Typical dioramas by his hand included the dramatic series of seascapes designed for *Harlequin and the Flying Chest; or, Malek and The Princess Schirine* (1823) – which incorporated scenes of the Plymouth Breakwater – and for *Harlequin Jack of All Trades* (1825), which included scenes of storms and shipwreck, a diorama for *The Queen Bee; or, Harlequin and the Fairy Hive* (1828), which presented a number of views of recognisable British coastlines, panoramas of the Simplon Pass for *Davy Jones* (1829), and an ambitious rendering of central Venice for *Harlequin and Little Thumb* (1831).

His designs for *Jack in the Box; or, Harlequin and the Princess of the Hidden Island* (1829) were made all the more dramatic by the use of 39 tuns of real water, with which he recreated the Falls of Virginia Water. Among others was a depiction of the battlefield of Waterloo, seen a full ten years after the real event in *The Man in the Moon* (1826).

As he became more famous as an easel painter and one of the greatest seascape artists (finally winning election to the Royal Academy in 1835), Stanfield (who left Drury Lane in 1834) did less work for the theatre, although Macready did persuade him to contribute scenes for productions at COVENT GARDEN. He also painted the scenery for some of the private theatricals organised by his friend CHARLES DICKENS at Tavistock House. He contributed his last theatrical scene in 1858, by which time he had created over 550 sets in all.

star trap A TRAP consisting of interlocking triangular segments (sometimes made of leather) that sprung open to allow a performer to make a dramatic rapid entrance through the stage floor. The mechanics of the trap (the operation of which required several stage crew and heavy counterweights) meant that the performer concerned could be propelled up to fourteen feet into the air before landing on the stage, by which time the trap had automatically closed. Such traps, which were once frequently used for entrances by the DEMON KING, were notorious for the injuries they caused (usually through an incorrectly positioned performer smashing into the side of the trap opening as he shot upwards). Such traps had fallen from use by the mid-20th century due to the danger they presented to performers; they were banned at DRURY LANE after complaints that they frightened children in the audience. Noted practitioners of the star trap included members of the Conquest and Lupino families.

Steele, Tommy (Thomas Hicks; 1936–) British pop singer and actor, born in Bermondsey, who became one of the most popular young stars of pantomime in the 1960s. Having become an idol of teenage pop audiences in the 1950s, he subsequently devoted himself to a stage career, specialising in light musical comedy, variety, and pantomime. His singing ability and lively cockney stage persona ensured his triumph in such roles as BUTTONS, which he played in Rodgers and Hammerstein's *CINDERELLA* at the LONDON COLISEUM in 1958 (the theatre refused to accept the show unless it included the character Buttons).

Subsequent pantomime successes included a television production of *DICK WHITTINGTON* (1964), which featured music and lyrics written by himself; he repeated the role at the LONDON PALLADIUM in 1969 to great acclaim, being described by some as the best performer of the part this century. Among his best roles since then have been the title part in Frank Loesser's musical *Hans Andersen* at the Palladium. He has also played a number of roles in 'straight' drama and has appeared in many films.

strobe A lighting unit (formally called a stroboscope) that produces a bright rapidly flashing beam. Strobe lighting is frequently employed in the pantomime, especially in CHASE SCENES as it creates the impression that the cast are moving in slow motion as though in a movie of the silent era, but is subject to various legal restrictions as such units can induce epileptic fits if used incorrectly.

superstitions A number of superstitions have attached themselves to the pantomime over the years. These include several common to other types of theatre, the best known of which is the convention that green is an unlucky colour on the stage. This particular taboo is especially relevant to productions of *BABES IN THE WOOD*, in which Robin Hood and his Merry Men are expected to appear in Lincoln Green; some actresses playing Robin have refused to wear a green costume and have come on instead in one of brown suede. Actors have also been known to refuse to accept scripts bound in green. This superstition about the colour green dates back to the days when stages were lit by LIMELIGHT, which cast a greenish glow over everything and had the tendency to make anything coloured green invisible to the audience. Other explanations suggest a link with the green stage carpet once traditionally used in performances of tragedy.

Other taboos concern the use of real flowers, peacock feathers, whistling (offenders must leave the dressing-room, turn round three times, and spit), and wishing an actor good luck – all of which are feared to threaten ill fortune. Among superstitions peculiar to the pantomime is the taboo against speaking the last line of the script in rehearsal (it is usually reserved for the PRINCIPAL BOY, who speaks it for the first time at the first performance). Of the pantomimes themselves, *ALI BABA AND THE FORTY THIEVES*, *BLUEBEARD*, and *The Fair One with the Golden Locks* are all considered unlucky. *See also* ENTRANCES.

Surrey Theatre Former theatre in Blackfriars Road, London, which became famous for its pantomimes in the latter half of the 19th century. The theatre began life as the Royal Circus, which was opened by CHARLES DIBDIN and Charles Hughes in 1782, and subsequently enjoyed great success as a home of melodrama before rebuilding after a fire in 1803.

The first pantomime to be staged there was *Harlequin and the Witch of Ludlow*, which was presented as early as 1809, under the management of Robert Elliston. Elliston was succeeded by THOMAS DIBDIN in 1816 and the theatre consolidated its reputation as a pantomime venue over the following decades (though Dibdin himself was ruined by the time he stepped down in 1823). The venue was destroyed by fire in 1865 but was rebuilt and prospered under the management of William Holland, who presented spectacular pun-laden pantomimes featuring such leading performers as NELLY POWER.

In 1880 the Surrey was taken over by GEORGE CONQUEST, who presented a highly popular repertory of melodramas and pantomimes (most of which were written by Conquest himself in collaboration with Henry Spry), winning the Surrey acclaim as one of the most popular pantomime venues in London (rivalling even DRURY LANE). Particularly notable were Conquest's two pantomimes featuring his discovery DAN LENO, who triumphed as Dame Durden in *JACK AND THE BEANSTALK* in 1886 and as Tinpanz the Tailor in *SINBAD AND THE LITTLE OLD MAN OF THE SEA* in 1887 before finally leaving the theatre in 1888 in order to appear at Drury Lane.

The theatre declined after Conquest died although the connection with the Conquest family continued under the management of his sons Fred and George. The Surrey was finally sold in 1925 in order to allow the neighbouring Royal Ophthalmic Hospital to expand and was demolished in 1934.

sweet-throwing It is customary at some point in the modern pantomime for the DAME or other leading members of the cast to step out of character and to interrupt the action in order to toss sweets to children in the audience. The practice has a long history and can be traced as far back as performances of the plays of Aristophanes, who was infuriated by it. In the late 19th century, it was usually CLOWN who undertook the task of tossing candies and nuts into the auditorium, shouting out the names of the sponsors of the show who had paid for the goodies as he did so. Sweet-throwing is now an essential part of the pantomime tradition and often takes place on the dame's first entrance.

T

tableau A grouping of motionless performers for visual effect, as practised on numerous occasions in the Victorian pantomime when such tableaux were a feature of the TRANSFORMATION SCENE. Examples of such dramatic scenes included a memorable representation of the Crystal Palace seen in a production of E. L. BLANCHARD's first pantomime at DRURY LANE, *Harlequin Hudibras; or, Old Dame Durden and the Droll Days of the Merry Monarch* (1852). More typically, such tableaux depicted fairies, nymphs, or other supernatural beings disporting themselves among magnificently painted scenery, which was gradually revealed as a succession of gauzes was slowly raised.

tabs *See* CURTAIN.

Ta-ra-ra-boom-de-ay One of the most famous songs to issue from the Victorian pantomime. This uproarious comic number was written by the US songwriter Harry Sayers for his minstrel troupe to sing in the course of a night-club show entitled *Tuxedo*, but it was not until LOTTIE COLLINS sang a spirited high-kicking English version of it at the Tivoli in October 1891 and subsequently in *DICK WHITTINGTON* that Christmas that it became a huge popular success (to the extent that many people complained of hearing it on every street corner). The song made Collins rich and remained one of the most performed pantomime numbers long after her death; other singers to deliver it with similar panache included MARIE LLOYD.

technical rehearsal A REHEARSAL that takes place (usually without the cast) shortly before the opening night of a production, during the course of which all the technical aspects are checked, including lighting, sound, and scene changing. It is not uncommon for such rehearsals to take all night long.

television The relationship between pantomime and television has grown increasingly close in recent decades as theatrical managements have capitalised upon the popularity of certain television performers by casting them in leading pantomime roles. This may have boosted takings at the box office and thus maintained the financial standing of the pantomime in British theatre, but it has also had an arguably less desirable effect in other ways. Since the 1960s, when theatre managers (who had previously seen television purely in terms of a commercial rival) first realised the potential television offered, stage actors of proven ability have frequently been passed over in favour of well-known television personalities, who all too often have turned out to lack the confidence and experience to succeed on stage. This in turn has subtly altered the balance of the pantomime's structure: with popular television stars (ranging from TV detectives to comedians and children's television presenters) typically taking the central heroic parts and more accomplished performers being cast in supporting comedy and villain roles, directors have accordingly allowed the latter parts, played by performers upon which they know they can rely, to expand.

Not all television performers have, of course, failed on the stage; among the legion of successful television personalities to appear with acclaim in the pantomime have been such illustrious names as Morecambe and Wise, Terry Scott and June Whitfield, Leslie Crowther, and Les Dawson. Writers are often required to build their pantomimes around a particular star, who may carry over his or her television persona virtually unchanged into the pantomime, inevitably leading to further distortion of accepted plots and characters.

A new breed of pantomime has also developed, with entire entertainments being built around fictional characters, including cartoons and puppets. Notable examples of such shows – which have particular appeal for the younger audience – have included in recent years those featuring such popular figures as Postman Pat, Firesam Sam, Noggin the Nog, Sooty, Basil Brush, and Emu (with his 'handler' Rod Hull). Some have condemned the mass invasion by Australian soap opera stars and children's television characters in recent decades as a perversion of the traditional pantomime (recalling the outrage expressed by many when the first MUSIC HALL stars were introduced towards the end of the 19th century). Others, bearing in mind the ever-changing nature of the pantomime over its 300-year history, have interpreted the fashion as just one more phase (for better or for worse) and a further proof of the pantomime's unique ability to prosper by responding to the tides of mass popular culture.

Television itself has returned the compliment over the years by presenting numerous pantomime entertainments starring casts of hugely popular television and stage performers around the Christmas season. The rising cost of such productions has, however, spelt the end of full-scale television pantomimes, although more modest shorter pantomime entertainments remain a feature of various festive children's programmes each year. What these truncated pantomimes lack in spontaneity and audience participation they often make up in special effects and the success they enjoy doubtless adds many to the theatre box office queues for the pantomime proper.

The relatively high production standards in British television may also have had a subtle effect upon the improvement of standards in the AMATEUR PANTOMIME (although television's role in the development of the 'three-minute culture', in which audiences are no longer expected to be able to concentrate on a single subject for more than three minutes at a time, has put new pressure on pantomime directors to keep audiences engaged in the action). The conventional one-hour length of much television drama may also have had an impact upon the pantomime and it is now usual for shows to be broken into two one-hour long acts to fit in with the audience's viewing habits.

Terriss, Ellaline (1871–1971) English actress, born in the Falkland Islands, whose many admired roles included CINDERELLA. The daughter of the actor William Terriss (who was murdered by a madman outside the ADELPHI THEATRE in 1897), she made her stage debut in 1888 at the HAYMARKET THEATRE. Her appearance as Cinderella in the Christmas pantomime at the LYCEUM THEATRE in 1894, when she was 23, caused a sensation and guaranteed the production's success. Praised for her youthful beauty as well as for her undoubted acting talents, she was the major pantomime attraction of the season and subsequently repeated the role in New York. Among her other famous parts were roles in the plays of her husband, Seymour Hicks, and in J. M. Barrie's *Quality Street* (1902).

Theatre Regulation Act *See* LICENSING ACT.

Thompson, Lydia (1836–1908) English actress, who excelled as a PRINCIPAL BOY in the Victorian pantomime. Her beauty and her talent made her a popular star in BURLESQUE and similar entertainments on both sides of the Atlantic and throughout Europe. She made her debut in the pantomime at the age of 16, playing Little Bo-Peep in *Little Silver Hair; or, Harlequin and the Three Bears* at Her Majesty's Theatre and subsequently made her first appearance as principal boy at the LYCEUM THEATRE at the age of 25, appearing in the part at DRURY LANE just a year later. Her most successful roles included ROBINSON CRUSOE and, by complete contrast, Goody Two-Shoes, which she played at Drury Lane in 1862. In the late 1860s she created a considerable stir in the USA after she was fined $2000 for horse-whipping a Chicago journalist who had criticised her touring company. She retired in 1899.

Thousand and One Nights, The *See* *ARABIAN NIGHTS ENTERTAINMENTS.*

Tilley, Vesta (Matilda Alice Powles; 1864–1952) English singer, who became a great star of the MUSIC HALL and one of the leading performers in the pantomime over a period of more than 30 years. Specializing in male impersonation, she was one of the most popular entertainers in the music hall between 1880 and her retirement in 1920, singing such songs as 'Berlington Bertie' and 'After the Ball'.

She made her debut in the role of PRINCIPAL BOY in 1877, playing ROBINSON CRUSOE, and subsequently appeared as principal boy at DRURY LANE, playing the Prince in *BEAUTY AND THE BEAST* (1890). This was her only appearance at the Lane, however, as she took exception to the heavy mask she had to wear and vowed never to perform there again.

Subsequently she spent much of her pantomime career in the provinces, where she had a huge following, and appeared at virtually all the leading pantomime venues throughout the country (most notably at Birmingham and Liverpool). Her star status was reflected in the fact that she was reputed to earn £500 a week in pantomime.

Tippity Witchet One of the most famous of all pantomime songs, which was one of the great favourites sung by JOSEPH GRIMALDI in the early 19th century. The song, written by CHARLES DIBDIN the younger, was first delivered during a performance of *Bang Up! or, Harlequin Prime* at SADLER'S WELLS in 1810 and proved an instant hit. The lyrics of the song, in which Grimaldi explained that he had taken a little too much brandy in his tea that morning, were enlivened by the great Clown with comical hiccups, sneezes, yawns, and helpless laughter.

Tom the Piper's Son A nursery rhyme, upon which a number of pantomimes have been based over the years. Early pantomimes using the rhyme as a basis included *Harlequin Tom, The Piper's Son Stole a Pig and Away he Ran*, which was staged at the OLYMPIC THEATRE in 1820, and *Harlequin Tom Tom, the Piper's Son, Pope Joan and Little Bo-Peep*, which was staged at ASTLEY'S AMPHITHEATRE in 1865. More recently, Norman Robbins figures among those who have constructed further pantomimes around the same rhyme.

Story In the original rhyme Tom the Piper's Son, who can only play one tune on his pipe, steals a pig (probably a reference to the sweetmeat pigs formerly sold by street vendors) and "away did run". Around this simple thread of a plot various writers have constructed elaborate stories in which many other nursery rhyme characters also appear (in the adaptation by Norman Robbins Georgie Porgie, Old King Cole, and the Knave of Hearts are among the characters who are involved in a simple plot about a kidnapped princess).

Origins It is thought that the nursery rhyme had its roots in an old English ballad dating back to the late 17th century (Tom being the usual nickname of pipers everywhere). The rhyme was elaborated into something more like a coherent story in CHAPBOOKS of the 19th century, adding the detail that when Tom played no one who heard him could stop themselves from dancing. Beatrix Potter also based *The Tale of Pigling Bland* upon the story.

Tom Thumb A fairytale about the adventures of a tiny man, which was frequently adapted as a pantomime in the 19th century. The figure of Tom Thumb made a stage appearance as early as 1730 in a satirical burlesque by Henry Fielding, which lampooned the conventions of heroic drama. Among later productions was DRURY LANE'S *Harlequin and Little Thumb; or, The Seven-Leagued Boots* (1831), which incorporated a diorama of Venice executed by CLARKSON STANFIELD, and *Harlequin Tom Thumb; or, Gog and Magog and Mother Goose's Garden*, which was staged at SADLER'S WELLS in 1853. Performers of the central role over the years have included the celebrated midget of the Victorian era, General Tom Thumb himself, and in the 20th century the television comedian Jimmy Clitheroe.

Story Tom Thumb is magically born to a penniless couple who have long wished for a child, even if no bigger than a man's thumb. The tiny, mischievous Tom then embarks on a series of adventures, which in the original tale include being sold to two strangers, being forced to help two robbers steal a parson's gold, and being eaten by a cow and a wolf in turn before being finally reunited with his rejoicing parents. In the pantomime, his adventures often begin when he is abandoned by his parents because they have no food and include battling with an ogre or joining a circus before finally restoring the family's fortunes (formerly at the conclusion of the harlequinade).

Origins There are many tales about a mythical tiny man in a number of European cultures as well as in the folklore of Japan and India (some being collected by the GRIMM BROTHERS). The English version was first recorded in print in 1579 and the story was widely known long before Fielding took it up. Subsequently compilations of fairytales and nursery rhymes for children were often put together under his name.

tongue-twisters *See* BARD, WILKIE.

topicality References to affairs of the day have always been an essential characteristic of the pantomime. Often, especially in the early 19th century, such references were deliberately aimed to "hold up to ridicule the monstrosities of the times" (as CHARLES DIBDIN explained) and the pantomime became a vessel for mild criticisms of the establishment in all its various manifestations, from the conduct of foreign affairs to the injustices of the Poor Laws and the hardships accompanying the advent of the Industrial Revolution (*see* SATIRE). More often, though, contemporary issues and fashions etc. have figured in the pantomime as incidental details, providing a novel opportunity for some new comic or visual invention without passing judgement on the moral issues involved.

This urge to relate the pantomime to the times dates back to the very earliest years. DRURY LANE's *Harlequin Incendiary; or, the Columbine Cameron* (1746) had a plot based upon the disturbances connected with the Jacobite Rebellion then in progress, while *The Siege of Quebec; or, Harlequin Emperor* (1760) commemorated the death of General Wolfe. Subsequently it became quite commonplace for authors to be asked to amend their scripts at the very last moment to incorporate some reference to recent events in the news and surviving scripts provide a lively source of information on public reactions to some of the great political and social issues of vanished eras.

Writers often structured scenes or even whole pantomimes around some topical story, as is the case in *The Birth of the Steam Engine, or Harlequin Locomotive and his Men*, the main character of which was the inventor James Watt, and John Thurmond's *Harlequin Sheppard* (1724), which told the life story of the recently-executed highwayman Jack Sheppard. A century later the Californian gold rush was one of the current events to inspire pantomime writers, who spotted the opportunity for some fabulous subterranean golden sets – as seen in such entertainments as *Harlequin and the Wild Fiend of California; or, the Demon of the Diggings and the Gnome Queen of the Golden Lake* at the GRECIAN THEATRE in 1849 and in *Harlequin and the Yellow Dwarf; or, the Enchanted Orange Tree and the King of the Golden Mines* at SADLER'S WELLS two years later.

Other products of their time included *Harlequin Genius; or, the Progress of Free Trade, the Spirit of Improvement, and the Great Exhibition of 1851* and *Uncle Tom and Lucy Neal; or, Harlequin Liberty and Slavery* (1852), which was just one of several pantomimes that year to capitalise upon the success of Harriet Beecher Stowe's anti-slavery novel *Uncle Tom's Cabin*.

A recurring theme of the mid-Victorian pantomime was the coming of the railways, which inspired such works as *Harlequin and the Steam King; or, Perroule's Wishes and the Fairy Frog*. Other technological sensations that were reflected in the preoccupations of pantomime writers included hot-air ballooning (a favourite of the writers connected with COVENT GARDEN) and travel by steam coaches, aeroplanes, cars (first seen in *CINDERELLA* at Drury Lane in 1895), and more recently spaceships. It was generally the case that such innovations were exploited for their comic possibilities and it was rare for new technological advances to be hailed rather than ridiculed.

In response to fashions of the time, DAMES have entered variously dressed as girl guides, Land Army girls, suffragettes, and air hostesses. Similarly, villains have appeared in the guise of hated national enemies, such as Napoleon or leaders of the Boers, and politicians from Benjamin Disraeli to Margaret Thatcher have regularly 'appeared' on the pantomime stage.

It remains customary for scripts to be tailored to include references to issues of purely local interest as well as to the films, pop idols, political scandals, and other issues and personalities currently capturing the headlines. *See also* ADVERTISING; SCENERY.

toy theatres The delightful miniature model theatres that were sold in their thousands throughout the 19th century and now constitute a valuable source of information about the staging of all types of drama, including the pantomime. These toy theatres varied in sophistication and could be added to by the purchase of one of the 300 or more sheets of figures or scenery based on famous theatrical productions that were produced specifically for use in the so-called **juvenile drama**. These sheets came in two forms, the **penny plain** and the **twopence coloured** varieties and included depictions of such famous performers as JOSEPH GRIMALDI.

Among the first pantomimes to be remodelled for toy theatres were *ALADDIN*, *BLUEBEARD*, and *TOM THUMB*, which were all rendered in miniature form as early as 1811. Subsequently virtually every major pantomime production seen in London found its way into the toy theatre.

transformation scene or **Grand Transformation** Traditionally, a climactic scene of the pantomime in which spectacular transformations of characters and scenery take place at a key point of the plot. Relatively modest transformations were a characteristic feature of the English court MASQUE in the Elizabethan era, when privileged audiences thrilled at the gradual transformation of barren deserts into leafy bowers and so forth in much the same way that spectators at the pantomime did several centuries later.

The productions of JOHN RICH in the early 18th century were much praised for their transformations of palaces into cottages and shops into snakes at the touch of Harlequin's magic bat and prepared the way for the stunning TRICKS OF CONSTRUCTION that were one of the great strengths of the pantomime dominated by JOSEPH GRIMALDI in the early 19th century. Such transformations subsequently assumed a new relevance later in the 18th century when more ambitious transformation scenes were enacted to bridge the gap between the otherwise unconnected narrative of the OPENING and the HARLEQUINADE that followed.

According to the convention that emerged, at a relatively early point in the pantomime, when the fortunes of the hero and his friends appeared impossibly lost, the Good Fairy or other supernatural figure (*see* BENEVOLENT AGENT) magically transformed the characters of the opening into the familiar figures of the harlequinade, who then set about the boisterous prank-making that audiences flocked to see. If the opening had been played with the cast wearing BIG HEADS then the transformation could be achieved by simply removing these, while outer costumes were rapidly stripped off by the use of hidden strings etc., disappearing through TRAPS in the stage floor to reveal the familiar harlequinade outfits beneath.

Audiences delighted in trying to guess which characters of the harlequinade the various figures in the opening would be transformed into and knew when they saw the cast surreptitiously loosening belts and buttons that the big change was imminent. Typically, the young lovers of the opening would emerge as Harlequin and Columbine, while Columbine's father became Pantaloon, the rival lover was turned into the Dandy Lover, and a comic old woman or official (or sometimes the rival suitor) took the role of Clown.

At this stage in the history of the pantomime the transformation was confined to characters alone and took place in front of a so-called DARK SCENE, although the Benevolent Agent might enter in a winged chariot or other spectacular conveyance to announce the change. The joining of the two distinct parts of the pantomime as it then existed through such transformations confused some playgoers (including Horace Walpole) but lent added purpose to the hectic pursuit of the harlequinade.

When the great age of Grimaldi passed and the comedy of the harlequinade faltered managements took note of the popularity of the EXTRAVAGANZA, which placed much greater emphasis upon scenic spectacle, and in the hands of such designers as WILLIAM BEVERLEY the transformation scene was born anew. Beverley's first transformation scene was designed for J. R. PLANCHÉ's *The Island of Jewels* at the LYCEUM THEATRE in 1849 and centred on the dramatic falling away of the leaves of a palm tree to reveal a group of six fairies holding up a spectacular coronet of jewels. The scene caused a sensation and the transformation scene became one of the principal attractions of the Victorian pantomime.

Utilising all manner of FALLING FLAPS, GAUZES, and other scenic devices gorgeous views were slowly revealed to admiring audiences, who were invited to marvel at the skills of the stage artists and carpenters. One method of enacting the scene was the so-called 'fan effect', in which the scenery slowly collapsed sideways in the manner of a folding fan to reveal further views behind. When the transformation of the scenery was complete, then the characters too would be transformed into the figures of the harlequinade.

Under Beverley's direction the emphasis was transferred from the transformation of the cast entirely to the transformation of the scenery, which typically evolved to depict a heavenly paradise or 'Bower of Bliss' populated by a tableau of motionless figures (generally fairies or other supernatural beings). The whole scene took place under ever-changing lighting and Victorian audiences frequently found such transformations breathtaking in their beauty and ingenuity, inspiring critics to describe such transformations as 'the essence of the pantomime itself'. Stage designers competed to find novel ways of effecting the change and considerable amounts of money were lavished upon it.

The scene did have its critics, however: W. S. GILBERT probably spoke for many when he once complained that the transformation scene had grown too ambitious, with some transformations taking 20 minutes to be completed. The 'Grand Transformation' of the Victorian pantomime moved closer to the end of the evening as the harlequinade contracted in length and the dark scene and concluding scene that followed were dropped altogether. AUGUSTUS HARRIS rang the changes towards the end of the century when he replaced the conventional transformation scene with huge processions of characters in lavish costumes, while at the same time bolstering the comedy element of the pantomime by importing leading comedians from the music hall.

Such moves served to distract attention somewhat from scenic effects and the death of the harlequinade contributed greatly to the decline of the tradition. In the interwar years the MELVILLE BROTHERS continued to present sumptuous transformation scenes, although they moved them from their usual place at the end of the pantomime to somewhere near the middle of the evening, arguing that there was no point in reserving such fireworks for that late stage of the performance when audiences were ready to go home.

Transformation scenes in the pantomime since World War II have generally been far more modest affairs than those staged in Victorian times. Typically the scene takes place at the end of the first act, just before the interval, when the stage is filled with performers in lavish costumes who strike a tableau against the newly-changed scenery. Among the more frequently seen examples of something approaching a transformation scene in the modern pantomime are the magical transformation of Cinderella's kitchen to Fairyland, the conversion of the dismal CAVE in *ALADDIN* into a dazzling treasure store, and the appearance of the beanstalk in *JACK AND THE BEANSTALK*.

transparency A piece of scenery that is totally or partially transparent in certain lighting. Such transparencies are of great scenic value in the pantomime, appearing solid until lit from a certain angle to reveal characters or further scenic items positioned behind. Early examples of the use of transparencies include the 1826 production of *Harlequin and Mother Shipton* at COVENT GARDEN, in which a transparency was used to depict 'flying demons'.

traps Concealed openings in the scenery and stage floor through which performers may make dramatic sudden entrances and exits. The use of traps in the pantomime was once a key element, although the risks involved and specialised skills required have led to a decline in their use. Such potentially dangerous traps as the STAR TRAP are now no longer used as a result of a ruling by the actors' union Equity after an accident to ARTHUR ASKEY involving a GRAVE TRAP. More modest traps let into the scenery and working as secret panels and hidden doors do, however, remain a stock feature of many modern productions, being usefully employed in the LAUNDRY SCENE in *ALADDIN*, for example.

In years gone by performers were highly praised for their agility in using traps, although many a performer – notably JOSEPH GRIMALDI – had to retire early because of the injuries they suffered in the execution of such acrobatics (*see also* ELLAR, THOMAS). Harlequin in particular was expected to execute a number of dramatic leaps through such traps, which might be disguised as mirrors, clockfaces, and shop windows; as he emerged on the other side of the set he would (all being well) be caught in a blanket held up for the purpose by a number of stagehands.

In the Victorian pantomime it was quite common for as many as a dozen traps to be in operation simultaneously. One of the masters of their use in that era was the remarkable GEORGE CONQUEST, who was reputed to use as many as 29 different traps as he leapt athletically about the stage in pantomimes at the

GRECIAN and SURREY theatres. *See* BRISTLE TRAP; CAULDRON TRAP; CORNER TRAP; DOWN-TRAP; GHOST GLIDE; SLOTE; SLOW TRAP; VAMP TRAP.

Tree of Truth The magical tree in one of the most famous traditional comic scenes of the pantomime. Seen in a number of different pantomimes, the Tree of Truth usually bears a good crop of grapefruit, coconuts, or other large fruit (originally they were acorns), which fall onto the head of anyone sitting below the tree who tells a lie. The comic possibilities are obvious and a Tree of Truth scene was for many years one of the most reliable stock comic scenes; it was seen at its best in the early years of the 20th century when those to sit beneath its loaded branches included DAN LENO and HERBERT CAMPBELL. It continues to be seen from time to time in the modern pantomime.

tricks of construction The ingenious manipulation of various miscellaneous items that was one of the prime features of the comedy of CLOWN. Such tricks of construction represented the height of comic invention and were frequently employed in the early pantomimes of JOHN RICH but were never better than when realised by JOSEPH GRIMALDI at COVENT GARDEN and SADLER'S WELLS in the early 19th century. A number of apparently unrelated odds and ends lying about the stage would be so arranged by Clown that they became something altogether different and often acquired a life of their own. Thus, in one of his most celebrated *coups de théâtre*, Grimaldi would fashion a pile of junk into a row of soldiers, which he would then pretend to drill (his horror would be without limit when – at Harlequin's command – these soldiers of barrels and broomsticks suddenly came to life).

Other notable tricks of construction devised by the great Clown included a hussar's uniform, which he assembled from pots, pans, and a muff (a bit of comic invention that is still sometimes revived for the scene in *CINDERELLA* during which BUTTONS seeks to cheer Cinders up). Grimaldi was also celebrated for his 'construction' of outlandish animals (built out of barrels and other objects), carriages (based on baby's cradles and pulled along by dogs), and exploding steamboats created from bath tubs.

trickwork The employment of TRAPS, acrobatics, special scenic devices, and sleights of hand etc. in the creation of stage illusions. Inventive physical humour has always been an essential feature of the pantomime, as it was in the *COMMEDIA DELL'ARTE*, and the manipulation of mechanical devices such as TRAPS as well as the mastery of leaps and rolls was once an indispensable part of the armoury of specialists in comic parts.

Injuries were frequent, even among skilled exponents of trickwork (*see* GRIMALDI, JOSEPH), but spectacular displays of seemingly impossible physical feats employing specially-prepared equipment were once expected by all pantomime audiences. Popular physical gags of ancient lineage included CLOWN'S attempts to eat a meal when first the table is hoisted high up in the air, and then, as the table descends, his own chair heads skywards. Many of the most spectacular examples of trickwork depended upon the use of ingeniously constructed stage props that could be magically transformed in a moment through the use of various FALLING FLAPS. Thus, houses turned into caves, tombs into fountains, carriages into wheelbarrows, sheep into soldiers, and pumpkins into coaches as if by a supernatural command, to the delight and amazement of countless Regency and Victorian audiences (and before them of spectators going back to the earliest days of the pantomime).

The convention had obvious potential as a vehicle for comic satire, with the most magnificent dwellings, for instance, being converted in a moment into hovels, or ruins, or prisons. In one of the most popular examples of such trickery, the watch house in which Clown took shelter was magically transmuted by Harlequin into the basket of a hot air balloon, which proceeded to carry the terrified Clown away.

The exact details of how such tricks were achieved are often shrouded in mystery as managements were intensely jealous of their technical secrets, upon which much of the success of their pantomimes depended. Grimaldi kept details of contemporary trickwork in a notebook, but this has long since vanished into unknown hands. In the modern era such demonstrations have been left largely to the circus, with contemporary comics confining themselves to relatively unadventurous clowning with custard pies etc., although the transformation of the pumpkin into the coach in *CINDERELLA* is among the scenes in the modern pantomime which continues to offer stage carpenters the opportunity to demonstrate their inventiveness. *See also* RISE-AND-SINK; TRICKS OF CONSTRUCTION.

Tripp, Jack (1922–) English comedian, who is celebrated as one of the most popular DAMES of the postwar era. He made his pantomime debut in the 1940s, when he played alongside DOUGLAS BYNG as the dame's son Billy in *GOODY TWO-SHOES*. Subsequently he quickly established himself in the role of dame, building his performance around his skill as a dancer and his rich comic talents.

In a pantomime career lasting 50 years, he has played virtually all the leading venues and, appearing in such parts as MOTHER GOOSE and DAME TROT, has carried on the tradition of the 'realistic' dame created by DAN LENO, giving the character a veneer of refinement yet creating an instant rapport with children in the audience. Highlights of his act include the SLOSH SCENE, which he has worked to a fine art in partnership with his colleague ROY HUDD. He has also enjoyed great success over the years in concert parties.

U

Ugly Sisters The vain, cruel, and ridiculous stepsisters of the heroine in *CINDERELLA*, who are among the most cherished of all pantomime characters. The names of the 'Uglies' (as they often referred to in the acting profession) have varied over the years, although they are often called Clorinda and Thisbe, as in the opera by Rossini (1807) and the classic 1860 BURLESQUE version by H. J. BYRON, in which the part of the elder sister Clorinda was played by a man (James Rogers); it was in this version that the two sisters became more than merely unkind and actually ugly. Other names under which they have appeared include Buttercup and Daisy, Snowdrop and Tulip, Phoebe and Fanny, Namby and Pamby, Tutti and Frutti, Euthanasia and Asphyxia, Valderma and Germolena, Salmonella and Lysteria, and (in the 1990s) Danii and Kylie (after the Minogue sisters).

Typically one of the sisters is tall, lean, and arrogant while the other is short, fat, and slow-witted, making the parts ideal for comedy double-acts. They wear some of the most bizarre and colourful costumes seen in pantomime, often designed to satirise contemporary fashions, and these are changed with virtually every appearance they make. The Ugly Sisters are the most popular characters in the story and writers generally devote around four scenes in each act to them. Among the usual highlights involving them are the make-up scene, in which there is much clowning with various messy props, and the slipper-fitting scene, in which the pair try all manner of tricks to make the slipper fit (including substituting one of their own feet with an artificial one); in early versions of the story, before the slipper was made of glass, one of the sisters cut off the shoe's heel and toes in an attempt to make it fit her foot.

Both roles are now traditionally played by male performers, although females are still cast from time to time. Notable combinations to appear in the parts over the years have included Ethel Revnell and Gracie West in the 1930s, Kenneth Williams and Ted Durante in the 1950s, Terry Scott and Hugh Lloyd in the 1960s, and more recently such pairs as Stanley Baxter and Walter Carr, and television's John Inman and Barry Howard.

ultraviolet or **UV** A form of lighting often used in the contemporary pantomime, which renders only specially painted details visible. Operating on a different wavelength to conventional lighting, ultraviolet light is typically used in short scenes to pick out the treated costumes of performers playing ghosts and skeletons. It is also of use in the TRANSFORMATION SCENE, when it can contribute to such illusions as the growing of the beanstalk in *JACK AND THE BEANSTALK*, for instance.

upper circle The uppermost tier of seating in theatres where there is more than one circle or balcony (the other being identified as the lower or dress circle).

US pantomime *See* BOWERY THEATRE; FOX, GEORGE WASHINGTON LAFAYETTE; *HUMPTY-DUMPTY*; *MOTHER GOOSE*; OLYMPIC THEATRE.

V

vamp trap A type of hinged TRAP, formally called a vampire trap, which enables a performer to appear to pass through the seemingly solid stage floor. Comprising a pair of sprung flaps, it was devised by the author J. R. PLANCHÉ for his melodrama *The Vampire; or, the Bride of the Isles* (1820) at the LYCEUM THEATRE and subsequently became one of the most frequently used traps in the pantomime, being specially effective for entrances by ghosts, sorcerers, etc.

variety A form of theatrical entertainment, similar to broad revue, which emerged as the successor to the MUSIC HALL (which was itself sometimes referred to as 'variety') in the 20th century. Like music hall, variety encompasses a wide range of acts, varying from singers and comedians to acrobats, jugglers, magicians, dance orchestras, and exotic dancers – though at the start at least variety was distinguished from its predecessor by the fact that it was deliberately less risqué and 'blue' material was precluded in an attempt to make such entertainment more respectable.

Variety turns are generally unrelated by any central theme and the audience is usually free to eat, drink, and smoke while a performance is in progress. The genre reached its peak in popularity in the 1930s before TELEVISION took a major hold. As regards the pantomime, variety has proved a further source of the SPECIALITY ACTS that have characterised panto productions since the very beginning.

Among the contemporary personalities who have made the leap from variety to pantomime with notable success may be included such figures as DANNY LA RUE, Lionel Blair, Jimmy Tarbuck, Canon and Ball, Jim Davidson, and Little and Large.

Vegetable Fairy The FAIRY in *JACK AND THE BEANSTALK*. A relatively recent addition to the traditional pantomime story, the Vegetable Fairy (often called Sweetcorn) was introduced in a version of the tale by JOHN MORLEY and has subsequently become a standard pantomime character.

Venus The Roman goddess of beauty and love, who often appeared as a character in early versions of the English pantomime. Central to the mythological tales presented by JOHN WEAVER, Venus remained a character in such stories as *CINDERELLA* until well into the 19th century, when the FAIRY GODMOTHER gradually took over her role as BENEVOLENT AGENT.

Vernon, Harriet (1852–1923) English actress, who was one of the most popular PRINCIPAL BOYS of the late Victorian pantomime. She began her theatrical career as a 'fancy skater' and sketch artiste before making her debut as principal boy at the Theatre Royal, Manchester in the 1870s. She went on to build a reputation as one of the most dashing principal boys of her day, often resplendent in magnificent costumes, playing such heroic parts as Robin Hood, in which role she appeared in *THE BABES IN THE WOOD* at DRURY LANE in 1888. Ill health dogged her later career, which closed with appearances on tour alongside other former pantomime and music hall stars.

verse Most modern pantomimes are written almost entirely in prose, but it was once conventional for much if not all of the DIALOGUE to be delivered in verse. The pantomime was silent in its early years, but gradually found its voice over the course of the 18th and early 19th centuries, with most long speeches being delivered in the form of elegant rhymed couplets.

Such writers as J. R. PLANCHÉ and E. L. BLANCHARD were celebrated for their charming rhymed scripts, although prose pantomimes became increasingly common towards the end of the century, with verse being reserved (as it often still is) for the IMMORTALS (such as the DEMON KING, FAIRIES, and other supernatural characters). J. HICKORY WOOD at the turn of the century confirmed the trend in his witty pantomimes, in which verse was rarely used by anyone but demons and fairies.

It is now a long-standing tradition that most pantomimes – and indeed scenes within them – end with a rhymed couplet delivered by the PRINCIPAL BOY (the final rhymed couplet of all being spoken for the first time in performance for fear that doing so in rehearsal will bring bad luck).

Vestris, Madame (Lucy Elizabeth Bartolozzi; 1797–1856) English actress, singer, and theatre manager, who enjoyed extraordinary success in the 1830s with her productions at the OLYMPIC THEATRE of the EXTRAVAGANZAS of J. R. PLANCHÉ. Vestris began her career as a dancer and opera singer, making her debut as an actress at DRURY LANE in 1817 (in a benefit performance for her first husband, Armand Vestris). Subsequently she became a popular star there and at COVENT GARDEN, winning admirers as much for her unequalled voice and refined acting ability as for her figure.

She made her first pantomime appearance in 1820 in *Shakespeare versus Harlequin*, attracting praise for both her dancing and her singing, and in the same year enjoyed huge success playing the 'breeches part' Don Giovanni in the extravaganza *Giovanni in London*. Her shapely legs became the talk of London and audiences demanded to see her in more male roles of a similar type, flocking to see her play such parts as Macheath in *The Beggar's Opera* at the HAYMARKET.

She took over the management of the Olympic in 1830, becoming the first woman theatre manager in London's history, and immediately began her celebrated collaboration with Planché, appearing in many of his entertainments herself to great acclaim (generally in male roles). She first appeared as a principal boy in a pantomime story in 1837, when she played Ralph in *PUSS IN BOOTS* and was still admired in such parts at the age of 50. To draw attention to her legs, she regularly gave them a hearty slap (ostensibly to emphasise some point in the dialogue), thus establishing one of the great traditions for actresses playing the role of principal boy.

Her management of the Olympic saw the extravaganza develop as the most popular form of theatrical entertainment in the capital, eclipsing the conventional pantomime, and in 1839 – after a US tour – Vestris and her second husband (the actor CHARLES MATHEWS) moved on to take over COVENT GARDEN. Over the next three years she repeated the success she had enjoyed at the Olympic, but ran into financial problems, which were largely a result of her insistence upon sparing no expense in the production of her shows. The Vestris-Mathews management ended in 1842 with both Vestris and her husband being declared bankrupt and spending a brief period in gaol for debt.

Subsequently they assumed control (1847–55) of the LYCEUM THEATRE, where they continued to stage highly successful extravaganzas, despite a gradual decline in Vestris's health and continued financial troubles, which culminated in another spell behind bars. Vestris herself made her last appearance on the stage in 1854, in a benefit on behalf of her husband.

The splendour of the Vestris productions was unsurpassed in her day and in that regard her style of theatre was to have a lasting effect upon the pantomime proper, which quickly learnt to mimic these extravaganzas. Her collaboration with Planché and with the celebrated scene designer WILLIAM BEVERLEY ushered in a new age in the history of the pantomime, which (in the wake of Grimaldi's retirement) had been showing signs of flagging.

Vestris is also remembered in the 'legitimate' theatre for the revolution in current stage practice that followed her introduction of realistic sets (including possibly the first use of a box set) and of historically accurate costumes.

Vokes family A celebrated English theatrical family, who enjoyed a long association with the Victorian pantomime. One of the best known pantomime families, the Vokes clan comprised **Frederick Vokes** (1846–88), the undisputed star of the group with his extraordinary eccentric dancing (being known as 'the man with elastic legs' and the world's greatest exponent of 'legmania'), **Jessie (Catherine Biddulph) Vokes** (1851–84), who took care of the troupe's business affairs, **Victoria Vokes** (1853–94), who first went on stage at the age of two and also excelled in melodrama and as a 'straight' actress, and **Rosina Vokes** (1854–94), who made her stage debut while still a baby and was later called 'the life and soul of that merry family'; another member, who took the name Vokes after joining the troupe, was **Walter Fawdon**.

The children of a theatrical costumier, the Vokeses – who were first seen in an act known as The Vokes Children – were popular stars of pantomime on both sides of the Atlantic for many years, winning acclaim as singers, dancers, actors, and acrobats. They made their debut at the LYCEUM THEATRE in *HUMPTY-DUMPTY* in 1865 and subsequently enjoyed a monopoly of virtually all the leading roles in the annual DRURY LANE pantomime (written by E. L. BLANCHARD) every year (except 1873 when they were on tour) between 1869 and 1879 – by which time audiences were tiring of them.

AUGUSTUS HARRIS ended their reign at Drury Lane shortly after he became manager and in 1880 they transferred to COVENT GARDEN. Rosina was eventually replaced by Fred's wife Bella and the group finally broke up in 1884 on the death of Jessie.

W

walkdown The reappearance of the cast at the end of a performance to receive the applause of the audience. Although methods of taking a bow vary in other forms of theatre, in the pantomime it is traditional for the leading members of the cast to enter (usually in pairs) and to walk down to the front of the stage to take a bow, then to retreat as other performers come on. Last to appear are always the two lovers around whose adventures the plot has revolved (no matter how well known the performer playing the dame or Simple Simon may be). The walkdown usually ends with the entire cast then taking one or more bows together (and possibly with a reprise of songs sung during the show).

walk-on A small acting part in which the performer makes an entrance but has no lines to say.

Wallace, Nellie (Eleanor Jane Wallace; 1870–1948) Scottish singer and comedian, who was one of the few successful female performers to appear in the role of DAME. Born in Glasgow, Wallace began her career while still a child, appearing as a clog dancer at various provincial venues and later winning popular acclaim with such songs as 'My Mother Said Always Look Under the Bed' and 'Three Cheers for the Red, White, and Blue'.

As dame, she carried over the eccentric and dilapidated spinster character she played in the music hall, complete with fur-piece ("her little bit of vermin") and moth-eaten clothes. Audiences seemed to accept her as a dame largely because of her unbecoming appearance and weird behaviour and were not offended by the sight of seeing a custard pie land in her face, as they would have been in the case of virtually any other female interpreter of the role. Billed 'The Essence of Eccentricity', she was also a star in revue.

wand *See* FAIRY GODMOTHER.

Ward, Dorothy (1895–) English actress, who became one of the most famous performers of all to appear in the role of PRINCIPAL BOY. She made her debut in her native city, Birmingham, in 1905 but did not appear as principal boy until the grand old age of 34; she was still appearing in the role with great success in 1960, despite her own protests that she was by then far too old.

More than any other performer of the role, she transformed the principal boy into the more feminine character of the contemporary pantomime, being the first to insist that her costumes were made by a dressmaker rather than a man's tailor. Though DICK WHITTINGTON was her favourite role, she was also especially acclaimed as JACK; her farewell scene with her mother's cow was so affecting that she was even asked to perform it at a Royal Command Performance.

She often appeared in pantomime in company with her husband SHAUN GLENVILLE as DAME.

wardrobe The COSTUME department of a theatre, which is usually supervised by a wardrobe mistress. The requirements of such major productions as pantomimes often necessitate the employment of a full-time wardrobe mistress and ancillary staff, although contemporary theatre managements frequently hire sets of costumes from outside, from specialist wardrobe companies.

Weaver, John (1673–1760) English dancing master, who revived the term 'pantomime' in the early 18th century as a description for his *ballets-pantomimes*. Weaver, who hailed from Shrewsbury (where he lived between engagements in London), was dancing master at DRURY LANE and often appeared on stage himself as a dancer.

His particular concern was that the art of dancing had been neglected in England for far too long and he sought to revive dance as a serious art form by linking his productions to the traditions of Classical times, which he described at length in a number of essays published between 1706 and 1728. Thus, his early entertainment *The Cheats; or, The Tavern Bilkers*, which was staged with only modest success possibly as early as 1702, claimed to be "an attempt in imitation of the ancient Pantomimes and the first of its kind that has appeared since the time of the Roman emperors" – even though the link between his piece and the art of the Roman *PANTOMIMUS* was remote in the extreme.

Weaver's most significant production was, however, *THE LOVES OF MARS AND VENUS*, another 'dance in character' which was staged in 1717 as an AFTERPIECE to one of the plays at Drury Lane. Consisting of a series of dances connected by a vague narrative derived from Classical mythology, this broke new ground in telling a rational story through mime and gesture alone and was the first entertainment in English theatrical history actually to be billed as a 'pantomime'. The production was doubly significant in that it also demonstrated how contemporary dance and mime techniques might be applied to source material drawn from ancient Classical legend or folklore – a concept that was crucial in the early development of the pantomime proper. Weaver's 'scenic dance' as he described it did not include any of the characters currently enjoying a vogue in performances of ITALIAN NIGHT SCENES (which he considered vulgar) at the LINCOLN'S INN FIELDS THEATRE, but it was inevitable that sooner or later he would have to succumb to popular taste; the following month he presented *The Shipwreck; or, Perseus and Andromeda*, in which the figures of HARLEQUIN and his confederates rubbed shoulders with characters from ancient legend.

Weaver's term 'pantomime' was quickly adopted by JOHN RICH (who lured Weaver to Lincoln's Inn that same year) to describe his own innovative productions, which were to mark the true beginnings of the modern pantomime.

Weldon, Harry (1881–1930) English comedian, who was a star of both the MUSIC HALL and pantomime. His comic verbal eccentricities started a national craze, with countless people mimicking his "S'no use" and "S'no good". He appeared many times under the management of the MELVILLE BROTHERS at the LYCEUM THEATRE and was particularly loved in the role of BUTTONS, in which he appeared in 1915. His other parts included IDLE JACK, which he played in *DICK WHITTINGTON* at the Palladium in 1923.

Whimsical Walker (1850–1934) English actor, who was one of the last great CLOWNS to appear at DRURY LANE. He began his career in the circus while still a child and eventually succeeded HARRY PAYNE as Clown at Drury Lane, going on to appear in 25 annual harlequinades there. He also attempted to present pantomime at a theatre in New York but lost all his money after a packed gallery collapsed during a performance. When the Drury Lane harlequinade came to an end, he continued to appear as Clown in the annual Christmas circus at Olympia for some years.

White Cat, The Fairytale that was regularly rendered as a pantomime on the Victorian stage. Early pantomime versions of the story included *The White Cat; or, Harlequin in Fairy Wood*, which was seen at DRURY LANE in 1811 and was particularly memorable for the fun the clown James Kirby had lampooning the elaborate army uniforms then in vogue (a theme subsequently taken up by JOSEPH GRIMALDI). J. R. PLANCHÉ based one of his most successful extravaganzas on the story in 1842, with MADAME VESTRIS winning acclaim in the role of Prince Paragon, while a later production seen at Drury Lane in 1877 featured members of the VOKES FAMILY in the leading parts.

The story has been seen much less often in the 20th century (perhaps because of the violence of the cat's death) and a version staged at Drury Lane in 1904 (immediately after the deaths of DAN LENO and HERBERT CAMPBELL) was not a success.

Story A king sets his three sons a challenge, promising that the son who brings him the handsomest dog after a year's travel will inherit the kingdom. The youngest son arrives at a mysterious castle inhabited by a magical White Cat who rewards him after a year with a dog that appears from an acorn, giving him easy victory. The king sets a second challenge, in which the sons must find a length of cloth fine enough to pass through the eye of a needle: again the White Cat enables the youngest son to win. Finally the king promises his throne to the son who returns with the most beautiful woman: the White Cat orders the youngest son to kill her and she is transformed into a beautiful princess (having been turned into a cat by wicked fairies many years before). The youngest son wins the contest while the other sons are made content with the gift of kingdoms that formerly belonged to the princess.

Origins The immediate source for the pantomime plot was a fairytale by MADAME D'AULNOY, which first appeared in English in 1698, although it was a subsequent translation by Elizabeth Newbery in 1795 that promoted the tale as one of the most popular pantomime stories of the 19th century.

Wicked Stepmother The archetypal villainess of many pantomimes, notably *SNOW WHITE AND THE SEVEN DWARFS* and – when she is included – *CINDERELLA* (*see* BARONESS). Psychologists have drawn a link between the many stories featuring a Wicked Stepmother with the confusion felt by every child when an otherwise kindly parent or guardian suddenly shows another angrier side to his or her character (often the result of some relatively insignificant incident); according to the theory, the child may interpret this new, threatening person to be quite different to the character he knows and loves and conclude that this is in fact a malevolent imposter.

Whatever the psychology behind the role, the part offers female performers excellent acting opportunities (something of a rarity in theatre as a whole) – although it is not unheard of for men to take the role (JOSEPH GRIMALDI and DAN LENO both appeared in the part). Among the latest generation of actresses to appear in the role are Kate O'Mara and Anita Dobson.

Widow Twankey The hero's mother in *ALADDIN* and possibly the best-loved of all pantomime DAMES. In the original Arabian story from which the pantomime was derived she is described as old and not at all beautiful, even as a girl. Nonetheless, indignant and irrepressible, the Widow Ching Mustapha (or Ching-Ching or simply Mustapha) as she was christened by CHARLES FARLEY in the COVENT GARDEN production of 1813, triumphs over all difficulties and in most versions of the tale is rewarded with wealth and sometimes even the hand of the Sultan himself.

In early pantomime productions she is the widow of a tailor, although by 1844 she was being described as a washerwoman and by the end of the 19th century had risen to the giddy heights of manageress of the royal laundry, in which she was assisted (or hindered) by WISHEE-WASHEE. It was H. J. BYRON who rechristened her Widow Twankey (or Twankay) in his BURLESQUE version of the story written in 1861, a full 73 years after the character first took the stage. Apparently Byron took his inspiration from Twankay tea, a green tea from the Tuon Ky district of China which was just then enjoying great popularity in London and had a somewhat glamorous image through its association with the great clipper vessels of the day that raced each other to bring their cargoes of tea from the Orient to the West.

By 1864 the tradition that men played the dame roles was well established and the first to breathe life into Byron's restyled character was the actor James Rogers. Many illustrious performers have followed in his footsteps, among them Charles Steyne (who played her in E. L. BLANCHARD's version in 1865), DAN LENO (who brought a new realism to the part at the turn of the century), and more recently ARTHUR ASKEY, BILLY DAINTY (who gave her a more vulgar edge), and DANNY LA RUE (in whose hands she became a more glamorous 'Merry Widow'). Before the part became as blousy and reliant upon slapstick comedy as it is today, women did occasionally appear in the role, notably in the early 1826 and 1836 productions at Covent Garden and again in 1874, when HARRIET COVENEY appeared in Blanchard's second version of the tale.

Wieland, 'Nimble' George (1810–47) English comedian, who won acclaim in the role of CLOWN in the 19th century. Wieland began his theatrical career while still a child and in time emerged as one of the most accomplished of JOSEPH GRIMALDI's successors, winning particular praise for his skill as a contortionist and acrobat. E. L. BLANCHARD for one considered him the finest Clown he had ever seen. His other comedy roles included that of the heroine Susan in a burlesque version of Douglas Jerrold's nautical drama *Black Ey'd Susan* (1830).

Wilton, Marie (Effie) (1839–1921) English actress, married to the famous actor-manager Squire Bancroft (1841–1926), who became a star of BURLESQUE and a popular PRINCIPAL BOY of the Victorian era.

Her pantomime roles included that of ALADDIN in the classic 1861 burlesque version of the story by H. J. BYRON. Billed 'The Queen of Burlesque' at the Strand Theatre, she took a share in the management of the theatre at the age of 25, when she became H. J. BYRON's partner there, and then turned the Prince of Wales Theatre into one of the leading venues in London.

She married Bancroft (who himself had made his stage debut in a pantomime in Birmingham) in 1867 and shared the management of the HAYMARKET with him before retiring in 1885. They are particularly remembered in the acting profession for their championship of the welfare of actors and for their promotion of higher performance standards (which included the use of authentic costumes and sets).

wings The pairs of flats that are arranged on either side of the stage, both to mask off the backstage area from the audience's view and also to complete a full set of scenery. It was once customary for the wings to run in grooves in the stage floor and to be supported overhead by rails running across the stage area. Wings could then be slid on and off the acting area at will and be interchanged with a minimum of difficulty.

Wisdom, Norman (1918–) English comedian, who became a highly popular star of the cinema and the pantomime in the 1950s. The diminutive slapstick comedian won almost overnight fame with the film *Trouble in Store* (1953) and, with his unique brand of pathos and rebelliousness, was quickly recognised as an ideal recruit for the pantomime. His performance in the title role of *ALADDIN* at the LONDON PALLADIUM in 1956–57 was particularly significant in that it began a new fashion for male PRINCIPAL BOYS, a trend that dominated the Palladium pantomimes (to the regret of many) until 1971. Wisdom's career faltered in the 1960s though he continued to be a popular star of pantomimes around the country.

Wishee-Washee The loyal but generally incompetent assistant to WIDOW TWANKEY in her laundry in *ALADDIN AND HIS WONDERFUL LAMP* (sometimes he is also identified as Aladdin's brother). Wishee-Washee (a Chinese equivalent of such figures as SIMPLE SIMON and IDLE JACK) was a relatively late addition to the tale, making his first appearance in 1889, reappearing at DRURY LANE in 1896, and subsequently becoming a standard character in the story (effectively replacing Abanazar's henchman Kasrac).

One of the greatest performers of the role, which was designed in part as a foil to the clowning of the DAME, was DAN LENO, who played Wishee-Washee in the 1896 production. More recent interpreters of the part have included the pop group The Shadows, who once appeared as Wishee, Washee, Noshee, and Poshee at the LONDON PALLADIUM.

witches The pantomime is populated with a number of singularly menacing wicked witches, the most well-known including those in *THE SLEEPING BEAUTY* (where she is more properly a Bad Fairy), *SNOW WHITE AND THE SEVEN DWARFS* (as the WICKED STEPMOTHER), and *HANSEL AND GRETEL*. Such characters are descended from the hags of countless folktales familiar in almost every culture; not all are bad, however.

Wolf The best known wolf in the pantomime is that in *LITTLE RED RIDING HOOD*, who threatens to devour both the heroine and her grandmother, although similar beasts have also appeared in a number of other pantomime stories. Performers of the role over the years have included no less a personage then SIR HENRY IRVING, the great actor who as a young man of 19 appeared as Scruncher, Captain of the Wolves, in a production of *LITTLE BO-PEEP* at the Theatre Royal, Edinburgh in the 1850s. In the celebrated 1892 production of *Little Bo-Peep, Little Red Riding-Hood and Hop o' My Thumb* at DRURY LANE the Wolf – much beaten by his wife – was somewhat unusually played as a drunken rascal professing to be a committed socialist (the Wolf and his wife being played by the GRIFFITHS BROTHERS comedy double act).

Wood, David (1944–) English playwright, who has established a reputation for plays for children and unconventional pantomimes. He began his career as an actor with the company of the Swan Theatre, Worcester, for which he wrote his first children's plays. *The Owl and the Pussycat* (1968) won great acclaim and was transferred to London, as were many of his subsequent works.

Rather than straight pantomimes he writes 'family musicals' in which the comic element is controlled and full emphasis is given to the plot (which may include ingenious new twists). They include *ALADDIN*, *BABES IN THE MAGIC WOOD*, *CINDERELLA*, *DICK WHITTINGTON AND WONDERCAT*, *Jack and the Giant*, *Mother Goose's Golden Christmas*, which is loosely based on the story of the Goose that Laid the Golden Eggs, OLD MOTHER HUBBARD, and (with Dave and Toni Arthur) *ROBIN HOOD*, *Jack the Lad*, which presents several of the various pantomime characters called Jack alongside other famous Jacks of myth and legend, and *THE PIED PIPER*.

Wood, J. Hickory (1859–1913) English author, who wrote many of the DRURY LANE pantomimes in which DAN LENO triumphed and who won recognition as the leading writer of early 20th-century pantomime. Born in Manchester, Wood worked as an insurance clerk before finding his ideal role as a writer for the pantomime, executing his first entertainments for provincial theatres and for the Garrick Theatre in London.

In 1900 he was recruited at the last minute to provide the script for *THE SLEEPING BEAUTY AND THE BEAST* for the management of ARTHUR COLLINS at Drury Lane; the show, which starred Leno and his partner HERBERT CAMPBELL as the King and Queen, proved a great success and Wood subsequently wrote the scripts for all the Lane's pantomimes for the next 12 years.

Critics praised his skill at combining well-known fairytales and his ability to devise new twists in old and sometimes stale stories; many pantomimes seen today still follow the patterns of Wood's versions. Unlike many other contemporary writers, he produced complete scripts that included the comic business usually left to the comedians to extemporise. Working closely with Leno and Collins, Wood provided scripts in which the conventional DAME became for the first time a fully-realised character of the type familiar to modern audiences. His other innovations included restricting rhymed couplets to the so-called 'Immortals' and dropping the HARLEQUINADE altogether.

Particularly successful was his reworking of *MOTHER GOOSE* (1902), which provided Leno with one of his most celebrated roles as dame and which is still used as the basis for most modern versions of the tale. Wood's pantomimes dominated the Edwardian pantomime and in 1911 no less than 33 of his creations were presented in professional productions throughout England and the British Empire.

Woodward, Henry (1720–77) English actor, who won acclaim in the role of HARLEQUIN in the pantomimes produced by DAVID GARRICK at DRURY LANE. Having begun his career as an actor while still a child, Woodward received his training in the part (from 1729) from no less an authority than JOHN RICH and was often billed as 'Lun Junior'. He had a hand in the writing of many of the pantomimes in which he appeared, including the first of those produced by Garrick – *Queen Mab* (1750) – in which his performance was greeted with rapturous applause.

Among the pantomimes he helped to create were early versions of *DICK WHITTINGTON*, *Robin Hood*, and *THE BABES IN THE WOOD*. He is also remembered for his performance in 1759 in what became known as 'Mr Garrick's Speaking Pantomime', more properly titled *Harlequin's Invasion*, in which he played Harlequin as usual, but was actually given lines to speak (in an attempt to steal the limelight from Rich himself). The pantomimes that he helped to write were significant in that they represented some of the earliest attempts to harness native English folklore as source material.

After his death Woodward was briefly replaced by RICHARD BRINSLEY SHERIDAN (with whom he had spent a year at the Smock Alley Theatre in Dublin) as writer of the Lane pantomimes. Outside pantomime, he created the role of Captain Absolute in Sheridan's *The Rivals* (1777).

Wylie, Julian (1878–1934) English theatre impresario, who exercised a considerable influence over the provincial pantomime in the 1920s and 1930s. An accountant by training, he formed a partnership with James W. Tate and concentrated upon pantomime after World War I. Under his guiding hand a new balance was struck between the MUSIC HALL element that had dominated the pantomime for too many years and the telling of the fairytales themselves.

Stars who appeared in the many pantomimes he produced included the actresses FAY COMPTON and Phyllis Neilson-Terry (his adventurous casting of US comedian and xylophone player Will Mahoney in *PUSS IN BOOTS* was a rare failure). It was through Wylie's efforts that pantomime was briefly restored to the bills at DRURY LANE in 1929.

XYZ

Yellow Dwarf, The Once-popular pantomime story about a wicked and lecherous dwarf. The tale was first adapted as a pantomime in 1807, when *Mother Bunch and the Yellow Dwarf* was staged; subsequently it was seen in another 16 versions before the end of the 19th century, including one by J. R. PLANCHÉ seen in 1854.

As *Harlequin and Mother Bunch; or, The Yellow Dwarf* by CHARLES FARLEY, the pantomime was presented at COVENT GARDEN in 1821, with JOSEPH GRIMALDI as the Yellow Dwarf. This version was notable also for its spectacular re-enactment of the Coronation of George IV that had recently taken place and for the incorporation of familiar London views in the scenery, which included such settings as Margate, London Bridge, Stamford Hill, the Bank of England, and New Cross.

The tale has long since vanished from the pantomime repertoire, largely because of the violence implicit in the plot and its negative view of the stereotypical wicked dwarf.

Story All-Fair is the beautiful only daughter of the queen. She refuses to marry various suitors and the queen sets off to seek advice from a bad fairy. She is attacked by lions and has to hide in an orange tree; in exchange for her life she promises her daughter's hand to the Yellow Dwarf, who lives in the tree. She does not tell her daughter what has happened and All-Fair herself goes to see the fairy. The Yellow Dwarf intercepts her and tells her that she must marry him.

In desperation, All-Fair agrees to marry a powerful king but the Yellow Dwarf kidnaps her while the bad fairy – having turned herself into a beautiful nymph – tries to capture the king. The king realises the trick when he sees the nymph's unchanged feet and escapes with the aid of a magic diamond sword. He fights his way to All-Fair but is killed by the Yellow Dwarf. All-Fair also dies and the fairy turns them both into palm trees (in the pantomime this unhappy ending was generally replaced with a happier one in which the king defeated the Yellow Dwarf and married All-Fair).

Origins The pantomime was based on a fairytale written by MADAME D'AULNOY, which was translated into English in 1721. Though the tale was largely her own invention, certain details of it were probably modelled on similar incidents in French folklore.

zanni The comic servant characters of the *COMMEDIA DELL'ARTE*, from which several of the main figures in the HARLEQUINADE developed. Initially there were usually just two of these clowns – ARLECCHINO, a greedy dolt, and BRIGHELLA, a dishonest rogue, who together formed a comedy double act that performed carefully rehearsed acrobatics and slapstick routines (*see* BURLA; LAZZI). Other servant characters sometimes counted among the *zanni* included PULCINELLA, a dimwitted peasant, and Scaramuccia (*see* SCARAMOUCHE), a comic valet. The *zanni* characters all wore distinctive masks and were responsible for most of the comedy and therefore the appeal of the *commedia dell'arte*. The word 'zany', meaning bizarre, is derived from *zanni*.

Appendix

Related children's entertainments

A number of children's plays and other Christmas entertainments are closely identified with the pantomime proper, though they do not strictly belong to the same tradition. Several of these works share many of the features of the pantomime and were intended by their authors to appeal to the same mixed audience. Such shows as *Peter Pan* and *Toad Hall* are regularly presented during the pantomime season even at venues that in other years would stage such accepted pantomimes as *Jack and the Beanstalk* and *Cinderella* and have on occasion been adapted in such a way that they are pantomimes in all but name, with all the usual elements of audience participation, cross-dressing, etc. (and, indeed, the same star names).

Notices of these entertainments appear alongside those of conventional pantomimes in the theatrical press as though they were one and the same thing and many children in the audience (and perhaps their parents) would find it hard to distinguish what is a 'proper' pantomime and what isn't.

The following section (with apologies to pantomime purists) gives details of a few of the best known of these now traditional 'almost-pantomimes', together with articles on the leading characters and other information. It may be that in years to come these productions will be thoroughly absorbed into the pantomime tradition: for now, it seems appropriate to include them as a sub-genre that enriches the 'pure' form, even as it trespasses on its territory.

* * *

Alice in Wonderland The classic children's story by Lewis Carroll (Charles Lutwidge Dodgson; 1832–98), which though not itself strictly a pantomime is often treated as one and regularly performed during the pantomime season (a Drury Lane pantomime procession at the end of thc 19th century placed Carroll's characters alongside those of more conventional fairytales).

Published in 1865, Carroll's story has many of the fantastical elements and exaggerated characters familiar from the pantomime proper and is usually produced in a broad pantomime style. Carroll himself approved of the tale's adaptation for the theatre and actively assisted in its first stage presentation – as an operetta by Henry Savile Clarke in 1886 (it had already been adapted as a play for children in a version by Kate Freilgrath-Kroeker in 1880). Since then the story has been adapted as a children's play many times. It has also been filmed (for the first time as early as 1906) and was the subject of an acclaimed Disney cartoon film (1951).

Story Alice is a wilful girl with a strong sense of curiosity. She follows a White Rabbit down a rabbit hole and thus embarks on a serious of remarkable and often hilarious and nonsensical adventures which bring her into contact with such unique figures as the Caterpillar, the Ugly Duchess, the Cheshire Cat, the Mad Hatter, the Mock Turtle, and the Queen of Hearts (usually treated as the dame role). The most famous scene both in the book and in performed versions remains the Mad Hatter's Tea Party.

Origins The way in which the tale developed is one of the great legends of modern literature. On 4 July 1862 Carroll and another university don took the ten-year-old Alice Liddell and her sisters Lorina and Edith – the offspring of the Dean of Christ Church, Oxford – on a boating trip during which he kept them entertained telling them the stories of a fictional Alice, which he made up as they went along. At Alice Liddell's request he subsequently committed the story – which in its original version was called *Alice's Adventures Under Ground* – to paper and submitted the manuscript for publication.

Critical reaction to the story was mixed but readers responded to Carroll's masterful combination of fantasy and nonsense and identified with his deliberate refusal to tell a tale with an obvious moral lesson (the case with most other contemporary children's stories). The book has since been translated into almost as many languages as the Bible. A sequel to the tale, *Alice's Adventures Through the Looking-Glass*, appeared in 1871 and most dramatisations of Alice's adventures include scenes taken from both volumes.

Christmas Carol, A A festive story by Charles Dickens, which is often staged as an alternative to the conventional pantomime during the pantomime season. Published in 1843, the dramatised version of the tale provides opportunities for the use of a large, lavishly costumed cast, although it can also be presented with a smaller ensemble if necessary.

The story depicts the conversion of the miserly Ebenezer Scrooge from his penny-pinching ways after he is visited by the ghost of the dead Jacob Marley and by the Spirits of Christmas Past, Christmas Present, and Christmas Yet To Come, who show him scenes of Christmas in the poor homes of his employees. There are a number of modern adaptations of Dickens's classic tale, among them versions by Christopher Bedloe, Shaun Sutton, and Kenelm Foss. The story is frequently staged in the USA as a standard Christmas entertainment.

Hook, Captain The villainous pirate captain and Peter's arch-enemy in J. M. Barrie's Christmas play *Peter Pan*. Hook offers one of the most relished parts in pantomime and related entertainments and has been played by a succession of famous performers, who have included Gerald du Maurier (father of the novelist Daphne du Maurier and the first to play the part), Ernest Lawford, Leslie Banks, Boris Karloff, Charles Laughton, Alastair Sim, and more recently Dustin Hoffman in the film *Hook*, and Brian Blessed. When Gerald du Maurier played Hook back in 1904 an extra carpenter's scene was added to cover a set change, in which Hook impersonated leading actors of the day. The actor playing Hook often doubles as Mr. Darling, the children's father, adding extra psychological impact.

Lion, the Witch, and the Wardrobe, The Children's novel by C. S. Lewis (1898–1963), which has been dramatised and presented as a Christmas entertainment alongside conventional pantomimes many times in recent years. The story (published as a novel in 1950) has established itself as one of the half-dozen or so alternatives to the pantomime that is capable of attracting a similar mixed audience of adults and children.

Story A group of four children (evacuees) discover that they can pass through a wardrobe into the imaginary land of Narnia, an icy wasteland that is populated by all manner of fantastical characters (among them the delightful Mr and Mrs Beaver and the compassionate faun Mr Tumnus). Here they become involved in a great struggle between good (personified by the lion-god Aslan) and evil (as embodied in the White Witch and her wolf pack) and have many adventures before finally returning home.

Origins Lewis invented the land of Narnia and its inhabitants after a nightmare about lions and devised his story to re-tell the most significant events in the life of Christ in a way that would be appealing to children. The original novel shows the influence of Hans Christian Andersen among other writers and, together with its six sequels, has inspired many adaptations both for the theatre and for television.

Peter Pan The central character around whom the action revolves in J. M. Barrie's *Peter Pan; or, The Boy Who Wouldn't Grow Up* (1904). Peter Pan, the wilful half-magical leader of the Lost Boys, is usually treated as a role for a female principal boy (as indeed were the parts of virtually all the children in early productions of the story). The first actress to take the part was Nina Boucicault, whose brother directed the first production.

Other actresses to win acclaim in the role have included Pauline Chase (who played it every year between 1906 and 1914), Jean Forbes-Robertson (who played it many times between 1927 and World War II), and, in the USA, Jean Arthur. A male actor, Miles Anderson, took the role in an acclaimed Royal Shakespeare Company production in 1982 and US film actor Robin Williams played a somewhat superannuated Peter in the film *Hook* (1992).

Peter Pan; or, The Boy Who Wouldn't Grow Up The children's fantasy by J. M. Barrie (1860–1937), which although not strictly a pantomime, has long been one of the most popular productions regularly presented during the pantomime season. Features the play shares in common with the pantomime include the principal boy (Peter Pan), principal girl (Wendy), a fairy (Tinkerbell), a Demon King equivalent (Captain Hook), and a version of the Broker's Men (Starkey and Smee).

Barrie's play was first seen in 1904 at the Duke of York's Theatre. The original production, staged by the impresario Charles Frohman, was spectacular, with not only impressive (and subsequently obligatory) flying effects but also such dramatic examples of trickwork as a working crocodile. Such was the enthusiasm with which the play was greeted that it was revived at the theatre every year until 1914 and then at other London theatres on an annual basis until 1939.

After World War II it was staged annually – still much as it was in 1904 – for another 20 years at the Scala Theatre. It has been revived regularly since then all around the country and in 1982 the Royal Shakespeare Company successfully presented a new production of the play (features of which included a male Peter Pan, new songs, and extracts from other related writings by Barrie). The play has also been successfully staged in the USA, the first production dating back to 1905.

At the author's request proceeds from the copyright in the production were from 1929 passed to the Great Ormond Street Children's Hospital in London, an arrangement that continued to be honoured even after the legal copyright ran out in the 1980s.

There have been several cinematic versions of the story, with the first silent rendering dating from 1924; subsequently Walt Disney made a popular full-length cartoon based on Barrie's work. A blockbuster film, *Hook* (1992) starring Robin Williams and Dustin Hoffman, dealt somewhat loosely with the original plot.

Story As the Darling children, Wendy (a name invented by Barrie himself), John, and Michael, lie in their nursery one night they are visited by Peter Pan, a wilful boy-cum-sprite with the power of flight. He teaches the children how to fly and takes them to Never Never Land, where he is the leader of a gang called the Lost Boys. There the children are captured by Peter Pan's arch-enemy, the evil Captain Hook (who now has a hook in the place of the right hand he once lost to a crocodile).

There follows a series of adventures as Peter (aided by the fairy Tinker Bell) pits his wits against the dastardly pirate captain and his crew (who include the comedy double-act Starkey and Smee) and finally overcomes his old adversary (who is consumed by the crocodile, which has waited all these years to get the rest of him). The children are reunited with their parents (and their Newfoundland dog-nursemaid Nana), although Wendy is allowed back to Never Never Land just once a year.

In the original production of the play, the story ended with a parade of 20 'Beautiful Mothers' applying to look after the Lost Boys. Barrie also intended that in a further concluding scene (never performed) Hook, having escaped from the crocodile, would menace the children at their home back in London until they eluded his clutches by being transformed into Harlequin and Columbine (illustrating Barrie's own identification of the play as a restyled pantomime).

Origins Barrie's play was based on his novel *The Little White Bird* and remains his single most well-known work. He was prompted to attempt such a piece partly by the success of Seymour Hicks's play *Bluebell in Fairyland* in London in 1901. Much speculation about the psychology behind the invention of 'the boy who never grew up' has taken place in recent decades and it is now generally agreed that in *Peter Pan* the author was voicing his own doubts about the superiority of an imperfect adult world over the escapist innocence of youth.

It also reflected his friendship with the children of the Llewelyn Davies family, who provided the models for the Darling children themselves (George Llewelyn Davies, who had provided the model for Peter, was killed in action at Flanders in 1915 during World War I). Never Never Land, incidentally, is the name of a district of Australia. Among Barrie's other works linked to the pantomime tradition was the play *A Kiss for Cinderella* (1916).

Pinocchio Fantasy story by the Italian writer Carlo Collodi (Carlo Lorenzini; 1826–90), which is frequently adapted as a children's play and staged during the traditional pantomime season. Published in 1883, the story of Pinocchio rapidly acquired the status of an international children's classic, inevitably attracting the attention of English pantomimists.

The story established itself as one of the small number of tales regularly revived in the 20th century pantomime and each year there are usually around half a dozen professional productions of it, often incorporating the use of puppets. Many children know the tale through an immensely successful (if sentimentalised) full-length cartoon made by Walt Disney in 1940. Recent stage dramatisations include one by John Morley.

Story Pinocchio is a talking wooden puppet fashioned by a penniless old puppet-maker called Gepetto, who longs for a son. The puppet's distinguishing feature is a long thin nose that grows longer whenever Pinocchio – who is wilful and badly behaved – tells a lie. He ignores the advice of Jiminy Cricket (who in the original version reappears as a ghost after Pinocchio kills him) to mend his ways and undergoes a series of hair-raising adventures (in company with the unruly Lampwick) before he learns to curb his reckless nature.

He is kidnapped by a puppet-master, robbed by a scheming Fox and Cat, escapes to 'Playland' (or 'Funland') where children play all day but are gradually turned into donkeys, is sold to a circus, and is only saved from destruction through the intervention of his guardian (the Blue Fairy). Eventually Pinocchio proves he has a loving heart by rescuing his creator-father Gepetto from the stomach of a whale; in reward he is forgiven his misdeeds and transformed by the fairy into a real boy.

Origins Collodi's story was written for a children's magazine and was first translated into English in 1892. Unfortunately, the author died before his remarkable tale (with some editing of the more cruel scenes) won recognition as a classic of modern children's literature.

Smee One of the pirate crew in J. M. Barrie's children's play *Peter Pan*. Smee, whose job it is to patch the clothes of the rest of the crew, was largely the invention of the actor George Shelton, who took the role in the original production (1904) and continued to appear in it in many later productions.

Snow Queen, The A fairytale by Hans Christian Andersen, which is regularly adapted as a children's play and presented during the pantomime season. Though requiring considerable inventiveness from writers to inject some frivolity into a relatively dour tale, the story has maintained its status as one of the more frequently seen Christmas shows (there were at least three professional productions of it in 1992–93 alone).

Story In Andersen's original tale, the Devil makes a mirror that has the effect of making all that is good appear evil and all that is bad appear good. The mirror breaks and splinters from it enter the eyes and heart of a small boy, Kai, who consequently turns against his friend Gerda and becomes hard and bitter. The beautiful but cruel Snow Queen takes him to her icy home but Gerda follows and after many adventures (including a brush with a gang of robbers) finds Kai and melts the splinters in his eyes and heart with her tears.

Origins Andersen's story was first published in 1846 and pulls together details of a number of myths; it remains one of his most effective and imaginative stories.

Tinder Box, The Fairytale by Hans Christian Andersen, which has on a number of occasions been adapted as a children's play and even as a pantomime. Andersen's story offers numerous opportunities for spectacular effects, with such details as the underground cavern and the three dogs.

Story A soldier returning from the wars meets a witch, who persuades him to go down a hollow tree into a cave to retrieve a tinder box she claims to have left there. The soldier descends and finds three chests of treasure guarded by three dogs with huge eyes. He uses a magic apron given to him by the witch to pacify the dogs and helps himself to the treasure. The witch refuses to tell him why she wants the tinder box and the soldier kills her (in most pantomime versions he frightens her away and she subsequently returns in disguise to attempt to steal the tinder box from him).

The soldier goes on to enjoy his new-found wealth and, with the aid of the three dogs (who are summoned up whenever he strikes the tinder box), replenishes his gold and enjoys secret visits from the princess, who is otherwise kept in seclusion in the royal palace. The queen learns about the liaison between her daughter and the soldier through the clever ruse of pinning a bag of flour with a hole in it to the princess's dress (thus leaving a trail that can be followed wherever she goes) and has the latter thrown into prison. He is sentenced to death but summons up the dogs, who kill the king and his men (in the pantomime they usually see off the witch, leaving the soldier free to marry the princess).

Origins Andersen's version was first published in 1836 and was translated into English in 1846. He based his story upon a traditional Scandinavian legend and may also have been influenced by his reading of *Aladdin* and similar tales by the Grimm brothers. In the original Scandinavian fairytale the tinder box is a candle and the role of the dogs is taken by an 'iron man'.

Tinker Bell The fairy in J. M. Barrie's *Peter Pan*. In the first production of the play, seen in 1904, and in many of the revivals seen since then the part was 'played' by a tiny point of light, which flitted restlessly around the stage (achieved by reflecting a spotlight beam with a small mirror). The part has, however, also been played by human performers, usually children. In the 1992 film *Hook* the part was played by a 'miniaturised' Julia Roberts.

Toad of Toad Hall Popular Christmas entertainment by A. A. Milne, which is often presented during the pantomime season, although it is not directly descended from that tradition. The play was first performed in London in 1930 and has since established itself as a regular feature of Christmas programmes everywhere, offering an alternative to the conventional pantomime. Among the many actors to enjoy great success in it over the years was Richard Goolden, who was still appearing as Mole after the age of 90. Other more recent versions of the story include one by John Morley.

Story Mole emerges from spring-cleaning his home to explore the river bank and meets Rat, who invites him to share a picnic and tells him all about the foolish and aristocratic Toad who flits from one craze to another. Toad invites them both to take a ride with him in his new gypsy caravan, but they are all flung into a ditch when a motor car rushes past. Toad is suitably impressed and is adamant that he must have a car of his own.

Mole sets off to visit Badger, who lives in the Wild Wood, but gets lost when snow falls and has to be rescued by Rat. Badger welcomes them both and they discuss Toad's latest mishaps on the road. Badger attempts to take Toad in hand but he escapes and steals a car and goes on a reckless joyride that ends in his arrest and trial. He escapes from prison disguised as a washerwoman and is reunited with his friends, who inform him that in his absence Toad Hall has been taken over by the 'Wild Wooders' (weasels and other creatures of the Wild Wood). Toad leads his friends in an attack on Toad Hall and the Wild Wooders are repulsed, leaving Toad a wiser animal.

Origins Milne's musical play was a dramatisation of the children's novel *The Wind in the Willows* (1908) by Kenneth Grahame. Grahame created the story as bedtime entertainment for his son Alastair, who requested a story about 'moles, giraffes, and water-rats', and based several of the characters upon real people. Milne's adaptation cut certain scenes from the original, notably that in which Mole and Rat have a vision of Pan, and added a more sentimental tone to the story as a whole.

Treasure Island The classic adventure story by Robert Louis Stevenson (1850–94), which continues to be regularly adapted as a Christmas entertainment alongside conventional pantomimes. Written in 1881 and published initially as a serial, the exotic location of most of the action and the inclusion of such colourful characters as Ben Gunn and Long John Silver permit theatre managements to present the story with a strong pantomime flavour. Notable among the many productions seen over the Christmas season in past decades have been the regular revivals of the tale that began in 1959 at the Mermaid Theatre in London, with Bernard Miles as Long John Silver himself. Walt Disney chose the story for his first full-length all-live action film (1950).

Story Young Jim Hawkins becomes embroiled in a tale of hidden treasure and piracy after a pirate named Billy Bones dies of fright at the inn run by Jim's mother on being shown the 'black spot' (a marked paper threatening death) by the menacing Blind Pew. A map showing the location of buried treasure on a desert island is discovered among Bones's effects and Jim joins the crew of the *Hispaniola* as one of the party organised to search for it.

When the ship arrives at the island there is a mutiny led by the rascally ship's cook, Long John Silver, a cunning, one-legged former crewmate of the notorious Captain Flint (after whom Silver's shanty-singing parrot is named). The subsequent search for the treasure is disrupted with all manner of violence, which includes Jim's kidnap by Long John Silver and a siege of the stockade in which Jim and his friends defend themselves against the mutineers. Other incidents include the discovery of the long-abandoned and now half-mad Ben Gunn and a final confrontation between the two parties as the treasure is dug up.

Origins Stevenson started to write the story after drawing a pirate map showing buried treasure with his 12-year-old stepson Lloyd Osborne. Some of the characters were drawn from life, with Long John Silver being based on the writer W. E. Henley and some details of Jim's adventures being borrowed from the career of Stevenson's own father. Other influences included Defoe's *Robinson Crusoe*.

Wizard of Oz, The A novel by the US writer Frank L(yman) Baum (1856–1919), which is frequently dramatised as a Christmas entertainment alongside conventional pantomimes. Written in 1900, the story is best known as a film (1939) starring Judy Garland as Dorothy and many of the songs used in that version are revived in stage adaptations. Baum himself devised a lively stage musical based on the novel as early as 1902; it reached Broadway and remained in production for many years. Writers of updated versions of the story include John Morley.

Story Dorothy, an orphan, and her dog Toto are carried in a cyclone from the farm in Kansas where they live to the land of Oz, where Dorothy meets the Scarecrow (in search of a brain), the Tin Woodman (in search of a heart), and the Cowardly Lion (in search of courage). They set off together down the Yellow Brick Road to find the Wizard of Oz, in the hope that he will grant them their wishes and return Dorothy to her home. After various adventures and surviving the threats of the Wicked Witch of the West, they meet the Wizard and discover he is a fraud, but nonetheless have their wishes fulfilled. Highlights of most performances of the tale customarily include entrances by trained dogs in the role of Toto and by legions of dancing children as the Munchkins.

Origins Baum conceived his story as a deliberate modern alternative to the familiar – and in his eyes – worn-out fairytales of the type collected by the Grimm brothers and Hans Christian Andersen. The tale was originally given the title *The Emerald City* but this was changed in deference to a popular superstition that it is unlucky to publish books with the name of a jewel in the title (the fact that emeralds are green also risks ill luck in theatrical folklore). It has been suggested that Baum, who added various sequels and other Oz stories, intended his tale to be an allegory about the nature of the so-called 'American Dream'.

Bibliography

Adams, W. Davenport, *A Book of Burlesque* (1891)
Arundell, Denis, *The Story of Sadlers Wells* (1978)
Beaumont, Cyril W., *The History of Harlequin* (London, 1926)
Beaver, Patrick, *Spice of Life*
Bettelheim, Bruno, *The Uses of Enchantment* (London, Thames and Hudson, 1976)
Blanchard, E. L., *The Life and Reminiscences of E. L. Blanchard* (London, 1891)
Brandreth, Gyles, *Discovering Pantomime* (Aylesbury, Shire Publications, 1973)
Brandreth, Gyles, *Funniest Man on Earth*
Brandreth, Gyles, *I Scream for Ice Cream*
British Pantomime Association, *Panto!*, 4 vols., London, (1972–75)
Broadbent, R. J., *A History of Pantomime* (London, Simpkin, Marshall, Hamilton, Kent, 1901)
Burnand, Sir Francis, *Records and Reminiscences* (1904)
Busby, Roy, *British Music Hall* (London, Paul Elek, 1976)
Clinton-Baddeley, V. C., *The Burlesque Tradition* (1952)
Clinton-Baddeley, V. C., *Some Pantomime Pedigrees* (London, Society for Theatre Research, 1963)
Coggin, F. M., *The Pantomimes of Augustus Harris* (Columbus, Ohio State University, 1973)
Dibdin, Charles, *Memoirs of Charles Dibdin* (Ed. Richard Findlater, London, MacGibbon and Kee, 1968)
Dibdin, Tom, *Reminiscences* (1837)
Dickens, Charles, *The Memoirs of Joseph Grimaldi* (Ed. Richard Findlater, London, MacGibbon and Kee, 1968)
Disher, Maurice Willson, *Clowns and Pantomimes* (London, Constable, 1925)
Eigner, Edwin M., *The Dickens Pantomime* (University of California Press, 1989)
Findlater, Richard, *Grimaldi; King of Clowns* (London, 1955)
Fleetwood, Frances, *Conquest: The Story of a Theatre Family* (London, W. H. Allen, 1953)
Frow, Gerald, *Oh, Yes It Is! A History of Pantomime* (London, BBC, 1985)
Halliday, Andrew, *Comical Fellows, or the History and the Mystery of the Pantomime* (London, J. H. Thomson, 1863)
Howard, Diana, *London Theatres and Music Halls*
Jackson, Allan S., *Production and Staging of the English Pantomime* (Columbus, Ohio State University, 1959)
Johnson, James, *An Account of Pantomimes* (1882)
Leno, Dan, *Hys Booke* (Intr. Roy Hudd, London, 1968)

Littler, Emile, *Emile Littler's Panto Pie* (London, Granthea, 1948)
McKechnie, Samuel, *Popular Entertainments Through the Ages*
Mander, Raymond, and Mitchenson, Joe, *Pantomime: A Story in Pictures* (London, Peter Davies, 1973)
Mayer, David, *Harlequin in His Element* (Cambridge (Mass.), Harvard University Press, 1969)
Mellor, Geoff J., *They Made Us Laugh* (Littleborough, George Kelsall, 1982)
Nagler, A. M., *A Source Book In Theatrical History* (New York, Dover, 1959)
Nicoll, Allardyce, *A History of Late 18th Century Drama; The World of Harlequin* (1963)
Niklaus, Thelma, *Harlequin Phoenix, or the Rise and Fall of a Bergamask Rogue* (London, 1956)
O'Keefe, John, *Recollections* (1826)
Planché, J. R., *The Recollections and Reflections of J. R. Planché* (London, 1872)
Pogson, Rex, *The Pantomime Story* (Manchester, Society for Theatre Research, 1956)
Pope, W. Macqueen, *Pillars of Drury Lane*
Pope, W. Macqueen, *Theatre Royal, Drury Lane* (1945)
Rowell, George, *The Victorian Theatre* Salberg, Derek, *Once Upon a Pantomime* (Luton, Cortney Publications, 1981)
Sand, Maurice, *The History of the Harlequinade* (London, Martin Secker, 1915)
Saxon, A. H., *The Life and Art of Andrew Ducrow and the Romantic Age of the English Circus* (Hamden, 1978)
Speaight, George, *The Book of Clowns*
Wagner, Leopold, *The Pantomimes and All About Them* (1881)
Weaver, John, *A History of Mimes and Pantomimes* (1728)
Wells, Mitchell P., *Pantomime and Spectacle on the London Stage* (Chapel Hill, University of North Carolina, 1934)
Williams, Clifford John, *Madame Vestris* (London, 1973)
Wilson, Albert Edward, *Christmas Pantomime* (London, Allen and Unwin, 1934)
Wilson, Albert Edward, *King Panto* (New York, E. P. Dutton, 1935)
Wilson, Albert Edward, *The Lyceum* (London, Dennis Yates, 1952)
Wilson, Albert Edward, *Pantomime Pageant* (London, Stanley Paul and Co. Ltd., 1946)
Wilson, Albert Edward, *The Story of Pantomime* (London, Home and Van Thal, 1949)

Index